ULTIMATE
IRA RESOURCE

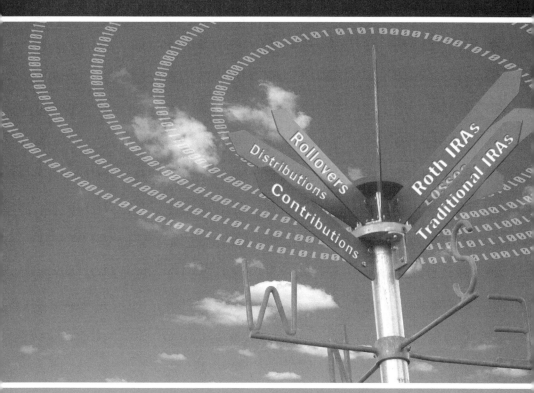

Including the
Ultimate IRA Calculator
Over 25 comprehensive, printer-friendly
calculations and explanations

William J. Wagner, J.D., LL.M., CLU

P.O. Box 14367
Cincinnati, OH 45250-0367
1-800-543-0874
www.NationalUnderwriter.com

The A Unit of Highline Media
National
Underwriter
Company
The Leader in Insurance and
Financial Services Information

ISBN: 0-87218-698-9

3rd Edition

Copyright © 1999, 2004, 2006
The National Underwriter Company
P.O. Box 14367, Cincinnati, Ohio 45250-0367

Printed in U. S. A.

About the Author

William J. Wagner, J.D., LL.M., CLU, is an Associate Editor with The National Underwriter Company. He is an editor of various tax, insurance, estate, and financial planning publications used by other professionals throughout the industry. These publications include *Tax Facts on Insurance and Employee Benefits* (Tax Facts 1), *Tax Facts on Investments* (Tax Facts 2), the *Advanced Sales Reference Service*, the monthly newsletter *TaxFacts News* and the website www.taxfactsonline.com. He is also the author of *The Ultimate Trust Resource* (including the *Trust Calculator* software) and the *IRA Calculator* software.

Bill received a J.D. degree from the University of Akron School of Law and an LL.M. in Estate Planning from the University of Miami (Florida) School of Law. Bill is admitted to the Ohio bar and a member of the American and Cincinnati Bar Associations, and is active in their Tax and Estate Planning Sections. Additionally, he is a member of the National Association of Estate Planners and the Cincinnati Estate Planning Council.

Table of Contents

Part III: IRA Planning

Appendices

Part

I

IRA Basics

Chapter 1

Introduction

In general, an individual retirement account (IRA) can be thought of as a tax-favored investment vehicle. Originally IRAs were intended as retirement accounts for individuals who were not covered by any employer retirement plan and into which deductible contributions could be made, but amounts were fully taxable when distributed. Over the years many changes have occurred with respect to IRAs; in recent years the changes have come increasingly frequently.

The types of IRAs have multiplied. Now there are traditional IRAs (see Chapter 4), Roth IRAs (see Chapter 5), SEP IRAs (including SAR-SEP IRAs – see Chapter 6), and SIMPLE IRAs (see Chapter 7). Each of these IRA types is discussed individually in Part II of this book. In addition, there are a few extras added by EGTRRA 2001 (see Chapter 8): a retirement savings contributions credit, deemed IRAs, and elective deferral Roth IRAs. Education IRAs have been appropriately renamed as education savings accounts and are no longer covered in this book.

Contributions can now be made on a nondeductible basis as well as a deductible basis. Employers can make contributions for employees. Employees can elect to make salary reduction contributions to certain IRAs. The amount that can be contributed on a deductible or nondeductible basis is now often subject to phaseout based upon the amount of an individual's income.

Amounts can generally be accumulated within an IRA on a tax-deferred (or possibly tax-free) basis. However, certain actions (e.g., loans) may be prohibited and certain investments are not permitted.

Distributions (see Chapter 13) from Roth IRAs may now be received tax-free in some circumstances. Otherwise, distributions from Roth IRAs are generally received tax-free to the extent of contributions. However, distributions from other IRAs are generally taxed on a pro-rated basis. Distributions made before age 59½ may be subject to an early distribution penalty tax. Required minimum distributions are generally required at the earlier of age 70½ or death. However, required minimum distributions from Roth IRAs are not required until after death.

Rollovers (see Chapter 11) are permitted on a tax-free basis between certain IRAs (as well as various other retirement plans) but not between others. However, a rollover or conversion (see Chapter 12) to a Roth IRA is generally a taxable event.

The balance of Part I of this book is devoted to comparing some of the variations in IRA features (see generally Chapter 2) or discussing some of the common features (see generally Chapter 3) discussed above, as well as other features such as how IRAs are taxed in the event of a divorce, what tax filings are required of an IRA participant, and what withholding is required with respect to IRAs.

IRAs can now be created for education purposes, for purchase of a home, as a disability fund, as a substitute for a qualified plan by employers, as a holding vehicle for amounts rolled over from a qualified plan, as a dynastic generational transfer device, as well as for retirement purposes. See Chapter 10 for certain special purpose planning with an IRA.

IRAs can be created for various purposes, but other factors may determine whether an individual can make use of an IRA and whether a particular type of IRA may be useful. See Chapter 9 for a discussion of how to select an IRA.

Choosing an IRA beneficiary (see Chapter 14) is important for a variety of reasons, including benefiting a loved one, minimizing the effect of the required minimum distributions rules, and general estate planning.

Much of the usefulness of IRAs is due to the relationship of IRAs with time, money, and taxes (see Chapter 15).

IRAs are potentially subject to multiple taxes (see Chapter 16). These include transfer taxes such as the gift tax (see Chapter 17), estate tax (see Chapter 18), and generation-skipping transfer tax (see Chapter 19).

Certain protections are provided for IRAs in bankruptcy (including sweeping changes made by the Bankruptcy Abuse Prevention and Consumer Protection Act of 2005), and against creditors and other claimants seeking to reach IRA assets and distributions (see Chapter 20).

Chapter 2

Comparison of IRAs

A number of IRA features that can vary depending on the type of IRA (i.e., traditional, Roth, SEP, or SIMPLE) are discussed below. These include the following:

- contributions to IRAs, including deductible contributions, nondeductible contributions, employer contributions, and excess contributions;

- the treatment of investment and accumulations within an IRA;

- distributions, including distributions includable in income, early distributions, and required distributions;

- rollovers; and

- withholding.

See Chapter 3 for a discussion of the following shared IRA features: the deduction of IRA expenses, who can be a trustee, payroll deduction, direct deposit of income tax refunds to IRAs, how investments accumulated in an IRA are taxed, early distributions, required minimum distributions, how IRAs are taxed in the event of a divorce, bankruptcy and asset protection for IRAs, and what tax filings are required of an IRA participant.

FIGURE 2.1

Comparison of IRAs

	Traditional IRAs	Roth IRAs
Deductible Contributions	Yes. $4,000 (2006-2007), subject to phaseout.	No
Nondeductible Contributions Amount	$4,000 (2006-2007), reduced by deductible contributions. Combined $4,000 limit for all traditional and Roth IRAs.	$4,000 (2006-2007), subject to phaseout. Combined $4,000 limit for all traditional and Roth IRAs.
Catch-up Contributions	$1,000 (2006). Deductible or nondeductible.	$1,000 (2006), subject to phaseout.
Contributions Phaseout	For deductible contributions only. Modified adjusted gross income in 2006 of: $50,000-$60,000 (single return) $75,000-$85,000 (joint return, active participant) $150,000-$160,000 (joint, non-active participant) $0-$10,000 (separate return)	Modified adjusted gross income in 2006 of: $150,000-$160,000 (joint return) $0-$15,000 (separate return) $95,000-$110,000 (all others)
Maximum Contribution Age	70½	None
Accumulations	Generally, tax-deferred.	Generally, tax-deferred (or tax-free).
Taxation of Distributions	Proration: nondeductible contributions excludable.	Contributions received tax-free. After 5 years: earnings tax-free after age 59½, after death, for disability, up to $10,000 lifetime for first-time homebuyer.
Early Distributions (10% penalty on amount includable in income)	Pre-age 59½ or death, unless an exception applies.	Pre-age 59½ or death, unless an exception applies.
Required Minimum Distributions (50% penalty for failure)	Generally, at age 70½, over life expectancy of owner (or owner and beneficiary).	After death of owner. Generally, over beneficiary's life expectancy.

FIGURE 2.2

Comparison of Employer-Provided IRAs

	SEP IRAs	SAR-SEP IRAs	SIMPLE IRAs
New Plans Permitted	Yes	No	Yes
Maximum Employees	NA	25	100
Salary Reduction	No	Yes, if 50% of employees elect and 1.25 deferral percentage test met.	Yes
Maximum Salary Reduction	NA	$15,000 (2006), overall elective deferral limit.	$10,000 (2006).
Catch-up Contributions (age 50)	NA	$5,000 (2006)	$2,000 (2006).
Other Employer Contributions	Nondiscriminatory definite written allocation formula. (25% of comp max) $44,000 (2006).	Nondiscriminatory definite written allocation formula. (25% of comp max) $44,000 (2006).	Matching (3% of comp) (see max above); or Nonelective (2% of comp) $4,400 (2006).
Maximum Contribution Age	None	None	None
Accumulations	Generally, tax-deferred.	Generally, tax-deferred.	Generally, tax-deferred.
Taxation of Distributions	Generally, fully taxable. Proration if nondeductible contributions.	Generally, fully taxable. Proration if nondeductible contributions.	Fully taxable.
Early Distributions (penalty on amount includable in income)	Pre-age 59½ or death, unless an exception applies. 10% penalty.	Pre-age 59½ or death, unless an exception applies. 10% penalty.	Pre-age 59½ or death, unless an exception applies. 10% penalty (25% first two years).
Required Minimum Distributions (50% penalty for failure)	Generally, at age 70½, over life expectancy of owner (or owner and beneficiary).	Generally, at age 70½, over life expectancy of owner (or owner and beneficiary).	Generally, at age 70½, over life expectancy of owner (or owner and beneficiary).

Contributions

Various types of contributions can be made to the different types of IRAs on either a deductible or a nondeductible basis. The different types of IRAs also have different maximum contribution amounts sometimes subject to various phaseouts based upon the amount of the individual's income. Certain IRAs are designed for employer contributions (including salary reduction contributions). Contributions to all IRAs must be made in cash. Excess contributions are generally subject to penalty taxes.

Each year, contributions for an individual to traditional IRAs and Roth IRAs and employee contributions to a SEP IRA are subject to a combined overall limitation of the lesser of the total contribution limit or includable compensation.[1] The total contribution limit consists of the sum of the regular contribution limit and the catch-up contribution limit.

The regular contribution limit is as follows.

Regular Contribution Limit

Year	Amount
2006-2007	$4,000
2008-	$5,000 *

*plus indexing for inflation after 2008

In addition, catch-up contributions can be made for individuals attaining age 50 before the end of the year. The catch-up contribution limit is as follows.

Catch-up Contribution Limit

Year	Amount
2006-	$1,000

The regular and catch-up contribution limits shown reflect changes made by PPA 2006. PPA 2006 eliminates the sunset after 2010 of scheduled increases in the contribution limits made by EGTRRA 2001.

While contributions to a particular type of these IRAs may be subject to phaseout based on the amount of the individual's income, the total contribution limit amount is not subject to such phaseout. Therefore, any individual who has not attained age 70½ may always make a contribution equal to the lesser of the total contribution limit or includable compensation to some IRA. In the case of an individual earning less than such individual's spouse, the compensation of the individual's spouse may be added to the individual's own compensation to the extent that the spouse's compensation is in excess of the sum for such spouse of contributions to traditional IRAs, employee contributions to SEP IRAs, and contributions to Roth IRAs.

Employers may make contributions (including salary reduction contributions) to IRAs for employees subject to the limitations described below.

Deductible Contributions

Deductible contributions can be made by an individual to a traditional IRA or a SEP IRA. However, a deduction cannot be taken for contributions made to a traditional or SEP IRA in taxable years once the individual has attained age 70½.[2] Furthermore, a deduction generally cannot be taken for contributions to an IRA inherited from another individual.[3] An IRA received by the spouse of the former IRA owner upon such owner's death is not treated as an inherited IRA.[4]

Deductible contributions to traditional IRAs and deductible employee contributions to a SEP IRA are subject to a combined overall limitation equal to the lesser of the total contribution limit (see above) or includable compensation per year per individual.[5] The compensation of the lower earning spouse may be supplemented with compensation of the other spouse. If the individual is an active participant in certain employer retirement plans, the total contribution limit is subject to phaseout based upon adjusted gross income for purposes of the deductible contribution limit.[6]

Thus, in the case of an active participant, the total contribution limit amount is reduced by an amount equal to such amount multiplied by the ratio of the individual's modified adjusted gross income (MAGI) in excess of an applicable dollar amount to $10,000 ($20,000 in the case of a joint return after 2006).

$$\text{total contribution limit} \times \frac{\underline{\text{MAGI - applicable dollar amount}}}{\$10,000} = \text{reduction}$$

Whenever the phaseout reduction is other than a multiple of $10, the reduction is rounded to the next lowest multiple of $10. However, where the total contribution limit amount adjusted for phaseout based upon adjusted gross income is between $0 and $200, $200 is allowable as a deduction.

In the case of a joint return, the applicable dollar amount and the corresponding amount at which total phaseout occurs equals:

Taxable Year	Applicable Dollar Amount	Total Phaseout
2006	$75,000	$85,000
2007-	$80,000 *	$100,000 *

*plus indexing for inflation after 2006

However, in the case of a joint return where one spouse is an active participant and the other is not, the applicable dollar amount with respect to the spouse who is not an active participant is increased to $150,000; however, the $10,000 phaseout band remains at $10,000 (it does not increase to $20,000 as in the case of a joint return after 2006).[7] Thus, in such case, total phaseout occurs at $160,000.

In the case of other than a joint return or a married filing separate return, the applicable dollar amount and the corresponding amount at which total phaseout occurs equals:

Taxable Year	Applicable Dollar Amount	Total Phaseout
2005-	$50,000 *	$60,000 *

*plus indexing for inflation after 2006

In the case of a married filing separate return of an active participant, the applicable dollar amount equals $0. Thus, in such case, total phaseout occurs at $10,000.

PPA 2006 provides for indexing of the phaseout limits for contributions after 2006. However, in the case of a joint return (see above), IRC Section 219(g)(3)(B)(i) already provided for an increased amount for 2007. A technical correction may be needed.

   Example. In 2006, a single taxpayer aged 55, who is an active participant in a retirement plan and has adjusted gross income of $54,500, can make a deductible contribution to a traditional IRA or SEP IRA of $2,750. This is calculated as follows:

This is calculated as follows:

total contribution limit x $\dfrac{\text{MAGI - applicable dollar amount}}{\$10,000}$ = reduction

round reduction down to next lowest multiple of $10

total contribution limit - reduction = amount deductible

regular contribution limit	$4,000
catch-up contribution limit	+ 1,000
total contribution limit	$5,000

$5,000 x $\dfrac{\$54,500 - \$50,000}{\$10,000}$ = $2,250

round $2,250 to $2,250

$5,000 - $2,250 = $2,750

For more information on deductible contributions to a traditional IRA, see Chapter 4. For more information on deductible employee contributions to a SEP IRA, see Chapter 6.

Nondeductible Contributions

In addition, nondeductible contributions can be made to traditional IRAs, nondeductible employee contributions to SEP IRAs, and nondeductible contributions to Roth IRAs. These contributions are also subject to limits and may be subject to phaseout.

Nondeductible contributions to traditional IRAs and nondeductible employee contributions to a SEP IRA are subject to a combined overall limitation equal to the lesser of the total contribution limit (see above) or compensation includable in income. This amount is reduced by any deductible contributions to a traditional IRA or SEP IRA.[8] However, nondeductible contributions to a traditional IRA or SEP IRA are not subject to any phaseout based upon modified adjusted gross income even if the individual or the individual's spouse is an active participant in certain employer retirement plans. Nevertheless, nondeductible deductions cannot be made to a traditional or SEP IRA in taxable years once the individual has attained age 70½.

For more information on nondeductible contributions to a traditional IRA, see Chapter 4. For more information on nondeductible employee contributions to a SEP IRA, see Chapter 6.

An individual can make nondeductible contributions to a Roth IRA up to the lesser of the total contribution limit (see above) or compensation includable in income. This amount is reduced by any contributions to a traditional IRA or employee contributions to a SEP IRA.[9] The total contribution limit amount is subject to phaseout based upon modified adjusted gross income (MAGI) for Roth IRA purposes.[10]

Thus, in the case of Roth IRAs, the applicable dollar amount and the corresponding amount at which total phaseout occurs equals:

Taxpayer Return	Applicable Dollar Amount	Total Phaseout
Married-Joint	$150,000 *	$160,000 *
Married-Separate	$0 *	$10,000 *
All Other	$95,000 *	$110,000 *

*plus indexing for inflation after 2006

PPA 2006 provides for indexing of the phaseout limits for contributions after 2006.

For more information on nondeductible contributions to a Roth IRA, see Chapter 5.

Employer Contributions

SEP IRAs and SIMPLE IRAs are designed for employer contributions (including salary reduction contributions in some cases). In addition, employer contributions can be made to traditional IRAs, Roth IRAs, or SEP IRAs as regular deductible or nondeductible contributions, subject to any limitations described above.

In the case of the special employer contributions (including salary reduction contributions), the employer takes a deduction for contributions and the employee excludes the employer contributions from income. In the case of regular employer deductible/nondeductible contributions, the employer takes a deduction for compensation paid the employee, the employee includes the compensation in income and the employee can take a deduction (see "Deductible Contributions," above), if the contribution is to a traditional IRA or SEP IRA, to the extent that the employee's deduction is not eliminated through phaseout.

An employer can take a deduction for contributions made to a SEP IRA during a year by the employer but not to exceed 25 percent of the employees' compensation.[11] In fact, in any year that the employer maintains a SEP IRA, the employer must contribute to the SEP IRA of any employee who (1) has attained age 21, (2) has performed service for the employer in at least three of the preceding five years, and (3) has compensation of at least $450 (as indexed for 2006). For this purpose, if the employee is eligible for salary reduction contributions to the SEP IRA for the year, the employer is considered to have contributed to the SEP IRA for the employee. Certain employees covered by collective bargaining and nonresident aliens can be excluded from required employer contributions to the SEP IRA.[12]

Employer contributions to a SEP IRA must be determined under a definite written allocation formula that specifies how an employee qualifies for employer contributions and how the amount of employer contributions is calculated.[13] Contributions to the SEP IRA by the employer may not discriminate in favor of any highly compensated employee. Contributions to the SEP IRA by the employer will generally be considered discriminatory unless contributions bear a uniform relationship to compensation (not to exceed $220,000 as indexed for 2006) of each employee maintaining a SEP IRA.[14]

Employer contributions to a SEP IRA, as well as annual additions to other defined contribution plans of the employer maintained for the employee, are subject to a combined overall limitation equal to the lesser of 100 percent of compensation or $44,000 (as indexed for 2006).

The employee can exclude employer contributions to a SEP IRA from income to the extent that such contributions do not exceed the lesser of 25 percent of compensation (determined without regard to the employer's contribution to the SEP IRA) or $44,000 (as indexed for 2006). There is also a $220,000 limitation (as indexed for 2006) on the amount of compensation that can be taken into account which would limit contributions to $55,000 (25% x $220,000) in 2006. However, since $44,000 is less than $55,000, the contribution limit is $44,000 in 2006. The dollar limitation is reduced in the case of highly compensated employees in a SEP IRA that is integrated with Social Security.[15]

In years after 1996, salary reduction contributions to a salary reduction SEP IRA (SAR-SEP IRA) can be made only by employers that had SAR-SEP IRAs that permitted salary reduction contributions as of December 31, 1996 (an existing SAR-SEP IRA). Existing SAR-SEP IRAs are grandfathered on an employer basis; an employer with existing SAR-SEP IRAs can add new employees to the plan.

A SAR-SEP IRA permits an employee to elect to have the employer either (1) make elective employer contributions to the SAR-SEP IRA on behalf of the employee or (2) distribute the amount in cash to the employee.[16] If the employee takes cash, the distribution is includable in the employee's income. If the employee chooses salary reduction, the employee excludes the amount of the salary reduction contribution from income for the year of contribution.

Salary reduction contributions to a SAR-SEP IRA, as well as all other elective deferrals to retirement plans, are subject to a combined overall elective deferral limitation in a year.[17] The elective deferral limits are as follows.

Elective Deferral Limit

Year	Amount
2006	$15,000
2007-	$15,000*

*plus indexing for inflation

In addition, elective deferral catch-up contributions can be made for individuals attaining age 50 before the end of the year. The elective deferral catch-up contribution limit is as follows.

Catch-up Contribution Limit

Year	Amount
2006	$5,000
2007-	$5,000*

*plus indexing for inflation

The elective deferral regular and catch-up contribution limits shown reflect changes made by PPA 2006. PPA 2006 eliminates the sunset after 2010 of scheduled increases in the contribution limits made by EGTRRA 2001.

The only contributions permitted to a SIMPLE IRA are salary reduction contributions made by the employer for an employee and certain matching or nonelective contributions by the employer.[18] The employer takes a deduction for the salary reduction, matching, and nonelective contributions.[19] The employee excludes the salary reduction, matching, and nonelective contributions from income.[20]

The amount of salary reduction contributions that can be made for any employee in any year to a SIMPLE IRA cannot exceed an applicable dollar amount.[21] The applicable dollar amount is as follows.

Salary Reduction Contribution Limit

Year	Amount
2006	$10,000
2007-	$10,000 *

*plus indexing for inflation

In addition, elective deferral catch-up contributions can be made for individuals attaining age 50 before the end of the year. The elective deferral catch-up contribution limit for SIMPLE IRAs is as follows.

Catch-up Contribution Limit

Year	Amount
2006	$2,500
2007-	$2,500 *

*plus indexing for inflation

The salary reduction regular and catch-up contribution limits shown reflect changes made by PPA 2006. PPA 2006 eliminates the sunset after 2010 of scheduled increases in the contribution limits made by EGTRRA 2001.

If the employer elects matching contributions, the employer must contribute to the SIMPLE IRA an amount equal to the lesser of (1) the amount of the salary reduction contribution to the IRA for the employee, or (2) the applicable percentage of compensation for the year. The applicable percentage is three percent unless the employer elects for any year to use a lower percentage of not less than one percent. An applicable percentage rate of less than three percent cannot be used more than twice during any five-year period.

Alternatively, if the employer elects to make nonelective contributions, the employer contributes to the SIMPLE IRA of each eligible employee with at least $5,000 of compensation from the employer for the year an amount equal to two percent of compensation (not to exceed $220,000 as indexed for 2006). If this election is made, this amount is contributed without regard to whether the elective salary reduction contributions have been made.

In general, all employees of the employer maintaining a SIMPLE IRA who received at least $5,000 in compensation from the employer for the two preceding years and are reasonably expected to have $5,000 in compensation from the employer for the current year must be eligible to either make a salary reduction contribution election or receive nonelective contributions. Certain employees covered by collective bargaining and nonresident aliens need not be covered under the SIMPLE IRA.[22]

Excess Contributions

Contributions to IRAs in excess of the limitations above are generally subject to penalty taxes until corrected. Excess contributions can generally be corrected in the current year by distributing the excess contributions plus earnings thereon during such year (often including a grace period thereafter). Excess contributions can also be carried over and corrected in a later year through distributions or by making less contributions than the maximum allowed in such later year.

In general, excess contributions to traditional IRAs and Roth IRAs are subject to a six percent penalty tax payable by the individual; excess contributions to SEP IRAs and SIMPLE IRAs are subject to a 10 percent penalty tax payable by the employer.

Accumulations/Investments

Amounts earned within IRAs generally accumulate on a tax-deferred basis. Earnings are generally not taxable until distributed from the IRA (and possibly not even then). However, an IRA is taxed if it has unrelated business taxable income. Furthermore, part or all of the IRA may be deemed distributed if the IRA owner engages in a prohibited transaction, borrows on an annuity contract, pledges the account as security for a loan, purchases an endowment contract, or invests in certain collectibles.[23] An IRA account cannot invest in life insurance contracts.[24] The IRA can be in the form of an individual retirement annuity.[25]

See Chapter 3 on Shared IRA Features for additional information.

Distributions

Distributions from an IRA may be subject to tax. Also, distributions may be subject to an early distribution penalty tax to the extent includable in income. Furthermore, certain distributions are required; a penalty tax may apply if the distribution is not made.

Distributions Includable in Income

Distributions from an IRA generally represent a return of contributions and earnings on contributions. Nondeductible contributions to an IRA are contributed on an after-tax basis; all other contributions and earnings on contributions have generally not been subject to tax. Therefore, the calculation of distributions from most IRAs is designed to prorate distributions to nondeductible contributions and exclude from income such portion of the distribution. The rules for Roth IRAs are generally more favorable and may even permit tax free distributions.

In general, the formula for calculating the portion of a distribution from a traditional IRA, SEP IRA, or SIMPLE IRA that is excludable from income as attributable to nondeductible contributions to the IRA is:

$$\frac{\text{Unrecovered Nondeductible Contributions}}{\substack{\text{Total Account Balance +} \\ \text{Distribution Amount +} \\ \text{Outstanding Rollover}}} \times \text{Distribution Amount}$$

All nonRoth IRAs (i.e., traditional, SEP, or SIMPLE) are treated as one in determining each of the above amounts. Unrecovered nondeductible contributions are generally determined as of the beginning of the year, but also include contributions made before the end of the current year. The total account balance is determined as of the end of the year (i.e., increased by contributions and rollovers to the IRA, but reduced by distributions and rollovers from the IRA). The distribution amount and outstanding rollover is the total of such transactions occurring during the current year.

Proration is required with respect to a traditional IRA if nondeductible contributions have been made to the traditional IRA. Otherwise, distributions from a traditional IRA are generally fully includable in income.

Distributions from SEP IRAs and SIMPLE IRAs will usually consist entirely of employer contributions and earnings on contributions. Therefore, distributions from SEP IRAs and SIMPLE IRAs will usually be fully includable in income. Proration could be required if the employee made nondeductible contributions to the SEP or SIMPLE IRA.

However, in the case of Roth IRAs, distributions are treated as being made from contributions first, and nontaxable to the extent made from contributions. Additionally, certain qualified distributions made at least five years after the first contribution to a Roth IRA can be received tax-free. These distributions include the following:

- made on or after the date the Roth IRA owner turns 59½;

- made after the death of the Roth IRA owner;

- attributable to disability of the Roth IRA owner; or

- made to the Roth IRA owner ($10,000 lifetime limit) for purchase of a first home by the IRA owner, the IRA owner's spouse, or children, grand-children, or ancestor of either.

Early Distributions

Distributions from an IRA made prior to age 59½ are subject to a 10 percent early distribution penalty to the extent includable in income unless an exception applies. Exceptions include distributions:

(1)   made after the death of the IRA owner;

(2)   attributable to the IRA owner's disability;

(3)   part of a series of substantially equal periodic payments (SEPPs) made for the life or the joint life of the IRA owner and a designated beneficiary;

(4)   made for medical care to the extent generally allowable as a medical expense deduction;

(5)   made to the IRA owner who is unemployed for payment of health insurance premiums;

(6)   made to the IRA owner for payment of qualified higher education expenses furnished to the IRA owner, the IRA owner's spouse, or children or grandchildren of either;

(7)   made to the IRA owner ($10,000 lifetime limit) for purchase of a first home by the IRA owner, the IRA owner's spouse, or children, grandchildren, or ancestor of either; or

(8)   made to a reservist while on active duty (commencing after September 11, 2001 and before 2008).

PPA 2006 adds an exception for distributions to a reservist while on active duty. Active duty must commmence after September 11, 2001 and before 2008. Furthermore, the reservist can recontribute such distributed amounts back to the IRA during a two-year period beginning on the day after active duty ends.

See Chapter 3 on Shared IRA Features for additional information.

Required Distributions

Certain distributions are required from a traditional IRA, Roth IRA, SEP IRA, or SIMPLE IRA or a 50 percent penalty tax applies. Such required minimum distributions must generally begin at age 70½ and distributions are generally made over the life expectancy of the IRA owner or the life expectancies of the IRA owner and designated beneficiary. In the case of a Roth IRA, required minimum distributions need not begin until after the death of the IRA owner. A spouse of an IRA owner who is the beneficiary of an IRA can generally elect to treat the IRA as the spouse's own at the death of the IRA owner.

See Chapter 3 on Shared IRA Features for additional information.

Rollovers

Rollovers are permitted between various IRAs, qualified plans, tax sheltered annuities, and eligible Section 457 governmental plans. In general, a rollover is a transfer of retirement assets from one plan to another by the participant or owner that is completed within 60 days of the distribution. The effect of a rollover is generally to avoid taxes and penalties upon what otherwise would be treated as a distribution.[26] See Chapter 11 regarding rollovers. Also, see Chapter 12 regarding conversions and Roth IRAs.

Withholding

When employer contributions (including salary reduction contributions) are made to a SEP IRA or SIMPLE IRA, such contributions may be subject to FICA (Social Security tax) or FUTA (federal unemployment tax). When distributions are made from any IRA, such distributions may be subject to income tax withholding.

Employer contributions to a SEP IRA are generally not subject to FICA or FUTA, or income tax withholding.[27] Salary reduction contributions to a SAR-SEP IRA are generally subject to FICA and FUTA, but not to income tax withholding.[28]

Salary reduction contributions to a SIMPLE IRA are not subject to income tax withholding; they are subject to FICA and FUTA.[29] Matching contributions and nonelective contributions to a SIMPLE IRA are not subject to FICA or FUTA, or to income tax withholding.[30]

Distributions from any IRA are distributions from a retirement plan subject to income tax withholding unless the individual elects to have withholding not apply. Thus, unless the election is made, periodic payments (annuity and similar payments) from an IRA are subject to withholding at regular withholding rates and nonperiodic payments from an IRA are subject to withholding at a 10 percent rate.[31]

However, a conversion of a traditional IRA, a SEP IRA, or a SIMPLE IRA into a Roth IRA (a qualified rollover) is a distribution for which income tax withholding is required, unless made in the form of a direct trustee-to-trustee transfer.[32]

Endnotes

1. IRC Secs. 219(b)(1), 219(b)(5), 408(o)(2), 408A(c)(2).
2. IRC Sec. 219(d)(1).
3. IRC Sec. 219(d)(4).
4. See IRC Sec. 408(d)(3)(C)(ii).
5. IRC Secs. 219(b)(1), 219(b)(5).
6. IRC Sec. 219(g).
7. IRC Sec. 219(g)(7).
8. IRC Sec. 408(o)(2).
9. IRC Secs. 408A(c)(2), 219.
10. IRC Sec. 408A(c)(3).
11. IRC Sec. 404(h).
12. IRC Secs. 408(k)(2), 408(k)(8).
13. IRC Sec. 408(k)(5).

14. IRC Sec. 408(k)(3).

15. IRC Secs. 404(h), 402(h)(2)(B).

16. IRC Sec. 408(k)(6).

17. IRC Secs. 402(g)(1), 414(v).

18. IRC Sec. 408(p)(1)(B).

19. IRC Sec. 404(m)(1).

20. IRC Secs. 402(k), 402(h)(1).

21. IRC Secs. 408(p)(2)(A)(ii), 408(p)(2)(E), 414(v).

22. IRC Sec. 408(p)(4).

23. IRC Secs. 408(e)(2), 408(m).

24. IRC Sec. 408(a)(3).

25. IRC Sec. 408(b).

26. See IRC Sec. 408(d)(3).

27. IRC Secs. 3121(a)(5)(C), 3306(b)(5)(C), 3401(a)(12)(C).

28. Ibid.

29. IRC Secs. 3121(a)(5)(H), 3306(b)(5)(H), 3401(a)(12)(D).

30. Ibid.

31. IRC Sec. 3405.

32. Treas. Reg. §1.408A-6 (A-13); IRC Sec. 3405(c).

Chapter 3

Shared IRA Features

Certain features shared by most IRAs are discussed below. These include the following:

- the deduction of IRA expenses,

- who can be a trustee,

- payroll deduction,

- direct deposit of federal income tax refund to IRA,

- how are investments accumulated in an IRA taxed,

- early distributions,

- required minimum distributions,

- how IRAs are taxed in the event of a divorce,

- bankruptcy and asset protection for IRAs, and

- what tax filings are required of an IRA participant.

See Chapter 2 for a comparison of certain IRA features: contributions to IRAs, including deductible contributions, nondeductible contributions, employer contributions, and excess contributions; distributions, including distributions includable in income, early distributions, and required distributions; rollovers; and withholding.

IRA Expense Deductions

Certain expenses incurred in creating and maintaining an IRA may be deductible. Certain IRA administrative or trustee fees can be claimed as miscellaneous itemized deductions. Interest on amounts borrowed to buy or carry the IRA may be deductible as investment interest expense.

If IRA administrative or trustee fees are separately billed and paid, they are generally deductible under IRC Section 212.[1] IRC Section 212 allows generally for the deduction of ordinary and reasonable expenses incurred for the production of income. However, such expenses are aggregated with other miscellaneous itemized expenses and deductible only to the extent that miscellaneous itemized expenses exceed two percent of adjusted gross income.[2] IRA administrative or trustee fees that are separately billed and paid are not treated as additional contributions to the IRA.

On the other hand, additional amounts contributed to an IRA to reimburse the IRA for a broker's commissions on transactions involving IRA assets were not deductible. Furthermore, such amounts were treated as additional contributions to the IRA.[3] Sales commissions on individual retirement annuities were similarly treated even though the commissions were separately billed and paid.[4]

The Service has ruled that interest borrowed to buy or carry an IRA is deductible under IRC Section 163; such interest is not allocable to tax-exempt income and, thus, it is not subject to the prohibition against deducting interest allocable to tax-exempt income.[5] However, interest borrowed to buy or carry an IRA is allocable to property held for investment. Such interest is aggregated with other investment interest and is deductible only to the extent of investment income; any excess investment interest can be carried over to later years.[6]

Trustee

An individual cannot be the trustee of an individual retirement account. The trustee must be a bank, a federally insured credit union, a building and loan association, or other person who satisfies requirements of the Internal Revenue Service.[7] A non-bank trustee must demonstrate the following characteristics to the IRS:

- fiduciary ability (including continuity of life, an established place of business in the United States where it is accessible during every business day, fiduciary experience, fiduciary responsibility, and financial responsibility),

- capacity to account for the interests of a large number of individuals,

- fitness to handle retirement funds,

- ability to administer fiduciary powers, and

- adequacy of net worth.[8]

In addition, the non-bank trustee must also provide the following:

- that audits will be conducted by a qualified public accountant at least once every 12 months,

- that funds will be kept invested as long as reasonable for the proper management of the account,

- that investments will not be commingled with other investments except in a common trust fund and investments will be safely maintained, and

- that separate fiduciary records will be maintained.[9]

For a discussion of selecting a trustee, see Chapter 9.

Payroll Deduction

An employer can set up direct deposits to traditional and Roth IRAs by way of payroll deduction so that individual employees can contribute to their own IRAs. The employee establishes the traditional or Roth IRA. The employer sets up the payroll deduction option. The employee determines how much to have deducted from pay (limited to the maximum annual contribution amounts for traditional and Roth IRAs). The only responsibility of the employer is to transmit the payroll deduction contribution to the traditional or Roth IRA selected by the employee.

The payroll deduction reduces pay received directly by the employee (and the employee's IRA is increased by the amount of the payroll deduction), but it does not reduce income reported to the IRS or the amount subject to tax. However, if the payroll deduction contribution is to a traditional IRA, the employee may be entitled to an income tax deduction on the employee's income tax return. It is the employee's responsibility to make sure that excess contributions are not made to the IRA (e.g., Roth maximum annual contribution amounts are subject to phaseout based on adjusted gross income).

Direct Deposit of Tax Refund to IRA

PPA 2006 Section 830 directs the IRS to make available a form (or modify an existing form) for individuals for the direct deposit of federal income tax refunds to an individual retirement plan. The form is to be made available for tax years beginning after 2006.

Such a deposit would be treated as a contribution to the IRA. If the contribution is to a traditional IRA, the individual may be entitled to an income tax deduction on his income tax return. It is the individual's responsibility to make sure that excess contributions are not made to the IRA.

Accumulations/Investments

Amounts earned within IRAs generally accumulate on a tax-deferred basis. Earnings are generally not taxable until distributed from the IRA (and possibly not even then). However, an IRA is taxed if it has unrelated business taxable income. Furthermore, part or all of the IRA may be deemed distributed if the IRA owner engages in a prohibited transaction, borrows on an annuity contract, pledges the account as security for a loan, purchases an endowment contract, or invests in certain collectibles.[10] An IRA account cannot invest in life insurance contracts.[11] The IRA can be in the form of an individual retirement annuity.[12]

An individual retirement annuity is an annuity contract or endowment contract issued by an insurance company meeting certain requirements: (1) the contract cannot be transferable by the owner; (2) the premiums may not be fixed; (3) the annual premium cannot exceed the regular annual limit on contributions; (4) any refund of premiums must be applied before the end of the next year to pay future premiums or to purchase additional benefits; (5) the required minimum distribution and minimum incidental death benefit rules apply; and (6) the entire interest of the owner must be nonforfeitable. For this purpose, an endowment contract cannot mature later than the taxable year in which the IRA owner reaches age 70½ and must be for the exclusive benefit of the IRA owner or beneficiary. Aggregate annual premiums for all endowment contracts purchased for the IRA owner cannot exceed the regular annual limit on contributions.

An IRA would generally be taxable as a trust to the extent that the IRA had unrelated business taxable income. IRAs typically invest in stocks, bonds, money markets, and mutual funds and do not have unrelated business taxable income.[13]

If the individual on behalf of whom an IRA is created or the beneficiary of such individual (disqualified persons) engage in a prohibited transaction with the IRA, the IRA will cease to qualify as an IRA and the entire IRA is treated as distributed at fair market value on the first day of the year in which the IRA ceased to qualify as an IRA. In general, prohibited transactions include the following:

- the sale, exchange, or leasing of property between the IRA and the disqualified person;

- the lending of money or other extension of credit between a plan and a disqualified person;

- the furnishing of goods, services, or facilities between the IRA and the disqualified person; and

- the transfer to, or use by or for the benefit of, the disqualified person of income or assets of the IRA.[14]

Where the owner of an individual retirement annuity borrows on the annuity, the IRA ceases to qualify as an IRA, and the full fair market value of the annuity is includable in income on the first day of the year.[15] (It appears that a technical correction is needed to permit the exclusion of nondeductible contributions.)

If the individual on behalf of whom the IRA is created pledges the account (or a portion thereof) as security for a loan, the portion pledged is treated as distributed.[16]

If the assets of an IRA are used to purchase an endowment contract for the benefit of the individual on behalf of whom the IRA is created, to the extent that the assets are used to purchase life, health, accident, or other insurance, such amounts are treated as distributed.[17] Apparently, such a deemed distribution would not be subject to the early distribution penalty tax; however, a technical correction is needed.

In general, IRAs cannot invest in collectibles. The acquisition by an IRA of a collectible is treated as a distribution from the IRA of an amount equal to the cost of the collectible. Collectibles mean works of art, rugs, antiques, metals, gems, stamps, coins, alcoholic beverages, and any other tangible personal property specified by the IRS. Certain coins and bullion are not treated as collectibles: certain gold, silver, or platinum U.S. coins; coins of the various states; and certain gold, silver, platinum, or palladium bullion if the bullion is in the physical possession of the IRA trustee.[18]

For a discussion of choosing the IRA investment vehicle, see Chapter 9.

Early Distributions

In general, distributions from an IRA received before age 59½ are subject to a 10 percent penalty tax on early distributions. However, the penalty tax only applies to the extent that the distribution is includable in income (see Chapter 13) and a number of exceptions to application of the penalty apply.[19] The early distribution penalty also applies to distributions of conversion contributions from a Roth IRA made within five years of the conversion to a Roth IRA (see Chapter 5).

The early distribution penalty tax does not apply to distributions from an IRA that are:

(1)   made after the death of the IRA owner;

(2)   attributable to the IRA owner's disability;

(3)   part of a series of substantially equal periodic payments (at least annually) made for the life (or life expectancy) or the joint life (or life expectancies) of the IRA owner and a designated beneficiary (the penalty tax plus interest is due if the substantially equal periodic payments are modified before the later of five years after payments have begun or the IRA owner reaches age 59½);

(4)   made for medical care to the extent generally allowable as a medical expense deduction (generally, unreimbursed medical expenses in excess of 7.5 percent of adjusted gross income; for this purpose, itemization of deductions is not required);

(5)   made to the IRA owner who is unemployed for payment of health insurance premiums;

(6)   made to the IRA owner for payment of qualified higher education expenses furnished to the IRA owner, the IRA owner's spouse, or children or grandchildren of either;

(7)   made to the IRA owner ($10,000 lifetime limit) for purchase of a first home by the IRA owner, the IRA owner's spouse, or children, grandchildren, or ancestor of either; or

(8)   made to a reservist while on active duty (commencing after September 11, 2001 and before 2008).

The IRS has approved three methods for calculating substantially equal periodic payments (SEPPs):

(1)   payments that satisfy the required minimum distributions method (see heading below);

(2)   amortization of payments over the life expectancy of the IRA owner or joint and survivor life expectancy of the IRA owner and beneficiary; and

(3)   annuitization of payments for the life of the IRA owner or the lives of the IRA owner and beneficiary.[20]

The first method requires recalculation of payments each year, while the second and third methods provide constant payments. A person using the second and third methods can elect to switch to the first method. In making these calculations, life expectancy and mortality are now based on the RMD tables (see Appendix D) and interest is generally limited to a maximum rate (which changes monthly).

For additional discussion of the early distribution penalty, and in particular, the three methods for calculating substantially equal periodic payments with examples, see Chapter 13.

Required Minimum Distributions

When a nonRoth IRA owner reaches age 70½, the IRA owner must begin taking required minimum distributions. In general, the required minimum distribution rules cause the IRA owner to withdraw the entire IRA account balance over the IRA owner's life or the lives of the IRA owner and a designated beneficiary. If there is more than one beneficiary other than the IRA owner, the oldest other beneficiary's life expectancy is used for the designated beneficiary. Special rules apply where the spouse of the IRA owner is the designated beneficiary. Failure to withdraw the required minimum distribution results in a 50 percent penalty tax on the amount by which the amount of the required minimum distribution exceeds the actual amount withdrawn.[21]

In the case of a Roth IRA, required minimum distributions need not begin until after the death of the Roth IRA owner (which includes the spouse of the original Roth IRA owner where the surviving spouse is the designated beneficiary and elects to treat the Roth IRA as the spouse's own.)[22] (See Chapter 5.)

An additional rule, the minimum distribution incidental benefit (MDIB) rule, is designed to insure that nonRoth IRA distributions are primarily for the benefit of the IRA owner. The rule does this, while the IRA owner is alive, by treating a beneficiary other than the spouse of the IRA owner as no more than 10 years younger than the IRA owner.[23] The Uniform Lifetime Table (see Appendix C) implements the MDIB rule. The minimum distribution incidental benefit rule does not apply to Roth IRAs.

In the case of a traditional, SEP, or SIMPLE IRA, required minimum distributions must begin by April 1 of the year following the year the IRA owner reaches age 70½. Generally, required minimum distributions must be made by December 31st of each year. However, in the year the IRA owner reaches age 70½, the required minimum distribution for that year need not be made until April 1st of the following year (the required beginning date).

Required minimum distributions may be calculated for each IRA and distributions made from each IRA as appropriate. Alternatively, required minimum distributions may be calculated for all IRAs within a category (e.g., Roth, nonRoth) owned by the individual and distributions made from whichever IRA or IRAs within the category the IRA owner chooses. However, an inherited IRA may not be aggregated with any other IRA within a category unless the other IRA was inherited from the same person. For this purpose, an IRA that a surviving spouse elects to treat as such spouse's own is not treated as being inherited from the decedent spouse.

The required minimum distribution for each year is generally calculated by dividing the IRA account balance as of the end of the previous year by the life expectancy of the IRA owner or the joint and survivor life expectancy of the IRA owner and a designated beneficiary.

Attained age is used for the age of the IRA owner and beneficiary in the appropriate year. Thus, a traditional, SEP, or SIMPLE IRA owner whose birthday is in the first half of the year (January-June) will be age 70 in the year the IRA owner turns 70½ and will enter the table using age 70. On the other hand, a traditional, SEP, or SIMPLE IRA owner whose birthday is in the second half of the year (July-December) will be age 71 in the year the IRA owner turns 70½ and will enter the table using age 71.

Distributions During Lifetime of Owner
(including the year of death)

Required minimum distributions during the lifetime of the owner (including the year of the death of the owner) of a traditional, SEP, or SIMPLE IRA (nonRoth IRAs), are generally determined using the Uniform Lifetime Table (see Appendix C). (Distributions from a Roth IRA are generally not required until after the deaths of the IRA owner and the spouse of the IRA owner.) The attained age of the IRA owner for the year is used, and the Uniform Lifetime Table treats the beneficiary as 10 years younger than the IRA owner. The Uniform Lifetime Table is used even if the IRA owner has not designated a beneficiary.

However, if the spouse of the IRA owner is the sole designated beneficiary of the IRA and the spouse is more than 10 years younger than the IRA owner, the joint and survivor life expectancy of the IRA owner and spouse is used. In this case, the attained ages of both the IRA owner and spouse for the year are used, and a factor from the RMD Joint and Survivor Table (see Appendix C) is used. This method produces higher RMD factors and lower required minimum distributions than using factors from the Uniform Lifetime Table.

Distributions After Death of Owner

The method for calculating required minimum distributions after the death of the IRA owner generally depends on whether a beneficiary has been designated by the time of the IRA owner's death and whether the spouse of the IRA owner is the designated beneficiary.

The method for calculating required minimum distributions after the death of the IRA owner may also depend on whether or not the IRA owner died before the *required beginning date*. For a traditional, SEP, or SIMPLE IRA, the required beginning date is April 1 of the year after the year in which the IRA owner would attain age 70½. For a Roth IRA, the owner is always treated as dying before the required beginning date.

The actual determination of the designated beneficiary can be determined as late as September 30 of the first year after the year of the owner's death. Thus, if a primary beneficiary disclaims an IRA, a contingent named beneficiary who receives the IRA would be treated as the designated beneficiary. Or, if there are two named beneficiaries of an IRA, and one beneficiary is cashed out, the remaining beneficiary is treated as the designated beneficiary.

Spouse Beneficiary. If the spouse of the IRA owner is the sole designated beneficiary, the spouse can elect to be treated as the owner of the IRA for purposes of the RMD rules. The election cannot be made if a trust is named beneficiary, even if the spouse is the sole beneficiary of the trust. (Under certain circumstances, it appears that a rollover to a spouse may be used to get around this limitation.) Also, if the IRA owner died prior to the year the IRA owner attained age 70½ and the spouse is the sole designated beneficiary, then required minimum distributions to the spouse do not have to begin until the year the IRA owner would have attained age 70½.

If the spouse does not elect to be treated as the owner of the IRA, then required minimum distributions must be made to the spouse over the single life expectancy of the spouse. In this case, the attained age of the spouse for the year is used, and a factor from the RMD Single Life Table (see Appendix C) is used. After the death of the spouse, distributions must continue using the remaining life expectancy of the spouse and the subtract one method. The life expectancy is determined using the attained age of the spouse for the year of the death of the spouse from the RMD Single Life Table (see Appendix C), and by subtracting one from that life expectancy for each year after the year of death.

If the spouse does not elect to be treated as the owner of the IRA, and the owner died on or after the required beginning date (see above), the life expectancy of the owner can be used in any year if it is greater than the life expectancy of the spouse (see preceding paragraph). The life expectancy of the owner is determined using the attained age of the owner for the year of the death of the IRA owner from the RMD Single Life Table (see Appendix C), and by subtracting one from that life expectancy for each year elapsed thereafter.

Nonspouse Beneficiary. Distributions to a designated nonspouse beneficiary after the death of the IRA owner depend on whether or not the IRA owner died before the required beginning date (see above).

If the IRA owner died *before* the required beginning date, distributions must be made over the remaining life expectancy of the beneficiary using the subtract one method. The life expectancy of the beneficiary is determined using the attained age of the beneficiary for the year after the year of the death of the IRA owner from the

RMD Single Life Table (see Appendix C), and by subtracting one from that life expectancy for each year elapsed thereafter.

If the IRA owner died *after* the required beginning date, distributions must be made over the longer of the remaining life expectancy of the owner or the beneficiary using the subtract one method. The life expectancy of the owner is determined using the attained age of the owner for the year of the death of the IRA owner from the RMD Single Life Table (see Appendix C), and by subtracting one from that life expectancy for each year elapsed thereafter. The life expectancy of the beneficiary is determined using the attained age of the beneficiary for the year after the year of the death of the IRA owner from the RMD Single Life Table (see Appendix C), and by subtracting one from that life expectancy for each year elapsed thereafter.

No Beneficiary. If there is no designated beneficiary, distributions after the death of the IRA owner depend on whether or not the IRA owner died before the required beginning date (see above).

If the IRA owner died *before* the required beginning date, the entire IRA account must be distributed under the five year rule (see below).

If the IRA owner died *after* the required beginning date, distributions must continue using the remaining life expectancy of the IRA owner and the subtract one method. The life expectancy is determined using the attained age of the IRA owner for the year of the death of the IRA owner from the RMD Single Life Table (see Appendix C), and by subtracting one from that life expectancy for each year after the year of death.

Five Year Rule. If the five year rule applies, the entire IRA account must be distributed by the end of the calendar year that contains the fifth anniversary of the date of death of the IRA owner. For example, if an IRA owner age 65 dies on January 1, 2003, then the entire account must be distributed by the end of 2008 if the five year rule applies.

The five year rule generally applies: if elected; if the IRA owner dies before the required beginning date (see above) and without a beneficiary; or if the IRA owner has a beneficiary and there is a failure to timely start distributions over the life expectancy of the beneficiary. Life expectancy distributions must generally start by December 31 of the year after the year of death of the IRA owner, but could start later if the spouse is the beneficiary.

For additional discussion of the required minimum distribution rules, including descriptions of the various methods available and examples of the calculations, see Chapter 13.

Divorce

If an interest in an IRA is transferred from one spouse to the other in connection with a divorce or separation, a gift may be made. However, a transfer of property to a spouse in settlement for his or her marital or property rights or for child support shall be deemed made for full and adequate consideration in money or money's worth if:

(1) the transfer is made pursuant to a written agreement between the husband and wife, and

(2) divorce occurs within the three-year period beginning on the date one year before the agreement is entered into.

Under this statutory provision, it is immaterial whether the agreement is approved by the divorce decree.[24]

Also, the transfer of an IRA from one spouse to the other in connection with a divorce or separation is generally not considered a taxable transfer for income tax purposes. The spouse to whom the IRA is transferred is thereafter treated as the IRA owner.[25]

Bankruptcy and Asset Protection

Certain protections are provided for IRAs in bankruptcy (including sweeping changes made by the Bankruptcy Abuse Prevention and Consumer Protection Act of 2005), and against creditors and other claimants seeking to reach IRA assets and distributions. The protection provided for SEP and SIMPLE IRAs is sometimes greater than that provided for traditional and Roth IRAs. Use of a spendthrift trust may offer additional protection for IRA beneficiaries. See Chapter 20.

Filing Requirements for IRA Participant

Generally, an individual who establishes an individual retirement plan does not need to file a return for the plan for any year in which there is no plan activity other than making contributions (other than rollover contributions) and making distributions. However, the individual does need to file a return if there is a tax due because of an excess contribution or an excess accumulation (i.e., failure to make a required minimum distribution).[26] Information on these additional taxes is reported on IRS Form 5329. The tax on early distributions is also reported on IRS Form 5329.

Also, if an individual makes a designated nondeductible contribution to a traditional or SEP IRA for any taxable year or takes a contribution from an IRA for any taxable year, the individual must include on his income tax return (or other form as the Secretary of the Treasury prescribes) the following information:

(1)	the amount of designated nondeductible contributions for the taxable year;

(2)	the amount of distributions from individual retirement plans for the taxable year;

(3)	the excess of the aggregate amount of designated nondeductible contributions for all preceding taxable years over the aggregate amount of distributions from individual retirement plans that was excludable from taxable income for such taxable years;

(4)	the aggregate balance of all individual retirement plans as of the close of the year in which the taxable year begins; and

(5)	any other information as the Secretary of the Treasury may prescribe.[27]

Overstatement of a designated nondeductible contribution for any year is subject to a penalty tax of $100 per overstatement. An individual who fails to file a form required by the Secretary of Treasury under IRC Section 408(o) incurs a penalty of $50 for each such failure unless it is shown that such failure is due to reasonable cause.[28]

IRS Form 8606 is the appropriate form for reporting designated nondeductible contributions and distributions.

Endnotes

1. Rev. Rul. 84-146, 1984-2 CB 61.
2. IRC Sec. 67.
3. Rev. Rul. 86-142, 1986-2 CB 60.
4. Let. Rul. 8747072.
5. Let. Rul. 8527082.
6. IRC Sec. 163(d).
7. IRC Secs. 408(a)(2), 408(n).
8. Regs. §§1.408-2(b)(2), 1.408-2(e).
9. Ibid.
10. IRC Secs. 408(e), 408(m).
11. IRC Sec. 408(a)(3).
12. IRC Sec. 408(b).
13. IRC Secs. 408(e), 511.
14. IRC Secs. 408(e)(2), 4975.
15. IRC Sec. 408(e)(3).
16. IRC Sec. 408(e)(4).
17. IRC Sec. 408(e)(5).
18. IRC Sec. 408(m).
19. IRC Sec. 72(t).
20. Rev. Rul. 2002-62, 2002-42 IRB 710; Notice 89-25 (A-12), 1989-1 CB 662.
21. IRC Secs. 408(a)(6), 408(b)(3), 401(a)(9), 4974(a).
22. IRC Sec. 408A(c)(5).
23. Treas. Reg. §1.401(a)(9)-5 (A-4).
24. IRC Sec. 2516.
25. IRC Sec. 408(d)(6).
26. IRC Secs. 6058(d), 6058(e).
27. IRC Sec. 408(o).
28. IRC Sec. 6693(b).

Part

II

IRA Types

Chapter 4

Traditional IRAs

Traditional IRAs have been particularly popular because deductible (as well as nondeductible) contributions can be made to such IRAs. The ability to make deductible (but not nondeductible) contributions to a traditional IRA is restricted if the individual is an active participant in certain employer retirement plans and the individual has certain thresholds (depending on taxpayer filing status) of income. Contributions to a traditional IRA must essentially be made from compensation received by the individual and cannot be made once the individual has attained age 70½.

Amounts contributed to a traditional IRA can be invested in a wide variety of investments. Such amounts grow within the IRA account on a tax-deferred basis; there is generally no taxation until amounts are distributed.

Amounts distributed from a traditional IRA are generally taxable on a pro-rated basis. Amounts distributed from a traditional IRA that are allocated to nondeductible contributions are excludable from income. Certain distributions from traditional IRAs to charity are not included in inome.

Distributions received before the individual reaches age 59½ are generally subject to an early distribution penalty tax to the extent the distribution is includable in income unless an exception applies. Once the individual reaches age 70½, required minimum distributions must be made from the traditional IRA or a different penalty tax applies.

Traditional IRAs are useful for receiving rollovers from a qualified retirement plan, a tax sheltered annuity, or an eligible Section 457 governmental plan. Such rollovered amounts can generally be: retained in a traditional IRA; rolled back to a qualified retirement plan, a tax sheltered annuity, or an eligible Section 457 governmental plan; or converted to a Roth IRA (generally a taxable event).

Roth IRAs compared. The development of Roth IRAs (see Chapter 5) may substantially cut into the popularity of traditional IRAs. No deduction is available for Roth IRAs; however, distributions from a Roth IRA can often be received tax-free. Therefore, it is generally preferable to make nondeductible contributions to a Roth IRA rather than nondeductible contributions to a traditional IRA unless contributions cannot be made to a Roth IRA because of the income thresholds for Roth IRAs. Furthermore, under some circumstances, it may be preferable to make nondeductible contributions to a Roth IRA rather than it is to make deductible contributions to a traditional IRA (see Chapter 9). Also, contributions can be made to a Roth IRA even after the individual has attained age 70½. And, finally, required minimum distributions from a Roth IRA can generally be postponed until after the death of the individual and the individual's spouse.

Contributions

An individual may generally make deductible and nondeductible contributions to a traditional IRA. In addition, an employer may make contributions to an employee's traditional IRA. Contributions may be subject to various limitations. A rollover (see heading below) to a traditional IRA is generally not treated as a contribution to a traditional IRA.

Contributions to a traditional IRA, as for all IRAs, must be made in cash.[1] Contributions for a taxable year may be made up until the time for filing the tax return for the year (not including extensions of time for filing): generally, April 15.[2] An IRA owner making a contribution between January 1 and April 15 should designate whether the contribution is made for the current year or the preceding year. If the year is not designated, the contribution is treated as made for the current year.

An individual may take a deduction from income in any taxable year for contributions the individual makes to a traditional IRA for up to the lesser of the total contribution limit or compensation includable in income.[3] However, a deduction cannot be taken for contributions made to a traditional IRA in taxable years once the individual has attained age 70½.[4] Furthermore, a deduction generally cannot be taken for contributions to an IRA inherited from another individual.[5]

The total contribution limit consists of the sum of the regular contribution limit and the catch-up contribution limit. The regular contribution limit is as follows.[6]

Regular Contribution Limit

Year	Amount
2005-2007	$4,000
2008-	$5,000*

*indexed for inflation after 2008

The regular contribution limit is indexed for inflation after 2008.[7]

In addition, catch-up contributions can be made for individuals attaining age 50 before the end of the year.[8] The catch-up contribution limit is as follows.

Catch-up Contribution Limit

Year	Amount
2006-	$1,000

The regular and catch-up contribution limits shown reflect changes made by PPA 2006. PPA 2006 eliminates the sunset after 2010 of sheduled increases in the contribution limits made by EGTRRA 2001.

In certain employer bankruptcy cases, PPA 2006 allows additional traditional and Roth IRA catchup contributions payments in 2007 through 2009. The provision is available for an individual who was a qualified participant in a 401(k) plan that provided an employer match of at least 50 percent of the employee's contribution in stock of the employer. In any taxable year preceding the taxable year in which the preceding sentence was applicable, the employer must have been a debtor in a case under Chapter 11 (bankruptcy) of federal law, or any similar federal or state law, and the employer (or any controlling corporation of such employer) was subject to an indictment or conviction relating to such case. The individual must have been a participant in the 401(k) plan on the date that is six months before the filing of the bankrupcty case. If the individual makes an election, the individual can contribute annually, in addition to the regular contribution amount above, an amount equal to three times the catch-up contribution amount above [$1,000 x 3 = $3,000]. This provision is not limited to individuals age 50 and older. However, the regular catch-up contribution provision is not available for the year if the election is made.[9]

Special rules apply to married individuals, or more specifically to an individual who files a joint return for the year where the individual's compensation includable in income for the year is less than the compensation includable in income for the year by the individual's spouse. In such case, a deduction from income may be taken for contributions the individual makes to a traditional IRA for up to the lesser of (1) the total contribution limit or (2) the sum of (a) compensation includable in such individual's income and (b) compensation includable in the income of such individual's spouse. For this purpose, the compensation included in the income of such individual's spouse is reduced by (1) any deductible or nondeductible contributions such spouse made to a traditional IRA and (2) any contribution to a Roth IRA for such spouse.[10]

This special rule is often referred to as allowing contributions to be made for a non-working spouse. However, the special rule may be of some use whenever one spouse has compensation of less than the total contribution limit. It can allow deductible contributions to be made for an individual with little or no compensation by taking into account compensation of such individual's spouse.

> *Example.* Bob and Sue (both age 45) file a joint return for 2006. Bob has compensation of $50,000 and Sue has no compensation. Bob has contributed $4,000 to a Roth IRA. A deduction can be taken for a $4,000 contribution to a traditional IRA for Sue. The deduction is equal to the lesser of (1) $4,000, or (2) the sum of (a) Sue's compensation ($0) and (b) Bob's compensation ($50,000) reduced by the $4,000 contribution to Bob's Roth IRA [($0 + $50,000) - $4,000 = $46,000]. Thus, Sue can make a deductible contribution of $4,000 to a traditional IRA even though she has no compensation.

If the individual is an active participant in certain employer retirement plans, the total contribution limit amount is subject to phaseout based upon adjusted gross income.[11] Deductible contributions to a traditional IRA are subject to this phaseout; nondeductible contributions (see below) to a traditional IRA are not subject to phaseout.

An individual is considered an active participant in an employer retirement plan if the individual is an active participant in a qualified corporate or Keogh pension, profit sharing, stock bonus, or annuity plan, in a simplified employee pension (SEP IRA), in a 403(b) tax sheltered annuity, SIMPLE IRA, or in a government plan. However, participation in Social Security, Railroad Retirement (tier I or II) or in a Section 457 deferred compensation plan is not taken into consideration. Active participants include any individual who is an active participant in a plan established for employees by the United States, a State or political subdivision thereof, or by an agency or instrumentality of any of the foregoing. Active participation is determined without regard to whether an individual's rights in the plan are nonforfeitable. However, certain members of the armed forces reserves and certain volunteer firemen covered under government plans are not considered active participants.[12]

In the case of an active participant, the total contribution limit amount (see above) is reduced by an amount equal to the total contribution limit amount multiplied by the ratio of the individual's modified adjusted gross income (MAGI, see below) in excess of an applicable dollar amount to $10,000 ($20,000 in the case of a joint return after 2006).

$$\text{total contribution limit} \times \frac{\text{MAGI - applicable dollar amount}}{\$10,000} = \text{reduction}$$

Whenever the phaseout reduction is other than a multiple of $10, the reduction is rounded to the next lowest multiple of $10. However, where the $2,000 amount adjusted for phaseout based upon adjusted gross income is between $0 and $200, $200 is the amount allowable as a deduction.[13]

Modified adjusted gross income (MAGI) for purposes of the phaseout of deductible contributions to traditional IRAs means adjusted gross income determined with certain adjustments. The deduction for contributions to traditional IRAs, which is being determined, is not taken into account. Also, MAGI includes social security and tier 1 railroad retirement benefits to the extent required to be included in income (see IRC Section 86); MAGI is determined after application of the passive loss rules (see IRC Section 469); and MAGI is not reduced by the exclusion for income from U.S. savings bonds used to pay higher education tuition and fees (see IRC Section 135), the exclusion for qualified adoption expenses (see IRC Section 137), the deduction for interest on a qualified education loan (see IRC Section 221), the deduction for qualified tuition and related expenses (see IRC Section 222), or the exclusion for certain citizens or residents living abroad (see IRC Section 911).[14]

In the case of a joint return, the applicable dollar amount equals:[15]

Taxable Year	Applicable Dollar Amount	Total Phaseout
2006	$75,000	$85,000
2007-	$80,000*	$100,000*

*plus indexing for inflation after 2006

Thus, in the case of a joint return of an active participant, the total contribution limit amount (see above) is not reduced for adjusted gross income of $75,000 and less for 2006, is reduced to $0 for adjusted gross income of $85,000 or more, and is proportionately reduced in the case of adjusted gross income between $75,000 and $85,000.

However, in the case of a joint return where one spouse is an active participant and the other is not, the applicable dollar amount with respect to the spouse who is not an active participant is increased to $150,000; however, the $10,000 phaseout band remains at $10,000 (it does not increase to $20,000 as in the case of a joint return after 2006).[16] Thus, in such case, the total contribution limit amount (see above) is not reduced for adjusted gross income of up to $150,000, is reduced to $0 for adjusted gross income of $160,000 or more, and is proportionately reduced in the case of adjusted gross income between $150,000 and $160,000.

In the case of other than a joint return or a married filing separate return, the applicable dollar amount equals:[17]

Taxable Year	Applicable Dollar Amount	Total Phaseout
2005-	$50,000*	$60,000*

*plus indexing for inflation after 2006

Thus, in the case of a single return or a head of household return of an active participant, the total contribution limit amount (see above) is not reduced for adjusted gross income of $50,000 and less for 2006, is reduced to $0 for adjusted gross income of $60,000 or more, and is proportionately reduced in the case of adjusted gross income between $50,000 and $60,000.

In the case of a married filing separate return of an active participant, the applicable dollar amount equals $0.[18] Thus, in such case, the total contribution limit amount (see above) is reduced to $0 for adjusted gross income of $10,000 or more, and is proportionately reduced in the case of adjusted gross income between $0 and $10,000. However, a married couple who file separate returns and live apart at all times during the year are not treated as married for purposes of the phaseout rules for deductible contributions to a traditional IRA.[19]

PPA 2006 provides for indexing of the phaseout limits for contributions after 2006.[20] The phaseout range ($10,000 or $20,000) is not indexed; the applicable dollar amount is indexed and the corresponding amount at which total phaseout occurs moves up with it. However, in the case of a joint return (see above), IRC Section 219(g)(3)(B)(i) already provided for an increased amount for 2007. A technical correction may be needed.

> *Example.* In 2006, a married individual (age 60) files a joint return, is an active participant in a retirement plan, and has adjusted gross income of $77,000. He can make a deductible contribution to a traditional IRA of $4,000. This is calculated as follows:
>
> total contribution limit x $\underline{\text{MAGI - applicable dollar amount}}$ = reduction
> $10,000
>
> round reduction down to next lowest multiple of $10
> total contribution limit - reduction = amount deductible
>
> regular contribution limit $4,000
> catch-up contribution limit   + 1,000
> total contribution limit $5,000
>
> $5,000 x $\underline{\$77,000 - \$75,000}$ = $1,000
> $10,000
>
> round $1,000 to $1,000
> $5,000 - $1,000 = $4,000 deductible

Figure 4.1 provides a phaseout table method for estimating the amount of deductible contributions that can be made to a traditional IRA where there is active participation. See Figure 4.2 for an example of using this method.

The deduction for a contribution to a traditional IRA is a deduction from gross income.[21] Therefore, the deduction can be taken whether or not the individual itemizes deductions and is not subject to any phaseout of itemized deductions.

A taxpayer can elect to have otherwise deductible contributions to a traditional IRA treated as nondeductible.[22] However, as noted below, it is usually better to make nondeductible contributions to a Roth IRA rather than to a traditional IRA. (For a discussion of whether it is better to make *deductible* contributions to a traditional IRA or nondeductible contributions to a Roth IRA, see Chapter 9.)

Nondeductible contributions to a traditional IRA must be reported on IRS Form 8606.

FIGURE 4.1

Traditional IRA Deductible Contributions
Phaseout Table Estimation Method

Traditional IRA Maximum Contribution

Year	Less Than Age 50	Age 50 or More
2006	4,000	5,000
2007	4,000	5,000
2008	5,000	6,000
20__	_____	_____

Phaseout Ranges (Active Participation)

Single/Head of Household

Year	Start	Range	End
2006	50,000	10,000	60,000
20__	_____	10,000	_____

Joint Return (Active Participant Spouse)

Year	Start	Range	End
2006	75,000	10,000	85,000
2007	80,000	20,000	100,000
20__	_____	20,000	_____

Joint Return (Non Active Participant Spouse)

Year	Start	Range	End
2006	150,000	10,000	160,000
20__	_____	10,000	_____

Separate Return

Year	Start	Range	End
2006-	0	10,000	10,000

FIGURE 4.1 (continued)

Worksheet

(1) Modified Adjusted Gross Income (MAGI)   _____
(2) Start of Phaseout Range (from above)   _____
     If (1) <= (2), then enter Maximum Contribution (see above)
     on Line 9.
     If (1) >= End of Phaseout Range (see above), then enter $0
     on Line 9.
(3) MAGI in Excess of Applicable Dollar Amount [(1) - (2)]   _____
(4) Phaseout Range (from above)   _____
(5) Maximum Contribution (from above)   _____
(6) Go to IRA Phaseout Table (Appendix B)
     with a phaseout range equal to (4)
(7) Go to column with maximum contribution equal to (5)
(8) Go to row with MAGI in excess of applicable dollar amount
     equal to (3)
(9) Phased Out Maximum Deductible Contribution Amount   _____

FIGURE 4.2

For example, assume the taxpayer, age 60, is an active participant in a retirement plan, files a joint return, and has modified adjusted gross income (MAGI) of $77,000 in 2006. The phased out maximum deductible contribution amount can be determined as follows.

Worksheet

(1) Modified Adjusted Gross Income (MAGI) $77,000
(2) Start of Phaseout Range (from above) $75,000
     If (1) <= (2), then enter Maximum Contribution (see above)
     on Line 9.
     If (1) >= End of Phaseout Range (see above), then enter $0
     on Line 9.
(3) MAGI in Excess of Applicable Dollar Amount [(1) - (2)] $2,000
(4) Phaseout Range (from above) $10,000
(5) Maximum Contribution (from above) $5,000
(6) Go to IRA Phaseout Table (Appendix B)
     with a phaseout range equal to (4)
(7) Go to column with maximum contribution equal to (5)
(8) Go to row with MAGI in excess of applicable dollar amount
     equal to (3)
(9) Phased Out Maximum Deductible Contribution Amount $4,000

An individual can also make nondeductible contributions to a traditional IRA up to the lesser of the total contribution limit (see above) or compensation includable in income. This amount is reduced by any deductible contributions made to a traditional IRA.[23] However, nondeductible contributions to a traditional IRA are not subject to any phaseout based upon adjusted gross income even if the individual is an active participant in certain employer retirement plans.

Nondeductible contributions can also be made to a Roth IRA (see Chapter 5). However, contributions that can be made to a Roth IRA are subject to phaseout based upon income and are reduced by contributions made to a traditional IRA. Because distributions from a Roth IRA are generally subject to much more favorable rules than are distributions from a traditional IRA, it is generally advisable to make nondeductible contributions to a Roth IRA rather than nondeductible contributions to a traditional IRA, except to the extent that the individual's permissible contributions to a Roth IRA are phased out by the limitations based on income.

In order to gain the more favorable rules for distributions from Roth IRAs, consideration can be given to converting the traditional IRA to a Roth IRA at a later time. The price of making such a qualified rollover to a Roth IRA (see Chapter 5) is that the amount in the traditional IRA is generally treated as distributed from the traditional IRA for income tax purposes in the year rolled over. In tax years before 2010, conversions to a Roth IRA are not allowed if the individual's adjusted gross income (AGI) for the year exceeds $100,000 or the individual is married and files a separate return. For tax years after 2009, these limitations do not apply. For conversions in 2010, the amount includable in income can be recognized ratably over 2011 and 2012, rather than in 2010. For additional discussion of conversions to a Roth IRA, including some analysis of whether to convert to a Roth IRA, see Chapter 12.

Contributions to traditional IRAs and Roth IRAs are subject to a combined overall limitation equal to the total contribution limit amount (see above).[24]

The trustee of a traditional IRA is required to report contributions to the IRA to the IRS and to the IRA owner on IRS Form 5498.

Return of Contributions

In general, a contribution (or portion of a contribution) to a traditional IRA for which a deduction has not been taken can be returned tax-free if it is returned, along with the income attributable to the contribution (see below), by the due date (including extensions) for filing a tax return for the year of the contribution.[25] However, the income returned is included in income for the year of the contribution. Also, the early distribution penalty tax (see heading below) applies to the income returned, unless an exception applies. The penalty tax on excess contributions (see heading below) does not apply to an excess contribution returned in this manner.

A return of a traditional IRA contribution after the due date (including extensions) for filing a tax return for the year of the contribution would generally be taxed as a distribution (see heading below). However, a return of an excess distribution (see heading below) for which a deduction has not been taken is not taxed even if it is returned after the due date (including extensions) for filing a tax return for the year of the contribution if total contributions to traditional and Roth IRAs for the year of return do not exceed the total contributions limit for such IRAs (see above).[26] An excess contribution returned in this manner could be subject to the penalty tax for excess contributions (see heading below) while it is held by the traditional IRA.

The net income (can be a loss if negative) attributable to a contribution is calculated using the following formula.

$$\text{Net Income} = \text{Contribution} \times \frac{\text{(Adjusted Closing Balance - Adjusted Opening Balance)}}{\text{Adjusted Opening Balance}}$$

The computation period means the period starting immediately prior to the contribution and ending immediately prior to the distribution of the contribution. The adjusted closing balance means the fair market value of the account balance at the end of the period, increased by distributions or transfers (including returned contributions and recharacterizations of contributions) from the IRA during the period. The adjusted opening balance means the fair market value of the account balance at the start of the period, increased by contributions or transfers (including any recharacterizations) to the account during the period. If an IRA asset is not valued daily, the most recent regularly determined fair market value on the same or an earlier date is used. The calculation is made only with respect to the traditional IRA from which the recharacterizing transfer is made. If more than one contribution was made to the traditional IRA for the year, the returned contribution is treated as being a return of the last contribution for the year.[27]

Recharacterization of Contributions

An IRA owner can also recharacterize a regular contribution made to a traditional IRA as being instead made to a Roth IRA (see Chapter 5) by transferring the contribution plus the income attributable to the contribution (see above) to the Roth IRA by the due date (including extensions) for filing a tax return for the year of the contribution.[28]

The individual makes the election to recharacterize by notifying both trustees that he has made such an election. The notification must include the following:

(1) the type and amount of contribution to the first IRA to be recharacter-ized;

(2) the date the contribution was made to the first IRA and the year for which it was made;

(3) a direction to the trustee of the first IRA regarding the amount of the contribution and income thereon to be transferred in a trustee-to-trustee transfer to the second IRA; and

(4) the name of both trustees and any additional information needed.[29]

The trustee of a traditional IRA is required to report recharacterized contributions to or from the IRA to the IRS and to the IRA owner on IRS Form 5498.

Excess Contributions

In the case of an excess contribution to a traditional IRA, there is imposed a six percent penalty tax.[30] In general, an excess contribution is any portion of a contri-bution to a traditional IRA in excess of the limitations described above. However, it is necessary to keep a running account of excess contributions; i.e., it is necessary to keep track of contributions and distributions for the current year and preceding years in order to determine if there is an excess contribution for the current year. A return of contributions (see above) can be used to reduce or eliminate the effect of the penalty tax on excess contributions.

More technically, an excess contribution for any taxable year equals the sum of (1) the excess of contributions to traditional IRAs over the lesser of the total contribution limit amount or the individual's compensation, and (2) amounts determined under this calculation for the preceding taxable year reduced by the sum of (a) distributions from traditional IRAs of amounts includable in income for the year, (b) distribu-tions from traditional IRAs of amounts not includable in income under IRC Section 408(d)(5) (i.e., distributions of amounts contributed that did not exceed the total contribution limit amount but did exceed the amount of compensation), and (c) the excess of the amount allowable as a deduction for contributions to a traditional IRA for the year over the amount contributed to traditional and Roth IRAs for the year. Thus, an excess contribution carried over from a previous year can be used up as a contribution in a subsequent year.[31]

Example. Ann (age 40) contributed $3,500 to a traditional IRA in 2004, resulting in an excess contribution of $500 ($3,500 - $3,000). Ann contributed $4,100 to the IRA in 2005, resulting in an excess contribution of $600 ([$4,100 - $4,000] plus the $500 carryover from 2004). In 2006, Ann does not contribute to the IRA. The $600 carryover from 2005 is treated as contributed (and deductible) in 2006 and is less than $4,000; there is no excess contribution.

Excess contributions to a traditional IRA must be reported on IRS Form 5329.

Employer Contributions

An employer can set up direct deposits to traditional IRAs by way of payroll deduction so that individual employees can contribute to their own IRAs.[32]

An employer may make contributions to an employee's traditional IRA. The employer takes a deduction for the contribution as compensation paid to the employee. The employer withholds any FICA (social security tax), FUTA (federal unemployment tax), and income tax as appropriate. The employee includes the contribution in income as compensation for the year in which the contribution was made.[33] The employee can then take a deduction for a contribution to a traditional IRA, subject to the limitations based upon active participation and income thresholds described above. The same overall contribution level described above also applies to contributions made by the employer.

The employer may also elect to treat part of a qualified employer plan as a deemed IRA (see Chapter 8) to which the employee makes contributions.

See the discussion of Simplified Employee Pensions (SEPs) in Chapter 6 and SIMPLE IRAs (Savings Incentive Match Plan for Employees IRA) in Chapter 7, for IRAs specifically designed for employer/employee programs.

Accumulations/Investments

Amounts earned within a traditional IRA generally accumulate on a tax-deferred basis. Earnings are generally not taxable until distributed from the traditional IRA. However, a traditional IRA is taxed if it has unrelated business taxable income. Furthermore, part or all of the traditional IRA may be deemed distributed if the IRA owner engages in a prohibited transaction, borrows on an annuity contract, pledges the account as security for a loan, purchases an endowment contract, or invests in certain collectibles.[34] A traditional IRA account, as with all IRAs, cannot invest in life insurance contracts.[35] The IRA can be in the form of an individual retirement annuity.[36]

An individual retirement annuity is an annuity contract or endowment contract issued by an insurance company meeting certain requirements: (1) the contract cannot be transferable by the owner; (2) the premiums may not be fixed; (3) the annual premium cannot exceed the total contribution limit amount (see above); (4) any refund of premiums must be applied before the end of the next year to pay future premiums or to purchase additional benefits; (5) the required minimum distribution and minimum distribution incidental death benefit rules apply; and (6) the entire interest of the owner must be nonforfeitable. For this purpose, an endowment contract cannot mature later than the taxable year in which the IRA owner reaches age 70½ and must be for the exclusive benefit of the IRA owner or beneficiary. Aggregate annual premiums for all endowment contracts purchased for the IRA owner cannot exceed the total contribution limit amount (see above).

See Chapter 3 for more information on limitations on accumulations in an IRA.

Distributions

Amounts distributed from a traditional IRA are includable in taxable income (on a prorated basis) to the extent distributions are from deductible contributions to the traditional IRA and earnings from the traditional IRA. Amounts distributed before the traditional IRA owner reaches age 59½ that are includable in income are subject to an early distribution penalty tax unless certain exceptions are met. Required minimum distributions must begin when the IRA owner reaches age 70½ or a penalty tax applies. A rollover (see heading below) from a traditional IRA is generally not treated as a distribution from a traditional IRA. Certain distributions from traditional IRAs to charity are not included in inome.

Part or all of the traditional IRA may be deemed distributed if the IRA owner engages in a prohibited transaction, borrows on an annuity contract, pledges the account as security for a loan, purchases an endowment contract, or invests in certain collectibles.[37]

Amounts distributed from a traditional IRA represent one of three categories: deductible contributions to the IRA, nondeductible contributions to the IRA, and earnings on contributions within the IRA. A deduction is taken when deductible contributions are made to the traditional IRA; therefore, deductible contributions represent property that has not been subjected to income tax. Earnings on contributions within the IRA generally accumulate tax-free (see above); therefore earnings on contributions also represent property that has not been subjected to income tax. However, nondeductible contributions to the IRA are contributed on an after-tax basis.

As a result, nondeductible contributions to a traditional IRA can be recovered tax-free from the IRA (similar to investment in the contract or basis). However, deductible contributions to a traditional IRA and earnings on contributions within a traditional IRA are includable in income upon distribution from a traditional IRA.

In order to calculate the part of a distribution from a traditional IRA that should be excluded from income, the annuity exclusion ratio rules are applied. Thus, gross income does not include the part of a distribution that bears the same ratio to such amount as the investment in the contract (i.e., nondeductible contributions) bears to expected return under the contract. For this purpose, all nonRoth IRAs (i.e., traditional, SEP, SIMPLE) are treated as one IRA, all distributions during the year are treated as one distribution, and the value of the contract, income on the contract, and investment in the contract is computed at the end of the calendar year in which the taxable year begins. The value of the contract is increased by any distribution during the calendar year.[38]

The value of the contract is also increased by any outstanding rollovers. An outstanding rollover is a distribution from the IRA during the current year that is rolled over within 60 days of the distribution but during the following year.

Thus, the formula for calculating the portion of a distribution from a traditional IRA that is excludable from income as attributable to nondeductible contributions to the IRA is:

$$\frac{\text{Unrecovered Nondeductible Contributions}}{\begin{array}{l}\text{Total Account Balance} + \\ \text{Distribution Amount} + \\ \text{Outstanding Rollover}\end{array}} \times \text{ Distribution Amount}$$

All nonRoth IRAs are treated as one in determining each of the above amounts. Unrecovered nondeductible contributions is generally determined as of the beginning of the year, but may be increased for contributions made during the current year. The total account balance is determined as of the end of the year (i.e., increased by contributions and rollovers to the IRA, but reduced by distributions and rollovers from the IRA). The distribution amount and outstanding rollover is the total of such transactions occurring during the current year.[39]

Example. John made $2,000 nondeductible contributions to a traditional IRA for 10 years. Unrecovered nondeductible contributions as of the beginning of 2006 equals $20,000. John withdraws $1,000 from the IRA in 2006. At the end of 2006, the IRA account balance equals $24,000. The amount of the distribution excludable from income equals $800; $200 is includable. Unrecovered nondeductible contributions as of the beginning of 2007 would equal $19,200 ($20,000 - $800).

$$\frac{\text{Unrecovered Nondeductible Contributions}}{\text{Total Account Balance} + \text{Distribution Amount} + \text{Outstanding Rollover}} \times \text{Distribution Amount} = \text{Amount Excludable}$$

Distribution Amount - Amount Excludable = Amount Includable

$$\frac{\$20,000}{\$24,000 + \$1,000 + \$0} \times \$1,000 = \text{Amount Excludable}$$

$800 = Amount Excludable

$1,000 - $800 = Amount Includable

$200 = Amount Includable

The trustee of a traditional IRA is required to report distributions from the IRA to the IRS and to the IRA owner on IRS Form 1099-R. Distributions from traditional IRAs are reported by the IRA owner or beneficiary on IRS Form 8606.

Qualified Charitable Distributions

PPA 2006 provides that certain distributions (qualified charitable distributions) from a traditional or Roth IRA made to charity in 2006 or 2007 are not included in income. The provision is not available for SEP and SIMPLE IRAs. The maximum annual amount that can be excluded under this provision is $100,000. The exclusion applies only to amounts otherwise includable in income. The distribution must be made directly from the IRA trustee to a 50% public charity (as described in IRC Section 170(b)(1)(A), other than a support organization or a donor advised fund). The distribution must be made after the IRA owner has attained age 70½. The entire contribution to charity must be otherwise deductible for income tax purposes, disregarding this provision and the charitable deduction percentage limitations based on income for this purpose. Adjustments are made to undistributed nondeductible contributions to reflect the qualified charitable distribution. An income tax charitable deduction is not available for the amount excluded from inome.[40]

For additional discussion of qualified charitable distributions, see Chapter 14.

Early Distributions

In general, distributions from a traditional IRA received before age 59½ are subject to a 10 percent penalty tax on early distributions. However, the penalty tax only applies to the extent that the distribution is includable in income and a number of exceptions to application of the penalty apply.[41]

The early distribution penalty tax does not apply to distributions from a traditional IRA that are:

(1) made after the death of the IRA owner;

(2) attributable to the IRA owner's disability;

(3) part of a series of substantially equal periodic payments (at least annually) made for the life (or life expectancy) or the joint life (or life expectancies) of the IRA owner and a designated beneficiary (the penalty tax plus interest is due if the substantially equal periodic payments are modified before the later of five years after payments have begun or the IRA owner reaches age 59½);

(4) made for medical care to the extent generally allowable as a medical expense deduction (generally, unreimbursed medical expenses in excess of 7.5 percent of adjusted gross income; for this purpose, itemization of deductions is not required);

(5) made to the IRA owner who is unemployed for payment of health insurance premiums;

(6) made to the IRA owner for payment of qualified higher education expenses furnished to the IRA owner, the IRA owner's spouse, or children or grandchildren of either;

(7) made to the IRA owner ($10,000 lifetime limit) for purchase of a first home by the IRA owner, the IRA owner's spouse, or children, grandchildren, or ancestor of either; or

(8) made to a reservist while on active duty (commencing after September 11, 2001 and before 2008).

The IRS has approved three methods for calculating substantially equal periodic payments (SEPPs):

(1)   payments that satisfy the required minimum distributions method (see heading below);

(2)   amortization of payments over the life expectancy of the IRA owner or joint and survivor life expectancy of the IRA owner and beneficiary; and

(3)   annuitization of payments for the life of the IRA owner or the lives of the IRA owner and beneficiary.[42]

The first method requires recalculation of payments each year, while the second and third methods provide constant payments. A person using the second and third methods can elect to switch to the first method. In making these calculations, life expectancy and mortality are now based on the RMD tables (see Appendix D) and interest is generally limited to a maximum rate (which changes monthly).

The additional tax on early distributions is reported either directly on IRS Form 1040 or on IRS Form 5329.

For additional discussion of the early distribution penalty, and in particular, the three methods for calculating substantially equal periodic payments, see Chapter 13.

Required Minimum Distributions

When a traditional IRA owner reaches age 70½, the IRA owner must begin taking required minimum distributions. In general, the required minimum distributions rules cause the IRA owner to withdraw the entire IRA account balance over the IRA owner's life or the lives of the IRA owner and a designated beneficiary. If there is more than one beneficiary other than the IRA owner, the oldest other beneficiary's life expectancy is used for the designated beneficiary. Special rules apply where the spouse of the IRA owner is the designated beneficiary. Failure to withdraw the required minimum distribution results in a 50 percent penalty tax on the amount by which the required minimum distribution exceeds the actual amount withdrawn.[43]

An additional rule, the minimum distribution incidental benefit rule, is designed to insure that the traditional IRA distributions are primarily for the benefit of the IRA owner. The rule does this, while the IRA owner is alive, by treating a beneficiary other than the spouse of the IRA owner as no more than 10 years younger than the IRA owner.[44] The Uniform Lifetime Table (see Appendix C) implements the MDIB rule.

In the case of a traditional IRA, required minimum distributions must begin by April 1 of the year following the year the IRA owner reaches age 70½. Generally, required minimum distributions must be made by December 31st of each year. However, in the year the IRA owner reaches age 70½, the required minimum distribution for that year need not be made until April 1st of the following year (the required beginning date).

Required minimum distributions may be calculated for each traditional IRA and distributions made from each IRA as appropriate. Alternatively, required minimum distributions may be calculated for all nonRoth IRAs (i.e., traditional, SEP, or SIMPLE) owned by the individual and distributions made from whichever nonRoth IRA or IRAs the IRA owner chooses. However, an inherited IRA may not be aggregated with any other IRA within a category unless the other IRA was inherited from the same person. For this purpose, an IRA that a surviving spouse elects to treat as such spouse's own is not treated as being inherited from the decedent spouse.

The required minimum distribution for each year is generally calculated by dividing the traditional IRA account balance as of the end of the previous year by the life expectancy of the IRA owner or the joint and survivor life expectancy of the IRA owner and a designated beneficiary.

Attained age is used for the age of the IRA owner and beneficiary in the appropriate year. Thus, an IRA owner whose birthday is in the first half of the year (January-June) will be age 70 in the year the IRA owner turns 70½ and will enter the table using age 70. On the other hand, an IRA owner whose birthday is in the second half of the year (July-December) will be age 71 in the year the IRA owner turns 70½ and will enter the table using age 71.

Distributions During Lifetime of Owner (including the year of death)

Required minimum distributions during the lifetime of the owner (including the year of the death of the owner) of a traditional IRA, are generally determined using the Uniform Lifetime Table (see Appendix C). The attained age of the IRA owner for the year is used, and the Uniform Lifetime Table treats the beneficiary as 10 years younger than the IRA owner. The Uniform Lifetime Table is used even if the IRA owner has not designated a beneficiary.

However, if the spouse of the IRA owner is the sole designated beneficiary of the IRA and the spouse is more than 10 years younger than the IRA owner, the joint and survivor life expectancy of the IRA owner and spouse is used. In this case, the attained ages of both the IRA owner and spouse for the year are used, and a factor from the

RMD Joint and Survivor Table (see Appendix C) is used. This method produces higher RMD factors and lower required minimum distributions than using factors from the Uniform Lifetime Table.

Distributions After Death of Owner

The method for calculating required minimum distributions after the death of the IRA owner generally depends on whether a beneficiary has been designated by the time of the IRA owner's death and whether the spouse of the IRA owner is the designated beneficiary.

The method for calculating required minimum distributions after the death of the IRA owner may also depend on whether or not the IRA owner died before the required beginning date. For a traditional IRA, the *required beginning date* is April 1 of the year after the year in which the IRA owner would attain age 70½.

If there are multiple designated beneficiaries of an IRA, the oldest beneficiary is treated as the designated beneficiary. Thus, the oldest beneficiary of a trust that is the beneficiary of an IRA is generally treated as the designated beneficiary of the IRA. If a person other than an individual is designated as beneficiary of an IRA, the IRA will be treated as having no beneficiary, even if an individual is also named beneficiary. For example, a charity is not an individual. Separate IRAs (and trusts) can be created with different designated beneficiaries.

The actual determination of the designated beneficiary can be determined as late as September 30 of the first year after the year of the owner's death. Thus, if a primary beneficiary disclaims an IRA, a contingent named beneficiary who receives the IRA would be treated as the designated beneficiary. Or, if there are two named beneficiaries of an IRA, and one beneficiary is cashed out, the remaining beneficiary is treated as the designated beneficiary.

Spouse Beneficiary. If the spouse of the IRA owner is the sole designated beneficiary, the spouse can elect to be treated as the owner of the IRA for purposes of the RMD rules. The election cannot be made if a trust is named beneficiary, even if the spouse is the sole beneficiary of the trust. (Under certain circumstances, it appears that a rollover to a spouse may be used to get around this limitation.) Also, if the IRA owner died prior to the year the IRA owner attained age 70½ and the spouse is the sole designated beneficiary, then required minimum distributions to the spouse do not have to begin until the year the IRA owner would have attained age 70½.

If the spouse does not elect to be treated as the owner of the IRA, then required minimum distributions must be made to the spouse over the single life expectancy of the spouse. In this case, the attained age of the spouse for the year is used, and a factor from the RMD Single Life Table (see Appendix C) is used. After the death of the spouse, distributions must continue using the remaining life expectancy of the spouse and the subtract one method. The life expectancy is determined using the attained age of the spouse for the year of the death of the spouse from the RMD Single Life Table (see Appendix C), and by subtracting one from that life expectancy for each year after the year of death.

If the spouse does not elect to be treated as the owner of the IRA, and the owner died on or after the required beginning date (see above), the life expectancy of the owner can be used in any year if it is greater than the life expectancy of the spouse (see preceding paragraph). The life expectancy of the owner is determined using the attained age of the owner for the year of the death of the IRA owner from the RMD Single Life Table (see Appendix C), and by subtracting one from that life expectancy for each year elapsed thereafter.

Nonspouse Beneficiary. Distributions to a designated nonspouse beneficiary after the death of the IRA owner depend on whether or not the IRA owner died before the required beginning date (see above).

If the IRA owner died *before* the required beginning date, distributions must be made over the remaining life expectancy of the beneficiary using the subtract one method. The life expectancy of the beneficiary is determined using the attained age of the beneficiary for the year after the year of the death of the IRA owner from the RMD Single Life Table (see Appendix C), and by subtracting one from that life expectancy for each year elapsed thereafter.

If the IRA owner died *after* the required beginning date, distributions must be made over the longer of the remaining life expectancy of the owner or the beneficiary using the subtract one method. The life expectancy of the owner is determined using the attained age of the owner for the year of the death of the IRA owner from the RMD Single Life Table (see Appendix C), and by subtracting one from that life expectancy for each year elapsed thereafter. The life expectancy of the beneficiary is determined using the attained age of the beneficiary for the year after the year of the death of the IRA owner from the RMD Single Life Table (see Appendix C), and by subtracting one from that life expectancy for each year elapsed thereafter.

No Beneficiary. If there is no designated beneficiary, distributions after the death of the IRA owner depend on whether or not the IRA owner died before the required beginning date (see above).

If the IRA owner died *before* the required beginning date, the entire IRA account must be distributed under the five year rule (see below).

If the IRA owner died *after* the required beginning date, distributions must continue using the remaining life expectancy of the IRA owner and the subtract one method. The life expectancy is determined using the attained age of the IRA owner for the year of the death of the IRA owner from the RMD Single Life Table (see Appendix C), and by subtracting one from that life expectancy for each year after the year of death.

Five Year Rule. If the five year rule applies, the entire IRA account must be distributed by the end of the calendar year that contains the fifth anniversary of the date of death of the IRA owner. For example, if an IRA owner age 65 dies on January 1, 2003, then the entire account must be distributed by the end of 2008 if the five year rule applies.

The five year rule generally applies: if elected; if the IRA owner dies before the required beginning date (see above) and without a beneficiary; or if the IRA owner has a beneficiary and there is a failure to timely start distributions over the life expectancy of the beneficiary. Life expectancy distributions must generally start by December 31 of the year after the year of death of the IRA owner, but could start later if the spouse is the beneficiary.

Miscellaneous

The trustee of a traditional IRA generally reports the fair market value of the IRA account as of the end of year. Fair market value may be as of the date of death if the IRA owner died. The fair market value of the account and whether a required minimum distribution is required is reported on IRS Form 5498. Required minimum distributions may be required even if not indicated on IRS Form 5498. The additional tax on failure to make required minimum distributions is reported on IRS Form 5329.

For additional discussion of the required minimum distribution rules, including descriptions of the various methods available and examples of the calculations, see Chapter 13.

Rollovers

Rollovers are permitted between various IRAs, qualified plans, tax sheltered annuities, and eligible Section 457 governmental plans. In general, a rollover is a transfer of retirement assets from one plan to another by the participant or owner that is completed within 60 days. The effect of a rollover is generally to avoid taxes and penalties upon what otherwise would be treated as a distribution.[45]

Rollovers are generally permitted from qualified retirement plans, tax sheltered annuities, and eligible Section 457 governmental plans to a traditional IRA. However, the qualified Roth contribution program portion of a 401(k) or 403(b) plan cannot be rolled over into a traditional IRA. Amounts rolled over from a qualified retirement plan, tax sheltered annuity, or eligible Section 457 governmental plan are subject to 20 percent withholding unless the rollover is made through a direct trustee-to-trustee transfer. Rollovers are generally permitted from a traditional IRA to qualified retirement plans, tax sheltered annuities, and eligible Section 457 governmental plans (but not to an elective deferral Roth).

If the amount rolled over from a qualified plan to a traditional IRA includes amounts that would be eligible for special tax treatment upon distribution from the qualified plan (e.g., income averaging or capital gains treatment), such special tax treatment will be lost. However, if the rolled over amounts are maintained in a separate conduit traditional IRA and rolled back to the qualified plan, the special tax treatment will be once again available for distributions of such amounts from the qualified plan.

Only one rollover is permitted from a particular IRA to any other IRA during the one-year period ending with the transfer from the first IRA. Also, in an IRA-to-IRA rollover, the receiving IRA cannot be an endowment contract. The one-year rollover limitation does not apply to trustee-to-trustee transfers.

Rollovers are permitted between traditional IRAs.

A rollover from a Roth IRA can be made only to another Roth IRA. Therefore, rollovers are not permitted from a Roth IRA to a traditional IRA (however, under certain circumstances, a Roth IRA can be recharacterized back as a traditional IRA – see Chapter 5). If a traditional IRA is rolled over to a Roth IRA, it is a taxable event and special provisions apply. See Chapter 5 on Roth IRAs.

Rollovers are permitted between a traditional IRA and a SEP IRA.

A rollover is not permitted from a SIMPLE IRA to a traditional IRA during the first two years that the individual participates in the SIMPLE IRA. The only rollover permitted to a SIMPLE IRA is from another SIMPLE IRA. Therefore, rollovers are not permitted from a traditional IRA to a SIMPLE IRA.

The trustee of an IRA is required to report rollovers to and from a traditional IRA to the IRS and to the IRA owner on IRS Form 5498.

See Chapter 11 for a more detailed discussion of rollovers.

Losses (Unrecovered Basis)

The Internal Revenue Code provides that if annuity payments from a traditional IRA end upon the death of the annuitant and there is still unrecovered investment in the contract (essentially unrecovered basis), the unrecovered investment in the contract is allowable as a deduction for the annuitant's final tax year. However, if refund payments are made to a beneficiary or the annuitant's estate after the annuitant's death, the deduction for unrecovered investment in the contract is taken by the person receiving the refund payments for the year in which received. The IRS provides additionally that when all amounts from all nonRoth IRAs (i.e., traditional, SEP, or SIMPLE) have been distributed and the amounts distributed are less than the unrecovered basis in nonRoth IRAs, a loss may be recognized.[46]

> *Example.* Jan contributes $2,000 (all nondeductible) to a traditional IRA in each of four years (a total of $8,000). The IRA earns $1,000 during the four years. Thus, the IRA account balance equals $9,000 ($8,000 + $1,000). Jan then withdraws $4,000. The amount excludable from income as investment in the contract equals $3,556 [($8,000 ÷ $9,000) x $4,000]. The unrecovered investment in the contract equals $4,444 ($8,000 - $3,556). The IRA account balance equals $5,000 ($9,000 - $4,000).

> The next year, the IRA account balance drops in value to $3,000 (i.e., a loss in value of $2,000). Jan withdraws the entire $3,000. No amount is includable in income. Furthermore, Jan may claim a loss of $1,444 ($4,444 - $3,000).

Withholding

Distributions from a traditional IRA are distributions from a retirement plan subject to income tax withholding unless the individual elects to have withholding not apply. Thus, unless the election is made, periodic payments from a traditional IRA are subject to withholding at regular withholding rates and nonperiodic payments from a traditional IRA are subject to withholding at a 10 percent rate.[47]

A conversion of a traditional IRA into a Roth IRA (a qualified rollover) is a distribution for which income tax withholding is required, unless made in the form of a direct trustee-to-trustee transfer.[48]

Transfer Taxes

A traditional IRA will generally be fully includable in the estate of the original IRA owner. A decedent's estate includes the value of an annuity or other payment receivable by reason of surviving the decedent where the decedent held certain interests in the property while alive. The amount includable is proportionate to the part of the purchase price contributed by the decedent. Any contribution by the employer of the decedent to the traditional IRA is treated as made by the employee for this purpose.[49] Thus, the original IRA owner will generally have contributed 100 percent of the contributions to the traditional IRA and the full value of the traditional IRA will be includable in the original owner's estate.

If upon the original owner's death the traditional IRA passes to the spouse of the original IRA owner, the transfer will generally qualify for the marital deduction (see Chapter 18). If the transfer to the surviving spouse qualified for the marital deduction, any amount still left in the traditional IRA at the surviving spouse's death will be includable in the surviving spouse's estate.

If the traditional IRA passes to a skip person (generally, a person two or more generations younger than the transferor), the generation-skipping transfer tax must be taken into consideration. See Chapter 19.

Endnotes

1. IRC Sec. 219(e)(1).
2. IRC Secs. 219(f)(3), 408(o)(3).
3. IRC Secs. 219(b)(1), 219(b)(5).
4. IRC Sec. 219(d)(1).
5. IRC Sec. 219(d)(4).
6. IRC Secs. 219(b)(5)(A), 219(b)(5)(D), as amended by PPA 2006.
7. IRC Sec. 219(b)(5)(D), as amended by PPA 2006.
8. IRC Sec. 219(b)(5)(B).
9. IRC Sec. 219(b)(5)(C), as added by PPA 2006.
10. IRC Sec. 219(c).
11. IRC Sec. 219(g).
12. IRC Secs. 219(g)(5), 219(g)(6).
13. IRC Sec. 219(g)(2).

14. IRC Sec. 219(g)(3)(A).
15. IRC Sec. 219(g)(3)(B)(i).
16. IRC Sec. 219(g)(7).
17. IRC Sec. 219(g)(3)(B)(ii).
18. IRC Sec. 219(g)(3)(B)(iii).
19. IRC Sec. 219(g)(4).
20. IRC Sec. 219(g)(8).
21. IRC Sec. 62(a)(7).
22. IRC Sec. 408(o)(2)(B)(ii).
23. IRC Sec. 408(o)(2).
24. IRC Secs. 219(b)(1), 408(o)(2), 408A(c)(2).
25. IRC Sec. 408(d)(4).
26. IRC Sec. 408(d)(5).
27. Treas. Reg. §1.408-11.
28. IRC Secs. 408A(d)(6), 408A(d)(7).
29. Treas. Reg. §1.408A-5(A-6).
30. IRC Sec. 4973(a).
31. IRC Secs. 4973(b), 219(f)(6).
32. Ann. 99-2, 1999-1 CB 305.
33. IRC Sec. 219(f)(5).
34. IRC Secs. 408(e), 408(m).
35. IRC Sec. 408(a)(3).
36. IRC Sec. 408(b).
37. IRC Secs. 408(e), 408(m).
38. IRC Secs. 408(d)(1), 408(d)(2), 72(b).
39. Notice 87-16(III), 1987-1 CB 446.
40. IRC sec. 408(d)(8).
41. IRC Sec. 72(t).
42. Rev. Rul. 2002-62, 2002-42 IRB 710; Notice 89-25(A-12), 1989-1 CB 662.
43. IRC Secs. 408(a)(6), 408(b)(3), 401(a)(9), 4974(a).
44. Treas. Reg. §1.401(a)(9)-5(A-4).
45. See IRC Sec. 408(d)(3).
46. IRC Sec. 72(b)(3); Notice 89-25(A-7), 1989-1 CB 662, clarifying Notice 87-16(D-5), 1987-1 CB 446.
47. IRC Sec. 3405.
48. Treas. Reg. §1.408A-6 (A-13); IRC Sec. 3405(c).
49. IRC Sec. 2039.

Chapter 5

Roth IRAs

Roth IRAs are a recent development that are popular for a number of reasons, most notably of which are: distributions from a Roth IRA can generally be arranged to be received tax-free, and required minimum distributions from a Roth IRA can be postponed until after the death of the individual and generally after the death of the individual's spouse.

Unlike with the traditional IRA (see Chapter 4), only nondeductible contributions can be made to a Roth IRA. The ability to make contributions to a Roth IRA is restricted if the individual has certain thresholds (depending on taxpayer filing status) of income. Contributions to a Roth IRA must essentially be made from compensation received by the individual. Unlike with the traditional IRA, contributions can be made to a Roth IRA even after the individual has attained age 70½.

Amounts contributed to a Roth IRA can be invested in a wide variety of investments. Such amounts grow within the IRA account on a tax-deferred (or possibly tax-free) basis; there may or may not be taxation when amounts are distributed.

Amounts distributed from a Roth IRA are generally received tax-free if the distribution is made more than five years after the creation of a Roth IRA and the distribution occurs after the individual turns age 59½, after the individual's death or disability, or if the distribution is for a first-time home purchase. Otherwise, distributions are generally treated as first made from nondeductible contributions and distributions attributable to nondeductible contributions are received tax-free. Also, certain distributions from Roth IRAs to charity are not included in inome.

Distributions received before the individual reaches age 59½ are generally subject to an early distribution penalty tax to the extent the distribution is includable in income unless an exception applies. Required minimum distributions must be made from a Roth IRA or a penalty tax applies. However, with the Roth IRA such required minimum distributions can be postponed until after the death of the individual and, generally, after the death of the individual's spouse. With the traditional IRA (see Chapter 4), such distributions must begin when the individual reaches age 70½.

Because distributions from a Roth IRA can often be received tax-free, it is generally preferable to make nondeductible contributions to a Roth IRA rather than nondeductible contributions to a traditional IRA (see Chapter 4) unless contributions cannot be made to a Roth IRA because of the income thresholds for Roth IRAs. Furthermore, under some circumstances it may be preferable to make nondeductible contributions to a Roth IRA rather than it is to make deductible contributions to a traditional IRA (see Chapter 9).

Generally, unless the Internal Revenue Code provides otherwise with respect to a Roth IRA, the general rules applicable to traditional IRAs (see Chapter 4) apply.[1]

The rules for elective deferral Roths (see Chapter 8) are not always the same as the rules for regular Roth IRAs.

Contributions

An individual may make nondeductible contributions to a Roth IRA. Unlike with a traditional IRA (see Chapter 4), deductible contributions cannot be made to a Roth IRA. In addition, an employer may make contributions to an employee's Roth IRA. Contributions may be subject to various limitations. A rollover (see heading below) to a Roth IRA is generally not treated as a regular contribution to a Roth IRA.

Contributions to a Roth IRA, as for all IRAs, must be made in cash.[2] Contributions for a taxable year may be made up until the time for filing the tax return for the year (not including extensions of time for filing): generally, April 15.[3] An IRA owner making a contribution between January 1 and April 15 should designate whether the contribution is made for the current year or the preceding year. If the year is not designated, the contribution is treated as made for the current year.

Unlike with traditional IRAs, contributions can be made to a Roth IRA even after the individual has attained age 70½.[4] However, the individual (or perhaps the individual's spouse) generally must have compensation in order to make contributions to a Roth IRA. Thus, the ability to make post age 70½ contributions to a Roth IRA is generally lost unless the individual (or perhaps the individual's spouse) continues to work.

An individual can make nondeductible contributions to a Roth IRA up to the lesser of the total contribution limit amount or compensation includable in income. (Contribution limits for elective deferral Roths are different from those for regular Roth IRAs. See Chapter 8.) This amount is reduced by any contributions to a traditional IRA or employee contributions to a SEP IRA.[5] Thus, the maximum amount that can be contributed to a Roth IRA equals the lesser of:

(1)   the lesser of total contribution limit amount or compensation, reduced by contributions to traditional IRAs and employee contributions to SEP IRAs; or

(2)   the total contribution limit amount as phased out based upon income (see below).[6]

The total contribution limit consists of the sum of the regular contribution limit and the catch-up contribution limit. The regular contribution limit is as follows.[7]

Regular Contribution Limit

Year	Amount
2005-2007	$4,000
2008-	$5,000*

*indexed for inflation after 2008

The regular contribution limit is indexed for inflation after 2008.[8]

In addition, catch-up contributions can be made for individuals attaining age 50 before the end of the year.[9] The catch-up contribution limit is as follows.

Catch-up Contribution Limit

Year	Amount
2006-	$1,000

The regular and catch-up contribution limits shown reflect changes made by PPA 2006. PPA 2006 eliminates the sunset after 2010 of scheduled increases in the contribution limits made by EGTRRA 2001.

In certain employer bankruptcy cases, PPA 2006 allows additional traditional and Roth IRA catchup contributions payments in 2007 through 2009. The provision is available for an individual who was a qualified participant in a 401(k) plan that provided an employer match of at least 50 percent of the employee's contribution in stock of the employer. In any taxable year preceding the taxable year in which the preceding sentence was applicable, the employer must have been a debtor in a case under Chapter 11 (bankruptcy) of federal law, or any similar federal or state law, and the employer (or any controlling corporation of such employer) was subject to an indictment or conviction relating to such case. The individual must have been a participant in the 401(k) plan on the date that is six months before the filing of the bankrupcty case. If the individual makes an election, the individual can contribute annually, in addition to the regular contribution amount above, an amount equal to three times the catch-up contribution amount above [$1,000 x 3 = $3,000]. This provision is not limited to individuals age 50 and older. However, the regular catch-up contribution provision is not available for the year if the election is made.[10]

Special rules apply to married individuals, or more specifically to an individual who files a joint return for the year where the individual's compensation includable in income for the year is less than the compensation includable in income for the year by the individual's spouse. In such case, a contribution can be made to a Roth IRA for up to the lesser of:

(1)   the total contribution limit amount, or

(2)   the sum of (a) compensation includable in such individual's income and (b) compensation includable in the income of such individual's spouse.

For this purpose, the compensation includable in the income of such individual's spouse is reduced by (1) any deduction taken for contributions such spouse made to a traditional IRA or SEP IRA and (2) any contribution to a Roth IRA for such spouse.[11]

This special rule is often referred to as allowing contributions to be made for a nonworking spouse. However, the special rule may be of some use whenever one spouse has compensation of less than the total contribution limit amount. It can allow contributions to be made for an individual with little or no compensation by taking into account compensation of such individual's spouse.

Example. Bob and Sue (both age 45) file a joint return for 2006. Bob has compensation of $80,000 and Sue has no compensation. Bob has contributed $4,000 to a Roth IRA. A $4,000 contribution can be made to a Roth IRA for Sue even though she has no compensation. The contribution is equal to the lesser of (1) $4,000, or (2) the sum of (a) Sue's compensation ($0) and (b) Bob's compensation ($80,000) reduced by the $4,000 contribution to Bob's Roth IRA [($0 + $80,000) - $4,000 = $76,000].

The total contribution limit amount is subject to phaseout based upon modified adjusted gross income (MAGI).[12] The total contribution limit amount is reduced by an amount equal to the total contribution limit amount multiplied by the ratio of the individual's modified adjusted gross income in excess of an applicable dollar amount to $15,000 ($10,000 in the case of a joint return or a married filing separate return).

$$\text{total contribution limit} \times \frac{\text{MAGI - applicable dollar amount}}{(\$15,000 \text{ if married})} = \text{reduction}$$

Whenever the phaseout reduction is other than a multiple of $10, the reduction is rounded to the next lowest multiple of $10. However, where the total contribution limit amount adjusted for phaseout based upon modified adjusted gross income is between $0 and $200, $200 can be contributed.

Modified adjusted gross income (MAGI) for purposes of the phaseout of contributions to Roth IRAs means adjusted gross income determined with certain adjustments. Any amount taken into income from a qualified rollover to a Roth IRA (see below) is not taken into account and any deduction for contributions to a traditional IRA is taken into account. Also, MAGI includes social security and tier 1 railroad retirement benefits to the extent required to be included in income (see IRC Section 86); MAGI is determined after application of the passive loss rules (see IRC Section 469); and MAGI is not reduced by the exclusion for income from U.S. savings bonds used to pay higher education tuition and fees (see IRC Section 135), the exclusion for qualified adoption expenses (see IRC Section 137), the deduction for interest on a qualified education loan (see IRC Section 221), the deduction for qualified tuition and related expenses (see IRC Section 222), or the exclusion for certain citizens or residents living abroad (see IRC Section 911).[13]

In the case of a joint return, the applicable dollar amount equals $150,000.[14] Thus, in such case, the total contribution limit amount is not reduced for modified adjusted gross income of $150,000 or less, is reduced to $0 for modified adjusted gross income of $160,000 or more, and is proportionately reduced in the case of modified adjusted gross income between $150,000 and $160,000.

In the case of a married filing separate return, the applicable dollar amount equals $0.[15] Thus, in such case, the total contribution limit amount is reduced to $0 for modified adjusted gross income of $10,000 or more, and is proportionately reduced in the case of modified adjusted gross income between $0 and $10,000. However, a married couple who file separate returns and live apart at all times during the year are not treated as married for purposes of the phaseout rules for contributions to a Roth IRA.[16]

In all other cases, the applicable dollar amount equals $95,000.[17] Thus, in the case of a single return or a head of household return, the total contribution limit amount is not reduced for modified adjusted gross income of $95,000 or less, is reduced to $0 for modified adjusted gross income of $110,000 or more, and is proportionately reduced in the case of modified adjusted gross income between $95,000 and $110,000.

PPA 2006 provides for indexing of the phaseout limits for contributions after 2006.[18] The phaseout range ($10,000 or $15,000) is not indexed; the applicable dollar amount is indexed and the corresponding amount at which total phaseout occurs moves up with it.

> *Example.* In 2006, a taxpayer (age 60) filing a joint return with modified adjusted gross income of $153,333, can make a contribution to a Roth IRA of $3,340. This is calculated as follows:
>
> total contribution limit x $\frac{\text{MAGI - applicable dollar amount}}{\$10,000}$ = reduction
>
> round reduction down to next lowest multiple of $10
>
> total contribution limit - reduction = permissible contribution amount
>
> | regular contribution limit | $4,000 |
> |---|---|
> | catch-up contribution limit | + 1,000 |
> | total contribution limit | $5,000 |
>
> $5,000 x $\frac{\$153,333 - \$150,000}{\$10,000}$ = $1,666
>
> round $1,666 to $1,660
> $5,000 - $1,660 = $3,340

FIGURE 5.1

Roth IRA Contributions
Phaseout Table Estimation Method

Roth IRA Maximum Contribution

Year	Less Than Age 50	Age 50 or more
2006	4,000	5,000
2007	4,000	5,000
2008	5,000	6,000
20__	_____	_____

Phaseout Ranges (Active Participation)

Single/Head of Household

Year	Start	Range	End
2006	95,000	15,000	110,000
20__	_____	15,000	_____

Joint Return

2006	150,000	10,000	160,000
20__	_____	10,000	_____

Separate Return

2006-	0	10,000	10,000

Worksheet

(1) Modified Adjusted Gross Income (MAGI) _____
(2) Start of Phaseout Range (from above) _____
  If (1) <= (2), then enter Maximum Contribution (see above)
  on Line 9.
  If (1) >= End of Phaseout Range (see above), then enter $0
  on Line 9.
(3) MAGI in Excess of Applicable Dollar Amount [(1) - (2)] _____
(4) Phaseout Range (from above) _____
(5) Maximum Contribution (from above) _____
(6) Go to IRA Phaseout Table (Appendix B)
  with a phaseout range equal to (4)
(7) Go to column with maximum contribution equal to (5)
(8) Go to row with MAGI in excess of applicable dollar amount
  equal to (3)
(9) Phased Out Maximum Roth Contribution Amount _____

FIGURE 5.2

For example, assume the taxpayer, age 45, files a single return, and has modified adjusted gross income (MAGI) of $98,000 in 2006. The phased out maximum Roth contribution amount can be determined as follows.

Worksheet

(1)	Modified Adjusted Gross Income (MAGI)	$98,000
(2)	Start of Phaseout Range (from above)	$95,000
	If (1) <= (2), then enter Maximum Contribution (see above) on Line 9.	
	If (1) >= End of Phaseout Range (see above), then enter $0 on Line 9.	
(3)	MAGI in Excess of Applicable Dollar Amount [(1) - (2)]	$3,000
(4)	Phaseout Range (from above)	$15,000
(5)	Maximum Contribution (from above)	$4,000
(6)	Go to IRA Phaseout Table (Appendix B) with a phaseout range equal to (4)	
(7)	Go to column with maximum contribution equal to (5)	
(8)	Go to row with MAGI in excess of applicable dollar amount equal to (3)	
(9)	Phased Out Maximum Roth Contribution Amount	$3,200

Figure 5.1 provides a phaseout table method for estimating the amount of contributions that can be made to a Roth IRA. See Figure 5.2 for an example of using this method.

Nondeductible contributions can also be made to a traditional IRA (see Chapter 4). However, contributions made to a traditional IRA are not subject to phaseout based upon income. Also, the amount that can be contributed to Roth IRAs may be reduced by contributions made to traditional IRAs (see above).

Because distributions from a Roth IRA (see below) are generally subject to much more favorable rules than are distributions from a traditional IRA, it is generally advisable to make nondeductible contributions to a Roth IRA rather than nondeductible contributions to a traditional IRA, except to the extent that the individual's permissible contributions to a Roth IRA are phased out by the limitations based on income. For example, although the taxpayer in the example above can contribute only $3,340 to a Roth IRA in 2006, the taxpayer could make a nondeductible contribution to a traditional IRA of the $1,660 amount ($5,000 - $3,340) phased out with respect to the Roth IRA.

In order to gain the more favorable rules for distributions from Roth IRAs, consideration can be given to converting a traditional IRA to a Roth IRA at a later time. The price of making such a qualified rollover to a Roth IRA is that the amount in the traditional IRA is generally treated as distributed from the traditional IRA for income tax purposes in the year rolled over. In tax years before 2010, conversions to a Roth IRA are not allowed if the individual's adjusted gross income (AGI) for the year exceeds $100,000 or the individual is married and files a separate return. For tax years after 2009, these limitations do not apply. For conversions in 2010, the amount includable in income can be recognized ratably over 2011 and 2012, rather than in 2010. Conversion to a Roth IRA is discussed under "Rollovers," below. For additional discussion of conversions to a Roth IRA, including some analysis of whether to convert to a Roth IRA, see Chapter 12.

For a discussion of whether it is better to make deductible contributions to a traditional IRA or nondeductible contributions to a Roth IRA, see Chapter 9.

Contributions to traditional IRAs and Roth IRAs are subject to a combined overall limitation equal to the total contribution limit amount.[19] Other IRAs, including elective deferral Roths, have their own limitations.

The trustee of a Roth IRA is required to report contributions to the IRA to the IRS and to the IRA owner on IRS Form 5498.

Return of Contributions

In general, a contribution (or a portion of a contribution) to a Roth IRA can be returned tax-free if it is returned, plus the income attributable to the contribution (a loss would reduce the amount that must be returned) (see below), by the due date (including extensions) for filing a tax return for the year of the contribution.[20] However, the income returned is included in income for the year of the contribution. Also, the early distribution penalty tax (see heading below) applies to the income returned, unless an exception applies. The penalty tax on excess contributions (see heading below) does not apply to an excess contribution returned in this manner.

A return of a Roth IRA contribution after the due date (including extensions) for filing a tax return for the year of the contribution would generally be taxed as a distribution (see heading below). However, a return of an excess contribution (see heading below) is not taxed even if it is returned after the due date (including extensions) for filing a tax return for the year of the contribution if total contributions to traditional and Roth IRAs for the year of return do not exceed the total contributions limit for such IRAs (see above).[21]An excess contribution returned in this manner could be subject to the penalty tax for excess contributions (see heading below) while it is held by the Roth IRA.

The net income (can be a loss if negative) attributable to a contribution is calculated using the following formula.

Net Income = Contribution x (Adjusted Closing Balance - Adjusted Opening Balance)
                                        Adjusted Opening Balance

The computation period means the period starting immediately prior to the contribution and ending immediately prior to the distribution of the returned contribution. The adjusted closing balance means the fair market value of the account balance at the end of the period, increased by distributions or transfers (including returned contributions and recharacterizations of contributions) from the IRA during the period. The adjusted opening balance means the fair market value of the account balance at the start of the period, increased by contributions or transfers (including any recharacterizations) to the account during the period. If an IRA asset is not valued daily, the most recent regularly determined fair market value on the same or an earlier date is used. The calculation is made only with respect to the Roth IRA from which the transfer is made. The IRA owner can choose the date and the dollar amount (but not specific assets) of the contribution to be recharacterized.[22]

Recharacterization of Contributions

An IRA owner can also recharacterize a regular contribution made to a Roth IRA as being instead made to a traditional IRA (see Chapter 4) by transferring the contribution plus the income attributable to the contribution (see above) to the traditional IRA by the due date (including extensions) for filing a tax return for the year of the contribution.[23] While a recharacterization can be done for any reason, it could be used to correct for a contribution to a Roth IRA which turns out to be phased out based on modified adjusted gross income (see above); nondeductible contributions to traditional IRAs are not subject to phaseout.

The individual makes the election to recharacterize by notifying both trustees that he has made such an election. The notification must include the following:

(1)   the type and amount of contribution to the first IRA to be recharacterized;

(2)   the date the contribution was made to the first IRA and the year for which it was made;

(3)   a direction to the trustee of the first IRA regarding the amount of the contribution and income thereon to be transferred in a trustee-to-trustee transfer to the second IRA; and

(4)   the name of both trustees and any additional information needed.[24]

The trustee of a Roth IRA is required to report recharacterized contributions to or from the IRA to the IRS and to the IRA owner on IRS Form 5498.

Excess Contributions

In the case of an excess contribution to a Roth IRA, there is imposed a six percent penalty tax.[25] In general, an excess contribution is any portion of a contribution to a Roth IRA in excess of the limitations described above. An excess contribution continues to be subject to the penalty tax each year until the excess contribution is corrected. Therefore, it is necessary to keep a running account of excess contributions (i.e., it is necessary to keep track of contributions and distributions for the current year and preceding years in order to determine if there is an excess contribution for the current year.) A return of contributions (see above) can be used to reduce or eliminate the effect of the penalty tax on excess contributions.

More technically, an excess contribution for any taxable year equals the sum of (1) the excess of contributions (does not include qualified rollovers, see heading below) to all Roth IRAs over the amount that can be contributed to all Roth IRAs for the year, and (2) amounts determined under this calculation for the preceding taxable year reduced by the sum of (a) distributions from Roth IRAs for the current year, and (b) the excess of the amount that can be contributed to all Roth IRAs for the year over the amount contributed to all Roth and traditional IRAs for the year. Thus, an excess contribution carried over from a previous year can be used up as a contribution in a subsequent year.[26]

> *Example.* Joe (age 45) contributes $4,000 to a Roth IRA in 2006. However, Joe is a single taxpayer and his modified adjusted gross income (MAGI) for 2006 is $98,000. His MAGI exceeds $95,000 by $3,000; thus, the maximum he can contribute to the Roth for 2006 is $3,200 (see Figure 5.2). Joe has an excess contribution of $800 for 2006.

> *Example.* Ann (age 40) contributed $3,500 to a Roth IRA in 2004, resulting in an excess contribution of $500 ($3,500 - $3,000). Ann contributed $4,100 to the IRA in 2005, resulting in an excess contribution

of $600 [($4,100 - $4,000) plus the $500 carryover from 2004]. In 2006, Ann does not contribute to the IRA. The $600 carryover from 2005 is treated as contributed in 2006 and is less than $4,000; there is no excess contribution.

Excess contributions to a Roth IRA must be reported on IRS Form 5329.

Employer Contributions

An employer can set up direct deposits to Roth IRAs by way of payroll deduction so that individual employees can contribute to their own IRAs.[27]

An employer may make contributions to an employee's Roth IRA. The employer takes a deduction for the contribution as compensation paid to the employee. The employer withholds any FICA (social security tax), FUTA (federal unemployment tax), and income tax as appropriate. The employee includes the contribution in income as compensation for the year in which the contribution was made.[28] The same overall contribution level described above also applies to contributions made by the employer, subject to the limitations based upon income thresholds described above.

The employer may also elect to treat part of a qualified employer plan as a deemed IRA (see Chapter 8) to which the employee makes contributions.

See the discussion of Simplified Employee Pensions (SEPs) in Chapter 6 and SIMPLE IRAs (Savings Incentive Match Plan for Employees IRAs) in Chapter 7, for IRAs specifically designed for employer/employee programs.

Elective Deferral Roth Contributions

After 2005, a qualified plan or tax sheltered annuity that accepts salary reduction contributions can include a qualified Roth contribution program.[29] Such a program essentially allows an employee to convert deductible contributions to nondeductible contributions, with more favorable rules for distributions.

In such a program, an employee can designate a portion of his elective deferral contributions as being made to a designated Roth account. Although the contribution is generally treated as a salary reduction contribution, the contribution is not excludable from income. It is a nondeductible contribution to a designated Roth account. However, the contribution limits for elective deferrals apply rather than those for Roth IRAs.

Distributions from the designated Roth account are partially taxable under the Roth IRA rules (see below) and partially under the proration rules that apply to IRAs other than Roth IRAs. Thus, qualified distributions can be received tax-free. Distributions treated as made from contributions are also received tax-free; however, distributions from a designated Roth account are treated as a return of contributions on a pro-rated basis, rather than on the contributions first basis generally applicable to Roth IRAs. Also, the five year period for qualified distributions that can be received tax-free from a Roth IRA does not start until the earlier of (1) the year of the first contribution to any designated Roth account for the employee in the qualified Roth contribution program, or (2) if another designated Roth account is rolled over to the designated Roth account, the year of the first contribution to such other account.

Such elective deferral Roth contributions are discussed in more detail in Chapter 8.

Accumulations/Investments

Amounts earned within a Roth IRA generally accumulate on a tax-deferred basis. As described below, distributions from a Roth IRA can generally be arranged so that earnings are not taxable even when distributed from the Roth IRA. However, a Roth IRA is taxed if it has unrelated business taxable income. Furthermore, part or all of the Roth IRA may be deemed distributed if the IRA owner engages in a prohibited transaction, borrows on an annuity contract, pledges the account as security for a loan, purchases an endowment contract, or invests in certain collectibles.[30] A Roth IRA account, as with all IRA accounts, cannot invest in life insurance contracts.[31] The IRA can be in the form of an individual retirement annuity.[32]

An individual retirement annuity is an annuity contract or endowment contract issued by an insurance company meeting certain requirements: (1) the contract cannot be transferable by the owner; (2) the premiums may not be fixed; (3) the annual premium cannot exceed the total contribution limit amount (see above); (4) any refund of premiums must be applied before the end of the next year to pay future premiums or to purchase additional benefits; (5) the required minimum distribution and minimum distribution incidental death benefit rules apply; and (6) the entire interest of the owner must be nonforfeitable. For this purpose, an endowment contract cannot mature later than the taxable year in which the IRA owner reaches age 70½ and must be for the exclusive benefit of the IRA owner or beneficiary. Aggregate annual premiums for all endowment contracts purchased for the IRA owner cannot exceed the total contribution limit amount (see above).

Distributions

Distributions of amounts from a Roth IRA can generally be arranged so that distributions are not taxable when distributed from the Roth IRA. Amounts distributed before the Roth IRA owner reaches age 59½ that are includable in income are subject to an early distribution penalty tax unless certain exceptions are met. Required minimum distributions do not have to begin until after the Roth IRA owner's death (i.e., distributions do not have to begin when the Roth IRA owner reaches age 70½). A rollover (see heading below) from a Roth IRA is generally not treated as a distribution from a Roth IRA. Certain distributions from Roth IRAs to charity are not included in inome.

Part or all of the Roth IRA may be deemed distributed if the IRA owner engages in a prohibited transaction, borrows on an annuity contract, pledges the account as security for a loan, purchases an endowment contract, or invests in certain collectibles.[33]

If the Roth owner makes a gift of the Roth IRA to another, the assets of the Roth IRA are deemed distributed from the Roth IRA.[34]

Amounts distributed from a Roth IRA generally represent one of two categories: contributions to the IRA, and earnings on contributions within the IRA. For this purpose, amounts rolled over to a Roth IRA are deemed contributions. Earnings on contributions within the IRA generally accumulate tax-free (see above); therefore earnings on contributions represent property that has not been subjected to income tax. However, nondeductible contributions to the IRA are contributed on an after-tax basis.

As a result, nondeductible contributions to a Roth IRA can be recovered tax-free from the IRA (similar to investment in the contract or basis). However, earnings on contributions within a Roth IRA are includable in income upon distribution from a Roth IRA unless the distribution is a "qualified distribution."[35]

A **qualified distribution** is excludable from income. A qualified distribution is a distribution from a Roth IRA that is made after the five-taxable-year period beginning in the year in which the first contribution was made to a Roth IRA and that is:

(1)   made on or after the date the Roth IRA owner turns age 59½;

(2)   made after the death of the Roth IRA owner (which means after the death of the surviving spouse where a surviving spouse elects to treat the deceased spouse's Roth IRA as the surviving spouse's own);

(3)   attributable to disability of the Roth IRA owner; or

(4)   made to the Roth IRA owner ($10,000 lifetime limit) for purchase of a first home by the IRA owner, the IRA owner's spouse, or children, grand-children, or ancestor of either.

An IRA owner attains age 59½ on the date that is six calendar months after the 59th anniversary of the IRA owner's birth. For example, if an IRA owner's date of birth was June 30, 1947, the 59th anniversary is June 30, 2006, and the IRA owner attains age 59½ on December 30, 2006.

The five-year period for qualified distribution purposes begins as soon as a con-tribution is made to a Roth IRA (a different five-year period applies to contributions attributable to a qualified rollover, see below). Therefore, it may be advisable for an individual to make a contribution to a Roth IRA in the first year possible to start the running of the five-year period. Note that a contribution made by April 15 of a year that is treated as made for the previous year is treated similarly for this purpose.

Example. John contributes $1,000 to a Roth IRA for 2001 by April 15, 2002. He makes additional contributions in later years. Starting in 2006 (the fifth year after 2001), John (or his survivor) can begin taking qualified distributions (assuming one of the other requirements – post age 59½, death, disability, or first time home purchase – is met) from the Roth IRA.

It is necessary to calculate the part of a distribution from a Roth IRA that can be excluded from income when the distribution is not a qualified distribution. For this purpose, distributions are generally treated as first coming from contributions (i.e., investment in the contract or the nontaxable part) and all Roth IRAs are treated as one.

More specifically, a distribution is treated as made from contributions to the extent that the amount of the distribution plus all previous distributions does not exceed aggregate contributions to the IRA. Distributions treated as made from contributions are then treated as made first from contributions other than a qualified rollover, and then from qualified rollover contributions (on a first-in, first-out basis). Qualified rollover contributions are treated as made from qualified rollover contributions includable in income and then from qualified rollover contributions not includable in income. An early distribution of a qualified rollover (see heading below) can result in imposition of the early distributions penalty tax (see below).[36]

Example. Mary contributes $2,000 to a Roth IRA in both 2000 and 2001. Mary makes no other contributions to a Roth IRA. In 2004, Mary withdraws $1,200 from the IRA in a nonqualified distribution. The full $1,200 is excludable from income ($1,200 does not exceed aggregate contributions of $4,000).

In 2005, Mary withdraws $1,900 from the Roth IRA in a qualified distribution. The distribution is excludable from income.

In 2006, Mary withdraws $1,500 from the Roth IRA in a nonqualified distribution. The distribution is excludable from income only to the extent of $900, and $600 is includable in income (distributions of $1,200 plus $1,900 plus $1,500 exceed aggregate contributions of $4,000 by $600).

The income tax basis of property distributed from a Roth IRA is its fair market value on the date of the distribution.[37]

The trustee of a Roth IRA is required to report distributions from the IRA to the IRS and to the IRA owner on IRS Form 1099-R. Distributions from Roth IRAs are reported by the IRA owner or beneficiary on IRS Form 8606.

Distributions from elective deferral Roths are taxed partially under the rules for Roth IRAs and partially under the rules applicable to IRAs other than Roth IRAs. See Chapter 8.

Qualified Charitable Distributions

PPA 2006 provides that certain distributions (qualified charitable distributions) from a traditional or Roth IRA made to charity in 2006 or 2007 are not included in income. The provision is not available for SEP and SIMPLE IRAs. The maximum annual amount that can be excluded under this provision is $100,000. The exclusion applies only to amounts otherwise includable in income. The distribution must be made directly from the IRA trustee to a 50% public charity (as described in IRC Section 170(b)(1)(A), other than a support organization or a donor advised fund). The distribution must be made after the IRA owner has attained age 70½. The entire contribution to charity must be otherwise deductible for income tax purposes, disregarding this provision and the charitable deduction percentage limitations based on income for this purpose. Adjustments are made to undistributed nondeductible contributions to reflect the qualified charitable distribution. An income tax charitable deduction is not available for the amount excluded from inome.[38]

The exclusion for qualified charitable distributions may have little impact on Roth IRAs. Distributions made on or after the date the Roth IRA owner turns age 59½ are generally treated as qualified distributions (see above) that are not includable in income. The excusion for qualified charitable contributions applies only to amounts includable in income and that are made after the IRA owner has attained age 70½. Distributions from a Roth made after age 70½ are not generally includable in income.

For additional discussion of qualified charitable distributions, see Chapter 14.

Early Distributions

In general, distributions from a Roth IRA received before age 59½ are subject to a 10 percent penalty tax on early distributions. However, the penalty tax only applies to the extent that the distribution is includable in income and a number of exceptions to application of the penalty apply.[39] In addition, distributions from a Roth IRA of rollover contributions within five years of the rollover to the Roth IRA are subject to the penalty tax to the extent that the distribution was includable in income as a result of the conversion (i.e., rollover) unless an exception applies.[40]

The early distribution penalty tax does not apply to distributions from a Roth IRA that are:

(1) made after the death of the IRA owner (the exception does not apply to distributions made to a surviving spouse who elects to treat the Roth IRA as his or her own);

(2) attributable to the IRA owner's disability;

(3) part of a series of substantially equal periodic payments (at least annually) made for the life (or life expectancy) or the joint life (or life expectancies) of the IRA owner and a designated beneficiary (the penalty tax plus interest is due if the substantially equal periodic payments are modified before the later of five years after payments have begun or the IRA owner reaches age 59½);

(4) made for medical care to the extent generally allowable as a medical expense deduction (generally, unreimbursed medical expenses in excess of 7.5 percent of adjusted gross income; for this purpose, itemization of deductions is not required);

(5)   made to the IRA owner who is unemployed for payment of health insurance premiums;

(6)   made to the IRA owner for payment of qualified higher education expenses furnished to the IRA owner, the IRA owner's spouse, or children or grandchildren of either;

(7)   made to the IRA owner ($10,000 lifetime limit) for purchase of a first home by the IRA owner, the IRA owner's spouse, or children, grandchildren, or ancestor of either; or

(8)   made to a reservist while on active duty (commencing after September 11, 2001 and before 2008).

The IRS has approved three methods for calculating substantially equal periodic payments (SEPPs):

(1)   payments that satisfy the required minimum distributions method (see heading below);

(2)   amortization of payments over the life expectancy of the IRA owner or joint and survivor life expectancy of the IRA owner and beneficiary; and

(3)   annuitization of payments for the life of the IRA owner or the lives of the IRA owner and beneficiary.[41]

The first method requires recalculation of payments each year, while the second and third methods provide constant payments. A person using the second and third methods can elect to switch to the first method. In making these calculations, life expectancy and mortality are now based on the RMD tables (see Appendix D) and interest is generally limited to a maximum rate (which changes monthly).

The additional tax on early distributions is reported either directly on IRS Form 1040 or on IRS Form 5329.

For additional discussion of the early distribution penalty, including examples of the three substantially equal payment methods, see Chapter 13.

Required Minimum Distributions

A Roth IRA owner does not have to begin taking required minimum distributions when the owner reaches age 70½. However, the required minimum distribution rules do apply once the IRA owner dies. (Elective deferral Roths are subject to the required minimum distribution rules even while the IRA owner is alive. See Chapter 8.) In general, the required minimum distribution rules cause the surviving designated beneficiary of the Roth IRA to withdraw the entire IRA account balance over the life of the designated beneficiary. If there is more than one beneficiary, the oldest beneficiary's life expectancy is used for the designated beneficiary. Special rules apply where the spouse of the IRA owner is the designated beneficiary. Failure to withdraw the required minimum distribution results in a 50 percent penalty tax on the amount by which the required minimum distribution exceeds the actual amount withdrawn.[42]

An additional rule, the minimum distribution incidental benefit rule, generally designed to insure that the IRA distributions are primarily for the benefit of the IRA owner, does not apply to a Roth IRA. This rule ordinarily applies while the IRA owner is alive, by treating a beneficiary other than the spouse of the IRA owner as no more than 10 years younger than the IRA owner. However, consistent with the required minimum distribution rules not applying until after the death of the Roth IRA owner, the minimum distribution incidental benefit rule does not apply to a Roth IRA.

In the case of a Roth IRA, required minimum distributions must begin after the death of the IRA owner. Generally, required minimum distributions must be made by December 31st of each year.

After the death of the Roth IRA owner, the entire IRA account must be distributed within five years of the owner's death unless the IRA owner has designated a beneficiary. Where the IRA owner has designated a beneficiary, distributions may be made over the life expectancy of the beneficiary as long as such distributions begin within one year of the owner's death.

However, where the spouse of the Roth IRA owner is the sole designated beneficiary, after the owner's death such spouse can generally elect to be treated as the owner of the Roth IRA for purposes of the required minimum distribution rules. If the surviving spouse elects to be treated as owner of the Roth IRA, required minimum distributions would not have to begin until after the death of such spouse. Even if the election were not made, such spouse could postpone required minimum distributions until such time as the former IRA owner would have reached age 70½.

Required minimum distributions are calculated for Roth IRAs separately from all other IRAs. Required minimum distributions for plans other than a Roth IRA cannot be made from a Roth IRA, nor can required minimum distributions for Roth IRAs be made from other plans. Furthermore, where minimum distributions are required of a beneficiary of a Roth IRA, required minimum distributions can be made from another Roth IRA only if the two Roth IRAs were inherited from the same decedent.[43]

The required minimum distribution for each year is generally calculated by dividing the Roth IRA account balance as of the end of the previous year by the life expectancy of the designated beneficiary. Life expectancies are based upon the RMD Single Life Table (see Appendix C).

The method for calculating required minimum distributions after the death of the IRA owner generally depends on whether a beneficiary has been designated by the time of the IRA owner's death and whether the spouse of the IRA owner is the designated beneficiary.

If there are multiple designated beneficiaries of an IRA, the oldest beneficiary is treated as the designated beneficiary. Thus, the oldest beneficiary of a trust that is the beneficiary of an IRA is generally treated as the designated beneficiary of the IRA. If a person other than an individual is designated as beneficiary of an IRA, the IRA will be treated as having no beneficiary, even if an individual is also named beneficiary. For example, a charity is not an individual. Separate IRAs (and trusts) can be created with different designated beneficiaries.

The actual determination of the designated beneficiary can be determined as late as September 30 of the first year after the year of the owner's death. Thus, if a primary beneficiary disclaims an IRA, a contingent named beneficiary who receives the IRA would be treated as the designated beneficiary. Or, if there are two named beneficiaries of an IRA, and one beneficiary is cashed out, the remaining beneficiary is treated as the designated beneficiary.

Spouse Beneficiary. If the spouse of the IRA owner is the sole designated beneficiary, the spouse can elect to be treated as the owner of the IRA for purposes of the RMD rules. The election cannot be made if a trust is named beneficiary, even if the spouse is the sole beneficiary of the trust. (Under certain circumstances, it appears that a rollover to a spouse may be used to get around this limitation.) If the election is made, distributions from a Roth IRA would not have to begin until after the spouse's death.

If the spouse does not elect to be treated as the owner of the Roth IRA, then required minimum distributions must be made to the spouse over the single life expectancy of the spouse. However, if the IRA owner died prior to the year the IRA owner attained age 70½ and the spouse is the sole designated beneficiary, then required minimum distributions to the spouse do not have to begin until the year the IRA owner would have attained age 70½.

If the election is not made, then the attained age of the spouse for the year is used, and a factor from the RMD Single Life Table (see Appendix C) is used. After the death of the spouse, distributions must continue using the remaining life expectancy of the spouse and the subtract one method. The life expectancy is determined using the attained age of the spouse for the year of the death of the spouse from the RMD Single Life Table (see Appendix C), and by subtracting one from that life expectancy for each year after the year of death.

Nonspouse Beneficiary. Distributions must be made over the remaining life expectancy of the beneficiary using the subtract one method. The life expectancy of the beneficiary is determined using the attained age of the beneficiary for the year after the year of the death of the Roth IRA owner from the RMD Single Life Table (see Appendix C), and by subtracting one from that life expectancy for each year elapsed thereafter.

No Beneficiary. The entire Roth IRA account must be distributed under the five year rule (see below).

Five Year Rule. If the five year rule applies, the entire IRA account must be distributed by the end of the calendar year that contains the fifth anniversary of the date of death of the IRA owner. For example, if an IRA owner age 65 dies on January 1, 2003, then the entire account must be distributed by the end of 2008 if the five year rule applies.

The five year rule generally applies: if elected; if the Roth IRA owner dies without a beneficiary; or if the Roth IRA owner has a beneficiary and there is a failure to timely start distributions over the life expectancy of the beneficiary. Life expectancy distributions must generally start by December 31 of the year after the year of death of the Roth IRA owner, but could start later if the spouse is the beneficiary.

Reporting. The trustee of a Roth IRA generally reports the fair market value of the IRA account as of the end of year. Fair market value may be as of the date of death if the IRA owner died. The fair market value of the account and whether a required minimum distribution is required is reported on IRS Form 5498. Required minimum distributions may be required even if not indicated on IRS Form 5498. The additional tax on failure to make required minimum distributions is reported on IRS Form 5329.

For additional discussion of the required minimum distribution penalty, including the different required minimum distribution methods and examples thereof, see Chapter 13.

Rollovers/Conversions

Rollovers are permitted between IRAs, qualified plans, tax sheltered annuities, and eligible Section 457 governmental plans. In general, a rollover is a transfer of retirement assets from one plan to another by the participant or owner that is completed within 60 days. The effect of a rollover is generally to avoid taxes and penalties upon what otherwise would be treated as a distribution. However, any rollover from an IRA other than a Roth IRA to a Roth IRA is a taxable event.[44] A rollover from an IRA other than a Roth IRA to a Roth IRA is also called a conversion.

Only one rollover is permitted from a particular IRA to any other IRA during the one-year period ending with the transfer from the first IRA. Also, in an IRA to IRA rollover, the receiving IRA cannot be an endowment contract. The one-year rollover limitation does not apply to trustee-to-trustee transfers.

Certain rollovers can be made to and from a Roth IRA. The only rollovers permitted to a Roth IRA before 2008 are from other Roth IRAs, traditional IRAs, SEP IRAs, SIMPLE IRAs, and elective deferral Roths. (An indirect rollover from qualified plans, tax sheltered annuities, or eligible Section 457 governmental plans may be accomplished through a rollover to a traditional IRA or SEP IRA followed by a rollover of the traditional IRA or SEP IRA to a Roth IRA.) PPA 2006 permits rollovers to a Roth IRA from qualified plans, tax sheltered annuities, or eligible Section 457 governmental plans after 2007. However, a rollover is not permitted from a SIMPLE IRA to any other IRA including a Roth IRA during the first two years that the individual participates in the SIMPLE IRA. (The only rollover permitted to an elective deferral Roth is from an elective deferral Roth of the same type (i.e., 401(k) to 401(k), or 403(b) to 403(b)). See Chapter 8.)

In general, rollovers to or from a Roth IRA are accomplished either by (1) having the trustee of the first IRA transfer IRA property directly to the trustee of the second IRA, or (2) having the trustee of the first IRA distribute the IRA property to the IRA owner who then transfers the IRA property to the trustee of the second IRA within 60 days of the distribution from the first IRA. In addition, a rollover to a Roth IRA can be accomplished by simply converting the other IRA into a Roth IRA. After 2007, a conversion of a qualified plan, tax sheltered annuity, or eligible Section 457 governmental plan to a Roth IRA can be accomplished by either (1) a direct trustee-to-trustee transfer, or (2) a 60-day rollover.

For tax years before 2010, an individual can generally rollover (or convert) an amount in one of these other IRAs (or qualified plans, tax sheltered annuities, or eligible Section 457 governmental plans after 2007 and before 2010) to a Roth IRA in a qualified rollover unless the individual's adjusted gross income (AGI) for the year exceeds $100,000 or the individual is married and files a separate return. (These limitations do not apply to a rollover of an elective deferral Roth to a Roth IRA.) For tax years after 2009, these limitations do not apply to any conversion to a Roth IRA. For tax years after 2004 (and before 2010), adjusted gross income does not include any required minimum distributions (see heading above) for this purpose. The primary reason for doing such a qualified rollover is to obtain the benefit of the generally more favorable rules for distributions from a Roth IRA. The price of making such a qualified rollover to a Roth IRA is that the amount in the other IRA (or qualified plans, tax sheltered annuities, or eligible Section 457 governmental plans after 2007) is treated as distributed from the other IRA for income tax purposes in the year rolled over.[45]

Thus, if a traditional IRA, SEP IRA, or SIMPLE IRA (or qualified plans, tax sheltered annuities, or eligible Section 457 governmental plans after 2007) is converted to a Roth IRA, the amount distributed from the other plan or IRA is includable in income for the year of distribution under the rules for such other plan or IRA. Actually, all distributions from all nonRoth IRAs for the year (including the amount being converted) would be aggregated together in determining the portion of the conversion that is taxable. However, the early distribution penalty tax does not apply to such distribution. Nevertheless, the early distribution rule will apply to any distribution from the Roth IRA made within the five-year period starting with the year of the rollover or conversion if the distribution is allocable to the qualified rollover contribution.

> *Example.* The only IRA Rachel has is a traditional IRA. Rachel converts her traditional IRA to a Roth IRA in 2006 in a qualified rollover. The account balance of the traditional IRA is equal to $100,000 and no nondeductible contributions have been made to the traditional IRA. Rachel includes in income for 2006 the full $100,000 distribution from the traditional IRA, but the early distribution penalty tax does not apply to the distribution.

If an elective deferral Roth is converted to a Roth IRA, the amount distributed from the elective deferral Roth is includable in income for the year of distribution under the rules for elective deferral Roths (see Chapter 8). The elective deferral Roth is treated as a separate contract for purpose of determining the taxation of distributions; it is not aggregated with other accounts or plans. To the extent the distribution from the elective deferral Roth is a qualified distribution, the distribution is not included in income. Nevertheless, the full qualified distribution is treated as a contribution to the Roth IRA for purposes of future distributions from the Roth IRA. For purposes of determining whether a distribution from a Roth IRA of an amount rolled over from an elective deferral Roth is a qualified distribution, the 5-year rule for Roth IRAs (see above) and the 5-year rule for elective deferral Roths (see Chapter 8) must be satisfied independently.[46]

For conversions to Roth IRAs in 2010, unless the taxpayer elects otherwise, the amount includable in income by reason of conversion to a Roth IRA is includable ratably in 2011 and 2012, rather than in 2010. However, income inclusion is accelerated if converted amounts are distributed from the Roth IRA before 2012. In such a case, the amount included in income for the year (2010 or 2011) is increased by the converted amount that is distributed from the Roth IRA. To avoid double inclusion of accelerated amounts, the converted amount included in income in subsequent years (2011 or 2012) is limited so as to not be in excess of the total conversion amount includable in income reduced by conversion amounts included in income in prior years.

> *Example.* Bob converts a traditional IRA to a Roth IRA in 2010. If Bob were to elect, $100 would be includable in income in 2010. No election is made, so $50 (one-half of $100) is includable in 2011 and $50 in 2012 (assuming no distribution of converted amounts before 2012). Later in 2010, Bob takes a distribution of $20 attributable to the converted amount. Bob must include the $20 in income in 2010. In 2011, Bob must include $50, which is the lesser of (1) $50 or (2) $70 [$100 total - $20 previously included]. In 2012, Bob must include $30, which is the lesser of (1) $50 or (2) $30 [$100 total - $70 previously included].

If the rollover from the traditional IRA, SEP IRA or SIMPLE IRA is not a qualified rollover, then the amount of the rollover is treated as distributed from the original IRA and subject to income tax based upon the rules for distributions from such IRA, including the penalty tax for early distributions if appropriate. The distributed amount is then treated as contributed to the Roth IRA. Most likely such a contribution to the Roth IRA would create an excess contribution subject to the excess contribution penalty tax until corrected.

An "unqualified" rollover to a Roth IRA can be a very taxing event. A taxpayer who makes a conversion to a Roth IRA and discovers that the rollover would not be qualified (e.g., adjusted gross income for the year exceeds $100,000 in 2006) can elect to recharacterize the contribution to the Roth IRA as being to a traditional IRA and avoid the "unqualified" rollover. The recharacterization must occur within the time for filing a tax return for the year of the original rollover to the Roth IRA.

Indeed, any person who converts a traditional, SEP, or SIMPLE IRA to a Roth IRA can recharacterize the contribution to the Roth IRA as being made instead back to such other IRA type and avoid the tax upon conversion to the Roth IRA. However, certain restrictions are placed upon a person who recharacterizes a contribution to a Roth IRA as being made to such other IRA type. The person can reconvert back to a Roth IRA but only after the later of (1) the beginning of the next year, or (2) 30 days after the recharacterization.[47]

When the stock market drops after a person has made a conversion to a Roth IRA, the person may wish to recharacterize the contribution back to the other type of IRA and then reconvert to a Roth IRA in order to reduce the amount taxable upon switching to a Roth IRA. The requirement that a person essentially wait until the later of the following year or 30 days to reconvert back to a Roth IRA reduces, but does not eliminate, the potential value of this technique.

For additional discussion of conversions to a Roth IRA, including some analysis of whether to convert to a Roth IRA, see Chapter 12.

A rollover from a Roth IRA can be made only to another Roth IRA. Thus, a regular Roth IRA cannot be rolled over to an elective deferral Roth.[48]

The trustee of an IRA is required to report rollovers to and from a Roth IRA and Roth conversions to the IRS and to the IRA owner on IRS Form 5498. A conversion from a traditional IRA, SEP IRA, or SIMPLE IRA to a Roth IRA is reported by the IRA owner on IRS Form 8606.

Losses (Unrecovered Basis)

The Internal Revenue Code provides that if annuity payments from an IRA end upon the death of the annuitant and there is still unrecovered investment in the contract, the unrecovered investment in the contract is allowable as a deduction for the annuitant's final tax year. However, if refund payments are made to a beneficiary or the annuitant's estate after the annuitant's death, the deduction for unrecovered investment in the contract is taken by the person receiving the refund payments for the year in which received. The IRS provides additionally that when all amounts from all Roth IRAs have been distributed and the amounts distributed are less than the unrecovered basis, a loss may be recognized.[49]

Example. Jan contributes $2,000 to a Roth IRA in each of four years (a total of $8,000). The IRA earns $1,000 during the four years. The IRA account balance is then $9,000 ($8,000 + $1,000). Jan then withdraws $3,000 in a nonqualified distribution. The amount excludable from income as investment in the contract equals $3,000 (distribution of $3,000 does not exceed aggregate contributions of $8,000). The unrecovered investment in the contract equals $5,000 ($8,000 - $3,000). The IRA account balance equals $6,000 ($9,000 - $3,000).

The next year, the IRA account balance drops in value to $4,000 (i.e., a loss in value of $2,000). Jan withdraws the entire $4,000 in a nonqualified distribution. No amount is includable in income (distributions of $3,000 plus $4,000 does not exceed aggregate contributions of $8,000). Furthermore, Jan may claim a loss of $1,000 ($5,000 - $4,000).

Withholding

Distributions from a Roth IRA are distributions from a retirement plan subject to withholding unless the individual elects to have withholding not apply. Thus, unless the election is made, periodic payments from a Roth IRA are subject to withholding at regular withholding rates and nonperiodic payments from a Roth IRA are subject to withholding at a 10 percent rate.[50]

A conversion of any other IRA into a Roth IRA (a qualified rollover) is a distribution for which income tax withholding is required, unless made in the form of a direct trustee-to-trustee transfer.[51]

Transfer Taxes

A Roth IRA will generally be fully includable in the estate of the original IRA owner. A decedent's estate includes the value of an annuity or other payment receivable by reason of surviving the decedent where the decedent held certain interests in the property while alive. The amount includable is proportionate to the part of the purchase price contributed by the decedent. Any contribution by the employer of the decedent to the Roth IRA is treated as made by the employee for this purpose.[52] Thus, the original IRA owner will generally have contributed 100 percent of the contributions to the Roth IRA and the full value of the Roth IRA will be includable in the original owner's estate.

If upon the original owner's death the Roth IRA passes to the spouse of the original IRA owner, the transfer will generally qualify for the marital deduction (see Chapter 18). If the transfer to the surviving spouse qualified for the marital deduction, any amount still left in the Roth IRA at the surviving spouse's death will be includable in the surviving spouse's estate.

If the Roth owner assigns his interest in the Roth IRA to another, the Roth IRA owner makes a gift of the Roth IRA (see Chapter 17). The first $10,000 as indexed of such a gift can generally qualify for the gift tax annual exclusion. If the donee is the spouse of the IRA owner, the gift should qualify for the gift tax marital deduction. However, if the Roth owner makes a gift of the Roth IRA to another, the assets of the Roth IRA are deemed distributed from the Roth IRA for income tax purposes.[53]

If the beneficiary of the Roth IRA following a gift or at death is two or more generations younger than the Roth IRA owner, there is a generation-skipping transfer subject to the generation-skipping transfer tax. A generation-skipping transfer tax exemption may be available to protect the transfer from the tax. See Chapter 19.

Endnotes

1. IRC Sec. 408A(a).
2. IRC Sec. 219(e)(1).
3. IRC Secs. 219(f)(3), 408(o)(3).
4. IRC Sec. 408A(c)(4).
5. IRC Secs. 408A(c)(2), 219(c).
6. Treas. Reg. §1.408A-3(A-3).
7. IRC Secs. 408A(c)(2)(A), 219(b)(5).
8. IRC Sec. 219(b)(5)(D), as amended by PPA 2006.
9. IRC Secs. 408A(c)(2)(A), 219(b)(5)(B).
10. IRC Sec. 219(b)(5)(C), as added by PPA 2006.
11. IRC Sec. 219(c).
12. IRC Sec. 408A(c)(3).
13. IRC Secs. 408A(c)(3)(C)(i), 219(g)(3)(A).
14. IRC Secs. 408A(c)(3)(C)(ii)(I).
15. IRC Secs. 408A(c)(3)(C)(ii)(III).
16. IRC Secs. 408A(c)(3)(D), 219(g)(4).
17. IRC Secs. 408A(c)(3)(C)(ii)(II).
18. IRC Sec. 408A(c)(3)(C).
19. IRC Secs. 219(b)(1), 408(o)(2), 408A(c)(2).
20. IRC Sec. 408(d)(4).
21. IRC Sec. 408(d)(5).

22. Treas. Reg. §1.408A-5(A-2)(c).
23. IRC Secs. 408A(d)(6), 408A(d)(7).
24. Treas. Reg. §1.408A-5(A-6).
25. IRC Sec. 4973(a).
26. IRC Secs. 4973(f), 219(f)(6).
27. Ann. 99-2, 1999-1 CB 305.
28. IRC Secs. 408A(a), 219(f)(5).
29. IRC Sec. 402A.
30. IRC Secs. 408(e), 408(m).
31. IRC Sec. 408(a)(3).
32. IRC Sec. 408(b).
33. IRC Secs. 408(e), 408(m).
34. Treas. Reg. §1.408A-6(A-19).
35. IRC Sec. 408A(d).
36. IRC Sec. 408A(d)(4).
37. Treas. Reg. §1.408A-6(A-16).
38. IRC Sec. 408(d)(8).
39. IRC Sec. 72(t).
40. IRC Sec. 408A(d)(3)(F).
41. Rev. Rul. 2002-62, 2002-42 IRB 710; Notice 89-25(A-12), 1989-1 CB 662.
42. IRC Secs. 408(a)(6), 408(b)(3), 401(a)(9), 4974(a).
43. Treas. Reg. §1.408A-6(A-15).
44. See IRC Sec. 408(d)(3).
45. IRC Sec. 408A(d)(3).
46. Treas. Prop. Reg. §1.408-10, A-3, A-4.
47. Treas. Reg. §1.408A-5(A-9).
48. Treas. Prop. Reg. §1.408-10, A-5.
49. IRC Sec. 72(b)(3); Notice 89-25(A-7), 1989-1 CB 662 clarifying Notice 87-16(D-5), 1987-1 CB 446.
50. IRC Sec. 3405.
51. Treas. Reg. §1.408A-6 (A-13); IRC Sec. 3405(c).
52. IRC Sec. 2039.
53. Treas. Reg. §1.408A-6(A-19).

Chapter 6

Simplified Employee Pension IRAs (SEP IRAs)

A simplified employee pension IRA (SEP IRA) is a way for an employer to offer an employee plan in the form of an IRA, but with higher contribution levels than for traditional and Roth IRAs, and without many of the restrictions applicable to qualified plans. An employer is not limited in the number of employees it may have in order to qualify for a SEP IRA. Employers with no more than 25 employees and who had salary reduction SEP IRAs (SAR-SEP IRAs) in effect prior to 1997 can offer employees an election to make current salary reduction contributions to such SAR-SEP IRAs. An employer with no more than 100 employees may prefer the alternative of a SIMPLE IRA (see Chapter 7), a recent creation that allows for higher contribution levels and salary reduction contributions while relaxing the rules for qualified plans.

An employer can take a deduction for contributions to a SEP IRA but not to exceed an amount equal to 25 percent of compensation paid to employees. The amount of the contribution must be determined under a definite written allocation formula that cannot discriminate in favor of the highly compensated. The employee, within limitations, excludes the contribution from income.

In the case of salary reduction contributions, the employer also takes a deduction and the employee excludes the contribution from income.

Amounts contributed to a SEP IRA can be invested in a wide variety of investments. Such amounts grow within the IRA account on a tax-deferred basis; there is generally no taxation until amounts are distributed.

Amounts distributed from a SEP IRA are generally taxable on a pro-rated basis. Amounts distributed from a SEP IRA allocated to nondeductible contributions to the SEP IRA can be excluded from income. Usually, all contributions to the SEP IRA are excluded from income when contributed and the full amount distributed from a SEP IRA is includable in income.

Distributions received before the individual reaches age 59½ are generally subject to an early distribution penalty tax to the extent the distribution is includable in income unless an exception applies. Once the individual reaches age 70½, required minimum distributions must be made from the SEP IRA or a penalty tax applies.

Contributions

Both employer and employee contributions may be made to a SEP IRA. Employer contributions to a SEP IRA are subject to their own set of rules including participation and nondiscrimination requirements. Employee contributions to a SEP IRA are essentially subject to the same rules as those for contributions to a traditional IRA. Additional rules apply to salary reduction contributions to a SAR-SEP IRA.

The trustee of an IRA is required to report contributions to a SEP IRA to the IRS and to the IRA owner on IRS Form 5498.

Employer Contributions

An employer can generally take a deduction for contributions made by the employer to a SEP IRA. The employee can generally exclude such employer contributions from income. Certain limitations apply and excess contributions are generally subject to a penalty tax. Salary reduction contributions to a SAR-SEP IRA are discussed under a separate heading below.

An employer can take a deduction for contributions made to a SEP IRA during a year by the employer but not to exceed an amount equal to 25 percent of the employees' compensation. The employer can use a calendar year or the employer's tax year as the SEP IRA's taxable year. Contributions for any year can be made up until the time for filing the return (including extensions) for the SEP IRA's taxable year. To the extent that contributions in any year exceed 25 percent of the employees' compensation, such excess may be carried forward and deducted in a later year, subject to the

25 percent limitation in such carryover year.[1] (The employer is also subject to a 10 percent penalty on such nondeductible contributions, see below).

To the extent that a deduction is taken for a SEP IRA, the deductible limitations for stock bonus and profit sharing plans are reduced. For purposes of the rules limiting deductible contributions where an employer contributes to a combination of defined contribution plans and defined benefit plans, a SEP IRA is treated as a separate stock bonus or profit sharing plan.

In any year that the employer maintains a SEP IRA, the employer must contribute to the SEP IRA of any employee who (1) has attained age 21, (2) has performed service for the employer in at least three of the preceding five years, and (3) has compensation of at least $450 (as indexed for 2006). For this purpose, if the employee is eligible for salary reduction contributions (see heading below) to the SEP IRA for the year, the employer is considered to have contributed to the SEP IRA for the employee. Employees covered by a collective bargaining agreement where retirement benefits were the subject of good faith bargaining can be excluded for purposes of the required employer contributions to the SEP IRA. Also, nonresident aliens with no U.S. source earned income from the employer can be excluded.[2]

Contributions to the SEP IRA by the employer may not discriminate in favor of any highly compensated employee. Contributions to the SEP IRA by the employer will generally be considered discriminatory unless contributions bear a uniform relationship to compensation (not to exceed $220,000 as indexed for 2006) of each employee maintaining a SEP IRA. Apparently, a contribution rate that decreases as compensation increases would also be permitted as nondiscriminatory. Certain disparity is permitted in plans that are integrated with Social Security.[3]

Employer contributions to a SEP IRA may not be conditioned on the employee retaining such contributions in the SEP IRA. Nor can the employer prohibit withdrawal of such contributions from the SEP IRA.[4]

Employer contributions to a SEP IRA must be determined under a definite written allocation formula that specifies how an employee qualifies for employer contributions and how the amount of employer contributions is calculated.[5]

Employer contributions to a SEP IRA, as well as annual additions to other defined contribution plans of the employer maintained for the employee, are subject to a combined overall limitation equal to the lesser of 100 percent of compensation or $44,000 (as indexed for 2006).[6]

In the case where an employer contributes more than it can deduct in a taxable year (i.e., a nondeductible contribution), a 10 percent penalty tax is imposed on the employer.[7] In general, a nondeductible contribution is any portion of a contribution to a SEP IRA by the employer in excess of the amount allowable as a deduction by the employer. However, it is necessary to keep a running account of such nondeductible contributions (i.e., it is necessary to keep track of contributions and distributions for the current year and preceding years in order to determine if there is a nondeductible contribution for the current year).

More technically, a nondeductible contribution for any taxable year equals the sum of (1) the excess of employer contributions to SEP IRAs and other retirement plans over the amounts allowable as a deduction for such contributions, and (2) amounts determined under this calculation for the preceding taxable year reduced by the sum of (a) such amounts returned to the employer during the current year, and (b) such amounts deductible for the current year. For this purpose, excess contributions from previous years are carried over and the amount allowable as a deduction in any year is treated as first consisting of carryovers from prior years (and from oldest carryovers first) and then from contributions made during the current year. Thus, a nondeductible contribution carried over from a previous year can be used up as a contribution in a subsequent year.[8]

> *Example.* Ann, who is not a highly compensated employee, has compensation of $50,000 in 2005 and 2006 from Company. The only retirement plan maintained by Company is a SEP IRA. Company contributed $13,000 to the SEP IRA for Ann in 2005, resulting in a nondeductible contribution of $500 [$13,000 - (25% x $50,000)]. In 2006, Company does not contribute to the SEP IRA. The $500 carryover from 2005 is treated as contributed (and deductible) in 2006 and is less than $12,500 (25% x $50,000); thus, there is no nondeductible contribution for 2006.

The employee can exclude employer contributions to a SEP IRA from income to the extent that such contributions do not exceed the lesser of 25 percent of compensation (determined without regard to the employer's contribution to the SEP IRA) or $44,000 (as indexed for 2006). There is also a $220,000 limitation (as indexed for 2006) on the amount of compensation that can be taken into account that would limit contributions to $55,000 (25% x $220,000) in 2006. However, since $44,000 (in 2006) is less than $55,000 (in 2006), the contribution limit is $44,000 in 2006. The dollar limitation is reduced in the case of highly compensated employees in a SEP IRA that is integrated with Social Security.[9]

Employer contributions to a SEP IRA are generally not subject to FICA (Social Security tax), FUTA (federal unemployment tax), or income tax withholding.[10]

See the discussion of SIMPLE IRAs (Savings Incentive Match Plan for Employees IRA) in Chapter 7 for other IRAs specifically designed for employer/employee programs.

Employee Contributions

An employee may generally make deductible and nondeductible contributions to a SEP IRA similar to those made to a traditional IRA. Contributions may be subject to various limitations. A rollover (see heading below) to a SEP IRA is generally not treated as a contribution to a SEP IRA. Salary reduction contributions to a SAR-SEP IRA are discussed under a separate heading below.

Contributions to a SEP IRA, as for all IRAs, must be made in cash.[11] Contributions for a taxable year may be made up until the time for filing the tax return for the year (not including extensions of time for filing): generally, April 15.[12]

A deduction cannot be taken for contributions made to a SEP IRA by the employee in taxable years once the employee has attained age 70½.[13] Furthermore, a deduction generally cannot be taken for contributions to an IRA inherited from another individual.[14]

An employee may take a deduction from income in any taxable year for contributions the employee makes to a SEP IRA for up to the lesser of the total contribution limit amount or compensation includable in income.[15] The total contribution limit consists of the sum of the regular contribution limit and the catch-up contribution limit. The regular contribution limit is as follows.[16]

Regular Contribution Limit

Year	Amount
2005-2007	$4,000
2008-	$5,000*

*indexed for inflation after 2008

In addition, catch-up contributions can be made for individuals attaining age 50 before the end of the year.[17] The catch-up contribution limit is as follows.

Catch-up Contribution Limit

Year	Amount
2006-	$1,000

The regular and catch-up contribution limits shown reflect changes made by PPA 2006. PPA 2006 eliminates the sunset after 2010 of sheduled increases in the contribution limits made by EGTRRA 2001.

However, if the employee is an active participant in certain employer retirement plans, including a SEP IRA, the total contribution limit amount is subject to phaseout based upon modified adjusted gross income (MAGI).[18] Modified adjusted gross income (MAGI) for this purpose means adjusted gross income determined with certain adjustments, including the deduction for contributions to traditional IRAs is not taken into account.[19] An employee is an active participant in a SEP-IRA if any employer contribution is made during the taxable year.[20]

In the case of an active participant, the total contribution limit amount (see above) is reduced by an amount equal to the total contribution limit amount multiplied by the ratio of the employee's modified adjusted gross income (MAGI) in excess of an applicable dollar amount to $10,000 ($20,000 in the case of a joint return after 2006).

$$\text{total contribution limit} \times \frac{\text{MAGI - applicable dollar amount}}{\$10,000} = \text{reduction}$$

Whenever the phaseout reduction is other than a multiple of $10, the reduction is rounded to the next lowest multiple of $10. However, where the total contribution limit amount adjusted for phaseout based upon adjusted gross income is between $0 and $200, $200 is the amount allowable as a deduction.[21]

In the case of a joint return, the applicable dollar amount equals:

Taxable Year	Applicable Dollar Amount	Total Phaseout
2006	$75,000	$85,000
2007-	$80,000*	$100,000 *

*plus indexing for inflation after 2006

Thus, in the case of a joint return of an active participant, the total contribution limit amount (see above) is not reduced for adjusted gross income of $75,000 or less for 2006, is reduced to $0 for adjusted gross income of $85,000 or more, and is proportionately reduced in the case of adjusted gross income between $75,000 and $85,000.

In the case of other than a joint return or a married filing separate return, the applicable dollar amount equals:

Taxable Year	Applicable Dollar Amount	Total Phaseout
2005-	$50,000*	$60,000*

*plus indexing for inflation after 2006

Thus, in the case of a single return or a head of household return of an active participant, the total contribution limit amount (see above) is not reduced for adjusted gross income of $50,000 or less for 2006, is reduced to $0 for adjusted gross income of $60,000 or more, and is proportionately reduced in the case of adjusted gross income between $50,000 and $60,000.

In the case of a married individual filing separate, the applicable dollar amount equals $0. Thus, in such case, the total contribution limit amount (see above) is reduced to $0 for adjusted gross income of $10,000 or more, and is proportionately reduced in the case of adjusted gross income between $0 and $10,000.

PPA 2006 provides for indexing of the phaseout limits for contributions after 2006.[22] The phaseout range ($10,000 or $20,000) is not indexed; the applicable dollar amount is indexed and the corresponding amount at which total phaseout occurs moves up with it. However, in the case of a joint return (see above), IRC Section 219(g)(3)(B)(i) already provided for an increased amount for 2007. A technical correction may be needed.

> *Example.* In 2006, a married individual (age 45) files a separate return, is an employee in a SEP IRA, and has adjusted gross income of $3,333. He can make a deductible contribution to the SEP IRA of $2,670. This is calculated as follows:
>
> total contribution limit x MAGI - applicable dollar amount = reduction
> $10,000
>
> round reduction down to next lowest multiple of $10
>
> total contribution limit - reduction = amount deductible
>
> | | |
> |---|---|
> | regular contribution limit | $4,000 |
> | catch-up contribution limit | + $0 |
> | total contribution limit | $4,000 |

$$\$4,000 \times \frac{\$3{,}333 - \$0}{\$10{,}000} = \$1{,}333.20$$

round $1,333.20 to $1,330
$4,000 - $1,330 = $2,670

Figure 4.1 in Chapter 4 provides a phaseout table method for estimating the amount of deductible employee contributions that can be made to a SEP IRA (or deductible contributions to a traditional IRA) where there is active participation. See Figure 4.2 in Chapter 4 for an example of using this method.

The deduction for a contribution to a SEP IRA by the employee is a deduction from gross income.[23] Therefore, the deduction can be taken whether or not the employee itemizes deductions and is not subject to any phaseout of itemized deductions.

An employee can elect to have otherwise deductible contributions to a SEP IRA by the employee treated as nondeductible.[24] However, as noted below, it is usually better to make nondeductible contributions to a Roth IRA rather than to a SEP IRA. (For a discussion of whether it is better for an employee to make *deductible* contributions to a SEP IRA or a traditional IRA or nondeductible contributions to a Roth IRA, see Chapter 9.)

An employee can also make nondeductible contributions to a SEP IRA up to the lesser of the total contribution limit amount (see above) or compensation includable in income. This amount is reduced by any deductible contributions made to a SEP IRA or traditional IRA.[25] However, nondeductible contributions to a SEP IRA or a traditional IRA are not subject to any phaseout based upon adjusted gross income even though the employee is an active participant.

Nondeductible contributions can also be made to a Roth IRA (see Chapter 5). However, contributions that can be made to a Roth IRA are subject to phaseout based upon income and are reduced by contributions made to a SEP IRA or a traditional IRA. Because distributions from a Roth IRA are generally subject to much more favorable rules than are distributions from a SEP IRA or traditional IRA, it is generally advisable to make nondeductible contributions to a Roth IRA rather than nondeductible contributions to a SEP IRA or traditional IRA, except to the extent that the individual's permissible contributions to a Roth IRA are phased out by the limitations based on income.

In order to gain the more favorable rules for distributions from Roth IRAs, consideration can be given to converting the SEP IRA to a Roth IRA at a later time.

The price of making such a qualified rollover to a Roth IRA (see Chapter 5) is that the amount in the SEP IRA is generally treated as distributed from the SEP IRA for income tax purposes in the year rolled over. In tax years before 2010, conversions to a Roth IRA are not allowed if the individual's adjusted gross income (AGI) for the year exceeds $100,000 or the individual is married and files a separate return. For tax years after 2009, these limitations do not apply. For conversions in 2010, the amount includable in income can be recognized ratably over 2011 and 2012, rather than in 2010. For additional discussion of conversions to a Roth IRA, including some analysis of whether to convert to a Roth IRA, see Chapter 12.

Employee contributions to a SEP IRA and contributions to traditional IRAs and Roth IRAs are subject to a combined overall limitation equal to the total contribution limit amount (see above).[26]

In the case of an excess contribution to a SEP IRA by the employee, there is imposed a six percent penalty tax.[27] In general, an excess contribution is any portion of a contribution to a SEP IRA by the employee in excess of the limitations on contributions by the employee described above. However, it is necessary to keep a running account of excess contributions (i.e., it is necessary to keep track of contributions and distributions for the current year and preceding years in order to determine if there is an excess contribution for the current year).

More technically, an excess contribution for any taxable year equals the sum of (1) the excess of employee contributions to SEP IRAs and contributions to traditional IRAs over the lesser of the total contribution limit amount or the employee's compensation, and (2) amounts determined under this calculation for the preceding taxable year reduced by the sum of (a) distributions from SEP IRAs and traditional IRAs of amounts includable in income for the year, (b) distributions from SEP IRAs (of employee contributions) and traditional IRAs of amounts not includable in income under IRC Section 408(d)(5) (i.e., distributions of amounts contributed that did not exceed the total contribution limit amount but did exceed the amount of compensation), and (c) the excess of the lesser of the total contribution limit amount or the employee's compensation over the amount of employee contributions to SEP IRAs and contributions to traditional and Roth IRAs for the year. Thus, an excess contribution carried over from a previous year can be used up as a contribution in a subsequent year.[28]

> *Example.* Ann (age 50) contributed $4,000 to a SEP IRA in 2004, resulting in an excess contribution of $500 ($4,000 - $3,500). Ann contributed $4,600 to the IRA in 2005, resulting in an excess contribution of $600 ([$4,600 - $4,500] plus the $500 carryover from 2004). In 2006, Ann

does not contribute to the IRA. The $600 carryover from 2005 is treated as contributed (and deductible) in 2006 and is less than $5,000; there is no excess contribution.

Salary Reduction Contributions: SAR-SEP IRAs

An employer can also make salary reduction contributions to an existing salary reduction SEP IRA (a SAR-SEP IRA) for an employee.[29] The employer takes a deduction for the salary reduction contributions. The employee excludes the salary reduction contribution from income. Certain limitations apply.

In years after 1996, salary reduction contributions to a SAR-SEP IRA can be made only by employers that had SAR-SEP IRAs that permitted salary reduction contributions as of December 31, 1996 (an existing SAR-SEP IRA). Existing SAR-SEP IRAs are grandfathered on an employer basis; an employer with existing SAR-SEP IRAs can add new employees to the plan. Salary reduction contributions can be made to SIMPLE IRAs (see Chapter 7). State and local governments and tax-exempt entities cannot have SAR-SEP IRAs.

Other than with regard to the special salary reduction provisions for contributions, a SAR-SEP IRA is generally treated like any other SEP IRA.

A SAR-SEP IRA permits an employee to elect to have the employer either (1) make elective employer contributions to the SAR-SEP IRA on behalf of the employee or (2) distribute the amount in cash to the employee.[30] If the employee takes cash, the distribution is includable in the employee's income. If the employee chooses salary reduction, the employee excludes the amount of the salary reduction contribution from income for the year of contribution. If the employee chooses salary reduction, taxation is generally deferred until distributions are made from the SAR-SEP IRA. Thus, salary reduction is a form of elective deferral or a cash or deferred arrangement.

The salary reduction provisions are not available in any year to a SAR-SEP IRA if the employer had more than 25 employees who were eligible to participate for the previous year. Also, the salary reduction provisions are not available in any year to a SAR-SEP IRA unless at least 50 percent of eligible employees elect the salary reduction option. Furthermore, the salary reduction provisions are not available in any year unless the deferral percentage of each highly compensated employee is not more than the average deferral percentages of all employees (other than highly compensated employees) multiplied by 1.25. The deferral percentage for a year is equal to the ratio of the actual amount of elective employer contributions paid to the SAR-SEP

IRA for the employee to the employee's compensation (not to exceed $220,000 as indexed for 2006).

Example. The average deferral percentages of all employees (other than highly compensated employees) covered under a SAR-SEP offered by employer equals six percent. If the deferral percentage of any highly compensated employee exceeds 7.5 percent (6% x 1.25), such employee's SAR-SEP does not qualify for salary reduction.

Salary reduction contributions to a SAR-SEP IRA, as well as all other elective deferrals to retirement plans, are subject to a combined overall limitation for elective deferrals in a year.[31] The elective deferral limits is as follows.

Elective Deferral Limit

Year	Amount
2006	$15,000
2007-	$15,000*

*plus indexing for inflation

In addition, elective deferral catch-up contributions can be made for individuals attaining age 50 before the end of the year. The elective deferral catch-up contribution limit is as follows.

Catch-up Contribution Limit

Year	Amount
2006	$5,000
2007-	$5,000*

*plus indexing for inflation

The elective deferral regular and catch-up contribution limits shown reflect changes made by PPA 2006. PPA 2006 eliminates the sunset after 2010 of sheduled increases in the contribution limits made by EGTRRA 2001.

An employer is not required to permit catch-up salary reduction contributions. However, if catch-up contributions are permitted, the option must be available to all eligible employees.

In the case of an excess contribution through salary reduction to a SAR-SEP IRA, there is imposed a 10 percent penalty tax on the employer.[32] In general, an excess contribution is any portion of a salary reduction contribution to a SAR-SEP IRA in excess of the "1.25" limitation described above. Distributions of excess contributions made within 2½ months after the end of the year can be treated as made during the preceding year. However, if the total amount of excess contributions (and any interest thereon) distributed in any year to an employee is less than $100, such excess contributions are treated as distributed in the year actually distributed.[33]

Salary reduction contributions to a SAR-SEP IRA are generally subject to FICA (Social Security tax) and FUTA (federal unemployment tax) tax withholding, but not to income tax withholding.[34]

See the discussion of SIMPLE IRAs (Savings Incentive Match Plan for Employees IRA) in Chapter 7 for other IRAs specifically designed for employer/employee programs.

Accumulations/Investments

Amounts earned within a SEP IRA generally accumulate on a tax-deferred basis. Earnings are generally not taxable until distributed from the SEP IRA. However, a SEP IRA is taxed if it has unrelated business taxable income. Furthermore, part or all of the SEP IRA may be deemed distributed if the SEP IRA owner engages in a prohibited transaction, borrows on an annuity contract, pledges the account as security for a loan, purchases an endowment contract, or invests in certain collectibles.[35] A SEP IRA account, as with all IRA accounts, cannot invest in life insurance contracts.[36] The IRA can be in the form of an individual retirement annuity.[37]

An individual retirement annuity is an annuity contract or endowment contract issued by an insurance company meeting certain requirements: (1) the contract cannot be transferable by the owner; (2) the premiums may not be fixed; (3) the annual premium cannot exceed the total contribution limit amount (see above); (4) any refund of premiums must be applied before the end of the next year to pay future premiums or to purchase additional benefits; (5) the required minimum distribution and minimum distribution incidental death benefit rules apply; and (6) the entire interest of the owner must be nonforfeitable. For this purpose, an endowment contract cannot mature later than the taxable year in which the SEP IRA owner reaches age 70½ and must be for the exclusive benefit of the SEP IRA owner or beneficiary. Aggregate annual premiums for all endowment contracts purchased for the SEP IRA owner cannot exceed the total contribution limit amount (see above).

See Chapter 3 for more information on limitations on accumulations in a SEP IRA.

Distributions

Amounts distributed from a SEP IRA are includable in taxable income (on a pro-rated basis) to the extent distributions are from employer contributions (including salary reduction contributions), employee deductible contributions to the SEP IRA, and earnings from the SEP IRA. Amounts distributed before the SEP IRA owner reaches age 59½ that are includable in income are subject to an early distribution penalty tax unless certain exceptions are met. Required minimum distributions must begin when the SEP IRA owner reaches age 70½ or a penalty tax applies. A rollover (see heading below) from a SEP IRA is generally not treated as a distribution from a SEP IRA.

Part or all of the SEP IRA may be deemed distributed if the SEP IRA owner engages in a prohibited transaction, borrows on an annuity contract, pledges the account as security for a loan, purchases an endowment contract, or invests in certain collectibles.[38]

Amounts distributed from a SEP IRA represent one of four categories: (1) employer contributions to the IRA (including salary reduction contributions), (2) deductible contributions to the IRA, (3) nondeductible contributions to the IRA, and (4) earnings on contributions within the IRA. Employer contributions to a SEP IRA are excludable from the employee's income when made; therefore, employer contributions represent property that has not been subjected to income tax. A deduction is taken when deductible contributions are made to the SEP IRA; therefore, deductible contributions represent property that has not been subjected to income tax. Earnings on contributions within the IRA generally accumulate tax-free (see above); therefore, earnings on contributions also represent property that has not been subjected to income tax. However, nondeductible contributions to the IRA are contributed on an after-tax basis.

As a result, nondeductible contributions to a SEP IRA can be recovered tax-free from the SEP IRA (similar to investment in the contract or basis). However, employer contributions and employee deductible contributions to a SEP IRA, as well as earnings on contributions within a SEP IRA, are includable in income upon distribution from a SEP IRA.

In order to calculate the part of a distribution from a SEP IRA that can be excluded from income, the annuity exclusion ratio rules are applied. Thus, gross income does not include the part of a distribution that bears the same ratio to such amount as the investment in the contract (i.e., nondeductible contributions) bears to expected return under the contract. For this purpose, all nonRoth IRAs (i.e., traditional, SEP, or SIMPLE) are treated as one IRA, all distributions during the year are treated as one distribution, and the value of the contract, income on the contract, and investment in the contract is computed at the end of the calendar year in which the taxable year begins. The value of the contract is increased by any distribution during the calendar year.[39]

The value of the contract is also increased by any outstanding rollovers. An outstanding rollover is a distribution from the SEP IRA during the current year that is rolled over within 60 days of the distribution but during the following year.

Thus, the formula for calculating the portion of a distribution from a SEP IRA that is excludable from income as attributable to nondeductible contributions to the SEP IRA is:

$$\frac{\text{Unrecovered Nondeductible Contributions}}{\text{Total Account Balance + Distribution Amount + Outstanding Rollover}} \times \text{Distribution Amount}$$

All nonRoth IRAs (i.e., traditional, SEP, or SIMPLE) are treated as one in determining each of the above amounts. The amount of unrecovered nondeductible contributions is generally determined as of the beginning of the year, but may be increased for contributions made during the current year. The total account balance is determined as of the end of the year (i.e., increased by contributions and rollovers to the IRA, but reduced by distributions and rollovers from the IRA). The distribution amount and outstanding rollover is the total of such transactions occurring during the current year.[40]

> *Example.* Jill made $2,000 nondeductible contributions to a SEP IRA for 10 years. Unrecovered nondeductible contributions as of the beginning of 2006 equals $20,000. Other contributions have been made to the SEP IRA. Jill withdraws $1,000 from the IRA in 2006. At the end of 2006, the IRA account balance equals $79,000. The amount of the distribution excludable from income equals $250; $750 is includable. Unrecovered nondeductible contributions as of the beginning of 2007 would equal $19,750 ($20,000 - $250).

$$\frac{\text{Unrecovered Nondeductible Contributions}}{\substack{\text{Total Account Balance +} \\ \text{Distribution Amount +} \\ \text{Outstanding Rollover}}} \times \text{Distribution Amount = Amount Excludable}$$

Distribution Amount - Amount Excludable = Amount Includable

$$\frac{\$20,000}{\$79,000 + \$1,000 + \$0} \times \$1,000 = \text{Amount Excludable}$$

$250 = Amount Excludable

$1,000 - $250 = Amount Includable

$750 = Amount Includable

The trustee of a SEP IRA is required to report distributions from the IRA to the IRS and to the IRA owner on IRS Form 1099-R. Distributions from SEP IRAs are reported by the IRA owner or beneficiary on IRS Form 8606.

Early Distributions

In general, distributions from a SEP IRA received before age 59½ are subject to a 10 percent penalty tax on early distributions. However, the penalty tax only applies to the extent that the distribution is includable in income and a number of exceptions to application of the penalty apply.[41]

A SAR-SEP IRA must prohibit a distribution from being made from the SAR-SEP IRA of any salary reduction contribution (or income thereon) before a determination has been made as to whether the deferral percentage requirement for such contributions has been met for the year.[42] Furthermore, where a distribution is made from a SAR-SEP IRA of any salary reduction contribution (or income thereon) before a determination has been made as to whether the deferral percentage requirement for such contributions has been met for the year, the early distribution penalty tax applies to such distribution without exception.[43]

Otherwise, the early distribution penalty tax does not apply to distributions from a SEP IRA that are:

(1) made after the death of the SEP IRA owner;

(2) attributable to the SEP IRA owner's disability;

(3)   part of a series of substantially equal periodic payments (at least annually) made for the life (or life expectancy) or the joint life (or life expectancies) of the SEP IRA owner and a designated beneficiary (the penalty tax plus interest is due if the substantially equal periodic payments are modified before the later of five years after payments have begun or the SEP IRA owner reaches age 59½);

(4)   made for medical care to the extent generally allowable as a medical expense deduction (generally, unreimbursed medical expenses in excess of 7.5 percent of adjusted gross income; for this purpose, itemization of deductions is not required);

(5)   made to the SEP IRA owner who is unemployed for payment of health insurance premiums;

(6)   made to the SEP IRA owner for payment of qualified higher education expenses furnished to the SEP IRA owner, the SEP IRA owner's spouse, or children or grandchildren of either;

(7)   made to the SEP IRA owner ($10,000 lifetime limit) for purchase of a first home by the SEP IRA owner, the SEP IRA owner's spouse, or children, grandchildren, or ancestor of either; or

(8)   made to a reservist while on active duty (commencing after September 11, 2001 and before 2008).

The IRS has approved three methods for calculating substantially equal periodic payments (SEPPs):

(1)   payments that satisfy the required minimum distributions method (see heading below);

(2)   amortization of payments over the life expectancy of the SEP IRA owner or joint and survivor life expectancy of the SEP IRA owner and beneficiary; and

(3)   annuitization of payments for the life of the SEP IRA owner or the lives of the SEP IRA owner and beneficiary.[44]

The first method requires recalculation of payments each year, while the second and third methods provide constant payments. A person using the second and third methods can elect to switch to the first method. In making these calculations, life expectancy and mortality are now based on the RMD tables (see Appendix D) and interest is generally limited to a maximum rate (which changes monthly).

For additional discussion of the early distribution penalty, including examples of the substantially equal periodic payment exceptions, see Chapter 13.

The additional tax on early distributions is reported either directly on IRS Form 1040 or on IRS Form 5329.

Required Minimum Distributions

When a SEP IRA owner reaches age 70½, the SEP IRA owner must begin taking required minimum distributions. In general, the required minimum distributions rules cause the SEP IRA owner to withdraw the entire SEP IRA account balance over the SEP IRA owner's life or the lives of the SEP IRA owner and a designated beneficiary. If there is more than one beneficiary other than the SEP IRA owner, the oldest other beneficiary's life expectancy is used for the designated beneficiary. Special rules apply where the spouse of the SEP IRA owner is the designated beneficiary. Failure to withdraw the required minimum distribution results in a 50 percent penalty tax on the amount by which the required minimum distribution exceeds the actual amount withdrawn.[45]

An additional rule, the minimum distribution incidental benefit (MDIB) rule, is designed to insure that the SEP IRA distributions are primarily for the benefit of the SEP IRA owner. The rule does this, while the SEP IRA owner is alive, by treating a beneficiary other than the spouse of the SEP IRA owner as no more than 10 years younger than the SEP IRA owner.[46] The Uniform Lifetime Table (see Appendix C) implements the MDIB rule.

In the case of a SEP IRA, required minimum distributions must begin by April 1 of the year following the year the SEP IRA owner reaches age 70½. Generally, required minimum distributions must be made by December 31st of each year. However, in the year the SEP-IRA owner reaches age 70½, the required minimum distribution for that year need not be made until April 1st of the following year (the required beginning date).

Required minimum distributions may be calculated for each SEP IRA and distributions made from each SEP IRA as appropriate. Alternatively, required minimum distributions may be calculated for all nonRoth IRAs (i.e., traditional, SEP, or SIMPLE) owned by the individual and distributions made from whichever nonRoth IRA or IRAs the IRA owner chooses. However, an inherited IRA may not be aggregated with any other IRA within a category unless the other IRA was inherited from the same person. For this purpose, an IRA that a surviving spouse elects to treat as such spouse's own is not treated as being inherited from the decedent spouse.

The required minimum distribution for each year is generally calculated by dividing the SEP IRA account balance as of the end of the previous year by the life expectancy of the SEP IRA owner or the joint and survivor life expectancy of the SEP IRA owner and a designated beneficiary.

Attained age is used for the age of the SEP IRA owner and beneficiary in the appropriate year. Thus, a SEP IRA owner whose birthday is in the first half of the year (January-June) will be age 70 in the year the SEP IRA owner turns 70½ and will enter the table using age 70. On the other hand, a SEP IRA owner whose birthday is in the second half of the year (July-December) will be age 71 in the year the SEP IRA owner turns 70½ and will enter the table using age 71.

Distributions During Lifetime of Owner (including the year of death)

Required minimum distributions during the lifetime of the owner (including the year of the death of the owner) of a SEP IRA are generally determined using the Uniform Lifetime Table (see Appendix C). The attained age of the IRA owner for the year is used, and the Uniform Lifetime Table treats the beneficiary as 10 years younger than the IRA owner. The Uniform Lifetime Table is used even if the IRA owner has not designated a beneficiary.

However, if the spouse of the IRA owner is the sole designated beneficiary of the IRA and the spouse is more than 10 years younger than the IRA owner, the joint and survivor life expectancy of the IRA owner and spouse is used. In this case, the attained ages of both the IRA owner and spouse for the year are used, and a factor from the RMD Joint and Survivor Table (see Appendix C) is used. This method produces higher RMD factors and lower required minimum distributions than using factors from the Uniform Lifetime Table.

Distributions After Death of Owner

The method for calculating required minimum distributions after the death of the IRA owner generally depends on whether a beneficiary has been designated by the time of the IRA owner's death and whether the spouse of the IRA owner is the designated beneficiary.

The method for calculating required minimum distributions after the death of the IRA owner may also depend on whether or not the IRA owner died before the required beginning date. For a SEP IRA, the *required beginning date* is April 1 of the year after the year in which the IRA owner would attain age 70½.

If there are multiple designated beneficiaries of an IRA, the oldest beneficiary is treated as the designated beneficiary. Thus, the oldest beneficiary of a trust that is the beneficiary of an IRA is generally treated as the designated beneficiary of the IRA. If a person other than an individual is designated as beneficiary of an IRA, the IRA will be treated as having no beneficiary, even if an individual is also named beneficiary. For example, a charity is not an individual. Separate IRAs (and trusts) can be created with different designated beneficiaries.

The actual determination of the designated beneficiary can be determined as late as September 30 of the first year after the year of the owner's death. Thus, if a primary beneficiary disclaims an IRA, a contingent named beneficiary who receives the IRA would be treated as the designated beneficiary. Or, if there are two named beneficiaries of an IRA, and one beneficiary is cashed out, the remaining beneficiary is treated as the designated beneficiary.

Spouse Beneficiary. If the spouse of the IRA owner is the sole designated beneficiary, the spouse can elect to be treated as the owner of the IRA for purposes of the RMD rules. The election cannot be made if a trust is named beneficiary, even if the spouse is the sole beneficiary of the trust. (Under certain circumstances, it appears that a rollover to a spouse may be used to get around this limitation.) Also, if the IRA owner died prior to the year the IRA owner attained age 70½ and the spouse is the sole designated beneficiary, then required minimum distributions to the spouse do not have to begin until the year the IRA owner would have attained age 70½.

If the spouse does not elect to be treated as the owner of the IRA, then required minimum distributions must be made to the spouse over the single life expectancy of the spouse. In this case, the attained age of the spouse for the year is used, and a factor from the RMD Single Life Table (see Appendix C) is used. After the death of the spouse, distributions must continue using the remaining life expectancy of the spouse and the subtract one method. The life expectancy is determined using the attained age of the spouse for the year of the death of the spouse from the RMD Single Life Table (see Appendix C), and by subtracting one from that life expectancy for each year after the year of death.

If the spouse does not elect to be treated as the owner of the IRA, and the owner died on or after the required beginning date (see above), the life expectancy of the owner can be used in any year if it is greater than the life expectancy of the spouse (see preceding paragraph). The life expectancy of the owner is determined using the attained age of the owner for the year of the death of the IRA owner from the RMD Single Life Table (see Appendix C), and by subtracting one from that life expectancy for each year elapsed thereafter.

Nonspouse Beneficiary. Distributions to a designated nonspouse beneficiary after the death of the IRA owner depend on whether or not the IRA owner died before the required beginning date (see above).

If the IRA owner died *before* the required beginning date, distributions must be made over the remaining life expectancy of the beneficiary using the subtract one method. The life expectancy of the beneficiary is determined using the attained age of the beneficiary for the year after the year of the death of the IRA owner from the RMD Single Life Table (see Appendix C), and by subtracting one from that life expectancy for each year elapsed thereafter.

If the IRA owner died *after* the required beginning date, distributions must be made over the longer of the remaining life expectancy of the owner or the beneficiary using the subtract one method. The life expectancy of the owner is determined using the attained age of the owner for the year of the death of the IRA owner from the RMD Single Life Table (see Appendix C), and by subtracting one from that life expectancy for each year elapsed thereafter. The life expectancy of the beneficiary is determined using the attained age of the beneficiary for the year after the year of the death of the IRA owner from the RMD Single Life Table (see Appendix C), and by subtracting one from that life expectancy for each year elapsed thereafter.

No Beneficiary. If there is no designated beneficiary, distributions after the death of the IRA owner depend on whether or not the IRA owner died before the required beginning date (see above).

If the IRA owner died *before* the required beginning date, the entire IRA account must be distributed under the five year rule (see below).

If the IRA owner died *after* the required beginning date, distributions must continue using the remaining life expectancy of the IRA owner and the subtract one method. The life expectancy is determined using the attained age of the IRA owner for the year of the death of the IRA owner from the RMD Single Life Table (see Appendix C), and by subtracting one from that life expectancy for each year after the year of death.

Five Year Rule. If the five year rule applies, the entire IRA account must be distributed by the end of the calendar year which contains the fifth anniversary of the date of death of the IRA owner. For example, if an IRA owner age 65 dies on January 1, 2003, then the entire account must be distributed by the end of 2008 if the five year rule applies.

The five year rule generally applies: if elected; if the IRA owner dies before the required beginning date (see above) and without a beneficiary; or if the IRA owner has a beneficiary and there is a failure to timely start distributions over the life expectancy of the beneficiary. Life expectancy distributions must generally start by December 31 of the year after the year of death of the IRA owner, but could start later if the spouse is the beneficiary.

Miscellaneous

The trustee of a SEP IRA generally reports the fair market value of the IRA account as of the end of year. Fair market value may be as of the date of death if the IRA owner died. The fair market value of the account and whether a required minimum distribution is required is reported on IRS Form 5498. Required minimum distributions may be required even if not indicated on IRS Form 5498. The additional tax on failure to make required minimum distributions is reported on IRS Form 5329.

For additional discussion of the required minimum distribution rules, including descriptions of the various methods available and examples of the calculations, see Chapter 13.

Rollovers

Rollovers are permitted between various IRAs, qualified plans, tax sheltered annuities, and eligible Section 457 governmental plans. In general, a rollover is a transfer of retirement assets from one plan to another by the participant or owner that is completed within 60 days of the distribution. The effect of a rollover is generally to avoid taxes and penalties upon what otherwise would be treated as a distribution.[47]

Rollovers are generally permitted from qualified retirement plans, tax sheltered annuities, and eligible Section 457 governmental plans to a SEP IRA. However, the qualified Roth contribution program portion of a 401(k) or 403(b) plan cannot be rolled over into a SEP IRA. Amounts rolled over from a qualified retirement plan, tax sheltered annuity, or eligible Section 457 governmental plan are subject to 20 percent withholding unless the rollover is made through a direct trustee-to-trustee transfer. Rollovers are generally permitted from a SEP IRA to qualified retirement plans, tax sheltered annuities, and eligible Section 457 governmental plans (but not to an elective deferral Roth).

If the amount rolled over from a qualified plan to a traditional IRA or SEP IRA includes amounts that would be eligible for special tax treatment upon distribution from the qualified plan (e.g., income averaging or capital gains treatment), such special tax treatment will be lost. However, if the rolled over amounts are maintained in a separate conduit traditional IRA and rolled back to the qualified plan, the special tax treatment will be once again available for distributions of such amounts from the qualified plan.

SEP IRAs do not make good conduit IRAs for qualified retirement plans because, in order to roll an amount back to a qualified retirement plan, no other amounts can be contributed or rolled over to the SEP IRA, which defeats the purpose for having a SEP IRA. Traditional IRAs (see Chapter 4) make much better conduit IRAs. A taxpayer can have many traditional IRAs, and create a conduit traditional IRA as needed.

Only one rollover is permitted from a particular IRA to any other IRA during the one-year period ending with the transfer from the first IRA. Also, in an IRA to IRA rollover, the receiving IRA cannot be an endowment contract. The one-year rollover limitation does not apply to trustee-to-trustee transfers.

Rollovers are permitted between SEP IRAs and traditional IRAs.

A rollover from a Roth IRA can be made only to another Roth IRA. Therefore, rollovers are not permitted from a Roth IRA to a SEP IRA. If a rollover is made from a SEP IRA to a Roth IRA, it is a taxable event and special provisions apply. See Chapter 5 on Roth IRAs.

Rollovers are permitted between SEP IRAs.

A rollover is not permitted from a SIMPLE IRA to a SEP IRA during the first two years that the individual participates in the SIMPLE IRA. The only rollover permitted to a SIMPLE IRA is from another SIMPLE IRA. Therefore, rollovers are not permitted from a SEP IRA to a SIMPLE IRA.

The trustee of an IRA is required to report rollovers to and from a SEP IRA to the IRS and to the IRA owner on IRS Form 5498.

Losses (Unrecovered Basis)

The Internal Revenue Code provides that if annuity payments from a SEP IRA end upon the death of the annuitant and there is still unrecovered investment in the contract, the unrecovered investment in the contract is allowable as a deduction for the annuitant's final tax year. However, if refund payments are made to a beneficiary or the annuitant's estate after the annuitant's death, the deduction for unrecovered investment in the contract is taken by the person receiving the refund payments for the year in which received. The IRS provides additionally that when all amounts from all nonRoth IRAs (i.e., traditional, SEP, or SIMPLE) have been distributed and the amounts distributed are less than the unrecovered basis, a loss may be recognized.[48]

An employee with a SEP IRA will generally have no basis in the SEP IRA because nondeductible contributions are not generally made to the SEP IRA. Therefore, there is generally no loss to be recognized with respect to a SEP IRA.

Withholding

Employer contributions to a SEP IRA are generally not subject to FICA (Social Security tax), FUTA (federal unemployment tax), or income tax withholding.[49]

Salary reduction contributions to a SAR-SEP IRA are generally subject to FICA (Social Security tax) and FUTA (federal unemployment tax) tax withholding, but not to income tax withholding.[50]

Distributions from a SEP IRA are distributions from an individual retirement plan subject to income tax withholding unless the individual elects to have withholding not apply. Thus, unless the election is made, periodic payments (annuity or similar payments) from a SEP IRA are subject to withholding at regular withholding rates and nonperiodic payments from a SEP IRA are subject to withholding at a 10 percent rate.[51]

A conversion of a SEP IRA into a Roth IRA (a qualified rollover) is a distribution for which income tax withholding is required, unless made in the form of a direct trustee-to-trustee transfer.[52]

Transfer Taxes

A SEP IRA will generally be fully includable in the estate of the original SEP IRA owner. A decedent's estate includes the value of an annuity or other payment receivable by reason of surviving the decedent where the decedent held certain interests in the property while alive. The amount includable is proportionate to the part of the purchase price contributed by the decedent. Any contribution by the employer of the decedent to the SEP IRA is treated as made by the employee for this purpose.[53] Thus, the original SEP IRA owner will generally have contributed 100 percent of the contributions to the SEP IRA and the full value of the SEP IRA will be includable in the original owner's estate.

If upon the original owner's death the SEP IRA passes to the spouse of the original SEP IRA owner, the transfer will generally qualify for the marital deduction (see Chapter 18). If the transfer to the surviving spouse qualified for the marital deduction, any amount still left in the SEP IRA at the surviving spouse's death will be includable in the surviving spouse's estate.

If the SEP IRA passes to a skip person (generally, a person two or more generations younger than the transferor), the generation-skipping transfer tax must be taken into consideration. See Chapter 19.

Endnotes

1. IRC Sec. 404(h).
2. IRC Secs. 408(k)(2), 408(k)(8).
3. IRC Sec. 408(k)(3).
4. IRC Sec. 408(k)(4).
5. IRC Sec. 408(k)(5).
6. IRC Sec. 415(a)(2)(C).
7. IRC Sec. 4972(a).
8. IRC Sec. 4972(b).
9. IRC Sec. 404(h).
10. IRC Secs. 3121(a)(5)(C), 3306(b)(5)(C), 3401(a)(12)(C).
11. IRC Sec. 219(e)(1).
12. IRC Secs. 219(f)(3), 408(o)(3).
13. IRC Sec. 219(d)(1).
14. IRC Sec. 219(d)(4).
15. IRC Sec. 219(b)(1).
16. IRC Secs. 219(b)(5)(A), 219(b)(5)(C).
17. IRC Sec. 219(b)(5)(B).
18. IRC Sec. 219(g).
19. IRC Sec. 219(g)(3)(A).
20. See Treas. Reg. §1.219-2(d)(1).
21. IRC Sec. 219(g)(2).
22. IRC Sec. 219(g)(8).
23. IRC Sec. 62(a)(7).
24. IRC Sec. 408(o)(2)(B)(ii).
25. IRC Sec. 408(o)(2).
26. IRC Secs. 219(b)(1), 408(o)(2), 408A(c)(2).

27. IRC Sec. 4973(a).

28. IRC Secs. 4973(b), 219(f)(6).

29. IRC Sec. 408(k)(6).

30. IRC Sec. 408(k)(6).

31. IRC Sec. 4979.

32. IRC Sec. 402(g)(1).

33. IRC Sec. 408(k)(6)(C).

34. IRC Secs. 3121(a)(5)(C), 3306(b)(5)(C), 3401(a)(12)(C).

35. IRC Secs. 408(e), 408(m).

36. IRC Sec. 408(a)(3).

37. IRC Sec. 408(b).

38. IRC Secs. 408(e), 408(m).

39. IRC Secs. 402(h)(3), 408(d)(1), 408(d)(2), 72(b).

40. Notice 87-16(III), 1987-1 CB 446.

41. IRC Sec. 72(t).

42. IRC Sec. 408(k)(6)(F)(ii).

43. IRC Sec. 408(d)(7).

44. Rev. Rul. 2002-62, 2002-42 IRB 710; Notice 89-25(A-12), 1989-1 CB 662.

45. IRC Secs. 408(a)(6), 408(b)(3), 401(a)(9), 4974(a).

46. Treas. Reg. §1.401(a)(9)-5(A-4).

47. See IRC Sec. 408(d)(3).

48. IRC Sec. 72(b)(3); Notice 89-25(A-7), 1989-1 CB 662, clarifying Notice 87-16(D-5), 1987-1 CB 446.

49. IRC Secs. 3121(a)(5)(C), 3306(b)(5)(C), 3401(a)(12)(C).

50. Ibid.

51. IRC Sec. 3405.

52. Treas. Reg. §1.408A-6(A-13).

53. IRC Sec. 2039.

Chapter 7

SIMPLE IRAs

A SIMPLE IRA is a relatively recent creation that allows for higher contribution levels than are permitted for traditional and Roth IRAs and permits salary reduction contributions while relaxing the rules for qualified plans. However, in order to qualify for a SIMPLE IRA, an employer can generally have no more than 100 employees. An employer with more than 100 employees may wish to consider a SEP IRA (see Chapter 6).

An employee can elect to make salary reduction contributions to a SIMPLE IRA. In addition, the employer makes either matching contributions or nonelective contributions that are not based upon salary reduction contributions. The employer takes a deduction for the salary reduction contributions, as well as the matching or nonelective contributions. The employee excludes such contributions from income.

Amounts contributed to a SIMPLE IRA can be invested in a wide variety of investments. Such amounts grow within the IRA account on a tax-deferred basis; there is generally no taxation until amounts are distributed.

Usually, all contributions to the SIMPLE IRA are excluded from income when contributed and the full amount distributed from a SIMPLE IRA is includable in income.

Distributions received before the individual reaches age 59½ are generally subject to an early distribution penalty tax to the extent the distribution is includable in income unless an exception applies. Once the individual reaches age 70½, required minimum distributions must be made from the SIMPLE IRA or a penalty tax applies.

Employer Requirements

An eligible employer for purposes of SIMPLE IRAs means an employer with no more than 100 employees with at least $5,000 of compensation from the employer for the preceding year.[1] Furthermore, the SIMPLE IRA must be the exclusive plan for the employer.[2] Certain transition rules are provided for an employer following an acquisition, disposition, or similar transaction.[3]

Contributions

The only contributions permitted to a SIMPLE IRA are salary reduction contributions made by the employer for an employee and certain matching or nonelective contributions by the employer.[4] The employer takes a deduction for the salary reduction, matching, and nonelective contributions.[5] The employee excludes the salary reduction, matching, and nonelective contributions from income.[6] Certain limitations apply and excess contributions are generally subject to a penalty tax.

A SIMPLE IRA provides that an employee can elect for any year to have the employer either (1) make elective employer contributions to the SIMPLE IRA on behalf of the employee or (2) distribute the amount in cash to the employee.[7] If the employee takes cash, the distribution is includable in the employee's income. If the employee chooses salary reduction, the employee excludes the amount of the salary reduction and taxation is generally deferred until distributions are made from the SIMPLE IRA. Thus, salary reduction is a form of elective deferral or a cash or deferred arrangement.

According to the Internal Revenue Code, the amount of salary reduction contributions that can be made for any employee in any year is required to be expressed as a percentage of the employee's compensation and cannot exceed an applicable dollar amount.[8] However, according to the Internal Revenue Service, the employer may permit the employee to express the level of salary reduction as a specific dollar amount, and the employer must not place any restrictions on the amount of the employee's salary reduction contributions other than the applicable dollar amount.[9]

The applicable dollar amount is as follows.

Regular Contribution Limit

Year	Amount
2005-2006	$10,000
2007-	$10,000*

*plus indexing for inflation

In addition, elective deferral catch-up contributions can be made for individuals attaining age 50 before the end of the year. The elective deferral catch-up contribution limit for SIMPLE IRAs is as follows.

Catch-up Contribution Limit

Year	Amount
2006	$2,500
2007-	$2,500*

*plus indexing for inflation

The sum of the regular and the catch-up contribution limits will be referred to as the total contributions limit. The regular and catch-up contribution limits shown reflect changes made by PPA 2006. PPA 2006 eliminates the sunset after 2010 of sheduled increases in the contribution limits made by EGTRRA 2001.

An employer is not required to permit catch-up salary reduction contributions. However, if catch-up contributions are permitted, the option must be available to all eligible employees. Also, an employer can, but is not required to, match catch-up contributions (within limits).

Each year each employee eligible to participate in the SIMPLE IRA can elect during the 60-day period preceding such year to participate in the salary reduction arrangement or to modify the amount subject to the arrangement.[10] The employee must be permitted to elect to have the salary reduction contributions made at the level specified by the employee, subject to the total contributions limit.[11] Where an employee was not previously eligible to participate, the employee can make the election during the 60-day period preceding the first day the employee is eligible.[12]

An employee can elect at any time during the year to terminate participation in the salary reduction arrangement. If the employee does so, the SIMPLE IRA can provide that the employee cannot resume participation until the following year.[13]

Salary reduction contributions to a SIMPLE IRA must be made by the employer no later than 30 days following the end of the month for which the contributions are to be made.[14]

Salary reduction contributions to a SIMPLE IRA are not subject to income tax withholding; they are subject to FICA (Social Security tax) and FUTA (federal unemployment tax).[15]

A SIMPLE IRA also provides that, for any year, the employer must make matching contributions on behalf of employees, or elect to make nonelective contributions.[16] (The term "nonelective contributions" refers to contributions being made without regard to whether salary reduction contributions have been elected by the employee.)

If the employer elects matching contributions, the employer must contribute to the SIMPLE IRA an amount equal to the lesser of (1) the amount of the salary reduction contribution to the IRA for the employee, or (2) the applicable percentage of compensation for the year. The applicable percentage is three percent unless the employer elects for any year to use a lower percentage of not less than one percent. An election to use an applicable percentage of less than three percent cannot be made for any year if the applicable percentage would be less than three percent in more than two years of the five-year period ending with such year. In other words, an applicable percentage rate of less than three percent can be used in no more than two years during any five-year period. For this purpose, the applicable percentage is deemed to have been three percent in years prior to the existence of the SIMPLE IRA.

For a person less than age 50 in 2006, the maximum that could be contributed to a SIMPLE IRA using matching contributions is $20,000: $10,000 maximum salary reduction + $10,000 matching contribution [$10,000 matching contribution would require approximately $333,333 of employee compensation with a three percent match (e.g., 3% x $333,333 = $10,000)].

For a person age 50 or more in 2006, the maximum that could be contributed to a SIMPLE IRA using matching contributions is $25,000: $12,500 maximum salary reduction + $12,500 matching contribution [$12,500 matching contribution would require approximately $416,667 of employee compensation with a three percent match (e.g., 3% x $416,667 = $12,500)].

Matching contributions made on behalf of a self-employed individual are not treated as elective employer contributions to a SIMPLE IRA.[17]

If the employer elects to make nonelective contributions, the employer contributes to the SIMPLE IRA of each eligible employee with at least $5,000 of compensation from the employer for the year an amount equal to two percent of compensation (not to exceed $220,000 as indexed for 2006). If this election is made, this amount is contributed without regard to whether salary reduction contributions have been elected.

For a person less than age 50 in 2006, the maximum that could be contributed to a SIMPLE IRA using nonelective contributions is $14,400: $10,000 maximum salary reduction + $4,400 nonelective contribution [(2% of maximum compensation of $220,000)]. For a person age 50 or more in 2006, the maximum that could be contributed to a SIMPLE IRA using nonelective contributions is $16,900: $12,500 maximum salary reduction + $4,400 nonelective contribution (2% of maximum compensation of $220,000).

Matching contributions and nonelective contributions to a SIMPLE IRA must be made by the employer no later than the time for filing the return for the taxable year (including extensions).[18]

Matching contributions and nonelective contributions to a SIMPLE IRA are not subject to FICA (Social Security tax), FUTA (federal unemployment tax), or income tax withholding.[19]

In general, all employees of the employer maintaining a SIMPLE IRA who received at least $5,000 in compensation from the employer for the two preceding years and are reasonably expected to have $5,000 in compensation from the employer for the current year must be eligible to either make a salary reduction contribution election or receive nonelective contributions. Certain employees covered by collective bargaining and nonresident aliens need not be covered under the SIMPLE IRA.[20]

The employee's rights to any contribution to a SIMPLE IRA must be nonforfeitable. Also, contributions to a SIMPLE IRA may not be conditioned on the employee retaining such contributions in the SIMPLE IRA. Nor can the employer prohibit withdrawal of such contributions from the SIMPLE IRA.[21]

The employer can make all SIMPLE IRA contributions to a designated financial institution. However, the employee must be notified in writing that the employee can have the employee's balance rolled over to another SIMPLE IRA or, if the rollover occurs after the two-year period beginning with the date the employee first participated in the salary reduction arrangement, to an IRA other than a SIMPLE IRA.[22]

In the case of a nondeductible contribution to a SIMPLE IRA by the employer, a 10 percent penalty tax is imposed on the employer.[23] In general, a nondeductible contribution is any portion of a contribution to a SIMPLE IRA by the employer in excess of the amount allowable as a deduction by the employer. However, it is necessary to keep a running account of such nondeductible contributions (i.e., it is necessary to keep track of contributions and distributions for the current year and preceding years in order to determine if there is a nondeductible contribution for the current year).

More technically, a nondeductible contribution for any taxable year equals the sum of (1) the excess of employer contributions to SIMPLE IRAs and other retirement plans over the amounts allowable as a deduction for such contributions, and (2) amounts determined under this calculation for the preceding taxable year reduced by the sum of (a) such amounts returned to the employer during the current year, and (b) such amounts deductible for the current year. For this purpose, nondeductible contributions from previous years are carried over and the amount allowable as a deduction in any year is treated as first consisting of carryovers from prior years (and from oldest carryovers first) and then from contributions made during the current year. Thus, a nondeductible contribution carried over from a previous year can be used up as a contribution in a subsequent year.[24]

> *Example.* The only plan maintained by Company is a SIMPLE IRA. Assume that the maximum permissible contribution to the SIMPLE IRA for Ann is $10,800 for all years. Company contributed $11,000 to the SIMPLE IRA for Ann in 2004, resulting in a nondeductible contribution of $200 ($11,000 - $10,800). Company contributed $12,000 to the SIMPLE IRA in 2005, resulting in a nondeductible contribution of $1,400 [($12,000 - $10,800) plus the $200 carryover from 2004]. In 2006, Company does not contribute to the SIMPLE IRA. The $1,400 carryover from 2005 is treated as contributed (and deductible) in 2006 and is less than $10,800; there is no nondeductible contribution.

The trustee of an IRA is required to report contributions to a SIMPLE IRA to the IRS and to the IRA owner on IRS Form 5498.

Accumulations/Investments

Amounts earned within a SIMPLE IRA generally accumulate on a tax-deferred basis. Earnings are generally not taxable until distributed from the SIMPLE IRA. However, a SIMPLE IRA is taxed if it has unrelated business taxable income.

Furthermore, part or all of the SIMPLE IRA may be deemed distributed if the SIMPLE IRA owner engages in a prohibited transaction, borrows on an annuity contract, pledges the account as security for a loan, purchases an endowment contract, or invests in certain collectibles.[25] A SIMPLE IRA account, as with all IRA accounts, cannot invest in life insurance contracts.[26] The IRA can be in the form of an individual retirement annuity.[27]

An individual retirement annuity is an annuity contract or endowment contract issued by an insurance company meeting certain requirements: (1) the contract cannot be transferable by the owner; (2) the premiums may not be fixed; (3) the annual premium cannot exceed the total contribution limit amount (see above); (4) any refund of premiums must be applied before the end of the next year to pay future premiums or to purchase additional benefits; (5) the required minimum distribution and minimum distribution incidental death benefit rules apply; and (6) the entire interest of the owner must be nonforfeitable. For this purpose, an endowment contract cannot mature later than the taxable year in which the SIMPLE IRA owner reaches age 70½ and must be for the exclusive benefit of the SIMPLE IRA owner or beneficiary. Aggregate annual premiums for all endowment contracts purchased for the SIMPLE IRA owner cannot exceed the total contribution limit amount (see above).

See Chapter 3 for more information on limitations on accumulations in an IRA.

Distributions

Amounts distributed from a SIMPLE IRA are generally fully includable in taxable income. Amounts distributed before the SIMPLE IRA owner reaches age 59½ that are includable in income are subject to an early distribution penalty tax unless certain exceptions are met. Amounts distributed within the first two years that an employee participates in a SIMPLE IRA are subject to an increased early distribution penalty tax. Required minimum distributions must begin when the SIMPLE IRA owner reaches age 70½ or a penalty tax applies. A rollover (see heading below) from a SIMPLE IRA is generally not treated as a distribution from a SIMPLE IRA.

Part or all of the SIMPLE IRA may be deemed distributed if the SIMPLE IRA owner engages in a prohibited transaction, borrows on an annuity contract, pledges the account as security for a loan, purchases an endowment contract, or invests in certain collectibles.[28]

Amounts distributed from a SIMPLE IRA generally represent one of two categories: employer contributions to the IRA (including salary reduction contributions, matching contributions, and nonelective contributions) and earnings on contributions within the IRA. Employer contributions to a SIMPLE IRA are excludable from the employee's income when made; therefore, employer contributions represent property that has not been subjected to income tax. Earnings on contributions within the IRA generally accumulate tax-free (see above); therefore earnings on contributions also represent property that has not been subjected to income tax.

If excess contributions were made to the SIMPLE IRA, such contributions would be treated as nondeductible contributions to the IRA (as well as being subject to the nondeductible contribution penalty tax, see above). Nondeductible contributions to the IRA are contributed on an after-tax basis. As a result, nondeductible contributions to a SIMPLE IRA can be recovered tax-free from the IRA (similar to investment in the contract or basis). Such nondeductible contributions would be excludable on a prorated basis (see discussion of distributions from a traditional IRA in Chapter 4).

However, employer contributions to a SIMPLE IRA, as well as earnings on contributions within a SIMPLE IRA, are includable in income upon distribution from a SIMPLE IRA. Thus, in the normal case the full amount of a distribution from a SIMPLE IRA will be includable in income. However, for purposes of calculating taxable distributions, all nonRoth IRAs are aggregated together and other nonRoth IRAs may have basis (see discussion of distributions from a traditional IRA in Chapter 4).

The trustee of a SIMPLE IRA is required to report distributions from the IRA to the IRS and to the IRA owner on IRS Form 1099-R. Distributions from SIMPLE IRAs are reported by the IRA owner or beneficiary on IRS Form 8606.

Early Distributions

In general, distributions from a SIMPLE IRA received before age 59½ are subject to a 10 percent penalty tax on early distributions. However, the penalty tax only applies to the extent that the distribution is includable in income and a number of exceptions to application of the penalty apply.[29] However, in the case of any amount received from a SIMPLE IRA within the first two years that an employee participates in the SIMPLE IRA, the 10 percent penalty tax on early distributions is increased to 25 percent.[30]

The early distribution penalty tax does not apply to distributions from a SIMPLE IRA that are:

(1)   made after the death of the SIMPLE IRA owner;

(2)   attributable to the SIMPLE IRA owner's disability;

(3)   part of a series of substantially equal periodic payments (at least annually) made for the life (or life expectancy) or the joint life (or life expectancies) of the SIMPLE IRA owner and a designated beneficiary (the penalty tax plus interest is due if the substantially equal periodic payments are modified before the later of five years after payments have begun or the SIMPLE IRA owner reaches age 59½);

(4)   made for medical care to the extent generally allowable as a medical expense deduction (generally, unreimbursed medical expenses in excess of 7.5 percent of adjusted gross income; for this purpose, itemization of deductions is not required);

(5)   made to the SIMPLE IRA owner who is unemployed for payment of health insurance premiums;

(6)   made to the SIMPLE IRA owner for payment of qualified higher education expenses furnished to the SIMPLE IRA owner, the SIMPLE IRA owner's spouse, or children or grandchildren of either;

(7)   made to the SIMPLE IRA owner ($10,000 lifetime limit) for purchase of a first home by the SIMPLE IRA owner, the SIMPLE IRA owner's spouse, or children, grandchildren, or ancestor of either; or

(8)   made to a reservist while on active duty (commencing after September 11, 2001 and before 2008).

The IRS has approved three methods for calculating substantially equal periodic payments (SEPPs):

(1)   payments which satisfy the required minimum distributions method (see heading below);

(2)   amortization of payments over the life expectancy of the SIMPLE IRA owner or joint and survivor life expectancy of the SIMPLE IRA owner and beneficiary; and

(3) annuitization of payments for the life of the SIMPLE IRA owner or the
lives of the SIMPLE IRA owner and beneficiary.[31]

The first method requires recalculation of payments each year, while the second
and third methods provide constant payments. A person using the second and third
methods can elect to switch to the first method. In making these calculations, life
expectancy and mortality are now based on the RMD tables (see Appendix D) and
interest is generally limited to a maximum rate (which changes monthly).

For additional discussion of the early distribution penalty, including examples of
the substantially equal periodic payment exceptions, see Chapter 13.

The additional tax on early distributions is reported either directly on IRS Form
1040 or on IRS Form 5329.

Required Minimum Distributions

When a SIMPLE IRA owner reaches age 70½, the SIMPLE IRA owner must
begin taking required minimum distributions. In general, the required minimum
distribution rules cause the SIMPLE IRA owner to withdraw the entire IRA account
balance over the SIMPLE IRA owner's life or the lives of the SIMPLE IRA owner and
a designated beneficiary. If there is more than one beneficiary other than the SIMPLE
IRA owner, the oldest other beneficiary's life expectancy is used for the designated
beneficiary. Special rules apply where the spouse of the SIMPLE IRA owner is the
designated beneficiary. Failure to withdraw the required minimum distribution
results in a 50 percent penalty tax on the amount by which the required minimum
distribution exceeds the actual amount withdrawn.[32]

An additional rule, the minimum distribution incidental benefit (MDIB) rule, is
designed to insure that the SIMPLE IRA distributions are primarily for the benefit of
the SIMPLE IRA owner. The rule does this, while the SIMPLE IRA owner is alive, by
treating a beneficiary other than the spouse of the SIMPLE IRA owner as no more
than 10 years younger than the SIMPLE IRA owner.[33] The Uniform Lifetime Table
(see Appendix C) implements the MDIB rule.

In the case of a SIMPLE IRA, required minimum distributions must begin by
April 1 of the year following the year the SIMPLE IRA owner reaches age 70½.
Generally, required minimum distributions must be made by December 31st of each
year. However, in the year the SIMPLE IRA owner reaches age 70½, the required
minimum distribution for that year need not be made until April 1st of the following
year (the required beginning date).

Required minimum distributions may be calculated for each SIMPLE IRA and distributions made from each IRA as appropriate. Alternatively, required minimum distributions may be calculated for all nonRoth IRAs (i.e., traditional, SEP, or SIMPLE) owned by the individual and distributions made from whichever nonRoth IRA or IRAs the IRA owner chooses. However, an inherited IRA may not be aggregated with any other IRA within a category unless the other IRA was inherited from the same person. For this purpose, an IRA that a surviving spouse elects to treat as such spouse's own is not treated as being inherited from the decedent spouse.

The required minimum distribution for each year is generally calculated by dividing the SIMPLE IRA account balance as of the end of the previous year by the life expectancy of the SIMPLE IRA owner or the joint and survivor life expectancy of the SIMPLE IRA owner and a designated beneficiary.

Attained age is used for the age of the SIMPLE IRA owner and beneficiary in the appropriate year. Thus, an SIMPLE IRA owner whose birthday is in the first half of the year (January-June) will be age 70 in the year the SIMPLE IRA owner turns 70½ and will enter the table using age 70. On the other hand, an SIMPLE IRA owner whose birthday is in the second half of the year (July-December) will be age 71 in the year the SIMPLE IRA owner turns 70½ and will enter the table using age 71.

Distributions During Lifetime of Owner
(including the year of death)

Required minimum distributions during the lifetime of the owner (including the year of the death of the owner) of a SIMPLE IRA, are generally determined using the Uniform Lifetime Table (see Appendix C). The attained age of the IRA owner for the year is used, and the Uniform Lifetime Table treats the beneficiary as 10 years younger than the IRA owner. The Uniform Lifetime Table is used even if the IRA owner has not designated a beneficiary.

However, if the spouse of the IRA owner is the sole designated beneficiary of the IRA and the spouse is more than 10 years younger than the IRA owner, the joint and survivor life expectancy of the IRA owner and spouse is used. In this case, the attained ages of both the IRA owner and spouse for the year are used, and a factor from the RMD Joint and Survivor Table (see Appendix C) is used. This method produces higher RMD factors and lower required minimum distributions than using factors from the Uniform Lifetime Table.

Distributions After Death of Owner

The method for calculating required minimum distributions after the death of the IRA owner generally depends on whether a beneficiary has been designated by the time of the IRA owner's death and whether the spouse of the IRA owner is the designated beneficiary.

The method for calculating required minimum distributions after the death of the IRA owner may also depend on whether or not the IRA owner died before the required beginning date. For a SIMPLE IRA, the *required beginning date* is April 1 of the year after the year in which the IRA owner would attain age 70½.

If there are multiple designated beneficiaries of an IRA, the oldest beneficiary is treated as the designated beneficiary. Thus, the oldest beneficiary of a trust that is the beneficiary of an IRA is generally treated as the designated beneficiary of the IRA. If a person other than an individual is designated as beneficiary of an IRA, the IRA will be treated as having no beneficiary, even if an individual is also named beneficiary. For example, a charity is not an individual. Separate IRAs (and trusts) can be created with different designated beneficiaries.

The actual determination of the designated beneficiary can be determined as late as September 30 of the first year after the year of the owner's death. Thus, if a primary beneficiary disclaims an IRA, a contingent named beneficiary who receives the IRA would be treated as the designated beneficiary. Or, if there are two named beneficiaries of an IRA, and one beneficiary is cashed out, the remaining beneficiary is treated as the designated beneficiary.

Spouse Beneficiary. If the spouse of the IRA owner is the sole designated beneficiary, the spouse can elect to be treated as the owner of the IRA for purposes of the RMD rules. The election cannot be made if a trust is named beneficiary, even if the spouse is the sole beneficiary of the trust. (Under certain circumstances, it appears that a rollover to a spouse may be used to get around this limitation.) Also, if the IRA owner died prior to the year the IRA owner attained age 70½ and the spouse is the sole designated beneficiary, then required minimum distributions to the spouse do not have to begin until the year the IRA owner would have attained age 70½.

If the spouse does not elect to be treated as the owner of the IRA, then required minimum distributions must be made to the spouse over the single life expectancy of the spouse. In this case, the attained age of the spouse for the year is used, and a factor from the RMD Single Life Table (see Appendix C) is used. After the death of the spouse, distributions must continue using the remaining life expectancy of the spouse and the subtract one method. The life expectancy is determined using the attained age of the spouse for the year of the death of the spouse from the RMD Single Life Table (see Appendix C), and by subtracting one from that life expectancy for each year after the year of death.

If the spouse does not elect to be treated as the owner of the IRA, and the owner died on or after the required beginning date (see above), the life expectancy of the owner can be used in any year if it is greater than the life expectancy of the spouse (see preceding paragraph). The life expectancy of the owner is determined using the attained age of the owner for the year of the death of the IRA owner from the RMD Single Life Table (see Appendix C), and by subtracting one from that life expectancy for each year elapsed thereafter.

Nonspouse Beneficiary. Distributions to a designated nonspouse beneficiary after the death of the IRA owner depend on whether or not the IRA owner died before the required beginning date (see above).

If the IRA owner died *before* the required beginning date, distributions must be made over the remaining life expectancy of the beneficiary using the subtract one method. The life expectancy of the beneficiary is determined using the attained age of the beneficiary for the year after the year of the death of the IRA owner from the RMD Single Life Table (see Appendix C), and by subtracting one from that life expectancy for each year elapsed thereafter.

If the IRA owner died *after* the required beginning date, distributions must be made over the longer of the remaining life expectancy of the owner or the beneficiary using the subtract one method. The life expectancy of the owner is determined using the attained age of the owner for the year of the death of the IRA owner from the RMD Single Life Table (see Appendix C), and by subtracting one from that life expectancy for each year elapsed thereafter. The life expectancy of the beneficiary is determined using the attained age of the beneficiary for the year after the year of the death of the IRA owner from the RMD Single Life Table (see Appendix C), and by subtracting one from that life expectancy for each year elapsed thereafter.

No Beneficiary. If there is no designated beneficiary, distributions after the death of the IRA owner depend on whether or not the IRA owner died before the required beginning date (see above).

If the IRA owner died *before* the required beginning date, the entire IRA account must be distributed under the five year rule (see below).

If the IRA owner died *after* the required beginning date, distributions must continue using the remaining life expectancy of the IRA owner and the subtract one method. The life expectancy is determined using the attained age of the IRA owner for the year of the death of the IRA owner from the RMD Single Life Table (see Appendix C), and by subtracting one from that life expectancy for each year after the year of death.

Five Year Rule. If the five year rule applies, the entire IRA account must be distributed by the end of the calendar year that contains the fifth anniversary of the date of death of the IRA owner. For example, if an IRA owner age 65 dies on January 1, 2003, then the entire account must be distributed by the end of 2008 if the five year rule applies.

The five year rule generally applies: if elected; if the IRA owner dies before the required beginning date (see above) and without a beneficiary; or if the IRA owner has a beneficiary and there is a failure to timely start distributions over the life expectancy of the beneficiary. Life expectancy distributions must generally start by December 31 of the year after the year of death of the IRA owner, but could start later if the spouse is the beneficiary.

Miscellaneous

The trustee of a SIMPLE IRA generally reports the fair market value of the IRA account as of the end of year. Fair market value may be as of the date of death if the IRA owner died. The fair market value of the account and whether a required minimum distribution is required is reported on IRS Form 5498. Required minimum distributions may be required even if not indicated on IRS Form 5498. The additional tax on failure to make required minimum distributions is reported on IRS Form 5329.

For additional discussion of the required minimum distribution rules, including descriptions of the various methods available and examples of the calculations, see Chapter 13.

Rollovers

Rollovers are permitted between various IRAs, qualified plans, tax sheltered annuities, and eligible Section 457 governmental plans. In general, a rollover is a transfer of retirement assets from one plan to another by the participant or owner that is completed within 60 days of the distribution. The effect of a rollover is generally to avoid taxes and penalties upon what otherwise would be treated as a distribution.[34]

The only rollover permitted from a SIMPLE IRA during the first two years that the individual participates in the SIMPLE IRA is to another SIMPLE IRA. After the individual has participated for two years in the SIMPLE IRA, rollovers can be made from the SIMPLE IRA to traditional IRAs, Roth IRAs, SEP IRAs, SIMPLE IRAs, qualified plans, tax sheltered annuities, and eligible Section 457 governmental plans (but not to an elective deferral Roth).

If a rollover is made from a SIMPLE IRA to a Roth IRA, it is a taxable event and special provisions apply. See Chapter 5 on Roth IRAs.

Only one rollover is permitted from a particular IRA to any other IRA during the one-year period ending with the transfer from the first IRA. Also, in an IRA to IRA rollover, the receiving IRA cannot be an endowment contract. The one-year rollover limitation does not apply to trustee-to-trustee transfers.

The only rollover permitted to a SIMPLE IRA is from another SIMPLE IRA.

The trustee of an IRA is required to report rollovers to and from a SIMPLE IRA to the IRS and to the IRA owner on IRS Form 5498.

Losses (Unrecovered Basis)

The Internal Revenue Code provides that if annuity payments from a SIMPLE IRA end upon the death of the annuitant and there is still unrecovered investment in the contract, the unrecovered investment in the contract is allowable as a deduction for the annuitant's final tax year. However, if refund payments are made to a beneficiary or the annuitant's estate after the annuitant's death, the deduction for unrecovered investment in the contract is taken by the person receiving the refund payments for the year in which received. The IRS provides additionally that when all amounts from all nonRoth IRAs (i.e., traditional, SEP, or SIMPLE) have been distributed and the amounts distributed are less than the unrecovered basis, a loss may be recognized.[35]

An employee with a SIMPLE IRA will have no basis in the SIMPLE IRA because only excludable contributions can be made to the SIMPLE IRA. Therefore, there is no loss to be recognized with respect to a SIMPLE IRA. However, for purposes of calculating taxable distributions and losses, all nonRoth IRAs are aggregated together and other nonRoth IRAs may have basis.

Withholding

Salary reduction contributions to a SIMPLE IRA are not subject to income tax withholding; they are subject to FICA (Social Security tax) and FUTA (federal unemployment tax).[36]

Matching contributions and nonelective contributions to a SIMPLE IRA are not subject to FICA (Social Security tax), FUTA (federal unemployment tax), or income tax withholding.[37]

Distributions from a SIMPLE IRA are distributions from a retirement plan subject to income tax withholding unless the individual elects to have withholding not apply. Thus, unless the election is made, periodic payments (annuity or similar payments) from a SIMPLE IRA are subject to withholding at regular withholding rates and nonperiodic payments from a SIMPLE IRA are subject to withholding at a ten percent rate.[38]

A conversion of a SIMPLE IRA into a Roth IRA (a qualified rollover) is a distribution for which income tax withholding is required, unless made in the form of a direct trustee-to-trustee transfer.[39]

Transfer Taxes

A SIMPLE IRA will generally be fully includable in the estate of the original SIMPLE IRA owner. A decedent's estate includes the value of an annuity or other payment receivable by reason of surviving the decedent where the decedent held certain interests in the property while alive. The amount includable is proportionate to the part of the purchase price contributed by the decedent. Any contribution by the employer of the decedent to the SIMPLE IRA is treated as made by the employee for this purpose.[40] Thus, the original SIMPLE IRA owner will generally have contributed 100 percent of the contributions to the SIMPLE IRA and the full value of the SIMPLE IRA will be includable in the original owner's estate.

If upon the original owner's death the SIMPLE IRA passes to the spouse of the original SIMPLE IRA owner, the transfer will generally qualify for the marital deduction (see Chapter 18). If the transfer to the surviving spouse qualified for the marital deduction, any amount still left in the SIMPLE IRA at the surviving spouse's death will be includable in the surviving spouse's estate.

If the SIMPLE IRA passes to a skip person (generally, a person two or more generations younger than the transferor), the generation-skipping transfer tax must be taken into consideration. See Chapter 19.

Endnotes

1. IRC Sec. 408(p)(2)(C)(i).
2. IRC Sec. 408(p)(2)(D).
3. IRC Sec. 408(p)(10).
4. IRC Sec. 408(p)(1)(B).
5. IRC Sec. 404(m)(1).
6. IRC Secs. 402(k), 402(h)(1).
7. IRC Sec. 408(p)(2)(A)(i).
8. IRC Secs. 408(p)(2)(A)(ii), 408(p)(2)(E); IR-2002-111.
9. Notice 98-4(D-2), 1998-2 CB 269.
10. IRC Sec. 408(p)(5)(C).
11. Notice 98-4(D-2), 1998-2 CB 269.
12. IRC Sec. 408(p)(5)(C).
13. IRC Sec. 408(p)(5)(B).
14. IRC Sec. 408(p)(5)(A)(i).
15. IRC Secs. 3121(a)(5)(H), 3306(b)(5)(H), 3401(a)(12)(D).
16. IRC Sec. 408(p)(2).
17. IRC Sec. 408(p)(9).
18. IRC Sec. 408(p)(5)(A)(ii).
19. IRC Secs. 3121(a), 3306(b)(5)(H), 3401(a)(12)(D).
20. IRC Sec. 408(p)(4).
21. IRC Secs. 408(p)(3), 408(k)(4).
22. IRC Secs. 408(p)(7), 408(d)(3)(g), 72(t)(6).
23. IRC Sec. 4972(a).
24. IRC Sec. 4972(b).
25. IRC Secs. 408(e), 408(m).
26. IRC Sec. 408(a)(3).
27. IRC Sec. 408(b).
28. IRC Secs. 408(e), 408(m).
29. IRC Sec. 72(t).
30. IRC Sec. 72(t)(6).
31. Rev. Rul. 2002-62, 2002-42 IRB 710; Notice 89-25(A-12), 1989-1 CB 662.
32. IRC Secs. 408(a)(6), 408(b)(3), 401(a)(9), 4974(a).
33. Treas. Reg. §1.401(a)(9)-5(A-4).
34. See IRC Sec. 408(d)(3).
35. IRC Sec. 72(b)(3); Notice 89-25(A-7), 1989-1 CB 662 clarifying Notice 87-16(D5), 1987-1 CB 446.
36. IRC Secs. 3121(a)(5)(H), 3306(b)(5)(H), 3401(a)(12)(D).

37. IRC Secs. 3121(a), 3306(b)(5)(H), 3401(a)(12)(D).

38. IRC Sec. 3405.

39. Treas. Regs. §§1.408A-4, A-4; 1.408A-6(A-13).

40. IRC Sec. 2039.

Chapter 8

EGTRRA Extras

The Economic Growth and Tax Relief Reconciliation Act of 2001 (EGTRRA 2001) made many changes that affect IRAs (e.g., increased contribution limits). Most of these are discussed throughout the book.

EGTRRA 2001 also created a retirement savings contributions credit, deemed IRAs, and elective deferral Roth IRAs. These are discussed here.

Retirement Savings Contributions Credit

A credit may be available for certain individuals who make contributions to IRAs.[1] PPA 2006 eliminates the termination of the credit after 2006 (as well as sunset of the credit after 2010 under EGTRRA 2001).

The maximum credit is $1,000 ($2,000 if married filing jointly). The credit is available to any individual who (1) has attained age 18 during the year, (2) is not claimed as a personal exemption on someone else's tax return (e.g., by a parent), and (3) is not a full-time student. However, the credit is limited to qualified retirement savings (not to exceed $2,000) multiplied by the applicable percentage of adjusted gross income.

Adjusted Gross Income (not over)

Joint Return	Head of Household	All Other	Applicable Percentage
30,000*	22,500*	15,000*	50%
32,500*	24,375*	16,250*	20%
50,000*	37,500*	25,000*	10%
....	....	....	0%

*plus indexing for inflation after 2006

PPA 2006 provides for indexing of the adjusted gross income amount limits for the credit after 2006.

> *Example.* Assume an individual makes qualified retirement savings contributions equal to $2,000. An individual who files a joint return and has adjusted gross income of $51,000 cannot take a credit (0% x $2,000 = $0).

> *Example.* Assume an individual who files as a head of household and has adjusted gross income of $25,000 makes qualified retirement savings contributions equal to $2,000. The credit is limited to $200 (10% x $2,000).

> *Example.* Assume an individual who files a single return and has adjusted gross income of $15,000 makes qualified retirement savings contributions equal to $2,000. The credit is limited to $1,000 (50% x $2,000).

> *Example.* Assume an individual who is married but files separate and has adjusted gross income of $16,000 makes qualified retirement savings contributions equal to $2,000. The credit is limited to $400 (20% x $2,000).

Qualified retirement savings contributions include contributions to traditional IRAs and Roth IRAs; salary reduction (elective deferral) contributions to SAR-SEP IRAs, SIMPLE IRAs, qualified plans, tax sheltered annuities, and eligible Section 457 governmental plans; and any voluntary employee contributions to a qualified plan or tax sheltered annuity.

In order to minimize the recycling of contributions as a way of obtaining the credit, qualified retirement savings contributions must be reduced by certain distributions during a testing period. The testing period includes (1) the year the credit would be claimed, (2) the two preceding years, and (3) the period after the year the credit would be claimed up until the due date (including extensions) for filing the return for such year.

Distributions for this purpose generally include any distribution (whether taxable or not) from any type of plan to which contributions could be made that could qualify for this credit. However, the following are not treated as distributions for this purpose: trustee to trustee transfers and rollovers that are not included in income; timely return of excess contributions and earnings thereon; and qualified rollovers to Roth IRAs.

For purposes of the testing period, an individual is treated as receiving distributions received by the individual's spouse if a joint return was filed with the spouse both for the year of distribution and the year for which a credit would be claimed.

The $2,000 limit on contributions that can be taken into account for purposes of the credit is applied after qualified retirement savings contributions are reduced by distributions.

The credit is reported on IRS Form 8880.

Deemed IRAs

In plan years beginning after 2002, a qualified plan, a tax sheltered annuity plan, or an eligible Section 457 governmental plan can elect to treat a separate account or annuity in the qualified employer plan as a deemed IRA. PPA 2006 eliminates the sunset of the deemed IRA provision after 2010 under EGTRRA 2001.

The deemed IRA must meet all the requirements for either a traditional IRA or a Roth IRA, except that the prohibition against commingling of IRA assets with other property except in a common trust or investment fund does not apply. The employee can make contributions to the IRA by designating any nonmandatory employee contribution as a voluntary employee contribution to the deemed IRA. In general, the deemed IRA is treated as an IRA rather than as a qualified plan.[2] However, the ERISA requirements relating to exclusive benefit, fiduciary responsibilities, and enforcement and administration apply to the deemed IRA.

The deemed IRA can be either a traditional IRA (see Chapter 4) or a Roth IRA (see Chapter 5). It cannot be a SEP IRA or a SIMPLE IRA.[3]

The provisions for the deemed IRA must be incorporated into the documents of the qualified employer plan. Also, the deemed IRAs must exist when the contributions are made.[4]

The availability of a deemed IRA is not treated as a benefit, right, or feature of a qualified employer plan. Therefore, it should not effect the nondiscrimination rules applicable to the qualified employer plan.[5]

If the qualified employer plan fails to meet its qualification requirements, the deemed IRA does not qualify as a deemed IRA. If so, the deemed IRA must therefore meet all the requirements of either a traditional IRA or a Roth IRA on its own (including the prohibition against commingling of assets). If any of the deemed IRAs fails to qualify as an IRA, the IRA is not a deemed IRA and the qualified employer plan fails to meet its qualification requirements.[6]

An employer can create IRAs for employees outside of a qualified employer plan. Why, then, might an employer decide to go the deemed IRA route? Perhaps there might be some minor administrative cost savings. Assets in the deemed IRA and the qualified employer plan could be commingled to some extent. Perhaps the combined deemed IRA and qualified employer plan would seem to be slightly more unified and cohesive.

In light of the harsh penalty to be paid if a deemed IRA or a qualified employer plan fails to qualify, it would appear generally to make sense to create the IRAs outside the qualified employer plan rather than as deemed IRAs inside the qualified employer plan. Little seems to be gained by going the deemed IRA route.

A discussion of the general application of the deemed IRA rules to contributions, investment/accumulation, distributions, and rollovers follows. With regard to the two types of deemed IRAs, traditional IRAs are discussed in detail in Chapter 4, and Roth IRAs are discussed in detail in Chapter 5.

Contributions

The amount that can be contributed (whether deductible or nondeductible) to a deemed IRA is the same as the contribution limits for all traditional IRAs (see Chapter 4) or Roth IRAs (see Chapter 5).[7] Thus, deductible contributions can be made to a traditional IRA up to the total contribution limit, subject to phaseout. Deductible contributions of an active participant in a qualified retirement plan may be phased out based on modified adjusted gross income (MAGI). Nondeductible contributions can be made to a traditional IRA to the extent that the total contribution limit exceeds the deductible contribution. However, contributions cannot be made to a traditional IRA once the individual reaches age 70½. Nondeductible contributions can be made to a Roth IRA to the extent that the total contribution limit exceeds all contributions to traditional IRAs. However the total contribution limit may be phased out based on modified adjusted gross income (MAGI) for this purpose.

Contributions for a taxable year may be made up until the time for filing the tax return for the year (not including extensions of time for filing): generally, April 15. The provision for employer contributions that provides that the employee includes the contribution in income as compensation for the year in which the contribution was made does not apply to employee contributions to a deemed IRA. Therefore, the employee will generally include the contribution in income in the year that the amount is withheld and paid by the employer, even if it is later than the year for which the contribution is made.[8]

> *Example.* Ann designates $4,000 of voluntary employee contribu-
> tions as a contribution to a deemed traditional IRA. Her employer with-
> holds the contribution and pays it to the deemed IRA in March 2006. She
> treats the contribution as having been made for 2005. If it is a deductible
> contribution, the deduction would be taken for 2005. Nevertheless, the
> contribution is not included in her income until 2006.

Accumulations/Investments

Amounts earned within a traditional IRA or deemed IRA generally accumulate on a tax-deferred basis (or perhaps tax-free).

The prohibition against commingling of IRA assets with other property except in a common trust or investment fund does not apply to a deemed IRA. Proposed regulations provide that this means that the IRA assets can be commingled with the assets of the qualified employer plan. However, the assets of the IRA and the qualified employer plan may not be commingled with nonplan assets.[9] Furthermore, the limitations on certain investments by IRAs (see Chapter 3) would still apply to the deemed IRA. For example, an IRA cannot invest in life insurance contracts.

The trust (or annuity) holding the IRA assets must be separate from the trust (or annuity) holding the assets of the qualified employer plan. There must be separate accounting for the interest of each participant.[10]

Distributions

The income tax rules applicable to distributions from traditional IRAs or Roth IRAs apply to distributions from a deemed IRA.[11] Part or all of the deemed IRA may be treated as distributed if the IRA owner engages in a prohibited transaction, borrows on an annuity contract, pledges the account as security for a loan, purchases an endowment contract, or invests in certain collectibles.

Distributions from traditional IRAs and Roth IRAs are generally excluded from income to the extent that distributions are made from unrecovered nondeductible contributions (i.e., basis). Distributions from traditional IRAs are treated as a return of nondeductible contributions on a prorated basis (see Chapter 4). Distributions from Roth IRAs are treated as first from a return of contributions, then from earnings. In addition, certain qualified distributions from Roth IRAs are not subject to income tax (see Chapter 5).

Distributions from IRAs and qualified retirement plans may be subject to an early distribution penalty tax if made before age 59½, death, or disability (see Chapter 13). The deemed IRA should be treated as separate from the qualified employer plan for this purpose. Thus, substantially equal periodic payments (an exception to the penalty) should be calculated separately for the deemed IRA and the qualified employer plan.

Distributions may be required from an IRA or a qualified retirement plan, or a penalty tax applies (see Chapter 13). Distributions are generally required from a traditional IRA at age 70½. Distributions from a Roth IRA are not required until after death. Distributions from a qualified retirement plan can often be postponed until the later of age 70½ or retirement. The amount required to be distributed is generally dependent on the life expectancy of the owner/participant and, perhaps, the life expectancy of a designated beneficiary. The calculation of required minimum distributions is made separately for the deemed IRA and the qualified employer plan.[12]

Rollovers

The rules applicable to IRA rollovers (see Chapter 11) applies to the deemed IRAs. Thus, an employee can request and receive a distribution from the deemed IRA even if distributions could not be received from the qualified employer plan.[13]

Elective Deferral Roths

After 2005, a qualified plan or tax sheltered annuity that accepts salary reduction contributions can include a qualified Roth contribution program.[14] Such a program essentially allows an employee to convert excludable (deductible) contributions to nondeductible contributions, with more favorable rules for distributions. Overall, if the employer adds the Roth option, the employee is generally given a choice of cash, regular elective deferrals, Roth elective deferrrals, or a combination of these. PPA 2006 eliminates the sunset of the elective deferral Roth provsions after 2010 under EGTRRA 2001.

In such a program, an employee can designate a portion of his elective deferral contributions as being made to a designated Roth account. Although the contribution is generally treated as a salary reduction contribution, the contribution is not excludable from income. It is a nondeductible contribution to a designated Roth account. However, the contribution limits for elective deferrals apply rather than those for Roth IRAs.

Distributions from the designated Roth account are generally taxable under the Roth IRA rules (see Chapter 5). Thus, contributions and qualified distributions can be received tax-free (although contributions are treated as returned on a pro-rated basis, rather than as contributions first). However, the five year period for qualified distributions that can be received tax-free from a Roth IRA does not start until the earlier of (1) the year of the first contribution to any designated Roth account for the employee in the same qualified Roth contribution program, or (2) if another designated Roth account is rolled over to the designated Roth account, the year of the first contribution to such other account. And the rules for required minimum distributions apply to a designated Roth account during the participant's lifetime.

Elective deferral Roths are subject to a combination of rules for qualified plans, such as 401(k) plans and 403(b) plans (depending on which type of elective deferral plan it is), and Roth IRAs. The rules for qualified plans are generally beyond the scope of this book on IRAs. The general rules for elective deferral Roths are discussed below, including a comparison with the rules for Roth IRAs.

Contributions

Contributions to an elective deferral Roth are included in income (unlike the exclusion for regular elective deferral contributions). They are, like contributions to a Roth IRA, nondeductible contributions. However, the contribution limits (including catch-up contributions) for elective deferrals, which are much higher than the contribution limits for Roth IRAs (see Chapter 5), apply to elective deferral Roths. (See, for example, elective deferral limits discussed in relation to SAR-SEPs in Chapter 6.) Also, there is no phaseout based on adjusted gross income for elective deferrral Roths, as there is for Roth IRAs. Contributions to an elective deferral Roth may be subject to other requirements applicable to elective deferral contributions made under a qualified cash or deferred arrangement, such as the actual deferral percentage (ADP) test applicable to 401(k) plans.[15]

An elective deferral Roth cannot be offered as a standalone plan. The employer must provide a regular elective deferral plan with the elective deferral Roth. However, the regular elective deferral account and the designated Roth account must be maintained and accounted for separately. The elective deferral Roth account must keep track of investment in the contract (i.e., undistributed contributions).[16]

In general, the employee makes an elective deferral election and elects whether the elective deferral is made as a regular contribution or as a Roth contribution. If the plan provides for automatic enrollment and the employee makes no election, the plan can specify the default deferral type as either regular or Roth. The employee must be given the same election frequency options and enrollment periods under the Roth account as are provided for the regular elective deferrals (generally, at least once a year).[17]

No contributions can be made to the designated Roth account other than designated Roth contributions (i.e., employee elective deferral contributions designated as Roth contributions) and rollovers (see below). Thus, forfeitures and matching contributions cannot be allocated to the designated Roth account.[18]

Distributions

If the terms of the plan so provides, a participant can choose whether distributions are made from the regular elective deferral account or the Roth elective deferral account.

Distributions from the designated Roth account are partially taxable under the Roth IRA rules and partially under the proration rules that apply to IRAs other than Roth IRAs (see Chapter 13 on distributions). Thus, qualified distributions can be received tax-free (see Chapter 5). Distributions treated as made from contributions are also received tax-free; however, distributions from a designated Roth account are treated as a return of contributions on a pro-rated basis under IRC Section 72 (see Chapter 4), rather on the contributions first basis generally applicable to Roth IRAs.

A designated Roth account is treated as a separate contract under IRC Section 72; it is not aggregated with other accounts or plans.[19]

In general, a qualified distribution is a distribution from a Roth IRA that is made after the five-taxable-year period beginning in the year in which the first contribution was made to a Roth IRA and that is made after age 59½ or death, on account of disability, or for cetain first home purchases. However, the five year period for qualified distributions which can be received tax-free from an elective deferral Roth does not start until the earlier of (1) the year of the first contribution to any designated Roth account for the employee in the same qualified Roth contribution program, or (2) if another designated Roth account is rolled over to the designated Roth account, the year of the first contribution to such other account.

Required minimum distribution rules for qualified plans, rather than for Roth IRAs, apply to the designated Roth account. Unlike with a Roth IRA, where distributions are not required during the IRA owner's lifetime, required minimum distributions from an elective deferral Roth must generally start at age 70½.[20]

Rollovers

Rollovers are permitted between various IRAs, qualified plans, tax sheltered annuities, and eligible Section 457 governmental plans. In general, a rollover is a transfer of retirement assets from one plan to another by the participant or owner that is completed within 60 days. The effect of a rollover is generally to avoid taxes and penalties upon what otherwise would be treated as a distribution.

The only rollover permitted from an elective deferral Roth is to a Roth IRA or to an elective deferral Roth of the same type (i.e., 401(k) to 401(k), or 403(b) to 403(b)). The only rollover permitted to an elective deferral Roth is from an elective deferral Roth of the same type. If any portion of the distribution from an elective deferral Roth is not includable in income (determined without regard to the rollover), a rollover to another elective deferral Roth can only be accomplished through a direct transfer to a plan that agrees to separately account for the amount not includable in income. Apparently, a rollover of an amount not includable in income cannot be made to a 403(b) plan.[21]

Endnotes

1. IRC Sec. 25B.
2. IRC Sec. 408(q).
3. Treas. Prop. Reg. §1.408(q)-1(b).
4. Treas. Prop. Reg. §1.408(q)-1(d)(1).
5. Treas. Reg. §1.408(q)-1(f)(5).
6. Treas. Reg. §1.408(q)-1(g).
7. Treas. Regs. §§1.408(q)-1(a), 1.408(q)-1(f)(3).
8. Treas. Reg. §1.408(q)-1(f)(3).
9. Treas. Reg. §1.408(q)-1(d)(2).
10. Treas. Reg. §1.408(q)-1(f)(2).
11. Treas. Reg. §1.408(q)-1(e).
12. Treas. Reg. §1.408(q)-1(e)(2).
13. Treas. Reg. §1.408(q)-1(f)(4).
14. IRC Sec. 402A.
15. Treas. Reg. §1.401(k)-1(f); Treas. Prop. Reg. §1.403(b)-3(c).
16. Treas. Reg. §1.401(k)-1(f)(2); Treas. Prop. Reg. §1.403(b)-3(c).
17. Treas. Reg. §1.401(k)-1(f)(4).
18. Treas. Reg. §1.401(k)-1(f)(2).
19. Treas. Prop. Reg. §1.402A-1, A-2, A-3.
20. Treas. Reg. §1.401(k)-1(f)(3): Treas. Prop. Reg. §1.403(b)-3(c)(2).
21. Treas. Prop. Reg. §1.408A-10.

Part

III

IRA Planning

Chapter 9

Selecting an IRA

Selecting an IRA generally involves choices regarding which type of IRA to use, what to invest the IRA in, and who to invest with.

For planning issues with IRAs regarding planning for education, purchase of a home, retirement, or spouses, or dynasty generational estate planning, see Chapter 10. Also, see Chapter 15 on IRAs, Time, Money, and Taxes.

Choosing IRA Type

Choosing an IRA type can depend on many factors. An employer can choose between a SEP IRA or a SIMPLE IRA as a substitute for more complex qualified plans. An employee covered by a SAR-SEP IRA or a SIMPLE IRA with limited funds may have to decide between contributions to the SAR-SEP IRA or SIMPLE IRA or to a Roth or traditional IRA. The amount of an individual's income can determine whether an individual can make deductible contributions to a traditional IRA and nondeductible contributions to a Roth IRA. The age of the IRA owner affects whether contributions can be made to a particular type of IRA and the amount that can be contributed. Age also affects when distributions are required from a particular type of IRA and the amount that must be distributed. Before a person makes a contribution to a traditional or Roth IRA, the person will probably want to know whether it is better from a time value of money standpoint to make deductible contributions to a traditional IRA or nondeductible contributions to a Roth IRA. All of these are discussed below.

The amount that a person can contribute to a particular type of IRA may also be a factor in choosing an IRA. These amounts are generally noted briefly throughout the discussion below. For a more detailed comparison of IRA contribution limits, see Chapter 2.

Employers

In general, an employer can create a SEP IRA or a SIMPLE IRA for the benefit of employees or contribute to traditional or Roth IRAs for the benefit of employees. Also, an employer with an existing SAR-SEP IRA can continue the SAR-SEP IRA. The employer takes a deduction for its contributions to such IRAs. An employer can also set up direct deposits to traditional and Roth IRAs by way of payroll deduction so that individual employees can contribute to their own IRAs.

An employer who wishes to provide a retirement plan to employees, but who wishes to avoid the complexity normally associated with qualified plans, could provide employees with a SEP IRA (including a SAR-SEP IRA) or a SIMPLE IRA. However, in general, an employer with a SAR-SEP IRA can have no more than 25 employees and an employer with a SIMPLE IRA can have no more than 100 employees; there are no limitations on the number of employees that an employer can have with a SEP IRA.

Employers can exclude from a SEP IRA employees who have not attained age 21, who have not performed services for the employer for at least three of the five preceding years, or whose compensation is less than $450 (as indexed for 2006). Employers can exclude from a SIMPLE IRA employees who have not received at least $5,000 in compensation from the employer in the past two years and are not expected to receive $5,000 for the current year. Certain employees covered by collective bargaining and nonresident aliens can be excluded from a SEP IRA or a SIMPLE IRA.

With a SEP IRA, contributions are made by an employer based upon a definite written allocation formula that specifies how an employee qualifies for employer contributions and how the amount of employer contributions is calculated. The employer's deduction for contributions to the SEP IRA is limited to 25 percent of the employee's compensation or $44,000 (as indexed for 2006). The amount of compensation taken into account of each employee cannot exceed $220,000 (as indexed for 2006). Thus, the employer's deduction and the resulting employee's exclusion from income is limited to $44,000 (in 2006 (or possibly less in case of certain highly compensated employees in a SEP IRA that is integrated with Social Security). Also, contributions must bear a uniform relationship (e.g., five percent) to compensation (not to exceed $220,000 as indexed for 2006) of each employee maintaining a SEP IRA. Other overall limitations on contributions to qualified plans may apply.

A SAR-SEP IRA is generally treated like a SEP IRA, except that an employee in a SAR-SEP IRA can make salary reduction contributions. Salary reduction essentially means that the employee can choose to receive cash that is immediately taxable or contributions to the SAR-SEP IRA that are generally tax deferred until distributed from the SAR-SEP IRA. Salary reduction contributions to a SAR-SEP IRA, as well as all other elective deferrals to retirement plans, are subject to a combined overall limitation for elective deferrals in a year.

The elective deferral limits is as follows.

Elective Deferral Limit

Year	Amount
2006	$15,000
2007-	$15,000*

*plus indexing for inflation

In addition, elective deferral catch-up contributions can be made for individuals attaining age 50 before the end of the year. However, an employer with a SAR-SEP IRA is not required to permit catch-up contributions. The elective deferral catch-up contribution limit is as follows.

Catch-up Contribution Limit

Year	Amount
2006	$5,000
2007-	$5,000*

*plus indexing for inflation

The elective deferral regular and catch-up contribution limits shown reflect changes made by PPA 2006. PPA 2006 eliminates the sunset after 2010 of scheduled increases in the contribution limits made by EGTRRA 2001.

With a SIMPLE IRA, the employer is required to make either matching contributions or nonelective contributions for employees. Matching contributions are generally equal to the lesser of three percent of an employee's compensation (an applicable percentage rate of less than three percent but no less than one percent can be used twice every five years) or the employee's salary reduction. An employee can generally elect a salary reduction amount up to an applicable dollar amount.

The applicable dollar amount is as follows.

Salary Reduction Contribution Limit

Year	Amount
2005-2006	$10,000
2007-	$10,000 *

*plus indexing for inflation

In addition, elective deferral catch-up contributions can be made for individuals attaining age 50 before the end of the year. However, an employer with a SIMPLE IRA is not required to permit catch-up contributions. Also, the employer can designate whether or not catch-up contributions will be matched. The elective deferral catch-up contribution limit for SIMPLE IRAs is as follows.

Catch-up Contribution Limit

Year	Amount
2006	$2,500
2007-	$2,500 *

*plus indexing for inflation

The salary reduction deferral regular and catch-up contribution limits shown reflect changes made by PPA 2006. PPA 2006 eliminates the sunset after 2010 of scheduled increases in the contribution limits made by EGTRRA 2001.

With matching contributions, the maximum employer contribution for an employee less than age 50 would be $10,000 in 2006; a $10,000 matching contribution would require at least $333,333 of employee compensation with a three percent match (3 percent x $333,333 = $10,000). The maximum employer contribution for an employee age 50 or more would be $12,500 in 2006; a $12,500 matching contribution would require at least $416,667 of employee compensation with a three percent match (3 percent x $416,667 = $12,500). However, matching contributions are made only for employees who elect salary reduction.

Alternatively, with a SIMPLE IRA, the employer can elect to make nonelective contributions rather than matching contributions. (The term "nonelective contributions" refers to contributions being made without regard to whether salary reduction contributions have been elected.) Nonelective contributions are made by the employer in an amount equal to two percent of compensation (not to exceed $220,000 as indexed for 2006).

Thus, with nonelective contributions, the maximum employer contribution for an employee is $4,400 in 2006 ($220,000 x 2 percent). However, as noted, nonelective contributions must be made whether or not the employee elects salary reduction.

An employer can also make contributions for an employee to a traditional IRA or a Roth IRA. The employer takes a deduction for the contribution as compensation paid to the employee and the employee includes the contribution in income as compensation. The employee is then treated as making a contribution to the traditional or Roth IRA. In the case of the traditional IRA, the employee may be entitled to a deduction for the contribution. Similar contributions can be made to a SEP IRA.

However, the maximum contributions that can be made to traditional IRAs, Roth IRAs, and SEP IRAs (disregarding employer contributions to a SEP IRA described above) may be much lower for any individual in any year (see below). For these types of contributions, the employer can choose whether or not to make a contribution for any particular employee.

An employer can also set up direct deposits to traditional and Roth IRAs by way of payroll deduction so that individual employees can contribute to their own IRAs. The employee establishes the traditional or Roth IRA. The employer sets up the payroll deduction option. The employee determines how much to have deducted from pay (limited to the maximum annual contribution amounts for traditional and Roth IRAs). The only responsibility of the employer is to transmit the payroll deduction contribution to the traditional or Roth IRA selected by the employee.

The payroll deduction reduces pay received directly by the employee (and the employee's IRA is increased by the amount of the payroll deduction), but it does not reduce income reported to the IRS or the amount subject to tax. However, if the payroll deduction contribution is to a traditional IRA, the employee may be entitled to an income tax deduction on the employee's income tax return. It is the employee's responsibility to make sure that excess contributions are not made to the IRA (e.g.,

Roth maximum annual contribution amounts are subject to phaseout based on adjusted gross income).

Employees

If an employee who is entitled to make salary reduction contributions to a SAR-SEP IRA or a SIMPLE IRA for which the employer will make matching contributions (see above) cannot afford to make both a salary reduction contribution and a regular contribution to a traditional or Roth IRA (see below), the employee should generally make the salary reduction contribution in order to obtain the employer matching contribution. If the employee can afford to make both types of contributions, then both types should be considered.

Amount of Income

The amount of an individual's modified adjusted gross income (MAGI) can determine whether an individual can make deductible contributions to a traditional IRA and nondeductible contributions to a Roth IRA. Also, contributions to a traditional IRA, whether deductible or not, and contributions to a Roth IRA can generally be made only to the extent of compensation. Furthermore, employees with small amounts of compensation can be excluded from participation in a SEP IRA or a SIMPLE IRA. Also, the amount that can be contributed to a SEP IRA or a SIMPLE IRA is generally limited to some percentage of compensation.

The total contribution limit for contributions to traditional and Roth IRAs consists of the sum of the regular contribution limit and the catch-up contribution limit. The regular contribution limit is as follows.

Regular Contribution Limit

Year	Amount
2005-2007	$4,000
2008-	$5,000*

*indexed for inflation after 2008

In addition, catch-up contributions can be made for individuals attaining age 50 before the end of the year. The catch-up contribution limit is as follows.

Catch-up Contribution Limit

Year	Amount
2006-	$1,000

The regular and catch-up contribution limits shown reflect changes made by PPA 2006. PPA 2006 eliminates the sunset after 2010 of scheduled increases in the contribution limits made by EGTRRA 2001.

A full deductible contribution equal to the total contribution limit amount can be made to a traditional IRA if the individual and the individual's spouse are not active participants in an employer retirement plan (assuming sufficient compensation). In the case of active participants, the total contribution limit amount is subject to phaseout based upon modified adjusted gross income (MAGI). For this purpose, modified adjusted gross income means adjusted gross income with certain adjustments, including that any deduction for contributions to a traditional IRA is not taken into account.

In the case of a joint return of an active participant in an employer retirement plan, a full deductible contribution can be made to a traditional IRA if adjusted gross income is $75,000 (in 2006, $80,000 in 2007) or less; and is fully phased out at $85,000 (in 2006, $100,000 in 2007). In the case of a joint return where one spouse is an active participant and the other is not, a full deductible contribution can be made to a traditional IRA with respect to the spouse who is not an active participant if adjusted gross income of the couple is $150,000 or less; and is fully phased out at $160,000. In the case of a married filing separate return of an active participant, phaseout of the deductible contribution begins with adjusted gross income of $0; and is fully phased out at $10,000. In the case of a single return or a head of household return of an active participant, a full deductible contribution can be made to a traditional IRA if adjusted gross income is $50,000 (in 2006) or less; and is fully phased out at $60,000 (in 2006). PPA 2006 provides for indexing of the phaseout limits for contributions after 2006.

Up to the total contribution limit amount (reduced by contributions to traditional IRAs) can be contributed to a Roth IRA. The total contribution limit amount (see above) is subject to phaseout based upon modified adjusted gross income (MAGI). For this purpose, modified adjusted gross income means adjusted gross income with certain adjustments, including that any amount taken into income from a qualified rollover to a Roth IRA (see Chapter 5) is not taken into account and any deduction for contributions to a traditional IRA is taken into account.

With respect to a Roth IRA: In the case of a joint return, the full total contribution limit amount is available if adjusted gross income is $150,000 or less; and is fully phased out at $160,000. In the case of a married filing separate return, the full total contribution limit amount starts to phaseout with adjusted gross income equal to $0; and is fully phased out at $10,000. In the case of a single return or a head of household return, the full total contribution limit amount is available if modified adjusted gross income is $95,000 or less; and is fully phased out at $110,000. PPA 2006 provides for indexing of the phaseout limits for contributions after 2006.

Nondeductible contributions of up to the total contribution limit amount (reduced by deductible contributions made to a traditional IRA) can be made to a traditional IRA (there is no phaseout of this total contribution limit amount; however, the total contribution limit amount (see above) is limited to compensation).

Because distributions from a Roth IRA are generally subject to much more favorable rules than are distributions from a traditional IRA, it is generally advisable to make nondeductible contributions to a Roth IRA rather than nondeductible contributions to a traditional IRA, except to the extent that the individual's permissible contributions to a Roth IRA are phased out by the limitations based on income. Consideration can be given to converting a traditional IRA to a Roth IRA at a later time. See Chapter 12.

For a discussion of whether to make deductible contributions to a traditional IRA or nondeductible contributions to a Roth IRA, see "Roth IRA vs. Traditional IRA," below.

Employers can exclude from a SEP IRA employees whose compensation is less than $450 (as indexed in 2006). Employers can exclude from a SIMPLE IRA employees whose compensation is less than $5,000. Also, the amount that can be contributed to a SEP IRA or a SIMPLE IRA is generally limited to some percentage of compensation. See heading, "Employers," above.

Age

The age of the IRA owner affects whether contributions can be made to a particular type of IRA and when distributions are required from a particular type of IRA. Also, additional catch-up contributions may be available starting at age 50.

Contributions cannot be made to a traditional IRA once the individual turns age 70½. Contributions to a Roth IRA are not so restricted (however, the individual is required to have compensation in order to make a contribution; so the ability to make contributions after age 70½ may be limited in many cases). Employers can exclude from a SEP Plan employees who have not attained age 21.

With traditional IRAs and Roth IRAs, catch-up contributions, in addition to regular contributions (see above), can be made for individuals attaining age 50 before the end of the year. The catch-up contribution limit is as follows.

Catch-up Contribution Limit

Year	Amount
2006-	$1,000

With SAR-SEP IRAs, elective deferral catch-up contributions, in addition to regular elective deferral contributions (see above), can be made for individuals attaining age 50 before the end of the year. The elective deferral catch-up contribution limit is as follows.

Catch-up Contribution Limit

Year	Amount
2006	$2,500
2007-	$2,500*

*plus indexing for inflation

With SIMPLE IRAs, elective deferral catch-up contributions, in addition to regular elective deferral contributions (see above), can be made for individuals attaining age 50 before the end of the year. The elective deferral catch-up contribution limit for SIMPLE IRAs is as follows.

Catch-up Contribution Limit

Year	Amount
2006	$5,000
2007-	$5,000*

*plus indexing for inflation

The catch-up contribution limits shown reflect changes made by PPA 2006. PPA 2006 eliminates the sunset after 2010 of scheduled increases in the contribution limits made by EGTRRA 2001.

Distributions from IRAs prior to age 59½ are subject to an early distribution penalty, unless an exception applies. See Chapter 13.

Distributions must generally begin from a traditional IRA, a SEP IRA (including a SAR-SEP IRA), or a SIMPLE IRA at the earlier of the death of the IRA owner or when the IRA owner turns age 70½. In the case of a Roth IRA, distributions are not required until after the death of the IRA owner. The actual amount required to be distributed is generally dependent on the age of the IRA owner or a beneficiary, or both. See Chapter 13.

Qualified charitable distributions can be made from a traditional IRA or a Roth IRA after the IRA owner attains age 70½ (for 2006 and 2007). See Chapter 14.

Traditional IRA vs. Roth IRA (Deductible v. Nondeductible)

The discussion here will deal with the issue of whether it is better from a time value of money standpoint to make deductible contributions to a traditional IRA or nondeductible contributions to a Roth IRA. As discussed under "Amount of Compensation," above, it is generally better to make nondeductible contributions to a Roth IRA rather than nondeductible contributions to a traditional IRA.

The total contribution limit for contributions to traditional and Roth IRAs consists of the sum of the regular contribution limit and the catch-up contribution limit. The regular contribution limit is as follows.

Regular Contribution Limit

Year	Amount
2005-2007	$4,000
2008-	$5,000*

*indexed for inflation after 2008

In addition, catch-up contributions can be made for individuals attaining age 50 before the end of the year. The catch-up contribution limit is as follows.

Catch-up Contribution Limit	
Year	**Amount**
2006-	$1,000

The catch-up contribution limits shown reflect changes made by PPA 2006. PPA 2006 eliminates the sunset after 2010 of scheduled increases in the contribution limits made by EGTRRA 2001. Deductible contributions to traditional IRAs and nondeductible contributions to Roth IRAs may be subject to phaseout based on modified adjusted gross income.

Due to possible rounding differences (as well as the general nature of projecting future results), insignificant differences between results under a deductible scenario and a nondeductible scenario can essentially be disregarded. Also, future value factors below and in Appendix E are shown rounded to 4 places. However, the future value factors actually used here, and generally throughout the *IRA Calculator* software, are essentially unrounded.

Comparisons of deductible and nondeductible scenarios, while helpful in making the decision of which IRA to contribute to, are generally theoretical. Comparisons are made on an isolated basis as if nothing else happens in the IRA world during the years between contribution and distribution, and as if no other contributions have ever been made to IRAs. However, for purposes of taxation of distributions, all non-Roth IRAs are generally grouped together and all Roth IRAs are grouped together. Other contributions, conversions, and distributions with respect to these or other IRAs could affect taxation of the IRAs being compared.

For purposes of the examples and comments below, assume the total contribution limit, the maximum amount of deductible contributions that can be made to traditional IRAs, and the maximum amount of nondeductible contributions that can be made to Roth IRAs are all $4,000. The comparisons would be made in a similar manner for other contribution limit amounts. The *IRA Calculator* software incorporates determination of the maximum contributions, as well as many other variables, into its "Deductible v. Nondeductible" contributions module.

If the annual deductible amount contributed to the traditional IRA is $4,000 or less and the corresponding amount as reduced by taxes (e.g., $4,000 x .75 = $3,000 in the case of a 25 percent tax bracket and a $4,000 contribution to a traditional IRA) is contributed to a Roth IRA, it does not make any difference what the taxpayer's tax bracket is (assuming the tax bracket stays constant); either IRA produces the same results. (It is assumed, for this purpose, that the Roth IRA will be received tax-free upon distribution.)

> *Example.* If a deductible contribution of $4,000 is made to a traditional IRA, and the $4,000 grows at 10 percent interest for 10 years, the $4,000 will have grown to $10,375 ($4,000 x 2.5937 future value of single sum factor at 10 percent and 10 years, see Appendix E). After taxes of $2,594 ($10,375 x 25 percent), $7,781 remains. On the other hand if $3,000 [$4,000 x (1 - 25 percent)] is contributed to a Roth IRA, and the $3,000 grows at 10 percent interest for 10 years, the $3,000 will have grown to $7,781 (3,000 x 2.5937), the same as with a traditional IRA.

> However, if the Roth IRA distribution was not a qualified distribution, only $6,586 would remain after tax [$7,881 - (($7,881 - $3,000) x 25 percent)]. Obviously, receipt of distributions as qualified distributions is important to the Roth IRA.

If a full $4,000 were to be contributed to the Roth IRA, for comparison purposes, a taxpayer should place an amount equal to the tax deduction for the contribution to a traditional IRA into a side fund that supplements the traditional IRA. For example, with respect to a $4,000 contribution to a traditional IRA, if the taxpayer is in a 25 percent tax bracket, $1,000 ($4,000 x 25 percent) is placed into a side fund.

For comparison purposes, if the amount contributed to the Roth IRA is less than $4,000, the traditional IRA is tentatively funded with an amount equal to the amount contributed to the Roth IRA divided by one minus the taxpayer's tax bracket. If the tentative amount is no greater than $4,000, such amount is contributed to the traditional IRA. However, if such tentative amount is greater than $4,000, the traditional IRA is funded with $4,000 and the excess of the tentative amount over $4,000 multiplied by one minus the taxpayer's tax bracket is placed in a side fund. For example, if $3,880 would be placed in a Roth IRA and the taxpayer is in a 25 percent tax bracket, the tentative comparable amount to be placed in the traditional IRA would be $5,173 [$3,800/(1 - 25 percent)]. However, only $4,000 can be placed in the traditional IRA, so $880 [($5,173 - $4,000) x (1 - 25 percent)] would be placed in a side fund.

When the taxpayer maintains a side fund for the tax savings attributable to the deduction for contribution to a traditional IRA, if the taxpayer were in the same tax bracket at time of contribution and at time of distribution and the side fund were not taxable, the traditional and Roth IRA would produce the same results. However, any tax on the side fund reduces the value of the traditional IRA plus side fund combination.

FIGURE 9.1

Deductible v. Nondeductible
(Traditional Plus Side Fund v. Roth)

IRA Contribution	4,000	Side Fund	1,000
Interest	10%	Years	10
Tax Rate at Contribution	25%		

At Distribution Tax Rate	Roth	Traditional Decreases	Traditional No Change	Traditional Increases
Tax Rate	NA	15%	25%	35%
IRA Balance	10,375	10,375	10,375	10,375
- Tax	NA	1,556	2,594	3,631
Net IRA	10,375	8,819	7,781	6,744
Side Fund (SF)				
No Tax	NA	2,594	2,594	2,594
After Tax	NA	2,355	2,196	2,036
IRA + SF				
SF No Tax	**10,375**	**11,413**	**10,375**	**9,338**
SF After Tax	**10,375**	**11,174**	**9,977**	**8,780**

Example. Assume a tax rate at time of contribution and at time of distribution equal to 25 percent. If $4,000 is contributed to a Roth IRA, and the $4,000 grows at 10 percent interest for 10 years, the $4,000 will have grown to $10,375 (4,000 x 2.5937 future value of single sum factor at 10 percent and 10 years, see Appendix E). On the other hand, if a deductible contribution of $4,000 is made to a traditional IRA, and the $4,000 grows at 10 percent interest for 10 years, the $4,000 will have grown to $10,375 ($4,000 x 2.5937). After taxes of $2,594 ($10,375 x 25 percent), $7,781 remains. If $1,000 (equal to the tax deduction of $4,000 x 25 percent for the contribution to the traditional IRA) is contributed to a side fund which grows at the same rate and the side fund is not taxable for 10 years, the side fund will grow to $2,594 ($1,000 x 2.5937). If there were no taxes on the side fund, after 10 years the traditional IRA plus side fund equals $10,375 ($7,781 + $2,594), the same as for the Roth IRA. After taxes of $398 (($2,594 - $1,000) x 25 percent), $2,196 remains in the side fund. Combining the traditional IRA with the side fund, $9,977 ($7,781 + $2,196) remains, less than the amount for the Roth IRA. See Figure 9.1.

Any increase in tax rates at the time of distribution as compared to the time of contribution works to the benefit of the Roth IRA. Any decrease in tax rates at the time of distribution as compared to the time of contribution works to the benefit of the traditional IRA plus side fund. However, any decrease in tax rates must still overcome any tax on the traditional IRA's side fund if the traditional IRA plus side fund is to be a better deal than the Roth IRA.

Example: Tax Rates Increase. Assume a tax rate at time of contribution equal to 25 percent and a tax rate at time of distribution equal to 35 percent. If $4,000 is contributed to a Roth IRA, and the $4,000 grows at 10 percent interest for 10 years, the $4,000 will have grown to $10,375 (4,000 x 2.5937 future value of single sum factor at 10 percent and 10 years, see Appendix E). On the other hand, if a deductible contribution of $4,000 is made to a traditional IRA, and the $4,000 grows at 10 percent interest for 10 years, the $4,000 will have grown to $10,375 ($4,000 x 2.5937). After taxes of $3,631 ($10,375 x 35 percent), $6,744 remains. If $1,000 (equal to the tax deduction of $4,000 x 25 percent for the contribution to the traditional IRA) is contributed to a side fund which grows at the same rate and the side fund is not taxable for 10 years, the side fund will grow to $2,594 ($1,000 x 2.5937). If there were no taxes on the side fund, after 10 years the traditional IRA plus side fund equals $9,338 ($6,744 + $2,594), less than the amount for a Roth IRA. If the side fund is subject to taxes, there is even less in the traditional IRA plus side fund combination. See Figure 9.1.

Example: Tax Rates Decrease. Assume a tax rate at time of contribution equal to 25 percent and a tax rate at time of distribution equal to 15 percent. If $4,000 is contributed to a Roth IRA, and the $4,000 grows at 10 percent interest for 10 years, the $4,000 will have grown to $10,375 (4,000 x 2.5937 future value of single sum factor at 10 percent and 10 years, see Appendix E). On the other hand, if a deductible contribution of $4,000 is made to a traditional IRA, and the $4,000 grows at 10 percent interest for 10 years, the $4,000 will have grown to $10,375 ($4,000 x 2.5937). After taxes of $1,556 ($10,375 x 15 percent), $8,819 remains. If $1,000 (equal to the tax deduction of $4,000 x 25 percent for the contribution to the traditional IRA) is contributed to a side fund which grows at the same rate and the side fund is not taxable for 10 years, the side fund will grow to $2,594 ($1,000 x 2.5937). If there were no taxes on the side fund, after 10 years the traditional IRA plus side fund equals $11,413 ($8,819 + $2,594), more than the amount for a Roth IRA.

If the side fund is subject to a single 25 percent tax, the side fund equals $2,196 [$1,000 + (($2,594 - $1,000) x (1 - 25 percent))], the traditional IRA and side fund combination equals $11,015 ($8,819 + $2,196), still more than the amount for a Roth IRA. If the side fund is subject to a single 35 percent tax, the side fund equals $2,036 [$1,000 + (($2,594 - $1,000) x (1 - 35 percent))], the traditional IRA and side fund combination equals $10,855 ($8,819 + $2,036), still more than the amount for a Roth IRA. See Figure 9.1.

For simplicity's sake, the above examples have shown a single tax on the side fund rather than a yearly, or other periodic, tax. Using a spreadsheet, one could increase the side fund for growth each year and then subtract out whatever tax was assumed to be payable for each year. A shortcut method might be to adjust the growth rate on the side fund to an after-tax rate. For example, if growth is assumed to be 10 percent per year and the income tax rate equal to 25 percent, an after-tax growth rate of 7.5 percent [10 percent x (1 - 25 percent)] could be used. The *IRA Calculator* software permits selection of a side fund that is tax free, tax deferred until distribution, or taxed annually in its "Deductible v. Nondeductible" module. Also, consider whether a lower tax rate should be used with the side fund (e.g., a capital gains tax rate or a blend of regular and capital gains tax rates).

The foregoing examples have demonstrated how to compare contributions to a Roth IRA as compared to contributions to a traditional IRA with a side fund (for tax deduction savings) based upon a single distribution. (Distributions from the Roth IRA have been assumed to be received tax-free, which is generally required for the success of a Roth IRA.) Comparisons can also be made of a person making periodic distributions for a number of years. Making periodic distributions may enable a person to keep income at lower tax rates than if the distribution is made all at once. However, the results above are no different if distributions are made comparably from either a Roth IRA or a traditional IRA with side fund and the tax rate used is appropriate under the circumstances.

The Roth IRA does have one advantage that is likely to be important if the IRA owner has sufficient other assets that the owner does not need to take distributions from the IRA. Required minimum distributions from a Roth IRA can be postponed until after the death of the IRA owner and, generally, the death of the spouse of the IRA owner. However, distributions from a traditional IRA must generally begin when the IRA owner attains age 70½.

Choosing the IRA Investment Vehicle

IRAs typically invest in stocks, bonds, money markets, and mutual funds. An IRA account cannot invest in life insurance contracts.[1] The IRA can be in the form of an individual retirement annuity. Certain investments in collectibles are not permitted.

Money market funds are invested in short term bank and corporate debt, and are essentially a cash equivalent.

Mutual funds can generally be classified by their investment objective: income, balanced, growth and income, growth, and aggressive growth. Income funds consist of fixed income funds that invest in bonds, and equity income funds that invest in stocks, especially preferred stock and blue chip common stocks, for their dividend yields. Balanced funds attempt to achieve some diversification between fixed income and equity investments. Growth and income funds attempt to achieve additional long term growth, with some current income. Growth funds seek long term growth, with little emphasis on income. Aggressive growth funds invest in stock with a high risk/high return focus. Primary research services covering mutual funds include *Morningstar Mutual Fund*, *ValueLine Mutual Fund Survey*, and *CDA/Wiesenberger Mutual Funds*.

An individual retirement annuity is an annuity contract or endowment contract issued by an insurance company meeting certain requirements: (1) the contract cannot be transferable by the owner; (2) the premiums may not be fixed; (3) the annual premium cannot exceed the total contribution limit amount; (4) any refund of premiums must be applied before the end of the next year to pay future premiums or to purchase additional benefits; (5) the required minimum distribution and minimum incidental death benefit rules apply; and (6) the entire interest of the owner must be nonforfeitable. For this purpose, an endowment contract cannot mature later than the taxable year in which the IRA owner reaches age 70½ and must be for the exclusive benefit of the IRA owner or beneficiary. Aggregate annual premiums for all endowment contracts purchased for the IRA owner cannot exceed the total contribution limit amount.[2]

However, an individual retirement annuity cannot be an endowment contract issued after November 6, 1978.[3] Also, if the assets of an IRA are used to purchase an endowment contract for the benefit of the individual on behalf of whom the IRA is created, to the extent that the assets are used to purchase life, health, accident, or other insurance, such amounts are treated as distributed.[4] Apparently, such a deemed distribution would not be subject to the early distribution penalty tax; however, a technical correction is needed.

In general, IRAs cannot invest in collectibles. The acquisition by an IRA of a collectible is treated as a distribution from the IRA of an amount equal to the cost of the collectible. Collectibles mean works of art, rugs, antiques, metals, gems, stamps, coins, alcoholic beverages, and any other tangible personal property specified by the IRS. Certain coins and bullion are not treated as collectibles: certain gold, silver, or platinum U.S. coins; coins of the various states; and certain gold, silver, platinum, or palladium bullion if the bullion is in the physical possession of the IRA trustee.[5]

Prior to April 30, 1982, certain retirement bonds were issued by the United States.[6] Such bonds can be used in individual retirement plans or redeemed at any time by their holders. Such a redemption would not be subject to the early distribution penalty tax.

Investing in real estate is not prohibited, but trustees are not required to offer real estate as an option. Because of administrative burdens, many IRA trustees do not permit IRA owners to invest IRA funds in real estate. The prohibited transactions rules (see Chapter 3 – Accumulations/Investments) prohibit many transactions typically undertaken with respect to real estate by individuals, including sales, exchanges, and leasing between the IRA owner and the IRA, and use of IRA assets by an IRA owner. Also, if the IRA invests directly in real estate or in a partnership, the IRA may be taxable as a trust to the extent that the IRA has unrelated business taxable income. Furthermore, many of the advantages typically associated with investing in real estate, such as leveraging purchases with loans, sheltering income, deferring tax, and turning ordinary income into capital gains, are generally unavailable or of little use within an IRA; earnings in an IRA are generally tax-deferred and taxed as ordinary income on distribution from the IRA (except for qualified distributions from Roth IRAs). As a result, investing in real estate is not that common in IRAs.

Choosing an IRA Trustee or Custodian

An individual cannot be the trustee of an individual retirement account. The trustee must be a bank, a federally insured credit union, a building and loan association, or other person who satisfies requirements of the Internal Revenue Service.[7] A non-bank trustee must demonstrate the following characteristics to the IRS:

- fiduciary ability (including continuity of life, an established place of business in the United States where it is accessible during every business day, fiduciary experience, fiduciary responsibility, and financial responsibility),

- capacity to account for the interests of a large number of individuals,

- fitness to handle retirement funds,

- ability to administer fiduciary powers, and

- adequacy of net worth.[8]

In addition, the non-bank trustee must also provide the following:

- that audits will be conducted by a qualified public accountant at least once every 12 months,

- that funds will be kept invested as long as reasonable for the proper management of the account,

- that investments will not be commingled with other investments except in a common trust fund and investments will be safely maintained, and

- that separate fiduciary records will be maintained.[9]

The IRS maintains a list of entities approved to act as a nonbank IRA trustee or custodian.[10]

An IRA can generally be invested in the form of an individual retirement annuity issued by an insurance company, but not in life insurance contracts (see heading, "Choosing The IRA Investment Vehicle," above). A number of companies rate insurance companies for their claims paying ability.

A.M. Best Company
Ambest Road
Oldwick, NJ 08858
(908) 439-2200
www.ambest.com

Standard & Poor's
55 Water Street
New York, NY 10041
(212) 438-1000
www.standardandpoors.com

Fitch Ratings
One State Street Plaza
New York, NY 10004
(212) 908-0500
www.fitchratings.com

Weiss Ratings Inc.
15430 Endeavour Drive
Jupiter, FL 33478
(800) 289-9222
www.weissratings.com

Moody's Investors Service
99 Church Street, 2nd Floor
New York, NY 10007
(212) 553-0377
www.moodys.com

Endnotes

1. IRC Sec. 408(a)(3).
2. IRC Secs. 408(b), 408A(a).
3. Treas. Reg. §1.408-3(e)(1)(ix).
4. IRC Sec. 408(e)(5).
5. IRC Sec. 408(m).
6. IRC Sec. 409, as in effect prior to TRA '84.
7. IRC Secs. 408(a)(2), 408(n).
8. Treas. Regs. §§1.408-2(b)(2), 1.408-2(e).
9. Ibid.
10. See. Ann. 2006-45, 2006-31 IRB 121.

Chapter 10

Special Purpose Planning

This chapter discusses planning for education with IRAs, planning for the purchase of a home with IRAs, planning for retirement with IRAs, planning for spouses with IRAs, and dynasty planning with IRAs.

For a discussion of various issues or factors in selecting an IRA, see Chapter 9. For a discussion of using an IRA as a tax favored accumulation vehicle, see Chapter 15.

Planning for Education with IRAs

The tax-deferred nature of earnings within IRAs can be used to provide for payment of education expenses. There are a wide variety of tax-favored vehicles other than IRAs that are designed specifically for payment of education expenses. Use of tax-favored vehicles, including IRAs as well as those designed specifically for payment of education expenses, takes on an even greater importance now that unearned income of a child under age 18 is generally taxed to the child at the parents' top tax rate under the kiddie tax.

First, it should be noted that Education IRAs have appropriately been renamed education savings accounts and are no longer covered in this book. Amounts earned within an education savings account generally accumulate on a tax-deferred basis and earnings from an education savings account are generally not taxable when distributed and used to pay qualified education expenses. Furthermore, the beneficiary of an education savings account need not have any compensation in order for contributions to be made to the education savings account.

Distributions from a Roth IRA are treated as being made from contributions first and thereafter from earnings. Contributions can be withdrawn tax-free from a Roth IRA. Therefore, a child with compensation could contribute to a Roth IRA for education purposes. When the time to withdraw for college came, the child could withdraw the contributions from the Roth IRA first, and then withdraw earnings thereafter. The earnings would grow on a tax-deferred basis until distributed, even if the distribution of earnings from the Roth IRA did not qualify as a qualified distribution excludable from income. IRA distributions included in income would generally be taxed at the low tax rates of the college student. Furthermore, amounts withdrawn from an IRA are not subject to the early distribution penalty tax (see next paragraph) if used for payment of qualified higher education expenses.

Distributions from an IRA made prior to age 59½ are generally subject to a 10 percent early distribution penalty to the extent includable in income unless an exception applies. However, an exception is provided for distributions made to the IRA owner for payment of qualified higher education expenses furnished to the IRA owner, the IRA owner's spouse, or children or grandchildren of either.

Similarly, a child with compensation could contribute deductible contributions to a traditional IRA for education purposes. The child gets an immediate tax deduction that can be put to work, possibly on a tax-deferred basis within the traditional IRA (or possibly in a side fund, where the contribution to the traditional IRA is maximized). Indeed, all earnings within the traditional IRA would grow on a tax-deferred basis until distributed when needed for college. However, distributions from a traditional IRA with only deductible contributions are fully includable in income. IRA distributions included in income would generally be taxed at the low tax rates of the college student. However, amounts withdrawn from a traditional IRA are also not subject to the early distribution penalty tax if used for payment of qualified higher education expenses.

There are a wide variety of other tax-favored ways to plan for education without using an IRA. These include: education savings accounts (formerly called Education IRAs), the Hope Scholarship Credit, the Lifetime Learning Credit, qualified state tuition programs, the deduction for payment of interest on student loans, and the exclusion from income for certain interest earned on qualified United States savings bonds used to pay qualified higher education expenses.[1]

Planning for the Purchase of a Home with IRAs

Among other features, Roth IRAs are designed specifically on a tax-favored basis to provide for the purchase of a first home. The tax-deferred nature of earnings within Roth and other IRAs can also be used to provide for the purchase of a home.

A qualified distribution from a Roth IRA is excludable from income. A qualified distribution is a distribution from a Roth IRA that is made after the five-taxable year period beginning in the year in which the first contribution was made to a Roth IRA and includes (among others) a distribution that is made to the Roth IRA owner ($10,000 lifetime limit) for the purchase of a first home by the IRA owner, the IRA owner's spouse, or children, grandchildren, or ancestor of either.

Distributions from a Roth IRA are treated as being made from contributions first and thereafter from earnings. Contributions can be withdrawn tax-free from a Roth IRA. Therefore, a person with compensation could contribute to a Roth IRA for future purchase of a home. When the time came to withdraw for the purchase of a home, the person could withdraw the contributions from the Roth IRA first, and then withdraw earnings thereafter. The earnings would grow on a tax-deferred basis until distributed, even if the distribution of earnings from the Roth IRA did not qualify as a qualified distribution excludable from income. If the IRA owner is the first time home buyer, it is likely the IRA owner will be in a low tax rate bracket when the home is purchased. Furthermore, within limitations, amounts withdrawn from an IRA are not subject to the early distribution penalty tax (see next paragraph) if used for purchase of a first home.

Distributions from an IRA made prior to age 59½ are generally subject to a 10 percent early distribution penalty to the extent includable in income unless an exception applies. However, an exception is provided for distributions made to the IRA owner ($10,000 lifetime limit) for the purchase of a first home by the IRA owner, the IRA owner's spouse, or children, grandchildren, or ancestor of either.

Note that this exemption from the early distribution penalty applies to more than Roth IRAs; for example, it also applies to traditional, SEP, and SIMPLE IRAs. Also, the exemption from the early distribution penalty applies to a Roth IRA even if the distribution from the Roth IRA is not a qualified distribution exempt from income (e.g., a distribution made within five years of the first contribution to a Roth IRA).

Similarly, a person with compensation could contribute deductible contributions to a traditional IRA. The person gets an immediate tax deduction that can be put to work, possibly on a tax-deferred basis within the traditional IRA (or possibly in a side fund, where the contribution to the traditional IRA is maximized). Indeed, all earnings within the traditional IRA would grow on a tax-deferred basis until distributed. However, distributions from a traditional IRA with only deductible contributions are fully includable in income. If the IRA owner is the first time home buyer, it is likely the IRA owner will be in a low tax rate bracket when the home is purchased. However, within limitations, amounts withdrawn from an IRA are not subject to the early distribution penalty tax if used for the purchase of a first home.

Planning for Retirement with IRAs

Some people may actually wish to use an IRA for retirement needs. Despite the many new provisions for IRAs such as for education, first time home purchase, and more, the "R" in IRAs does stand for retirement.

The need for saving for retirement is greater than ever. Defined benefit retirement plans are disappearing. The future of goverment programs such as Social Security is in question. People are living longer in retirement. Expenses for health care in retirement are likely to only increase. It becomes increasingly important for individuals to find tax favored ways to save for retirement. For a discussion of using an IRA as a tax favored accumulation vehicle, see Chapter 15.

IRAs are a tax favored vehicle designed specifically for providing for retirement needs. In general, contributions can be made on a tax deductible (or exclusionary) basis to a traditional IRA, a SEP IRA, or a SIMPLE IRA. Assets in an IRA accumulate on a tax-deferred, or possibly tax-free, basis in an IRA. A qualified distribution from a Roth IRA is excludable from income. Even if distributions from an IRA are includable in income, for many individuals taxable income and tax rates will likely be lower in retirement than while the individual is working.

The taxation of distributions is always a concern, especially at retirement. A person seeking to retire early (before age 59½) may need to plan around the early distribution penalty tax. The required minimum distribution penalty is a concern at older ages (age 70½ and older).

Distributions from a traditional IRA, a SEP IRA, or a SIMPLE IRA are includable in income on a prorated basis to the extent that the distribution is made from deductible contributions or earnings from the IRA. If nondeductible contributions have not been made to such an IRA, distributions are fully includable in income.

A qualified distribution from a Roth IRA is excludable from income. A qualified distribution is a distribution from a Roth IRA that is made after the five-taxable year period beginning in the year in which the first contribution was made to a Roth IRA and that is (1) made on or after the date the Roth IRA owner turns age 59½; (2) made after the death of the Roth IRA owner; (3) attributable to disability of the Roth IRA owner; or (4) made to the Roth IRA owner ($10,000 lifetime limit) for the purchase of a first home by the IRA owner, the IRA owner's spouse, or children, grandchildren, or ancestor of either.

Otherwise, distributions from a Roth IRA are includable in income except to the extent that the distribution is made from contributions. Distributions from a Roth IRA are treated as made first from contributions and then from earnings.

If the Roth IRA owner is at least age 59½, distributions are generally received tax-free. Even if the Roth IRA owner is less than age 59½ and the owner is not disabled, the owner can still withdraw contributions tax-free. If earnings are then withdrawn after age 59½, such earnings could generally be received tax-free at such time.

A person seeking to retire before age 59½ and take distributions from his IRA must plan around the early distribution penalty tax. A distribution from an IRA prior to the IRA owner reaching age 59½ is subject to a 10 percent early distribution penalty tax to the extent the distribution is includable in income (see above) unless an exception applies. In general, the early distribution penalty does not apply to distributions:

(1) to a beneficiary or the individual's estate, made on or after the death of the individual;

(2) attributable to the individual's disability;

(3) which are part of a series of substantially equal periodic payments (SEPPs);

(4) made for medical care, to the extent that the payment for medical care would be deductible (i.e., such expenses are deductible only to the extent in excess of 7.5 percent of adjusted gross income) without regard as to whether the individual itemizes deductions;

(5) made by an unemployed individual for the payment of health insurance premiums;

(6) made to pay qualified higher education expenses;

(7)   made for first-time homebuyers; or

(8)   made to a reservist while on active duty (commencing after September 11, 2001 and before 2008).

Unless the person is disabled, the primary means for a person seeking to retire before age 59½ while taking distributions from his IRA and avoiding the early distribution penalty tax is to take distributions that are part of a series of substantially equal periodic payments made (at least annually) for the life or the life expectancy of the individual or for the lives or the life expectancies of the individual and the individual's designated beneficiary. (As noted above, distributions of contributions from a Roth IRA can be another useful strategy for taking distributions before age 59½.) If the series of substantially equal periodic payments are modified (other than by reason of death or disability) before the individual reaches age 59½, or after the individual reaches age 59½ if within five years of the first payment, the early distribution penalty tax that would have applied except for the exemption plus interest for the deferral period is added to tax in the year of the modification.

The IRS has approved three methods for calculating substantially equal periodic payments. These methods and factors that should be considered in selecting a method are discussed in detail in Chapter 13.

In selecting a substantially equal periodic payment method to use, it is often useful to select the method that comes closest to withdrawing from the IRA the amount that is desired. The required minimum distribution method must be recalculated each year, whereas the amortization and annuitization methods need to be calculated only once. Also, a person using the amortization or annuitization methods can elect to switch to the required minimum distribution method.

Distributions must generally begin from a traditional IRA, SEP IRA (including a SAR-SEP IRA), or SIMPLE IRA at the earlier of the death of the IRA owner or when the IRA owner turns age 70½. In the case of a Roth IRA, distributions are not required until after the death of the IRA owner (which includes the spouse of the original Roth IRA owner where the surviving spouse is the designated beneficiary and elects to treat the Roth IRA as the spouse's own). These rules are generally referred to as the required minimum distribution rules and are discussed in detail in Chapter 13. A 50 percent penalty applies to the extent a required minimum distribution is not made.

Required minimum distributions are generally calculated in ways designed to cause an IRA to be distributed during the lifetime of the IRA owner or the lifetime of the IRA owner and a designated beneficiary. However, the required minimum distribution methods do not provide for level payments.

An IRA owner who wishes reasonably level payments may wish to annuitize distributions. This can be done (1) by using an individual retirement annuity or (2) by making distributions equal to the greater of the required minimum distribution amount or an annuitized amount (taking out more than the required minimum distribution is generally acceptable; taking out less is not). In the annuitized distribution method, the annuitized amount could be periodically adjusted (the required minimum distribution calculation is adjusted every year to reflect the account balance at the beginning of the year) to reflect the actual experience of the IRA plan. For an example of making annuitized distributions, see Chapter 13.

Alternatively, a person who wishes reasonably level income for retirement and who has other assets could take distributions from the other assets to supplement the required minimum distributions from the IRAs. This might enable the tax deferral of the IRAs to be stretched while still maintaining a reasonably level income. See Chapter 15.

Planning for Spouses with IRAs

Where the IRA owner has a spouse, it is often useful to plan around that spouse. For one, a person's spouse is typically the most important person that a married person wishes to provide for. Also, special income tax provisions are available when the beneficiary is the spouse of the IRA owner. Similarly, an estate tax deduction is generally available if the IRA passes to the spouse of the IRA owner. And special income and gift tax provisions may be available in case of divorce.

The ability to make a contribution to a traditional IRA or a Roth IRA depends on the IRA owner having compensation. Special rules apply to married individuals, or more specifically to an individual who files a joint return for the year where the individual's compensation includable in income for the year is less than the compensation includable in income for the year by the individual's spouse. In such case, contributions are generally allowed to be made for an individual with little or no compensation by taking into account the compensation of such individual's spouse.

Furthermore, one spouse can give the other spouse money free of gift tax using the gift tax annual exclusion or marital deduction. The other spouse can then make contributions to an IRA (assuming the compensation requirement for such spouse have been met).

Where the spouse of the IRA owner is named as the sole beneficiary of the IRA, after the IRA owner's death the spouse can usually elect to treat the IRA as her own for income tax purposes. The election is usually made whenever required minimum distributions can be postponed further by making the election. For example, a spouse who elects to treat the IRA owner's account as the spouse's own could postpone distributions from the IRA until after the spouse reaches age 70½, in the case of a traditional IRA, a SEP IRA, or SIMPLE IRA, or until after the spouse's death in the case of a Roth IRA. Furthermore, the life expectancy of the spouse and a beneficiary could be used rather than the life expectancy of the IRA owner and beneficiary.

Also, where the spouse of the IRA owner is named as the sole beneficiary of the IRA and the IRA owner dies before reaching age 70½, the spouse can postpone receiving required minimum distributions until after the IRA owner would have reached age 70½. This rule can generally be taken advantage of where the IRA owner was younger than the spouse.

Where the spouse of the IRA owner is named as the beneficiary of the IRA, the IRA can usually be made to qualify for the estate tax marital deduction. A marital deduction trust could also be the beneficiary of the IRA. Where a marital deduction trust is used, the IRA should generally provide for distributions (at least annually) to the trust equal to at least the greater of income on the undistributed IRA (for marital deduction purposes) or the required minimum distribution and the marital deduction trust should generally provide for distributions to the spouse of all trust income. See Chapter 14 on choosing a beneficiary and Chapter 18 on the estate tax.

However, certain required minium distribution options are not available with a marital deduction trust: (1) the spouse cannot elect to treat the IRA owner's account as the spouse's own, and (2) the spouse cannot postpone receiving required minimum distributions until after the IRA owner would have reached age 70½. Required minimum distributions from an IRA with a marital deduction trust as beneficiary would generally use the life expectancy of the spouse. If required minimum distributions began before the IRA owner died, the life expectancy of the IRA owner can be used if that is longer. The life expectancy of younger trust beneficiaries, such as children, cannot be used.

If required minimum distribution concerns outweigh use of a marital deduction trust, consideration should be given to rolling the IRA over to the spouse after the IRA owner's death. The more favorable rules for required minimum distributions where the spouse is the sole beneficiary would be available, as well as the marital deduction. However, the benefits of using a trust would be lost.

The effect of using a traditional IRA, SEP IRA, or SIMPLE IRA to fund the marital deduction is generally to create a wasting asset. As the IRA is distributed to the spouse, the spouse is required to pay income taxes. Therefore, the amount remaining at the spouse's death that is subject to estate tax has been reduced by the income tax paid by the spouse.

Where a credit shelter trust is named as the beneficiary of the IRA, the spouse will not be given an interest sufficient to allow the spouse to treat the IRA as her own. (The spouse may be given the right to distributions of income, and a limited withdrawal right.) Therefore, if required minimum distributions did not begin before the IRA owner died, distributions must generally be made over the life expectancy of the oldest beneficiary of the credit shelter trust (who is often the spouse). If required minimum distributions began before the IRA owner died, the life expectancy of the IRA owner can be used if that is longer.

If an interest in an IRA is transferred from one spouse to the other in connection with a divorce or separation, a gift may be made. However, a transfer of property to either spouse in settlement for his or her marital or property rights or for child support shall be deemed made for full and adequate consideration in money or money's worth if: (1) the transfer is made pursuant to a written agreement between the husband and wife, and (2) divorce occurs within the three-year period beginning on the date one year before the agreement is entered into. Under this statutory provision, it is immaterial whether the agreement is approved by the divorce decree.[2]

Also, the transfer of an IRA from one spouse to the other in connection with a divorce or separation is generally not considered a taxable transfer for income tax purposes. The spouse to whom the IRA is transferred is thereafter treated as the IRA owner.[3]

Dynasty Planning with IRAs

Dynasty planning is generally thought of as passing interests in property, generally in a trust, down through generations while minimizing the taxes, especially the transfer taxes (gift tax, estate tax, and generation-skipping transfer tax) on the property. The ability to do dynasty planning with IRAs is sometimes compromised by the required minimum distribution rules.

In dynasty planning, the object is generally to give as many interests as possible to as many generations as is possible, while minimizing exposure to transfer tax at each level. Dynasty plans with trusts are often made to last as many generations as possible, limited generally only by the rule against perpetuities. In general, the rule against perpetuities requires that interests vest no later than a life in being plus 21 years. The rule against perpetuities has even been eliminated in a few states.

Distributions must generally begin from a traditional IRA, SEP IRA (including a SAR-SEP IRA), or SIMPLE IRA at the earlier of the death of the IRA owner or when the IRA owner turns age 70½. In the case of a Roth IRA, distributions are not required until after the death of the IRA owner (which includes the spouse of the original Roth IRA owner where the surviving spouse is the designated beneficiary and elects to treat the Roth IRA as the spouse's own). These rules are generally referred to as the required minimum distribution rules and are discussed in detail in Chapter 13. A 50 percent penalty applies to the extent a required minimum distribution is not made.

Thus distributions from a traditional IRA, SEP IRA (including a SAR-SEP IRA), or SIMPLE IRA must generally be made for the life expectancy of the IRA owner and a designated beneficiary starting at the earlier of the death of the IRA owner or when the IRA owner turns age 70½. If there is more than one beneficiary, the oldest beneficiary's age is used. Furthermore, while the IRA owner (other than the owner of a Roth IRA) is alive, a beneficiary other than the spouse of the IRA owner is generally treated as being no more than 10 years younger than the IRA owner. In the case of a Roth IRA, distributions must generally be made for the life expectancy of a designated beneficiary starting at the death of the IRA owner. If the spouse of the IRA owner is the designated beneficiary, the spouse can elect to treat the IRA as the spouse's own; the required minimum distribution rules would then be applied as if the spouse is the IRA owner.

Required minimum distributions must be made or a 50 percent penalty tax applies. Even though required minimum distributions must generally be paid to the trust, the trust is not generally required to make distributions from the trust of the required minimum distributions. Whether distributions from the trust are required generally depend on the trust document and state law. Note that if income is required to be distributed from the trust, the IRA distributions to the trust generally consist of both income and principal.

It is possible to move an IRA down generations with a dynasty trust. With a dynasty trust, distributions can generally be sprayed around to many different beneficiaries and generations as is typically done in dynasty planning. However, the IRA must be distributed to the trust generally within a time period limited to the beneficiary's life expectancy. And as noted above, in the case of multiple beneficiaries the oldest beneficiary's age is used. This requirement could conflict with the desire to have older generations as potential beneficiaries.

Multiple IRAs with a different beneficiary for each IRA can reduce the problem with the oldest beneficiary's life being used for required minimum distribution purposes, but generally with a reduction in flexibility of spraying benefits. However, use of separate IRAs with separate trusts can also facilitate use of the generation-skipping transfer tax annual exclusion. A typical dynasty trust often relies on use of the generation-skipping transfer tax exemption rather than the annual exclusion, because of the separate share requirements for the annual exclusion.

Multiple IRAs with an IRA and a trust for each generation might also be used. This would allow each IRA to use the life expectancy of the oldest beneficiary in a generation (rather than the oldest overall beneficiary). However, the flexibility of spraying benfits would be limited within that generation. Also, the generation-skipping transfer tax annual exclusion would not be available if there is more than one beneficiary in a generation (separate trusts for each beneficiary would be required).

Multiple IRAs with separate trusts can also facilitate allocations of the generation-skipping transfer tax exemption. The exemption could be allocated to trusts with potential generation-skipping transfers (e.g., trust for grandchildren), but not to trusts with no generation-skipping potential (e.g., trust for children). Similarly, distributions from trusts to which the exemption has been allocated could be made to skip persons (e.g., grandchildren) while distributions from trusts to which no exemption has been allocated could be made to nonskip persons (e.g., children).

It may also be useful to move IRAs down generations by giving a child with a small estate a general power of appointment to appoint the IRA (or perhaps a power to appoint a trust to which the IRA is payable) to the child's estate or to children of the child (or perhaps to a trust). The IRA owner does not need to allocate the generation-skipping transfer tax exemption to the transfer to the child because the child is not a skip person. The IRA (or trust) is included in the child's estate but the child's estate is small enough so that there is no estate tax. The IRA (or trust) then passes to the IRA owner's grandchildren without the need for allocation of the generation-skipping transfer tax exemption to the transfer because the children of the IRA owner's child are not skip persons relative to the IRA owner's child (the transferor at child's death).

Therefore the ability to do dynasty planning with IRAs must sometimes weigh the ability to prolong distributions under the required minimum distribution rules with a somewhat reduced flexibility to spray distributions.[4]

Dynasty planning will often use reverse QTIP trusts. The effect of making the reverse QTIP election is generally to have the decedent (rather than the surviving spouse) treated as the transferor for generation-skipping purposes. Such an election would generally be used to insure that a decedent's GST exemption was not wasted.

> *Example.* In 2006, decedent (who has made $500,000 of taxable gifts protected by the unified credit) with a $4,000,000 estate leaves $1,500,000 in a credit shelter trust and $2,500,000 to his surviving spouse in a QTIP trust, reducing his taxable estate to zero. [Assume each trust would be subject to GST tax to the extent that the $2,000,000 (in 2006) GST exemption is not allocated to such trust.] The executor allocates $1,500,000 of the decedent's $2,00,000 GST tax exemption to the credit shelter trust and makes a reverse QTIP election as to $500,000 of the QTIP property so that the decedent's full $2,000,000 exemption can be used. The surviving spouse's $2,000,000 exemption amount may then be used to protect the remaining $2,000,000 of property, and the entire $4,000,000 has escaped GST tax (assuming separate QTIP trusts of $2,000,000 and $500,000 are created).

For more on the generation-skipping transfer tax, see Chapter 19.

Endnotes

1. See *Tax Facts on Insurance and Employee Benefits* (Tax Facts 1) and *Tax Facts on Investments* (Tax Facts 2), published annually by The National Underwriter Company, for the taxation of such other tools that can be used in planning for education.

2. IRC Sec. 2516.

3. IRC Sec. 408(d)(6).

4. For more on dynasty trusts, see *The Ultimate Trust Resource*, by William J. Wagner, published by The National Underwriter Company.

Chapter 11

Rollovers

Rollovers are permitted between various IRAs, qualified plans, tax sheltered annuities, and eligible Section 457 governmental plans. In general, a rollover is a transfer of retirement assets from one plan to another by the participant or owner that is completed within 60 days. The effect of a rollover is generally to avoid taxes and penalties upon what otherwise would be treated as a distribution. The rolled over amounts are then generally subject to the rules of the plan to which rolled over.[1]

In general, an IRA that is inherited from another by other than the surviving spouse cannot receive a rollover or be rolled over.[2] However, PPA 2006 provides that, after 2006, a nonspouse beneficiary can generally roll over an inherited eligible retirement plan (an IRA, qualified plan, tax sheltered annuity, or Section 457 governmental plan) to an IRA created to receive the inherited eligible retirement plan in a direct trustee-to-trustee transfer. Nevertheless, as described below, there are various limitations on what can be rolled over and which type of retirement plans rollovers can be made between. The new IRA is treated as an inherited IRA and the required minimum distribution rules are applied accordingly.[3]

Required minimum distributions (see Chapter 13, generally) from a qualified plan, tax sheltered annuity, eligible Section 457 governmental plan, or IRA cannot be rolled over.[4]

Only one rollover is permitted from a particular IRA to any other IRA during the one-year period ending with the transfer from the first IRA. The Internal Revenue Code appears to limit a taxpayer to one rollover from all of the taxpayer's IRAs in any one-year period.[5] However, proposed regulations would treat each IRA as separate and permit one rollover from a particular IRA during the one-year period ending with the transfer from such IRA. For example, a rollover could be made from IRA 1 to IRA 3 and another rollover from IRA 2 to IRA 3, even though the rollover from IRA 2 to IRA 3 occurred within one year of the rollover from IRA 1.[6] However, an IRS publication states that a rollover cannot then be made from IRA 3 during the one-year period.[7] Similarly, one court case held that where IRA 1 was rolled over to IRA 2, a rollover was not permitted from IRA 2 during the one-year period after the rollover from IRA 1 to IRA 2.[8]

Direct trustee-to-trustee transfers are not treated as rollovers for purpose of the one rollover per year requirement. A rollover from a traditional, SEP, or SIMPLE IRA to a Roth IRA does not count as a rollover for this purpose.[9]

A rollover from any traditional, SEP, or SIMPLE IRA (or qualified plan, tax sheltered annuity, or eligible Section 457 governmental plan after 2007) to a Roth IRA is a conversion subject to tax. See Chapter 12.

The distributee of a qualified plan, tax sheltered annuity, eligible Section 457 governmental plan, or IRA has only 60 days after a distribution to complete a rollover.[10] The 60-day period (1) does not include any period during which the amount transferred to the employee is in a frozen deposit, and (2) does not end earlier than 10 days after the amount ceases to be frozen. A frozen deposit means the distributee is unable to withdraw the property to be rolled over because the property is deposited in an institution in bankruptcy or insolvency.[11]

If property is distributed, a rollover can be completed by rolling over the property or by selling the property and rolling over the cash proceeds. However, if the proceeds are used to purchase other property; such property cannot be rolled over. Distributions that are not rolled over are generally subject to income tax. In addition, the sale of property whose proceeds are not rolled over can also be a taxable event.

For an overview of IRA rollovers available, see Figure 11.1.

FIGURE 11.1

IRA Rollovers[1]

From –>	To	From –>	To
traditional IRA, SEP IRA, SIMPLE IRA[2], qualified plan[3], tax sheltered annuity, eligible Sec. 457 gov. plan	traditional IRA	traditional IRA, SEP IRA, Roth IRA[4], qualified plan, tax sheltered annuity, eligible Sec. 457 gov. plan	
Roth IRA; traditional IRA, SEP IRA, SIMPLE IRA,[2] elective deferral Roth (in a qualified rollover[4]); qualified plan, tax sheltered annuity, eligible Sec. 457 gov. plan (in a qualified rollover[4] after 2007)	Roth IRA	Roth IRA	
SEP IRA, traditional IRA, SIMPLE IRA[2], qualified plan, tax sheltered annuity, eligible Sec. 457 gov. plan	SEP IRA	SEP IRA, traditional IRA, Roth IRA[4], qualified plan, tax sheltered annuity, eligible Sec. 457 gov. plan	
SIMPLE IRA	SIMPLE IRA[2]	SIMPLE IRA, traditional IRA, Roth IRA[4], SEP IRA, qualified plan, tax sheltered annuity, eligible Sec. 457 gov. plan	
elective deferral Roth[6]	elective deferral Roth[5]	Roth IRA, elective deferral Roth[5]	

1. Only one rollover is permitted from a particular IRA to any other IRA during the one-year period ending with the transfer from the first IRA. Direct trustee-to-trustee transfers are not treated as rollovers for this purpose.

2. A rollover is not permitted from a SIMPLE IRA to anything but a SIMPLE IRA during the first two years that the individual participates in the SIMPLE IRA.

3. A separately maintained traditional IRA can be used as a conduit IRA to later transfer assets back to the same or another qualified plan where plan distribution would be entitled to special tax benefits (e.g., income averaging or capital gains).

4. A qualified rollover is a taxable event and special provisions apply (see Chapter 5).

5. Rollover to elective deferral Roth permitted only to one of the same type (i.e., 401(k) to 401(k), or 403(b) to 403(b)).

Qualified Plans

Before 2008, the only rollovers permitted from a qualified plan to an IRA are to a traditional IRA or a SEP IRA. Rollover of a qualified plan to a Roth IRA can be accomplished indirectly by first rolling the qualified plan over to a traditional IRA or SEP IRA and then rolling the traditional IRA or SEP IRA over to a Roth IRA. After 2007, PPA 2006 provides that a qualified plan can also be rolled over to a Roth IRA (see below), but it is a taxable event.

Amounts rolled over from a qualified plan are subject to 20 percent withholding unless the rollover is made through a direct trustee-to-trustee transfer.[12]

The following cannot be rolled over from a qualified plan:

(1)   payments that are part of a series of substantially equal periodic payments for the life (or life expectancy) of the employee or the lives (or joint life expectancy) of the employee and a designated beneficiary, or for a specified period of 10 years or more;

(2)   required minimum distributions; and

(3)   hardship distributions from a 401(k) plan (or tax sheltered annuity).[13]

Amounts that would not be includable in income (i.e., nondeductible employee contributions) can be rolled over to a traditional IRA or SEP IRA, but cannot be rolled back to a qualified plan (see below).

Note that the rule for required minimum distributions from qualified plans differs from the general rule for IRAs: required minimum distributions from qualified plans can generally be postponed until the later of retirement or attainment of age 70½. A person who plans on working after age 70½ and who does not wish to take required minimum distributions should consider delaying a rollover from a qualified plan until a later date (perhaps until retirement). Distributions from a Roth IRA are not required until after the IRA owner's death and distributions after age 59½ are generally not included in income; however, a conversion to a Roth IRA is a taxable event.

In addition, regulations provide that the following cannot be rolled over from a qualified plan:

(1)   the Table 2001 or P.S. 58 cost of life insurance;

(2)   loans that are treated as deemed distributions under Section 72(p);

(3)   dividends paid on employer securities under Section 404(k); and

(4)   corrective distributions of excess contributions or deferrals.[14]

Life insurance contracts cannot be rolled over to an IRA account; an IRA account is not permitted to invest in a life insurance contract.[15]

Any traditional IRA, SEP IRA, or SIMPLE IRA can be rolled over to a qualified plan, if the qualified plan permits rollovers to it. (A qualified plan is not required to permit rollovers to it.) However, the amount that can be rolled over is limited to amounts that would be included in income if distributed. Thus, nondeductible contributions cannot be rolled over from a traditional IRA or SEP IRA (SIMPLE IRAs cannot have nondeductible contributions) to a qualified plan.

If the amount rolled over from a qualified plan to a traditional IRA or SEP IRA includes amounts that would be eligible for special tax treatment upon distribution from the qualified plan (e.g., income averaging or capital gains treatment), such special tax treatment will be lost. However, if the rolled over amounts are maintained in a separate conduit traditional IRA and rolled back to the qualified plan, the special tax treatment will be once again available for distributions of such amounts from the qualified plan.

If the spouse of an employee receives a distribution attributable to the employee after the death of the employee, the spouse is treated the same as the employee. Therefore, the spouse can roll over the distribution to a traditional IRA or SEP IRA and then roll it back to a qualified plan.

A spouse or former spouse who receives a distribution as an alternate payee pursuant to a qualified domestic relations order can roll over the distribution to an IRA or a qualified plan.[16] (It would appear that similar rules should apply to distributions from tax sheltered annuities to surviving spouses and alternate payee spouses, but technical corrections are needed.[17])

Different rules apply to elective deferral Roths (see below).

Tax Sheltered Annuities

A tax sheltered annuity can be rolled over to a traditional IRA or SEP IRA, and a traditional IRA, SEP IRA, or SIMPLE IRA can be rolled over to a tax sheltered annuity.[18] The rules are generally the same as for qualified plans (see above). However, there are no special tax benefits to be preserved using a conduit traditional IRA with a tax sheltered annuity. After 2007, PPA 2006 provides that a tax sheltered annuity can also be rolled over to a Roth IRA (see below), but it is a taxable event.

Different rules apply to elective deferral Roths (see below).

Eligible Section 457 Governmental Plans

An eligible Section 457 governmental plan can be rolled over to a traditional IRA or SEP IRA, and a traditional IRA, SEP IRA, or SIMPLE IRA can be rolled over to an eligible Section 457 governmental plan.[19] The rules are generally the same as for qualified plans (see above) except that an eligible Section 457 governmental plan cannot accept rollovers from a traditional IRA, SEP IRA, or SIMPLE IRA unless the eligible Section 457 governmental plan agrees to separately account for the amounts rolled over from the traditional IRA, SEP IRA, or SIMPLE IRA.[20] Also, there are no special tax benefits to be preserved using a conduit traditional IRA with an eligible Section 457 governmental plan. Rollovers are not permitted between eligible Section 457 governmental plans and elective deferral Roths. After 2007, PPA 2006 provides that an eligible Section 457 governmental plan can also be rolled over to a Roth IRA (see below), but it is a taxable event.

Traditional IRAs

Rollovers are permitted between traditional IRAs.[21] Rollovers are also permitted between a traditional IRA and each of the following: a SEP IRA (see below), a qualified plan (see above), a tax sheltered annuity (see above), and an eligible Section 457 governmental plan (see above). After the individual has participated for two years in a SIMPLE IRA (see below), a SIMPLE IRA can be rolled over to a traditional IRA. However, a traditional IRA cannot be rolled over to a SIMPLE IRA. A traditional IRA can be rolled over to a Roth IRA (see below), but it is a taxable event. A Roth IRA cannot be rolled over to a traditional IRA. Rollovers are not permitted between traditional IRAs and elective deferral Roths.

Only one rollover is permitted from a particular IRA to any other IRA during the one-year period ending with the transfer from the first IRA.[22] Direct trustee-to-trustee transfers are not treated as rollovers for this purpose. Neither does a rollover from a traditional IRA to a Roth IRA count as a rollover for this purpose.

In general, an IRA that is inherited from another by other than the surviving spouse cannot receive a rollover or be rolled over.[23] However, PPA 2006 provides that, after 2006, a nonspouse beneficiary can generally roll over a traditional IRA, SEP IRA, SIMPLE IRA, qualified plan, tax sheltered annuity, or Section 457 governmental plan to a traditional IRA created to receive the inherited eligible retirement plan in a direct trustee-to-trustee transfer (other limitations may apply). The new IRA is treated as an inherited IRA and the required minimum distribution rules are applied accordingly.[24]

Roth IRAs

A rollover from a Roth IRA can be made only to another Roth IRA. Therefore, rollovers are not permitted from a Roth IRA to any other type of IRA (including an elective deferral Roth). If a traditional IRA, SIMPLE IRA, or SEP IRA is rolled over to a Roth IRA (a qualified rollover, or conversion), it is a taxable event and special provisions apply.[25] See Chapter 12. Rollover of a qualified plan, a tax sheltered annuity, or an eligible Section 457 governmental plan to a Roth IRA can be accomplished indirectly by first rolling the qualified plan or tax sheltered annuity to a traditional IRA or SEP IRA and then rolling the traditional IRA or SEP IRA over to a Roth IRA. An elective deferral Roth can be rolled over to a Roth IRA. PPA 2006 provides that, after 2007, a qualified plan, a tax sheltered annuity, or an eligible Section 457 governmental plan can also be rolled over to a Roth IRA, but it is a taxable event.

Only one rollover is permitted from a particular IRA to any other IRA during the one-year period ending with the transfer from the first IRA.[26] Direct trustee-to-trustee transfers are not treated as rollovers for this purpose.[27]

SEP IRAs

Rollovers are permitted between SEP IRAs.[28] Rollovers are also permitted between a SEP IRA and each of the following: a traditional IRA (see above), a qualified plan (see above), a tax sheltered annuity (see above), and an eligible Section 457 governmental plan (see above). After the individual has participated for two years in a SIMPLE IRA (see below), a SIMPLE IRA can be rolled over to a SEP IRA. However, a SEP IRA cannot be rolled over to a SIMPLE IRA. A SEP IRA can be rolled over to a Roth IRA (see above), but it is a taxable event. A Roth IRA cannot be rolled over to a SEP IRA. Rollovers are not permitted between SEP IRAs and elective deferral Roths.

Only one rollover is permitted from a particular IRA to any other IRA during the one-year period ending with the transfer from the first IRA.[29] Direct trustee-to-trustee transfers are not treated as rollovers for this purpose. A rollover from a SEP IRA to a Roth IRA does not count as a rollover for this purpose.[30]

SIMPLE IRAs

The only rollover permitted from a SIMPLE IRA during the first two years that the individual participates in the SIMPLE IRA is to another SIMPLE IRA. A 25 percent early distribution penalty applies to any amount received from a SIMPLE IRA during the first two years that the individual participates in the SIMPLE IRA.[31] After the individual has participated for two years in the SIMPLE IRA, rollovers can be made from the SIMPLE IRA to traditional IRAs (see above), Roth IRAs (see above), SEP IRAs (see above), SIMPLE IRAs, qualified plans (see above), tax sheltered annuities (see above), and eligible Section 457 governmental plans (see above).[32] Rollovers are not permitted between SIMPLE IRAs and elective deferral Roths. The only rollover permitted to a SIMPLE IRA is from another SIMPLE IRA.

Only one rollover is permitted from a particular IRA to any other IRA during the one-year period ending with the transfer from the first IRA.[33] Direct trustee-to-trustee transfers are not treated as rollovers for this purpose. Neither does a rollover from a SIMPLE IRA to a Roth IRA count as a rollover for this purpose.[34]

Elective Deferral Roth

The only rollover permitted from an elective deferral Roth is to a Roth IRA or to an elective deferral Roth of the same type (i.e., 401(k) to 401(k), or 403(b) to 403(b)). The only rollover permitted to an elective deferral Roth is from an elective deferral Roth of the same type.

Endnotes

1. See IRC Secs. 402(c), 403(b)(8), 408(d)(3), 408A(c)(6).
2. IRC Sec. 408(d)(3)(C).
3. IRC Sec. 402(c)(11).
4. IRC Secs. 402(c)(4)(B), 403(b)(8), 408(d)(3)(E).
5. IRC Secs. 408(d)(3)(B), 408A(a).
6. Treas. Prop. Reg. §1.408-4(b)(4)(ii).
7. IRS Pub. 590.
8. *Martin v. Comm.*, TC Memo 1992-331.
9. IRC Sec. 408A(e).
10. IRC Secs. 402(c)(3), 403(b)(8), 408(d)(3).
11. IRC Secs. 402(c)(7), 403(b)(8), 408(d)(3)(F).

12. IRC Sec. 3405(c).

13. IRC Secs. 402(c)(4), 403(b)(8).

14. Treas. Reg. §1.402(c)-2(A-4).

15. IRC Sec. 408(a)(3).

16. IRC Sec. 402(e)(1); Treas. Reg. §1.402(c)-2(A-12).

17. See IRC Sec. 403(b)(8)(C) prior to amendment by the Unemployment Compensation Act of 1992.

18. IRC Secs. 408(d)(3), 402(c)(8)(vi).

19. IRC Secs. 408(d)(3), 402(c)(8)(v).

20. IRC Sec. 402(c)(10).

21. IRC Sec. 408(d)(3).

22. IRC Sec. 408(d)(3)(B).

23. IRC Sec. 408(d)(3)(C).

24. IRC Sec. 402(c)(11).

25. IRC Sec. 408(d)(3)(C).

26. IRC Secs. 408A(d)(3), 408A(c)(6), 408A(e).

27. IRC Sec. 408(d)(3)(B).

28. IRC Sec. 408(d)(3).

29. IRC Sec. 408(d)(3)(B).

30. IRC Sec. 408A(e).

31. IRC Sec. 72(t)(6).

32. IRC Sec. 408(d)(3)(G).

33. IRC Sec. 408(d)(3)(B).

34. IRC Sec. 408A(e).

Chapter 12

Conversions

A traditional, SEP, or SIMPLE IRA can be converted into a Roth IRA if certain conditions are met. A conversion also includes a rollover from a traditional, SEP, or SIMPLE IRA (or a qualified plan, tax sheltered annuity, or eligible Section 457 governmental plan after 2007) to a Roth IRA. However, unlike the usual situation with rollovers, a conversion to a Roth IRA is a taxable event. Within certain limitations, a Roth IRA can be recharacterized back into the IRA type from which it was converted and then reconverted to a Roth IRA at a later time. Special rules apply to valuing an annuity contract in connection with a conversion.

Before 2008, the only conversions permitted to a Roth IRA are from Roth IRAs, traditional IRAs, SEP IRAs, and SIMPLE IRAs. However, a rollover is not permitted from a SIMPLE IRA to any other IRA including a Roth IRA during the first two years that the individual participates in the SIMPLE IRA. After 2007, qualified plans, tax sheltered annuities, and eligible Section 457 governmental plans may also be rolled over to a Roth IRA.

Prior to 2008, an indirect conversion from qualified plans, tax sheltered annuities, and eligible Section 457 governmental plans may be accomplished through a rollover to a traditional IRA (see Chapter 4) or SEP IRA (see Chapter 6) followed by a conversion of the traditional IRA or SEP IRA to a Roth IRA.

Rollovers are permitted between various IRAs, qualified plans, tax sheltered annuities, and eligible Section 457 governmental plans (see Chapter 11). In general, a rollover is a transfer of retirement assets from one plan to another by the participant or owner that is completed within 60 days of the distribution. The effect of a rollover is generally to avoid taxes and penalties upon what otherwise would be treated as a distribution. However, any rollover from an IRA other than a Roth IRA (or a qualified plan, tax sheltered annuity, or eligible Section 457 governmental plan after 2007) to a Roth IRA is a taxable event. The term conversion, as used in this chapter, will include rollovers to a Roth IRA.[1]

A rollover from a Roth IRA can be made only to another Roth IRA. Such a rollover is not a taxable event.

In general, conversions to a Roth IRA are accomplished either by (1) having the trustee of the first IRA transfer IRA property directly to the trustee of the second IRA, (2) having the trustee of the first IRA distribute the IRA property to the IRA owner who then transfers (rolls over) the IRA property to the trustee of the second IRA within 60 days of the distribution from the first IRA, or (3) simply converting the other IRA into a Roth IRA.[2] After 2007, a conversion of a qualified plan, tax sheltered annuity, or eligible Section 457 governmental plan to a Roth IRA can be accomplished by either (1) a direct trustee-to-trustee transfer, or (2) a 60-day rollover.

For tax years before 2010, an individual can generally convert an amount in one of these other IRAs (or a qualified plan, tax sheltered annuity, or eligible Section 457 governmental plan in 2008 and 2009) to a Roth IRA unless the individual's adjusted gross income for the year exceeds $100,000 or the individual is married and files a separate return. For tax years after 2009, these limitations do not apply. For tax years after 2004 (and before 2010), adjusted gross income will not include any required minimum distributions (see Chapter 13) for purposes of the $100,000 limitation. The primary reason for doing such a conversion is to obtain the benefit of the generally more favorable rules for distributions from a Roth IRA. The price of making such a conversion to a Roth IRA is that the amount in the other IRA (or a qualified plan, tax sheltered annuity, or eligible Section 457 governmental plan after 2007) is treated as distributed from the other IRA (or other plan) for income tax purposes. For conversions in 2010, the amount otherwise includable in income can be included in income over a two-year period.[3]

Thus, if a traditional IRA, SEP IRA, or SIMPLE IRA (or a qualified plan, tax sheltered annuity, or eligible Section 457 governmental plan after 2007) is converted to a Roth IRA, the amount distributed from the other IRA (or other plan) is generally includable in income for the year of distribution under the rules for such other IRA. Actually, all distributions from all nonRoth IRAs for the year (including the amount being converted) would be aggregated together in determining the portion of the conversion of nonRoth IRAs that is taxable. However, the early distribution penalty tax does not apply to such distribution. Nevertheless, the early distribution rule will apply to any distribution from the Roth IRA made within the five-year period starting with the year of the conversion if the distribution is allocable to the qualified rollover contribution.

> *Example.* The only IRA Rachel has is a traditional IRA. Rachel converts her traditional IRA to a Roth IRA in 2006 in a qualified rollover. The account balance of the traditional IRA is equal to $75,000 and no nondeductible contributions have been made to the traditional IRA. Rachel includes in income for 2006 the full $75,000 distribution from the traditional IRA, but the early distribution penalty tax does not apply to the distribution.

For conversions to Roth IRAs in 2010, unless the taxpayer elects otherwise, the amount includable in income by reason of conversion to a Roth IRA is includable ratably in 2011 and 2012, rather than in 2010. However, income inclusion is accelerated if converted amounts are distributed from the Roth IRA before 2012. In such a case, the amount included in income for the year (2010 or 2011) is increased by the converted amount that is distributed from the Roth IRA. To avoid double inclusion of accelerated amounts, the converted amount included in income in subsequent years (2011 or 2012) is limited so as to not be in excess of the total conversion amount includable in income reduced by conversion amounts included in income in prior years.

> *Example.* Bob converts a traditional IRA to a Roth IRA in 2010. If Bob were to elect, $100 would be includable in income in 2010. No election is made, so $50 (one-half of $100) is includable in 2011 and $50 in 2012 (assuming no distribution of converted amounts before 2012). However, later in 2010, Bob takes a distribution of $20 attributable to the converted amount. Bob must include the $20 in income in 2010. In 2011, Bob must include $50, which is the lesser of (1) $50 or (2) $80 [$100 total - $20 previously included]. In 2012, Bob must include $30, which is the lesser of (1) $50 or (2) $30 [$100 total - $70 previously included].

Unqualified Rollovers, Recharacterizations, and Reconversions

If the rollover from the traditional IRA, SEP IRA or SIMPLE IRA is not a qualified rollover, then the amount of the rollover is treated as distributed from the original IRA and subject to income tax based upon the rules for distributions from such IRA, including the penalty tax for early distributions if appropriate. The distributed amount is then treated as contributed to the Roth IRA. Most likely such a contribution to the Roth IRA would create an excess contribution subject to the excess contribution penalty tax until corrected.

An "unqualified" rollover to a Roth IRA can be a very taxing event. A taxpayer who makes a conversion to a Roth IRA and discovers that the rollover would not be qualified (e.g., adjusted gross income for the year exceeds $100,000 in 2006) can elect to recharacterize the contribution to the Roth IRA as being to a traditional IRA and avoid the "unqualified" rollover. The recharacterization must generally occur within the time for filing a tax return (including extensions) for the year of the original rollover to the Roth IRA.[4]

An election to recharacterize a contribution cannot be revoked once elected. The individual making the election must report the recharacterization to the IRS and all income tax reporting must be consistent with the recharacterization having been made. A recharacterization (which is a trustee-to-trustee transfer) is not treated as a rollover for purposes of the limitation to one rollover per year from a particular IRA.[5]

A recharacterization is accomplished by having the trustee of the first IRA transfer the conversion contribution to be recharacterized along with any income attributable to the contribution to the trustee of the second IRA. The net income attributable to a recharacterized conversion contribution is calculated using the following formula.

$$\text{Net Income} = \text{Contribution} \times \frac{(\text{Adjusted Closing Balance} - \text{Adjusted Opening Balance})}{\text{Adjusted Opening Balance}}$$

The computation period means the period starting immediately prior to the conversion contribution and ending immediately prior to the distribution of the contribution (recharacterizing transfer). The adjusted closing balance means the fair market value of the account balance at the end of the period, increased by distributions or transfers (including returned contributions and recharacterizations of contributions) from the IRA during the period. The adjusted opening balance means the fair market value of the account balance at the start of the period, increased by contributions or transfers (including the amount being recharacterized and any other recharacterizations) to the account during the period. If an IRA asset is not valued daily, the most recent regularly determined fair market value on the same or an earlier date is used. The calculation is made only with respect to the IRA from which the recharacterizing transfer is made. The IRA owner can choose the date and the dollar amount (but not specific assets) of the contribution to be recharacterized.[6]

The individual makes the election to recharacterize by notifying both trustees that he has made such an election. The notification must include the following:

(1)   the type and amount of contribution to the first IRA to be recharacterized;

(2)   the date the contribution was made to the first IRA and the year for which it was made;

(3)   a direction to the trustee of the first IRA regarding the amount of the contribution and income thereon to be transferred in a trustee-to-trustee transfer to the second IRA; and

(4)   the name of both trustees and any additional information needed.[7]

Indeed, any person who converts a traditional, SEP, or SIMPLE IRA to a Roth IRA can recharacterize the contribution to the Roth IRA as being made instead back to such other IRA type and avoid the tax upon conversion to the Roth IRA. However, certain restrictions are placed upon a person who recharacterizes a contribution to a Roth IRA as being made to such other IRA type. The person can reconvert back to a Roth IRA but only after the later of (1) the beginning of the next year, or (2) 30 days after the recharacterization.[8]

When the stock market (or the value of the property converted) drops after a person has made a conversion to a Roth IRA, the person may wish to recharacterize the contribution back to the other type of IRA and then reconvert to a Roth IRA in order to reduce the amount taxable upon switching to a Roth IRA. The requirement that a person essentially wait until the later of the following year or 30 days to reconvert back to a Roth IRA reduces, but does not eliminate, the potential value of this technique.

The IRS will most likely adopt similar rules for rollovers of qualified plans, tax sheltered annuities, or eligible Section 457 governmental plans to Roth IRAs after 2007.

Annuities

The IRS has issued some special rules for valuing an annuity contract for purpose of determining the amount includable in income as a result of a conversion to a Roth IRA. The rules apply whether the IRA being converted is an annuity contract (i.e., an individual retirement annuity) or includes an annuity contract as an IRA asset. The rules are intended to prevent the undervaluation of annuity contracts on conversion, such as where the annuity has a temporarily artificially reduced cash surrender value due to surrender penalties in the early years of the contract that are unlikely to be paid.

In general, the amount treated as distributed is the fair market value of the annuity contract. If an individual retirement annuity is converted to a Roth IRA, fair market value on the day the annuity contract is converted is used. If an annuity is treated as distributed from a nonRoth IRA on conversion, fair market value on the date of distribution is used. Fair market value is determined as follows.[9]

1.   If the conversion occurs soon after the contract was purchased and there have been no material changes in market conditions, fair market value equals premiums paid.

2.   If the conversion occurs some time after the contract was purchased and no further premiums are to be paid, fair market value equals the single premium the company would charge for a comparable contact.

3.   If the conversion occurs some time after the contract was purchased and further premiums are to be paid, fair market value equals the interpolated terminal reserve at the date of conversion, plus the value of the unearned portion of the last premium. However, this method cannot be used if the reserve does not reflect all relevant features of the contract.

If there is a complete surrender of the annuity, extinguishing all benefits and characteristics of the annuity, and the cash proceeds are reinvested in the Roth IRA, the value of the distribution for purposes of the conversion is the cash proceeds.

Until further guidance is issued, the following safe harbor can be used to value an annuity that has not yet been annuitized.[10] Fair market value equals the sum of the following:

1. The dollar amount credited under the contract. This amount cannot be reduced by any surrender charges under the contract.

2. The actuarial present value of any additional benefits that will be provided under the contract. These might include: survivor benefits in excess of the account balance; any guaranteed minimum benefits; and any charges that are expected to be refunded, rebated, or otherwise reversed at a later date.

For purpose of this safe harbor, the following rules apply:

1. All front-end loads and other non-recurring charges assessed in the 12 months immediately preceding the conversion must be added to the account value.

2. Future distributions are not to be assumed in determing the actuarial present value of additional benefits.

Reporting Conversions

The trustee of an IRA is required to report rollovers to and from a Roth IRA and Roth conversions to the IRS and to the IRA owner on IRS Form 5498. A conversion from a traditional IRA, SEP IRA, or SIMPLE IRA to a Roth IRA is reported by the IRA owner on IRS Form 8606.

To Convert or Not?

Should a traditional IRA be converted into a Roth IRA? If the taxpayer expects to be in the same tax bracket at the time of possible conversion as at the time of distributions, there may be no real advantage to converting or not converting. If the taxpayer expects to be in a higher tax bracket later, it probably makes sense to convert now. If the taxpayer expects to be in a lower tax bracket later, it may make no sense to convert. Keep in mind that making a conversion may push a taxpayer into a higher tax bracket in the year of conversion than if no conversion were made. (Comparisons have been made based upon distributions at comparable times. The Roth IRA does have the advantage that required minimum distributions can generally be postponed until both the IRA owner and the spouse of the IRA owner are dead, thus generally permitting a longer tax-free growth period.)

For a conversion in 2010, income attributable to the conversion is generally pro-rated over the years 2011 and 2012, rather than included in full in 2010, unless the IRA owner elects otherwise. For a conversion in 2010, where the income is prorated over 2011 and 2012, the deferral of payment of tax on the conversion works to the advantage of converting to a Roth IRA. In addition, prorating the income attributable to conversion over 2011 and 2012 may keep the IRA owner in a lower tax bracket than if all of the income was included in 2010. But making a conversion may push a taxpayer into a higher tax bracket in 2011 and 2012 than if no conversion were made.

An IRA owner generally has substantial control over whether, when, and how much of, an amount is rolled over or converted to a Roth IRA. Consider making conversions in years in which the taxpayer is in a lower tax bracket. In some cases, it could make sense to do a series of conversions over a number of years in order to keep the taxpayer in lower tax brackets.

Notes About Examples. Due to possible rounding differences (as well as the general nature of projecting future results), insignificant differences between results under a Roth conversion scenario and a no conversion scenario can essentially be disregarded. Also, future value factors below and in Appendix E are shown rounded to 4 places. However, the future value factors actually used here, and generally throughout the *IRA Calculator* software, are essentially unrounded.

For simplicity's sake, the examples shown below all assume that no nonductible contributions have been made to the traditional IRA. If nondeductible contributions have been made to the traditional IRA, the taxable amount at conversion would have to be calculated and the amount of tax on conversion would be different. Otherwise, the comparisons would still be made in the same manner. The *IRA Calculator* software incorporates calculation of the amount taxable at conversion and the amount of the tax, as well as many other variables, into its "To Convert or Not" module.

Comparisons of Roth conversion and no conversion scenarios, while helpful in making the decision to convert or not, are generally theoretical. Comparisons are made on an isolated basis as if nothing else happens in the IRA world during the years between conversion and distribution. However, for purposes of taxation of distributions, all nonRoth IRAs (i.e., traditional, SEP, or SIMPLE) are generally grouped together and all Roth IRAs are grouped together. Contributions, conversions, and distributions with respect to other IRAs could affect taxation of the IRAs being compared.

Example: Taxes Paid From Outside of IRA. A traditional IRA containing $100,000 is converted into a Roth IRA in 2006. Assume $25,000 of income tax (25 percent tax rate) is paid from funds outside the IRA leaving $100,000 inside the IRA. If the $100,000 grows at 10 percent for 10 years, the Roth IRA grows to $259,374 [$100,000 x 2.5937 future value of single sum factor (10 percent, 10 years), see Appendix E]. Assuming the $259,374 can be withdrawn in a qualified distribution, the taxpayer has $259,374.

If on the other hand the traditional IRA is not converted, the traditional IRA would grow at 10 percent for 10 years to $259,374 [$100,000 x 2.5937 future value of single sum factor (10 percent, 10 years), see Appendix E]. If $68,844 ($259,374 x 25 percent tax rate) of tax is paid, the taxpayer has $194,531 ($259,374 - $68,844) remaining from the IRA. In addition, in comparison with the conversion, the taxpayer has the $25,000 of taxes that were saved by not converting to a Roth IRA. The $25,000 will be placed in a side fund. At 10 percent for 10 years, the $25,000 will have grown to $64,844 [$25,000 x 2.5937 future value of single sum factor (10 percent, 10 years), see Appendix E]. If the growth portion of the $64,844 is not subject to tax, the taxpayer has $259,374 under either scenario.

However, if the growth portion of the $68,844 is subject to tax, the taxpayer has a greater amount under the Roth IRA conversion scenario. For example, if taxation of the growth portion of the $68,044 is deferred for 10 years and the side fund is then taxed at 25 percent, $249,413 remains under the no conversion scenario [$194,5371 + ($68,844 - (($68,844 - $25,000) x 25 percent))]. Or, if growth in the side fund was taxed annually at 25 percent, $246,056 remains under the no conversion scenario. See Figure 12.1.

However, if the $259,374 in the Roth IRA conversion scenario is not received in a qualified distribution, $39,844 of tax would be due on distribution [($259,374 - $100,000) x 25 percent tax rate]. Only $219,531 ($259,374 - $39,844) would remain after tax. This is less than any of the no conversion scenarios above. Obviously, receipt of distributions as qualified distributions is important to the Roth IRA.

FIGURE 12.1

To Convert or Not
(Roth v. Traditional Plus Side Fund)

IRA Balance	100,000	Side Fund	25,000
Interest	10%	Years	10
Tax Rate at Conversion	25%	Tax Paid	Outside

At Distribution Tax Rate	Roth	Traditional Decreases	Traditional No Change	Traditional Increases
Tax Rate	NA	15%	25%	35%
IRA Balance	259,374	259,374	259,374	259,374
- Tax	NA	38,906	64,844	90,781
Net IRA	259,374	220,468	194,531	168,593
Side Fund (SF)				
No Tax	NA	64,844	64,844	64,844
After Tax	NA	58,867	54,883	50,899
IRA + SF				
SF No Tax	**259,374**	**285,312**	**259,375**	**233,437**
SF After Tax	**259,374**	**279,335**	**249,414**	**219,492**

Example: Taxes Paid From Within IRA. A traditional IRA containing $100,000 is converted into a Roth IRA in 2006. Assume $25,000 of income tax (25 percent tax rate) is paid from within the IRA leaving $75,000 inside the IRA. (A penalty tax for an early distribution may also be due on the amount withdrawn to pay taxes.) If the $75,000 grows at 10 percent for 10 years, the Roth IRA grows to $194,531 [$75,000 x 2.5937 future value of single sum factor (10 percent, 10 years), see Appendix E]. Assuming the $194,531 can be withdrawn in a qualified distribution, the taxpayer has $194,531.

If on the other hand the traditional IRA is not converted, the traditional IRA would grow at 10 percent for 10 years to $259,374 [$100,000 x 2.5937 future value of single sum factor (10 percent, 10 years), see Appendix E]. If $64,844 ($259,374 x 25 percent tax rate) of tax is paid, the taxpayer has $194,531 ($259,370 - $64,844) remaining from the IRA. Thus, the taxpayer has $194,531 under either scenario.

The amount remaining if taxes are paid from within the IRA is significantly less than if taxes were paid from outside the IRA. This could possibly be offset by putting an amount equal to the tax at conversion in this example in a side fund. However, the value of using an IRA may be reduced by paying taxes from inside the IRA on conversion.

Example: Lower Tax Rate Later. A traditional IRA containing $100,000 is converted into a Roth IRA in 2006. Assume $25,000 of income tax (25 percent tax rate) is paid from funds outside the IRA leaving $100,000 inside the IRA. If the $100,000 grows at 10 percent for 10 years, the Roth IRA grows to $259,374 [$100,000 x 2.5937 future value of single sum factor (10 percent, 10 years), see Appendix E]. Assuming the $259,374 can be withdrawn in a qualified distribution, the taxpayer has $259,374.

If on the other hand the traditional IRA is not converted, the traditional IRA would grow at 10 percent for 10 years to $259,374 [$100,000 x 2.5937 future value of single sum factor (10 percent, 10 years), see Appendix E]. If $38,906 ($259,374 x 15 percent tax rate) of tax is paid, the taxpayer has $220,468 ($259,374 - $38,906) remaining from the IRA. In addition, in comparison with the conversion, the taxpayer has the $25,000 of taxes that were saved by not converting to a Roth IRA. At 10 percent for 10 years, the $25,000 will have grown to $68,844 [$25,000 x 2.5937 future value of single sum factor (10 percent, 10 years), see Appendix E]. If the growth portion of the $68,844 is not subject to tax, the taxpayer has $285,312 under the "no conversion/lower taxes later" scenario.

However, if the growth portion of the $68,844 is subject to tax, the advantage under the "no conversion/lower taxes later" scenario would be less or eliminated. For example, the taxpayer has $279,335 if the growth portion were subject to a 15 percent tax [$220,468 + ($25,000 + ((1 - .25) x ($68,844 - $25,000)))]. See Figure 12.1.

Example: Higher Tax Rate Later. A traditional IRA containing $100,000 is converted into a Roth IRA in 2006. Assume $25,000 of income tax (25 percent tax rate) is paid from funds outside the IRA leaving $100,000 inside the IRA. If the $100,000 grows at 10 percent for 10 years, the Roth IRA grows to $259,374 [$100,000 x 2.5937 future value of single sum factor (10 percent, 10 years), see Appendix E]. Assuming the $259,374 can be withdrawn in a qualified distribution, the taxpayer has $259,374.

If on the other hand the traditional IRA is not converted, the traditional IRA would grow at 10 percent for 10 years to $259,374 [$100,000 x 2.5937 future value of single sum factor (10 percent, 10 years), see Appendix E]. If $90,781 ($259,374 x 35 percent tax rate) of tax is paid, the taxpayer has $168,593 ($259,374 - $90,781) remaining from the IRA. In addition, in comparison with the conversion, the taxpayer has the $25,000 of taxes that were saved by not converting to a Roth IRA. At 10 percent for 10 years, the $25,000 will have grown to $68,844 [$25,000 x 2.5937 future value of single sum factor (10 percent, 10 years), see Appendix E]. If the growth portion of the $68,844 is not subject to tax, the taxpayer has $233,437 under the "no conversion/higher taxes later" scenario. However, if the growth portion of the $68,844 is subject to tax, the taxpayer has even less. See Figure 12.1.

For simplicity's sake, the above examples have generally shown a single tax on the side fund rather than a yearly, or other periodic, tax. Using a spreadsheet, one could increase the side fund for growth each year and then subtract out whatever tax was assumed to be payable for each year. A shortcut method might be to adjust the growth rate on the side fund to an after-tax rate. For example, if growth is assumed to be 10 percent per year and the income tax rate equal to 25 percent, an after-tax growth rate of 7.5 percent [10 percent x (1 - 25 percent)] could be used. The *IRA Calculator* software permits selection of a side fund that is tax free, tax deferred until distribution, or taxed annually in its "To Convert or Not" module. Also, consider whether a lower tax rate should be used with the side fund (e.g., a capital gains tax rate or a blend of regular and capital gains tax rates).

The foregoing examples have demonstrated how to compare conversion to a Roth IRA as compared to no conversion of a traditional IRA with a side fund (for tax savings from not converting) based upon a single distribution. (Distributions from the Roth IRA have generally been assumed to be received tax-free, which is generally required for the success of a Roth IRA.) Comparisons can also be made of a person making periodic distributions for a number of years. Making periodic distributions may enable a person to keep income at lower tax rates than if the distribution is made all at once. However, the results above are no different if distributions are made comparably from either a Roth IRA or a traditional IRA with side fund and the tax rate used is appropriate under the circumstances.

The Roth IRA does have one advantage that is likely to be important if the IRA owner has sufficient other assets that the owner does not need to take distributions from the IRA. Required minimum distributions from a Roth IRA can be postponed until after the death of the IRA owner and, generally, the death of the spouse of the

IRA owner. However, distributions from a traditional IRA must generally begin when the IRA owner attains age 70½.

Endnotes

1. See IRC Sec. 408(d)(3).
2. Treas. Reg. §1.408A-4(A-1).
3. IRC Sec. 408A(d)(3).
4. Treas. Reg. §1.408A-5.
5. Treas. Reg. §1.408A-5.
6. Treas. Reg. §1.408A-5(A-2)(c).
7. Treas. Reg. §1.408A-5(A-6).
8. Treas. Reg. §1.408A-5(A-9).
9. Treas. Temp. Reg. §1.408A-4T, A-14.
10. Rev. Rul. 2006-13, 2006-3 IRB 315.

Chapter 13

Distributions

$\mathbf{A}$ good deal of planning with respect to distributions from an IRA involves arranging distributions before age 59½ so that the early distribution penalty tax does not apply, and after age 70½ so as to postpone distributions as long as possible under the required minimum distribution rules. But, first, an overview of when IRA distributions are includable in income is in order.

IRA Distributions Includable in Income

Distributions from a traditional IRA, a SEP IRA (including a SAR-SEP IRA), or a SIMPLE IRA (collectively, nonRoth IRAs) are includable in income on a prorated basis to the extent that the distribution is made from deductible contributions or earnings from the IRA. If nondeductible contributions have not been made to such an IRA, distributions are fully includable in income.

A qualified distribution from a Roth IRA is excludable from income. A qualified distribution is a distribution from a Roth IRA that is made after the five-taxable year period beginning in the year in which the first contribution was made to a Roth IRA and that is:

(1)   made on or after the date the Roth IRA owner turns age 59½;

(2)   made after the death of the Roth IRA owner;

(3) attributable to disability of the Roth IRA owner; or

(4) made to the Roth IRA owner ($10,000 lifetime limit) for purchase of a first home by the IRA owner, the IRA owner's spouse, or children, grand-children, or ancestor of either.

Otherwise, distributions from a Roth IRA are includable in income except to the extent that the distribution is made from contributions. Distributions from a Roth IRA are treated as made first from contributions and then from earnings.

The timing of Roth IRA distributions can be extremely important.

For example, assume contributions of $2,000 have been made to a Roth IRA that is now worth $4,000. If a nonqualified distribution is made of $2,000 in 2005, the distribution is a nontaxable return of $2,000 of contributions. If a qualified distribution is then made of the remaining $2,000 in 2006, none of the $4,000 is subject to income tax.

On the other hand, if a qualified distribution of $2,000 is made in 2005, the qualified distribution would be treated as withdrawing $2,000 of contributions. Then, if a nonqualified distribution is made of the remaining $2,000 in 2006, the full amount of the nonqualified distribution is subject to income tax.

Early Distribution Penalty Tax

A distribution from an IRA prior to the IRA owner reaching age 59½ is subject to a 10 percent early distribution penalty tax to the extent the distribution is includable in income (see above) unless an exception applies. An IRA owner attains age 59½ on the date that is six calendar months after the 59th anniversary of the IRA owner's birth. For example, if an IRA owner's date of birth was June 30, 1947, the 59th anniversary is June 30, 2006, and the IRA owner attains age 59½ on December 30, 2006.

In general, the early distribution penalty does not apply to distributions:

(1) to a beneficiary or the individual's estate, made on or after the death of the individual;

(2) attributable to the individual's disability;

(3)   that are part of a series of substantially equal periodic payments (an important exception that is discussed in detail below);

(4)   made for medical care, to the extent that the payment for medical care would be deductible (i.e., such expenses are deductible only to the extent in excess of 7.5 percent of adjusted gross income) without regard as to whether the individual itemizes deductions;

(5)   made by an unemployed individual for the payment of health insurance premiums;

(6)   made to the IRA owner for payment of qualified higher education expenses furnished to the IRA owner, the IRA owner's spouse, or children or grandchildren of either;

(7)   made to the IRA owner ($10,000 lifetime limit) for purchase of a first home by the IRA owner, the IRA owner's spouse, or children, grandchildren, or ancestor of either; or

(8)   made to a reservist while on active duty (commencing after September 11, 2001 and before 2008).[1]

Where the spouse of the IRA owner is the sole designated beneficiary after the IRA owner's death, such spouse can generally elect to be treated as the owner of the IRA (see the discussion of required minimum distributions below). If the election is made, the spouse is treated as the owner and the exception for distributions made after the death of the IRA owner is not available until after the spouse dies. So, if the spouse is younger than age 59½, the early distribution penalty tax could apply to distributions unless another exception applies. If the election is not made, the exception for distributions made after the death of the original IRA owner would be available.

Substantially Equal Periodic Payments (SEPPs)

An important exception to the early distribution penalty tax is for distributions that are part of a series of substantially equal periodic payments made (at least annually) for the life or the life expectancy of the individual or for the lives or the life expectancies of the individual and the individual's designated beneficiary. If the series of substantially equal periodic payments are modified (other than by reason of death or disability) before the individual reaches age 59½, or after the individual reaches age 59½ if within five years of the first payment, the early penalty tax that would have applied except for the exemption plus interest for the deferral period is added to tax in the year of the modification.

The IRS has approved three methods for calculating substantially equal periodic payments (SEPPs) under IRC Section 72(t):

(1)   where the payment is determined using a method that would be acceptable for minimum required distributions purposes (requires annual calculations);

(2)   where the payment is determined by amortizing the IRA account balance over the number of years equal to the life expectancy of the account owner or the life expectancies of the account owner and beneficiary; and

(3)   where the payment is determined by dividing the IRA account balance by an annuity factor.[2]

The first method requires recalculation of payments each year, while the second and third methods provide constant payments. A person using the second and third methods can elect to switch to the first method. In making these calculations, life expectancy and mortality are now based on the RMD tables (see Appendix D) and interest is generally limited to a maximum rate (which changes monthly).

The interest rate that is used in the amortization and annuitization methods cannot exceed 120 percent of the federal midterm rate under IRC Section 1274(d) for either of the two months immediately preceding the month in which the substantially equal periodic payments start. This rate is essentially the same as the IRC Section 7520 interest rate except that the Section 7520 rate is rounded to the nearest 2/10 of one percent. The IRS publishes these applicable federal rates (AFRs) monthly in a revenue ruling. They are also available at www.taxfactsonline.com.

The IRA account balance must be determined in a reasonable manner based on facts and circumstances. Generally, this means that the account can be valued as of December 31 of the prior year or on a date that is within a reasonable period before the date of the first distribution during a year.

A number of factors should be considered in selecting between the three substantially equal periodic payment methods. These include:

•   In selecting a method to use, it is often useful to select the method that comes closest to withdrawing from the IRA the amount that is desired.

- The required minimum distribution method must be recalculated each year, whereas the amortization and annuitization methods need to be calculated only once.

- A person using the amortization or annuitization methods can elect to switch to the required minimum distribution method.

- The amount that can be withdrawn under the amortization or annuitization methods depends on the interest rate used; the required minimum distribution method does not take interest into account. Under the amortization or annuitization methods, higher interest rates result in higher payments; lower interest rates result in lower payments.

- Under all three methods, having a designated beneficiary reduces the amount of the payments (calculations are based upon two lives rather than one). In general, where there is a designated beneficiary, a younger designated beneficiary results in lower payments; an older designated beneficiary results in higher payments.

- The IRA owner can select which of his IRA accounts are to be taken into consideration for purposes of calculating substantially equal periodic payments and payments can be made from one or more of the selected IRAs. Selecting IRA accounts with a lower aggregate account balance results in lower payments; selecting IRA accounts with a higher aggregate account balance results in higher payments. In general, the IRA owner can adjust the account balance of his IRAs by splitting IRAs or through rollovers to other IRAs.

Required Minimum Distribution (RMD) Method

Using the required minimum distribution method can be as simple as dividing the account balance as of the end of the prior year by the life expectancy (RMD Single Life Table, see Appendix C) of the IRA account holder.

> *Example.* Assume the IRA account holder is age 40 and the IRA account balance is $100,000. At age 40 life expectancy is 43.6, so dividing the account balance of $100,000 by 43.6 indicates a distribution of $2,294 is required. (If payments are quarterly, simply dividing $2,294 by 4 produces quarterly payments of $573.) The next year, at age 41 life expectancy is 42.7 and the account balance is $98,000, so dividing the account balance of $98,000 by 42.7 indicates a distribution of $2,295 is required, and so on.

For purposes of substantially equal periodic payments, the following rules apply under the RMD method. The RMD method can be based on the Uniform Lifetime Table (treats beneficiary as being 10 years younger than IRA owner), the RMD Single Life Table, or the RMD Joint and Survivor Table (see Appendix C). In general, the same table that is used in the first year must be used in future years. However, the RMD Joint and Survivor Table can only be used if there is an actual designated beneficiary on January 1 of the year of distribution. If there are multiple beneficiaries of the IRA, the oldest beneficiary is used. If the RMD Joint and Survivor Table is being used and there ceases to be a designated beneficiary, the single life expectancy (RMD Single Life Table) of the owner must be used.

For more on required minimum distributions, see heading below.

Amortization Method

The payment is determined by amortizing the IRA account balance over the number of years equal to the life expectancy of the account owner (RMD Single Life Table, see Appendix C) or the life expectancies of the account owner and beneficiary (RMD Joint and Survivor Table, see Appendix C) using an appropriate interest rate on the date payments begin. Apparently the age of the beneficiary can also be deemed to be 10 years younger then the IRA owner (RMD Uniform Lifetime Table, see Appendix C). The payment stays constant; it is not recalculated each year.[3]

The basic amortization formula equals:

$$(1 - (1 \div ((1 + i)^{le}))) \div i$$

where i = interest rate and le = life expectancy

The basic amortization factor is then multiplied by a factor from the Annuity Adjustment Factors Table A (if payments are at the beginning of each period) or Annuity Adjustment Factors Table B (if payments are at the end of each period) to produce an amortization factor adjusted for frequency of payments. See Appendix D for annuity adjustment factors.

The IRA account balance at the beginning of the series of payments is then divided by the frequency adjusted amortization factor to determine the aggregate distribution required each year. If payments are other than annual, divide the aggregate distribution required each year by the number of payments each year.

Example. Assume the IRA account holder is age 40, a reasonable interest rate is 5 percent, and the IRA account balance is $100,000. The RMD Single

Life Table life expectancy for age 40 is 43.6. Quarterly distributions payable at the end of each quarter that qualify as substantially equal periodic payments are calculated as follows:

$$\text{basic amortization factor} = (1 - (1 \div ((1 + i)^{le}))) \div i$$
$$\text{basic amortization factor} = (1 - (1 \div ((1 + 5\%)^{43.6}))) \div 5\%$$
$$\text{basic amortization factor} = 17.6167$$

Annuity Adjustment Factors Table A (Quarterly, 5%) = 1.0186
frequency adjusted amortization factor = 17.6167 x 1.0186
frequency adjusted amortization factor = 17.9444

aggregate yearly distribution = $100,000 ÷ 17.9444
aggregate yearly distribution = $5,573

quarterly distributions = $5,573 ÷ 4
quarterly distributions = $1,393

A present value term certain annuity factor table (see Term Certain Annuity Factor tables in Appendix D) can be used instead of the basic amortization factor formula above. Where life expectancy is between table factors for years, interpolation is generally required. For example, if life expectancy is 42.5, a term certain annuity factor halfway between the table factors for 42 years and 43 years would be used.

Example. Assume the IRA account holder is age 40, a reasonable interest rate is 5 percent, and the IRA account balance is $100,000. The RMD Single Life Table life expectancy for age 40 is 43.6. [A partial year equal to .6 (43.6 - 43) is used in the interpolation below.] Quarterly distributions payable at the end of each quarter that qualify as substantially equal periodic payments are calculated as follows:

Term Certain Annuity Factor (43 years, 5%) = 17.5459
Term Certain Annuity Factor (44 years, 5%) = 17.6628
basic amortization factor = 17.5459 + ((17.6628 - 17.5459) x .6)
basic amortization factor = 17.6160

Annuity Adjustment Factors Table A (Quarterly, 5%) = 1.0186
frequency adjusted amortization factor = 17.6160 x 1.0186
frequency adjusted amortization factor = 17.9437

aggregate yearly distribution = $100,000 ÷ 17.9437
aggregate yearly distribution = $5,573

quarterly distributions = $5,573 ÷ 4
quarterly distributions = $1,393

Annuitization Method

In general, payment is determined by dividing the IRA account balance by an annuity factor (including a factor from the RMD Single Life Annuity Factors table and a factor from Annuity Adjustment Factors Table A, see Appendix D) using an appropriate interest rate on the date payments begin. The annuity factor can be based upon the age of the IRA account holder or the ages of the IRA account holder and a beneficiary. The *IRA Calculator* software has and uses (where selected) RMD Joint and Survivor Annuity Factors for two lives.

For example, assume the IRA account holder is age 40, a reasonable interest rate is 5 percent, and the IRA account balance is $100,000. Quarterly distributions payable at the end of each quarter that qualify as substantially equal periodic payments are calculated as follows:

> Single Life Annuity Factor (age 40, 5%) = 17.0946
> Annuity Adjustment Factors Table A (Quarterly, 5%) = 1.0186
> combined annuity factor = 17.0946 x 1.0186
> combined annuity factor = 17.4126
>
> aggregate yearly distribution = $100,000 ÷ 17.4126
> aggregate yearly distribution = $5,743
>
> quarterly distributions = $5,743 ÷ 4
> quarterly distributions = $1,436

If payments in the example were at the beginning of each period, an adjustment must be made for the first payment. Quarterly distributions payable at the beginning of each quarter that qualify as substantially equal periodic payments are calculated as follows:

> Single Life Annuity Factor (age 40, 5%) = 17.0946
> Annuity Adjustment Factors Table A (Quarterly, 5%) = 1.0186
> combined annuity factor = 17.0946 x 1.0186
> combined annuity factor = 17.4126
>
> first payment adjustment factor = 1 ÷ number of payments in year
> first payment adjustment factor = 1 ÷ 4
> first payment adjustment factor = .25
>
> adjusted combined annuity factor = 17.4126 + .25
> adjusted combined annuity factor = 17.6626
>
> aggregate yearly distribution = $100,000 ÷ 17.6626
> aggregate yearly distribution = $5,662

quarterly distributions = $5,662 ÷ 4
quarterly distributions = $1,415

Required Minimum Distributions

Distributions must generally begin from a traditional IRA, SEP IRA (including a SAR-SEP IRA), or SIMPLE IRA (collectively, nonRoth IRAs) at the earlier of the death of the IRA owner or when the IRA owner turns age 70½. (See next paragraph regarding Roth IRAs.) These rules are generally referred to as the required minimum distribution rules and are discussed in detail, including examples, below. A 50 percent penalty applies to the extent a required minimum distribution is not made.

In the case of a Roth IRA, required minimum distributions need not begin until after the death of the Roth IRA owner (which includes the spouse of the original Roth IRA owner where the surviving spouse is the designated beneficiary and elects to treat the Roth IRA as the spouse's own).[4] However, elective deferral Roth distributions (see Chapter 8) must generally begin at the earlier of the death of the IRA owner or when the IRA owner turns age 70½.

When a traditional IRA, SEP IRA, or SIMPLE IRA owner reaches age 70½, the IRA owner must begin taking required minimum distributions. In general, the required minimum distribution rules cause the IRA owner to withdraw the entire IRA account balance over the IRA owner's life or the lives of the IRA owner and a designated beneficiary. If there is more than one beneficiary other than the IRA owner, the oldest other beneficiary's life expectancy is used for the designated beneficiary. Special rules apply where the spouse of the IRA owner is the designated beneficiary. Failure to withdraw the required minimum distribution results in a 50 percent penalty tax on the amount by which the required minimum distribution exceeds the actual amount withdrawn.[5]

An additional rule, the minimum distribution incidental benefit (MDIB) rule, is designed to insure that traditional, SEP IRA, or SIMPLE IRA distributions are primarily for the benefit of the IRA owner. The rule does this, while the IRA owner is alive, by treating a beneficiary other than the spouse of the IRA owner as no more than 10 years younger than the IRA owner.[6] If there is no designated benficiary while the IRA owner is alive, there will be deemed to be a beneficiary 10 years younger than the IRA owner.

In the case of a traditional, SEP, or SIMPLE IRA, required minimum distributions generally must begin when the IRA owner reaches age 70½. Ordinarily, required minimum distributions must be made by December 31st of each year. However, in the year the IRA owner reaches age 70½, the required minimum distribution for that year need not be made until April 1st of the following year (the required beginning date). Two distributions in a single year would be required where the distribution for the year the IRA owner turns 70½ (first year) is made in the following year (second year): the distribution for the first year must be made by April 1 and the one for the second year by December 31.

The April 1st required beginning date should generally be viewed as a grace period for age 70½, allowing the distribution for the first year distributions are required to be made after the end of the first year. This may be useful where there is a late realization that distributions are required starting at age 70½. It also provides a slight deferrral of when the distribution will be subject to income tax. From an income tax planning perspective, consideration should be given to what other income, deductions, and credits the IRA owner has in the two years (the year the IRA owner turns age 70½ and the next year). As appropriate, the distribution required for the year the IRA owner turns age 70½ can be made (and taxed) in the first year, in the second year, or split between the two years (as long as the total required distribution for the first year is made by April 1st of the second year). If the IRA owner dies before the required beginning date, no distribution is required until at least the year after death (see below).

Required minimum distributions may be calculated for each IRA and distributions made from each IRA as appropriate. Alternatively, required minimum distributions may be calculated for each IRA within a category (e.g., Roth, nonRoth) owned by the individual and totalled, and distributions made from whichever IRA or IRAs within the category the IRA owner chooses.[7] However, an inherited IRA may not be aggregated with any other IRA within a category unless the other IRA was inherited from the same person. For this purpose, an IRA that a surviving spouse elects to treat as such spouse's own is not treated as being inherited from the decedent spouse.

Generally, the oldest beneficiary of a trust is treated as the designated beneficiary for RMD purposes. It appears that the adverse affect of this rule can be avoided if separate trusts or shares of trusts and separate IRAs or IRA accounts are created for each beneficiary. See Chapter 14 regarding choosing a beneficiary and trusts.

If a person other than an individual is designated as beneficiary of an IRA, the IRA will be treated as having no beneficiary for RMD purposes, even if an individual is also named beneficiary. A charity is not an individual. Therefore, if a charity is named as a beneficiary of an IRA, or a trust with a charitable beneficiary is named as a beneficiary of an IRA, the IRA will be treated as having no beneficiary. It appears that the adverse effect of this rule can be avoided if separate IRAs are created and a separate IRA transferred outright to the charity. See Chapter 14 regarding choosing a beneficiary, including a charity.

The required minimum distribution for each year is generally calculated by dividing the IRA account balance as of the end of the previous year by the life expectancy of the IRA owner or the joint and survivor life expectancy of the IRA owner and a designated beneficiary. During the owner's lifetime (or possibly the lifetime of the owner's spouse), including the year of death, life expectancy is based upon the Uniform Lifetime Table or the RMD Joint and Survivor Table (where the spouse is the sole beneficiary and more than 10 years younger than the IRA owner). After the death of the IRA owner (or possibly the death of the owner's spouse), life expectancy is based on the RMD Single Life Table. The RMD Tables are in Appendix C.

Attained age is used for the age of the IRA owner and beneficiary in the appropriate year. Thus, an IRA owner whose birthday is in the first half of the year (January-June) will be age 70 in the year the IRA owner turns 70½ and will enter the table using age 70. On the other hand, an IRA owner whose birthday is in the second half of the year (July-December) will be age 71 in the year the IRA owner turns 70½ and will enter the table using age 71.

While the traditional, SEP or SIMPLE IRA owner is alive, a designated beneficiary other than the spouse of the IRA owner is treated as no more than 10 years younger than the IRA owner under the minimum distribution incidental benefit (MDIB) rule. If the amount determined under the minimum distribution incidental benefit rule is higher than the regular required minimum distribution, the higher amount is required to be distributed. In essence, the minimum distribution incidental benefit rule attempts to insure that distributions are primarily for the benefit of the owner of the traditional, SEP, or SIMPLE IRA. The rule does so by preventing distributions from being excessively spread out over many years through the use of a beneficiary (except in the case of the spouse of the IRA owner) who is much younger than the IRA owner. The MDIB rule is implemented by using the Uniform Lifetime Table (see Appendix C), which lists RMD factors for the IRA owner and a beneficiary deemed 10 years younger than the IRA owner. The Uniform Lifetime Table is also used while the owner is alive if there is no designated beneficiary.

For example, if the owner of the traditional, SEP, or SIMPLE IRA is age 70 and the designated beneficiary (who is not the spouse of the IRA owner) is age 40, the joint and survivor life expectancy for a person age 70 and a person age 40 would ordinarily be 44.0 (see RMD Joint and Survivor Table). However, the minimum distribution incidental benefit rule would treat the designated beneficiary as being age 60 (70

- 10), and the resulting joint and survivor life expectancy for a person age 70 and a person age 60 would be 27.4. The factor for calculating the required minimum distribution is the lower of the regular factor (44.0) or the MDIB factor (27.4), or 27.4. As a shortcut to all this, the Uniform Lifetime Table provides a factor for an IRA owner age 70 of 27.4. The results would be the same if there is no designated beneficiary.

While the traditional, SEP or SIMPLE IRA owner is alive, the Uniform Lifetime Table is also used where the spouse is the beneficiary and is not more than 10 years younger than the IRA owner. The RMD Joint and Survivor table is only used if the spouse is more than 10 years younger than the owner. Thus, the best of either table (i.e., the highest RMD factor) is obtained with a spouse beneficiary.

If the traditional, SEP, or SIMPLE IRA owner dies on or after the required beginning date (generally, April 1st of the year after reaching age 70½), required minimum distributions generally must continue at least as rapidly as under the method used (or required) while the IRA owner was alive. If there is no beneficiary, distributions in years after the owner's death are based on the life expectancy of the IRA owner in the year of death. The life expectancy factor is reduced by one for each year after the year of the owner's death. For example, if the owner died in the year he attained (or would have attained) age 80, life expectancy in the year of death is 10.2 (RMD Single Life Table). The RMD factor in the year after death is 9.2 (10.2 - 1), 8.2 (9.2 - 1) the next year, 7.2 the next year, and so on.

If the traditional, SEP, or SIMPLE IRA owner dies on or after the required beginning date (generally, April 1st of the year after reaching age 70½) and there is a beneficiary, distributions may generally be distributed over the longer of the life expectancy of the IRA owner (as described in the preceding paragraph) or the life expectancy of the beneficiary. The life expectancy of a beneficiary other than the spouse is determined in the year after the death of the IRA owner, and is reduced by one for each year after the year of the owner's death. For example, if the beneficiary attained (or would have attained) age 40 in the year after the owner's death, the life expectancy of the beneficiary in the year after death is 43.6 (RMD Single Life Table). The RMD factor in the next year is 42.6 (43.6 - 1), 41.6 (42.6 - 1) the next year, 40.6 the next year, and so on.

However, where the spouse of the IRA owner is the sole designated beneficiary after the owner's death, such spouse can generally elect to be treated as the owner of the IRA for purposes of the required minimum distribution rules. If the election is made, the RMD rules would generally treat the spouse as the IRA owner, rather than as an IRA beneficiary. Also, where the spouse of the IRA owner is the sole designated beneficiary after the owner's death, such spouse can postpone required minimum distributions until such time as the former IRA owner would have reached age 70½.

If the spouse is the sole designated beneficiary, and the spouse does not elect to treat the IRA as the spouse's own, the life expectancy of the spouse is used. During the lifetime of the spouse, the spouse's life expectancy is redetermined each year based upon the attained age of the spouse. In years after the death of the spouse, required minimum distributions are based on the life expectancy of the spouse in the year of death. The life expectancy factor is reduced by one for each year after the year of the spouse's death. For example, if the spouse died in the year he attained (or would have attained) age 80, life expectancy in the year of death is 10.2 (RMD Single Life Table). The RMD factor in the year after death is 9.2 (10.2 - 1), 8.2 (9.2 - 1) the next year, 7.2 the next year, and so on. If the traditional, SEP, or SIMPLE IRA owner dies on or after the required beginning date (generally, April 1st of the year after reaching age 70½), the life expectancy of the IRA owner (as described above) can be used in any year if greater than the life expectancy of the spouse.

If the traditional, SEP, or SIMPLE IRA owner dies before the required beginning date (generally, April 1st after reaching age 70½), the entire IRA account must be distributed by December 31 of the year that contains the fifth anniversary of the owner's death unless the IRA owner has designated a beneficiary.[8] Where the IRA owner has designated a beneficiary, distributions may be made over the life expectancy (RMD Single Life Table) of the beneficiary as long as such distributions begin no later than December 31 of the year following the IRA owner's death.[9] Required minimum distributions are generally calculated the same as where the owner dies on or after the required beginning date with a beneficiary (including a spouse) (see above), except that use of the IRA owner's life expectancy is not available (even if the beneficiary is older than the IRA owner).

Where the spouse of the IRA owner is the sole designated beneficiary after the owner's death, such spouse can generally elect to be treated as the owner of the IRA for purposes of the required minimum distribution rules. In the case of a Roth IRA, such an election would permit required minimum distributions to be postponed until after the death of the spouse. In the case of a traditional, SEP, or SIMPLE IRA, such an election would permit distributions to be postponed until the spouse reaches age 70½. Also, where the spouse of the IRA owner is the sole designated beneficiary, after the owner's death such spouse could postpone required minimum distributions until such time as the former IRA owner would have reached age 70½.

Summary of RMD Methods

If there are multiple designated beneficiaries of an IRA, the oldest beneficiary is treated as the designated beneficiary. Thus, the oldest beneficiary of a trust that is the beneficiary of an IRA is generally treated as the designated beneficiary of the IRA. If a person other than an individual is designated as beneficiary of an IRA, the IRA will be treated as having no beneficiary, even if an individual is also named beneficiary. For example, a charity is not an individual. Separate IRAs (and trusts) can be created with different designated beneficiaries.

Distributions During Lifetime of Owner
(including the year of death)

Required minimum distributions during the lifetime of the owner (including the year of the death of the owner) of a nonRoth IRA are generally determined using the Uniform Lifetime Table (see Appendix C). The attained age of the IRA owner for the year is used, and the Uniform Lifetime Table treats the beneficiary as 10 years younger than the IRA owner. The Uniform Lifetime Table is used even if the IRA owner has not designated a beneficiary. [See Figures 13.2 to 13.5 for examples using the Uniform Lifetime Table].

However, if the spouse of the IRA owner is the sole designated beneficiary of the IRA and the spouse is more than 10 years younger than the IRA owner, the joint and survivor life expectancy of the IRA owner and spouse is used. In this case, the attained ages of both the IRA owner and spouse for the year are used, and a factor from the RMD Joint and Survivor Table (see Appendix C) is used [see Figures 13.8 to 13.9 for examples using the RMD Joint and Survivor Table]. This method produces higher RMD factors and lower required minimum distributions than using factors from the Uniform Lifetime Table.

In the case of a Roth IRA, distributions are not required during the lifetime of the IRA owner (including a spouse who elects to treat a Roth IRA as the spouse's own).

Distributions After Death of Owner

The method for calculating required minimum distributions after the death of the IRA owner generally depends on whether a beneficiary has been designated by the time of the IRA owner's death and whether the spouse of the IRA owner is the designated beneficiary.

The method for calculating required minimum distributions after the death of the IRA owner may also depend on whether or not the IRA owner died before the required beginning date. For a traditional IRA, the required beginning date is April 1 of the year after the year in which the IRA owner would attain age 70½. For a Roth IRA, the owner is always treated as dying before the required beginning date.

The actual determination of the designated beneficiary can be determined as late as September 30 of the first year after the year of the owner's death. Thus, if a primary beneficiary disclaims an IRA, a contingent named beneficiary who receives the IRA would be treated as the designated beneficiary. Or, if there are two named beneficiaries of an IRA, and one beneficiary is cashed out, the remaining beneficiary is treated as the designated beneficiary.

Spouse Beneficiary. If the spouse of the IRA owner is the sole designated beneficiary, the spouse can elect to be treated as the owner of the IRA for purposes of the RMD rules [see Figures 13.14 to 13.15, and 13.19, for examples with a spousal election]. The election cannot be made if a trust is named beneficiary, even if the spouse is the sole beneficiary of the trust. (Under certain circumstances, it appears that a rollover to a spouse may be used to get around this limitation.) Also, if the IRA owner died prior to the year the IRA owner attained age 70½ and the spouse is the sole designated beneficiary, then required minimum distributions to the spouse do not have to begin until the year the IRA owner would have attained age 70½ [see Figure 13.13 for an example of this].

If the spouse is the sole designated beneficiary and does not elect to be treated as the owner of the IRA, then required minimum distributions must generally be made to the spouse over the single life expectancy of the spouse. In this case, the attained age of the spouse for the year is used, and a factor from the RMD Single Life Table (see Appendix C) is used. After the death of the spouse, distributions must continue using the remaining life expectancy of the spouse and the subtract one method. The life expectancy is determined using the attained age of the spouse for the year of the death of the spouse from the RMD Single Life Table (see Appendix C), and by subtracting one from that life expectancy for each year after the year of death. [See Figures 13.11 to 13.13 for examples of this method]

If the spouse does not elect to be treated as the owner of the IRA, and the owner died on or after the required beginning date (see above), the life expectancy of the owner can be used in any year if it is greater than the life expectancy of the spouse (see preceding paragraph). The life expectancy of the owner is determined using the attained age of the owner for the year of the death of the IRA owner from the RMD Single Life Table (see Appendix C), and by subtracting one from that life expectancy for each year elapsed thereafter. [See Figure 13.12 for an example of this.]

Nonspouse Beneficiary. Distributions to a designated nonspouse beneficiary after the death of the IRA owner depend on whether or not the IRA owner died before the required beginning date (see above).

If the IRA owner died *before* the required beginning date, distributions must be made over the remaining life expectancy of the beneficiary using the subtract one method [see Figure 13.6 for an example of this method]. The life expectancy of the beneficiary is determined using the attained age of the beneficiary for the year after the year of the death of the IRA owner from the RMD Single Life Table (see Appendix C), and by subtracting one from that life expectancy for each year elapsed thereafter.

If the IRA owner died *on or after* the required beginning date, distributions must be made over the longer of the remaining life expectancy of the owner or the beneficiary using the subtract one method [see Figures 13.4 and 13.5 for examples of this subtract one method]. The life expectancy of the owner is determined using the attained age of the owner for the year of the death of the IRA owner from the RMD Single Life Table (see Appendix C), and by subtracting one from that life expectancy for each year elapsed thereafter. The life expectancy of the beneficiary is determined using the attained age of the beneficiary for the year after the year of the death of the IRA owner from the RMD Single Life Table (see Appendix C), and by subtracting one from that life expectancy for each year elapsed thereafter.

No Beneficiary. If there is no designated beneficiary, distributions after the death of the IRA owner depend on whether or not the IRA owner died before the required beginning date (see above).

If the IRA owner died *before* the required beginning date, the entire IRA account must be distributed under the five year rule (see below) [see Figures 13-1 and 13-16].

If the IRA owner died *on or after* the required beginning date, distributions must continue using the remaining life expectancy of the IRA owner and the subtract one method [see Figures 13.2 and 13.3 for examples of this subtract one method]. The life expectancy is determined using the attained age of the IRA owner for the year of the death of the IRA owner from the RMD Single Life Table (see Appendix C), and by subtracting one from that life expectancy for each year after the year of death.

Five Year Rule. If the five year rule applies, the entire IRA account must be distributed by the end of the calendar year that contains the fifth anniversary of the date of death of the IRA owner. For example, if an IRA owner age 65 dies on January 1,

2003, then the entire account must be distributed by the end of 2008 if the five year rule applies.

The five year rule generally applies: if elected; if the IRA owner dies before the required beginning date (see above) and without a beneficiary; or if the IRA owner has a beneficiary and there is a failure to timely start distributions over the life expectancy of the beneficiary. Life expectancy distributions must generally start by December 31 of the year after the year of death of the IRA owner, but could start later if the spouse is the beneficiary.

Methodology For Making RMD Calculations

A methodology for making required minimum distribution calculations, including projections of account balances and distributions for future years, follows. It must be remembered that calculations for future years are just projections; required minimum distributions must be calculated each year based upon the actual account balance as of the end of the previous year. The account may grow at a faster or a slower rate than projected. In any year, an amount larger than the required minimum distribution may be taken out. Taking out an amount less than the required minimum distribution is disastrous – a 50 percent penalty applies to the shortfall. Furthermore, death can cause a change in the calculation.

In the "IRA Required Minimum Distributions" spreadsheets that follow (and in the *IRA Calculator*), the columns are as described below.

Year. The year of the required minimum distribution (or potential required minimum distribution) is shown in the first column.

Age. In general, depending on whether the calculation is based on one life (generally, the owner) or two lives (the owner and a beneficiary), for each succeeding year the age of the owner is shown in one column and the age of the beneficiary in the next column (where applicable). Angle brackets, <>, indicate a switch in beneficiaries (e.g., when a spousal election is made, or when a spouse beneficiary predeceases the IRA owner). Square brackets, [], indicates the owner or the owner's spouse died in a prior year. A negative age indicates a beneficiary who is not yet born.

Account Balance (Balance), Balance Plus Interest (Balance +). Following the age column(s) is the "account balance" column. The account balance here is as of December 31 of the preceding year. The account balance is increased by interest in the "balance plus interest" column to show the growth of the account balance during the year prior to the required minimum distribution at the end of the year. The account balance at the beginning of the next year is then equal to the "balance plus interest" reduced by the required minimum distribution (RMD).

RMD Factors (Factor). Factors are based on either the Uniform Lifetime Table, the RMD Single Life Table, or the RMD Joint and Survivor Table. The actual factor used will depend on the RMD method being used at any time. Factors are dependent on the age of the owner (and, possibly, the beneficiary); however, the factor may not correspond to the age in the year being calculated because artificial ages (e.g., the Uniform Lifetime Table treats the beneficiary as being 10 years younger than the IRA owner) and subtract one methods (generally, for distributions after death) are sometimes used.

Required Minimum Distribution (RMD). The required minimum distribution is determined by dividing the "account balance" as of the end of the preceding year by the RMD factor. If the amount determined in this fashion exceeds the amount in the "balance plus interest" column, the required minimum distribution equals the "balance plus interest." If the factor is zero (division by zero is not permissible), the amount distributed also equals the "balance plus interest."

A total is provided at the bottom of the "IRA Required Minimum Distributions" spreadsheets for the total required minimum distributions for the years shown. This is a simple total of the benefit provided from the IRA during those years.

Illustrative Calculations

The following figures show a number of examples of required minimum distribution calculations for nonRoth IRAs [see Figures 13.1 to 13.15] and Roth IRAs [see Figures 13.16 to 13.19]; where the IRA owner's starting age is 70 [see Figure 13.2] or 71 [see Figure 13.3]; where there is no beneficiary [see Figures 13.1 to 13.3, and 13.16], a nonspouse beneficiary [see Figures 13.4 to 13.6], or a spouse beneficiary [see Figures 13.7 to 13.15, and 13.18 to 13.19]; where a spouse is beneficiary but predeceases the IRA owner [see Figures 13.7 to 13.9]; where a spousal election is made [see Figures 13.14 to 13.15, and 13.18 to 13.19] or is not made [see Figures 13.11 to 13.13]; where the spouse has a beneficiary [see Figures 13.15 to 13.16, and 13.19] or doesn't have a beneficiary [see Figure 13.14]; where a spouse is beneficiary but disclaims [see Figure 13.10]; where payments are annuitized [see Figure 13.20]; and more.

FIGURE 13.1

NonRoth IRA, No Beneficiary, Owner Dies Before RBD

In the case of a nonRoth IRA, the required beginning date (RBD) is generally April 1 of the year after the IRA owner attains age 70½. If the owner's birthday is in January through June, the owner attains 70½ in the year the owner is 70. If the owner's birthday is in July through December, the owner attains 70½ in the year the owner is 71.

If the IRA owner does not have a designated beneficiary and dies before the required beginning date, the entire account balance must be distributed by the end of the calendar year that contains the fifth anniversary of the owner's death. For example, if an IRA owner aged 65 dies on January 1, 2003, then the entire account must be distributed by the end of 2008.

FIGURE 13.2

NonRoth IRA, No Beneficiary, Owner Dies on or After RBD

This figure is an example of a nonRoth IRA where there is no beneficiary and the IRA owner dies on or after the required beginning date. The owner's starting age is 70 (an owner born in the second half of the year would have a starting age of 71) and the starting IRA account balance is $100,000. The Uniform Lifetime Table factor for a person age 70 equals 27.4. (Note that the Uniform Lifetime Table is used even though there is no designated beneficiary.) Adding interest at 6 percent to the starting account balance produces a "balance plus 6 percent" equal to $106,000 ($100,000 x 1.06). The required minimum distribution equals $3,650 ($100,000 ÷ 27.4).

The account balance as of the end of the first year is $102,350 ($106,000 - $3,650). The Uniform Lifetime Table factor for a person age 71 equals 26.5. Adding interest at 6 percent to the account balance produces a "balance plus 6 percent" equal to $108,491 ($102,350 x 1.06). The required minimum distribution equals $3,862 ($102,350 ÷ 26.5).

The IRA owner's age in the year of death is 87. The RMD Single Life Table factor at age 87 is 6.7. Therefore, the RMD factor in the year after death is 5.7 (6.7 - 1), and the factor is reduced by one for each year thereafter.

FIGURE 13.2 (continued)

IRA Required Minimum Distributions

IRA Type:	NonRoth	Year:	2006
Account Balance:	$100,000	Account Growth Rate:	6%
Beneficiary:	None		

IRA Owner (Current Age: 70; Age at Death: 87)

Date of Birth:	6/30/1936	Date of Death:	3/31/2023

Year	Age	Age	Account Balance	RMD Factor	Balance Plus 6%	RMD
2006	70	NA	100,000	27.4	106,000	3,650
2007	71	NA	102,350	26.5	108,491	3,862
2008	72	NA	104,629	25.6	110,907	4,087
2009	73	NA	106,820	24.7	113,229	4,325
2010	74	NA	108,904	23.8	115,438	4,576
2011	75	NA	110,862	22.9	117,514	4,841
2012	76	NA	112,673	22.0	119,433	5,122
2013	77	NA	114,311	21.2	121,170	5,392
2014	78	NA	115,778	20.3	122,725	5,703
2015	79	NA	117,022	19.5	124,043	6,001
2016	80	NA	118,042	18.7	125,125	6,312
2017	81	NA	118,813	17.9	125,942	6,638
2018	82	NA	119,304	17.1	126,462	6,977
2019	83	NA	119,485	16.3	126,654	7,330
2020	84	NA	119,324	15.5	126,483	7,698
2021	85	NA	118,785	14.8	125,912	8,026
2022	86	NA	117,886	14.1	124,959	8,361
2023	87	NA	116,598	13.4	123,594	8,701
2024	[88]	NA	114,893	5.7	121,787	20,157
2025	[89]	NA	101,630	4.7	107,728	21,623
2026	[90]	NA	86,105	3.7	91,271	23,272
2027	[91]	NA	67,999	2.7	72,079	25,185
2028	[92]	NA	46,894	1.7	49,708	27,585
2029	[93]	NA	22,123	0.7	23,450	23,450
					Total	248,874

FIGURE 13.3

NonRoth IRA, No Beneficiary, Owner Dies on or After RBD, Owner Age 71

This figure is an example of a nonRoth IRA where there is no beneficiary and the IRA owner dies on or after the required beginning date. The owner's starting age is 71 (an owner born in the first half of the year would have a starting age of 70) and the starting IRA account balance is $100,000. The Uniform Lifetime Table factor for a person age 71 equals 26.5. (Note that the Uniform Lifetime Table is used even though there is no designated beneficiary.) Adding interest at 6 percent to the starting account balance produces a "balance plus 6 percent" equal to $106,000 ($100,000 x 1.06). The required minimum distribution equals $3,774 ($100,000 ÷ 26.5).

The account balance as of the end of the first year is $102,226 ($106,000 - $3,774). The Uniform Lifetime Table factor for a person age 72 equals 25.6. Adding interest at 6 percent to the account balance produces a "balance plus 6 percent" equal to $108,360 ($102,226 x 1.06). The required minimum distribution equals $3,993 ($102,226 ÷ 25.6).

The IRA owner's age in the year of death is 87. The RMD Single Life Table factor at age 87 is 6.7. Therefore, the RMD factor in the year after death is 5.7 (6.7 - 1), and the factor is reduced by one for each year thereafter.

FIGURE 13.3 (continued)

IRA Required Minimum Distributions

IRA Type:	NonRoth	Year:	2006
Account Balance:	$100,000	Account Growth Rate:	6%
Beneficiary:	None		

IRA Owner (Current Age: 71; Age at Death: 87)

Date of Birth:	7/1/1935	Date of Death:	3/31/2022

Year	Age	Age	Account Balance	RMD Factor	Balance Plus 6%	RMD
2006	71	NA	100,000	26.5	106,000	3,774
2007	72	NA	102,226	25.6	108,360	3,993
2008	73	NA	104,367	24.7	110,629	4,225
2009	74	NA	106,404	23.8	112,788	4,471
2010	75	NA	108,317	22.9	114,816	4,730
2011	76	NA	110,086	22.0	116,691	5,004
2012	77	NA	111,687	21.2	118,388	5,268
2013	78	NA	113,120	20.3	119,907	5,572
2014	79	NA	114,335	19.5	121,195	5,863
2015	80	NA	115,332	18.7	122,252	6,167
2016	81	NA	116,085	17.9	123,050	6,485
2017	82	NA	116,565	17.1	123,559	6,817
2018	83	NA	116,742	16.3	123,747	7,162
2019	84	NA	116,585	15.5	123,580	7,522
2020	85	NA	116,058	14.8	123,021	7,842
2021	86	NA	115,179	14.1	122,090	8,169
2022	87	NA	113,921	13.4	120,756	8,502
2023	[88]	NA	112,254	5.7	118,989	19,694
2024	[89]	NA	99,295	4.7	105,253	21,127
2025	[90]	NA	84,126	3.7	89,174	22,737
2026	[91]	NA	66,437	2.7	70,423	24,606
2027	[92]	NA	45,817	1.7	48,566	26,951
2028	[93]	NA	21,615	0.7	22,912	22,912

Total   239,593

FIGURE 13.4

NonRoth IRA, Nonspouse Beneficiary, Owner Dies on or After RBD

This figure is an example of a nonRoth IRA where there is a beneficiary other than the spouse and the IRA owner dies on or after the required beginning date. The owner is age 80 and is projected to die at age 85. The beneficiary is age 50. (If the beneficiary is the same age or older than the IRA owner, see Figure 13.5.) The starting IRA account balance is $100,000. The Uniform Lifetime Table factor for a person age 80 equals 18.7. (Note that the Uniform Lifetime Table is used and the age of the nonspouse beneficiary does not matter while the IRA owner is alive.) Adding interest at 6 percent to the starting account balance produces a "balance plus 6 percent" equal to $106,000 ($100,000 x 1.06). The required minimum distribution equals $5,348 ($100,000 ÷ 18.7).

The account balance as of the end of the first year is $100,652 ($106,000 - $5,348). The Uniform Lifetime Table factor for a person age 81 equals 17.9. Adding interest at 6 percent to the account balance produces a "balance plus 6 percent" equal to $106,691 ($100,652 x 1.06). The required minimum distribution equals $5,623 ($100,652 ÷ 25.6).

The beneficiary's age in the year after the death of the IRA owner is 56. The RMD Single Life Table factor at age 56 is 28.7. Therefore, the RMD factor in the year after death is 28.7, and the factor is reduced by one for each year thereafter.

FIGURE 13.4 (continued)

IRA Required Minimum Distributions

IRA Type:	NonRoth	Year:	2006
Account Balance:	$100,000	Account Growth Rate:	6%
Beneficiary:	Other Than Spouse		

IRA Owner (Current Age: 80; Age at Death: 85)

Date of Birth:	6/30/1926	Date of Death:	3/31/2011

Owner's Other Beneficiary (Current Age: 50)	Date of Birth:	6/30/1956

Year	Age	Age	Account Balance	RMD Factor	Balance Plus 6%	RMD
2006	80	50	100,000	18.7	106,000	5,348
2007	81	51	100,652	17.9	106,691	5,623
2008	82	52	101,068	17.1	107,132	5,910
2009	83	53	101,222	16.3	107,295	6,210
2010	84	54	101,085	15.5	107,150	6,522
2011	85	55	100,628	14.8	106,666	6,799
2012	[86]	56	99,867	28.7	105,859	3,480
2013	[87]	57	102,379	27.7	108,522	3,696
2014	[88]	58	104,826	26.7	111,116	3,926
2015	[89]	59	107,190	25.7	113,621	4,171
2016	[90]	60	109,450	24.7	116,017	4,431
2017	[91]	61	111,586	23.7	118,281	4,708
2018	[92]	62	113,573	22.7	120,387	5,003
2019	[93]	63	115,384	21.7	122,307	5,317
2020	[94]	64	116,990	20.7	124,009	5,652
2021	[95]	65	118,357	19.7	125,458	6,008
2022	[96]	66	119,450	18.7	126,617	6,388
2023	[97]	67	120,229	17.7	127,443	6,793
2024	[98]	68	120,650	16.7	127,889	7,225
2025	[99]	69	120,664	15.7	127,904	7,686
2026	[100]	70	120,218	14.7	127,431	8,178
2027	[101]	71	119,253	13.7	126,408	8,705
2028	[102]	72	117,703	12.7	124,765	9,268
2029	[103]	73	115,497	11.7	122,427	9,872
2030	[104]	74	112,555	10.7	119,308	10,519
2031	[105]	75	108,789	9.7	115,316	11,215
2032	[106]	76	104,101	8.7	110,347	11,966
2033	[107]	77	98,381	7.7	104,284	12,777
2034	[108]	78	91,507	6.7	96,997	13,658
2035	[109]	79	83,339	5.7	88,339	14,621
2036	[110]	80	73,718	4.7	78,141	15,685
2037	[111]	81	62,456	3.7	66,203	16,880
2038	[112]	82	49,323	2.7	52,282	18,268
2039	[113]	83	34,014	1.7	36,055	20,008
2040	[114]	84	16,047	0.7	17,010	17,010
					Total	309,533

FIGURE 13.5

NonRoth IRA, Same Age or Older
Nonspouse Beneficiary

This figure is an example of a nonRoth IRA where there is a beneficiary, other than the spouse, who is the same age or older than the IRA owner and the IRA owner dies on or after the required beginning date. The owner is age 80 and is projected to die at age 85. The beneficiary is age 83. The starting IRA account balance is $100,000. The Uniform Lifetime Table factor for a person age 80 equals 18.7. (Note that the Uniform Lifetime Table is used and the age of the nonspouse beneficiary does not matter while the IRA owner is alive.) Adding interest at 6 percent to the starting account balance produces a "balance plus 6 percent" equal to $106,000 ($100,000 x 1.06). The required minimum distribution equals $5,348 ($100,000 ÷ 18.7).

The account balance as of the end of the first year is $100,652 ($106,000 - $5,348). The Uniform Lifetime Table factor for a person age 81 equals 17.9. Adding interest at 6 percent to the account balance produces a "balance plus 6 percent" equal to $106,691 ($100,652 x 1.06). The required minimum distribution equals $5,623 ($100,652 ÷ 17.9).

The RMD Single Life Table factor for the owner in the year of death is 7.6. The RMD factor for the owner in the year after death would be 6.6 (7.6 - 1). The beneficiary's age in the year after the death of the IRA owner is 89. The RMD Single Life Table factor at age 89 is 5.9. The RMD factor in the year after death is the higher of the two factors, or 6.6, and the factor is reduced by one for each year thereafter.

FIGURE 13.5 (continued)

IRA Required Minimum Distributions

IRA Type:		NonRoth	Year:		2006	
Account Balance:		$100,000	Account Growth Rate:		6%	
Beneficiary:		Other Than Spouse				

IRA Owner (Current Age: 80; Age at Death: 85)

Date of Birth:	6/30/1926	Date of Death:	3/31/2011

Owner's Other Beneficiary (Current Age: 83)		Date of Birth:	6/30/1923

Year	Age	Age	Account Balance	RMD Factor	Balance Plus 6%	RMD
2006	80	83	100,000	18.7	106,000	5,348
2007	81	84	100,652	17.9	106,691	5,623
2008	82	85	101,068	17.1	107,132	5,910
2009	83	86	101,222	16.3	107,295	6,210
2010	84	87	101,085	15.5	107,150	6,522
2011	85	88	100,628	14.8	106,666	6,799
2012	[86]	89	99,867	6.6	105,859	15,131
2013	[87]	90	90,728	5.6	96,172	16,201
2014	[88]	91	79,971	4.6	84,769	17,385
2015	[89]	92	67,384	3.6	71,427	18,718
2016	[90]	93	52,709	2.6	55,872	20,273
2017	[91]	94	35,599	1.6	37,735	22,249
2018	[92]	95	15,486	0.6	16,415	16,415

	Total	162,784

FIGURE 13.6

NonRoth IRA, Nonspouse Beneficiary, Owner Dies Before RBD

This figure is an example of a nonRoth IRA where there is a beneficiary other than the spouse and the IRA owner dies before the required beginning date. The owner would be age 60 and died at age 59. The beneficiary is age 65. The starting IRA account balance is $100,000.

The beneficiary's age in the year after the death of the IRA owner is 65. The RMD Single Life Table factor at age 65 is 21.0. Therefore, the RMD factor in the year after death is 21.0, and the factor is reduced by one for each year thereafter.

The RMD Single Life Table factor for the owner in the year of death would be 26.1. The RMD factor for the owner in the year after death would be 25.1 (26.1 - 1). However, since the IRA owner died before the required beginning date, the RMD factor for the owner cannot be used even though it is higher than the RMD factor for the beneficiary. See Figure 13.5.

FIGURE 13.6 (continued)

IRA Required Minimum Distributions

IRA Type:	NonRoth	Year:	2006
Account Balance:	$100,000	Account Growth Rate:	6%
Beneficiary:	Other Than Spouse		

IRA Owner (Current Age: 60; Age at Death: 59)

Date of Birth:	6/30/1946	Date of Death:	3/31/2005

Owner's Other Beneficiary (Current Age: 65)		Date of Birth:	6/30/1941

Year	Age	Age	Account Balance	RMD Factor	Balance Plus 6%	RMD
2006	[60]	65	100,000	21.0	106,000	4,762
2007	[61]	66	101,238	20.0	107,312	5,062
2008	[62]	67	102,250	19.0	108,385	5,382
2009	[63]	68	103,003	18.0	109,183	5,722
2010	[64]	69	103,461	17.0	109,669	6,086
2011	[65]	70	103,583	16.0	109,798	6,474
2012	[66]	71	103,324	15.0	109,523	6,888
2013	[67]	72	102,635	14.0	108,793	7,331
2014	[68]	73	101,462	13.0	107,550	7,805
2015	[69]	74	99,745	12.0	105,730	8,312
2016	[70]	75	97,418	11.0	103,263	8,856
2017	[71]	76	94,407	10.0	100,071	9,441
2018	[72]	77	90,630	9.0	96,068	10,070
2019	[73]	78	85,998	8.0	91,158	10,750
2020	[74]	79	80,408	7.0	85,232	11,487
2021	[75]	80	73,745	6.0	78,170	12,291
2022	[76]	81	65,879	5.0	69,832	13,176
2023	[77]	82	56,656	4.0	60,055	14,164
2024	[78]	83	45,891	3.0	48,644	15,297
2025	[79]	84	33,347	2.0	35,348	16,674
2026	[80]	85	18,674	1.0	19,794	18,674
2027	[81]	86	1,120	0.0	1,187	1,187
					Total	205,893

FIGURE 13.7

NonRoth IRA, Spouse Beneficiary Predeceases, No Secondary Beneficiary

This figure is an example of a nonRoth IRA where there is a spouse beneficiary, the spouse predeceases the IRA owner, and the IRA owner dies on or after the required beginning date but without a secondary beneficiary. The owner is age 80 and dies at age 85. The spouse beneficiary is age 75 and dies at age 78. The starting IRA account balance is $100,000.

The Uniform Lifetime Table factor for a person age 80 equals 18.7. (The Uniform Lifetime Table is used because the spouse is not more than 10 years younger than the IRA owner. If the spouse is more than 10 years younger than the IRA owner, see Figure 13.8.)

After the spouse dies at age 78, the Uniform Lifetime Table continues to be used while the IRA owner is alive. Therefore, since the IRA owner is age 84 in the year after the spouse's death, the RMD factor for that year is 15.5.

The IRA owner's age in the year of death is 85. The RMD Single Life Table factor at age 85 is 7.6. Therefore, the RMD factor in the year after death is 6.6 (7.6 - 1), and the factor is reduced by one for each year thereafter.

FIGURE 13.7 (continued)

IRA Required Minimum Distributions

IRA Type:			NonRoth	Year:		2006
Account Balance:			$100,000	Account Growth Rate:		6%
Beneficiary:			Spouse	Secondary Beneficiary:		No

IRA Owner (Current Age: 80; Age at Death: 85)
Date of Birth:		6/30/1926	Date of Death:	3/31/2011

Spouse Beneficiary (Current Age: 75; Age at Death: 78)
Date of Birth:		6/30/1931	Date of Death:	3/31/2009
Spouse Election:		NA	Spouse Predeceases:	NA

Year	Age	Age	Account Balance	RMD Factor	Balance Plus 6%	RMD
2006	80	75	100,000	18.7	106,000	5,348
2007	81	76	100,652	17.9	106,691	5,623
2008	82	77	101,068	17.1	107,132	5,910
2009	83	78	101,222	16.3	107,295	6,210
2010	84	NA	101,085	15.5	107,150	6,522
2011	85	NA	100,628	14.8	106,666	6,799
2012	[86]	NA	99,867	6.6	105,859	15,131
2013	[87]	NA	90,728	5.6	96,172	16,201
2014	[88]	NA	79,971	4.6	84,769	17,385
2015	[89]	NA	67,384	3.6	71,427	18,718
2016	[90]	NA	52,709	2.6	55,872	20,273
2017	[91]	NA	35,599	1.6	37,735	22,249
2018	[92]	NA	15,486	0.6	16,415	16,415

Total	162,784

FIGURE 13.8

NonRoth IRA, Much Younger Spouse Beneficiary Predeceases, No Secondary Beneficiary

This figure is an example of a nonRoth IRA where there is a spouse beneficiary who is more than 10 years younger than the IRA owner, the spouse predeceases the IRA owner, and the IRA owner dies on or after the required beginning date but without a secondary beneficiary. The owner is age 80 and dies at age 85. The spouse beneficiary is age 67 and dies at age 70. The starting IRA account balance is $100,000.

The RMD Joint and Survivor Table factor for two persons age 80 and 67 equals 20.6. [The RMD Joint and Survivor Table is used instead of the Uniform Lifetime Table (the ULT factor would only be 18.7) because the spouse is more than 10 years younger than the IRA owner. If the spouse is not more than 10 years younger than the IRA owner, see Figure 13.7.]

After the spouse dies at age 70, the Uniform Lifetime Table is then used while the IRA owner is alive. Therefore, since the IRA owner is age 84 in the year after the spouse's death, the RMD factor for that year is 15.5.

The IRA owner's age in the year of death is 85. The RMD Single Life Table factor at age 85 is 7.6. Therefore, the RMD factor in the year after death is 6.6 (7.6 - 1), and the factor is reduced by one for each year thereafter.

FIGURE 13.8 (continued)

IRA Required Minimum Distributions

IRA Type:	NonRoth	Year:	2006
Account Balance:	$100,000	Account Growth Rate:	6%
Beneficiary:	Spouse	Secondary Beneficiary:	No

IRA Owner (Current Age: 80; Age at Death: 85)

Date of Birth:	6/30/1926	Date of Death:	3/31/2011

Spouse Beneficiary (Current Age: 67; Age at Death: 70)

Date of Birth:	6/30/1939	Date of Death:	3/31/2009
Spouse Election:	NA	Spouse Predeceases:	NA

Year	Age	Age	Account Balance	RMD Factor	Balance Plus 6%	RMD
2006	80	67	100,000	20.6	106,000	4,854
2007	81	68	101,146	19.8	107,215	5,108
2008	82	69	102,107	19.0	108,233	5,374
2009	83	70	102,859	18.2	109,031	5,652
2010	84	NA	103,379	15.5	109,582	6,670
2011	85	NA	102,912	14.8	109,087	6,954
2012	[86]	NA	102,133	6.6	108,261	15,475
2013	[87]	NA	92,786	5.6	98,353	16,569
2014	[88]	NA	81,784	4.6	86,691	17,779
2015	[89]	NA	68,912	3.6	73,047	19,142
2016	[90]	NA	53,905	2.6	57,139	20,733
2017	[91]	NA	36,406	1.6	38,590	22,754
2018	[92]	NA	15,836	0.6	16,786	16,786

| | | | | | Total | 163,850 |

FIGURE 13.9

NonRoth IRA, Spouse Beneficiary Predeceases, Secondary Beneficiary

This figure is an example of a nonRoth IRA where there is a spouse beneficiary who predeceases the IRA owner, and the IRA owner dies on or after the required beginning date with a secondary beneficiary. The owner is age 80 and dies at age 85. The spouse beneficiary is age 67 and dies at age 70. The secondary beneficiary is age 50. The starting IRA account balance is $100,000.

The RMD Joint and Survivor Table factor for two persons age 80 and 67 equals 20.6. [The RMD Joint and Survivor Table is used instead of the Uniform Lifetime Table (the ULT factor would only be 18.7) because the spouse is more than 10 years younger than the IRA owner. If the spouse is not more than 10 years younger than the IRA owner, see Figure 13.7.]

After the spouse dies at age 70, the Uniform Lifetime Table is then used while the IRA owner is alive. Therefore, since the IRA owner is age 84 in the year after the spouse's death, the RMD factor for that year is 15.5.

The RMD Single Life Table factor for the owner in the year of death would be 7.6. The RMD factor for the owner in the year after death would be 6.6 (7.6 - 1). The beneficiary's age in the year after the death of the IRA owner is 56. The RMD Single Life Table factor at age 56 is 28.7. Therefore, the RMD factor in the year after death is the higher of the two factors, or 28.7, and the factor is reduced by one for each year thereafter.

FIGURE 13.9 (continued)

IRA Required Minimum Distributions

IRA Type:		NonRoth	Year:		2006	
Account Balance:		$100,000	Account Growth Rate:		6%	
Beneficiary:		Spouse	Secondary Beneficiary:		Yes	

IRA Owner (Current Age: 80; Age at Death: 85)
Date of Birth: 6/30/1926   Date of Death: 3/31/2011

Spouse Beneficiary (Current Age: 67; Age at Death: 70)
Date of Birth: 6/30/1939   Date of Death: 3/31/2009
Spousal Election: NA   Spouse Predeceases: NA

Owner's Other Beneficiary (Current Age: 50)   Date of Birth: 6/30/1956

Year	Age	Age	Account Balance	RMD Factor	Balance Plus 6%	RMD
2006	80	67	100,000	20.6	106,000	4,854
2007	81	68	101,146	19.8	107,215	5,108
2008	82	69	102,107	19.0	108,233	5,374
2009	83	70	102,859	18.2	109,031	5,652
2010	84	<54>	103,379	15.5	109,582	6,670
2011	85	<55>	102,912	14.8	109,087	6,954
2012	[86]	<56>	102,133	28.7	108,261	3,559
2013	[87]	<57>	104,702	27.7	110,984	3,780
2014	[88]	<58>	107,204	26.7	113,636	4,015
2015	[89]	<59>	109,621	25.7	116,198	4,265
2016	[90]	<60>	111,933	24.7	118,649	4,532
2017	[91]	<61>	114,117	23.7	120,964	4,815
2018	[92]	<62>	116,149	22.7	123,118	5,117
2019	[93]	<63>	118,001	21.7	125,081	5,438
2020	[94]	<64>	119,643	20.7	126,822	5,780
2021	[95]	<65>	121,042	19.7	128,305	6,144
2022	[96]	<66>	122,161	18.7	129,491	6,533
2023	[97]	<67>	122,958	17.7	130,335	6,947
2024	[98]	<68>	123,388	16.7	130,791	7,389
2025	[99]	<69>	123,402	15.7	130,806	7,860
2026	[100]	<70>	122,946	14.7	130,323	8,364
2027	[101]	<71>	121,959	13.7	129,277	8,902
2028	[102]	<72>	120,375	12.7	127,597	9,478
2029	[103]	<73>	118,119	11.7	125,206	10,096
2030	[104]	<74>	115,110	10.7	122,017	10,758
2031	[105]	<75>	111,259	9.7	117,935	11,470
2032	[106]	<76>	106,465	8.7	112,853	12,237
2033	[107]	<77>	100,616	7.7	106,653	13,067
2034	[108]	<78>	93,586	6.7	99,201	13,968
2035	[109]	<79>	85,233	5.7	90,347	14,953
2036	[110]	<80>	75,394	4.7	79,918	16,041
2037	[111]	<81>	63,877	3.7	67,710	17,264
2038	[112]	<82>	50,446	2.7	53,473	18,684
2039	[113]	<83>	34,789	1.7	36,876	20,464
2040	[114]	<84>	16,412	0.7	17,397	17,397
					Total	313,927

FIGURE 13.10

NonRoth IRA, Spouse Beneficiary Disclaims, No Secondary Beneficiary

This figure is an example of a nonRoth IRA where there is a spouse beneficiary who survives the IRA owner but disclaims the IRA, and the IRA owner dies on or after the required beginning date but without a secondary beneficiary. The owner is age 80 and dies at age 85. The spouse beneficiary is age 75 and disclaims the IRA after the death of the IRA owner. The starting IRA account balance is $100,000.

The Uniform Lifetime Table factor for two persons age 80 and 70 equals 18.7. (The RMD Joint and Survivor Table is not used because the spouse is not more than 10 years younger than the IRA owner.)

Since the spouse beneficiary disclaims the IRA after the death of the IRA owner, the spouse is treated as dying on the same day as the IRA owner and as predeceasing the IRA owner.

The RMD Single Life Table factor for the owner in the year of death would be 7.6. The RMD factor for the owner in the year after the owner's death would be 6.6 (7.6 - 1), and the factor is reduced by one for each year thereafter.

If there was a secondary beneficiary after the death of the IRA owner, the IRA could be distributed over the longer of the life expectancy of the IRA owner or the life expectancy of the beneficiary.

FIGURE 13.10 (continued)

IRA Required Minimum Distributions

IRA Type:	NonRoth	Year:	2006
Account Balance:	$100,000	Account Growth Rate:	6%
Beneficiary:	Spouse	Secondary Beneficiary:	No

IRA Owner (Current Age: 80; Age at Death: 85)

| Date of Birth: | 6/30/1926 | Date of Death: | 3/31/2011 |

Spouse Beneficiary (Current Age: 70; Age at Death: 75)

| Date of Birth: | 6/30/1936 | Date of Death: | 3/31/2011 |
| Spousal Election: | No | Spouse Predeceases: | Yes |

Year	Age	Age	Account Balance	RMD Factor	Balance Plus 6%	RMD
2006	80	70	100,000	18.7	106,000	5,348
2007	81	71	100,652	17.9	106,691	5,623
2008	82	72	101,068	17.1	107,132	5,910
2009	83	73	101,222	16.3	107,295	6,210
2010	84	74	101,085	15.5	107,150	6,522
2011	85	75	100,628	14.8	106,666	6,799
2012	[86]	NA	99,867	6.6	105,859	15,131
2013	[87]	NA	90,728	5.6	96,172	16,201
2014	[88]	NA	79,971	4.6	84,769	17,385
2015	[89]	NA	67,384	3.6	71,427	18,718
2016	[90]	NA	52,709	2.6	55,872	20,273
2017	[91]	NA	35,599	1.6	37,735	22,249
2018	[92]	NA	15,486	0.6	16,415	16,415

| | | | | | Total | 162,784 |

FIGURE 13.11

NonRoth IRA, Spouse Beneficiary Without Election, No Secondary Beneficiary

This figure is an example of a nonRoth IRA where there is a spouse beneficiary who survives the IRA owner but no spousal election is made, and the IRA owner dies on or after the required beginning date but without a secondary beneficiary. The owner is age 80 and dies at age 85. The spouse beneficiary is age 75 and dies at age 88. The starting IRA account balance is $100,000.

The Uniform Lifetime Table factor for an IRA owner age 80 equals 18.7. (The RMD Joint and Survivor Table is not used because the spouse is not more than 10 years younger than the IRA owner.)

The RMD Single Life Table factor for the owner in the year of death would be 7.6. The RMD factor for the owner in the year after the owner's death would be 6.6 (7.6 - 1). The spouse is age 81 in the year after the IRA owner's death. Therefore, the RMD Single Life Table factor for the spouse for that year would be 9.7. Since 9.7 is greater than 7.6, the RMD Single Life Table using the spouse's age is then used while the spouse is alive. (If the RMD life expectancy factor for the IRA owner in the year after the owner's death were greater than the RMD life expectancy factor for the spouse, see Figure 13.12.)

The RMD Single Life Table factor for the spouse in the year of death is 6.3. Therefore, the RMD factor in the year after the spouse's death is 5.3 (6.3 - 1), and the factor is reduced by one for each year thereafter.

FIGURE 13.11 (continued)

IRA Required Minimum Distributions

IRA Type:	NonRoth	Year: 2006
Account Balance:	$100,000	Account Growth Rate: 6%
Beneficiary:	Spouse	Secondary Beneficiary: NA

IRA Owner (Current Age: 80; Age at Death: 85)

Date of Birth:	6/30/1926	Date of Death:	3/31/2011

Spouse Beneficiary (Current Age: 75; Age at Death: 88)

Date of Birth:	6/30/1931	Date of Death:	3/31/2019
Spousal Election:	No	Spouse Predeceases:	NA

Year	Age	Age	Account Balance	RMD Factor	Balance Plus 6%	RMD
2006	80	75	100,000	18.7	106,000	5,348
2007	81	76	100,652	17.9	106,691	5,623
2008	82	77	101,068	17.1	107,132	5,910
2009	83	78	101,222	16.3	107,295	6,210
2010	84	79	101,085	15.5	107,150	6,522
2011	85	80	100,628	14.8	106,666	6,799
2012	[86]	81	99,867	9.7	105,859	10,296
2013	[87]	82	95,563	9.1	101,297	10,501
2014	[88]	83	90,796	8.6	96,244	10,558
2015	[89]	84	85,686	8.1	90,827	10,579
2016	[90]	85	80,248	7.6	85,063	10,559
2017	[91]	86	74,504	7.1	78,974	10,494
2018	[92]	87	68,480	6.7	72,589	10,221
2019	[93]	88	62,368	6.3	66,110	9,900
2020	[94]	[89]	56,210	5.3	59,583	10,606
2021	[95]	[90]	48,977	4.3	51,916	11,390
2022	[96]	[91]	40,526	3.3	42,958	12,281
2023	[97]	[92]	30,677	2.3	32,518	13,338
2024	[98]	[93]	19,180	1.3	20,331	14,754
2025	[99]	[94]	5,577	0.3	5,912	5,912
					Total	187,800

FIGURE 13.12

NonRoth IRA, Older Spouse Beneficiary
Without Election

This figure is an example of a nonRoth IRA where there is an older spouse beneficiary who survives the IRA owner but no spousal election is made, and the IRA owner dies on or after the required beginning date. The owner is age 80 and dies at age 85. The spouse beneficiary is age 83 and dies at age 92. The starting IRA account balance is $100,000.

The Uniform Lifetime Table factor for two persons age 80 and 75 equals 18.7. (The RMD Joint and Survivor Table is not used because the spouse is not more than 10 years younger than the IRA owner.)

The RMD Single Life Table factor for the owner in the year of death would be 7.6. The RMD factor for the owner in the year after the owner's death would be 6.6 (7.6 - 1). The spouse is age 89 in the year after the IRA owner's death. Therefore, the RMD Single Life Table factor for the spouse for that year would be 5.9. The RMD factor for the year after the IRA owner's death is the greater of the two factors, or 6.6.

For the next year (2013), the RMD factor for the owner would be 5.6 (6.6 - 1). The spouse is age 90 in that year. Therefore, the RMD Single Life Table factor for the spouse for that year would be 5.5. The RMD factor for year 2013 is the greater of the two factors, or 5.6.

For the next year (2014), the RMD factor for the owner would be 4.6 (5.6 - 1). The spouse is age 91 in that year. Therefore, the RMD Single Life Table factor for the spouse for that year would be 5.2. Since 5.2 is greater than 4.6, the RMD Single Life Table using the spouse's age is then used while the spouse is alive.

The RMD Single Life Table factor for the spouse in the year of death is 4.9. The RMD factor for the spouse in the year after death is 3.9 (4.9 - 1). Therefore, the RMD factor in the year after the spouse's death is 3.9, and the factor is reduced by one for each year thereafter.

FIGURE 13.12 (continued)

IRA Required Minimum Distributions

| IRA Type: | NonRoth | Year: | 2006 |
IRA Type:		Year:	
IRA Type:	NonRoth	Year:	2006
Account Balance:	$100,000	Account Growth Rate:	6%
Beneficiary:	Spouse	Secondary Beneficiary:	NA

IRA Owner (Current Age: 80; Age at Death: 85)

Date of Birth:	6/30/1926	Date of Death:	3/31/2011

Spouse Beneficiary (Current Age: 83; Age at Death: 92)

Date of Birth:	6/30/1923	Date of Death:	3/31/2015
Spousal Election:	No	Spouse Predeceases:	NA

Year	Age	Age	Account Balance	RMD Factor	Balance Plus 6%	RMD
2006	80	83	100,000	18.7	106,000	5,348
2007	81	84	100,652	17.9	106,691	5,623
2008	82	85	101,068	17.1	107,132	5,910
2009	83	86	101,222	16.3	107,295	6,210
2010	84	87	101,085	15.5	107,150	6,522
2011	85	88	100,628	14.8	106,666	6,799
2012	[86]	89	99,867	6.6	105,859	15,131
2013	[87]	90	90,728	5.6	96,172	16,201
2014	[88]	91	79,971	5.2	84,769	15,379
2015	[89]	92	69,390	4.9	73,553	14,161
2016	[90]	[93]	59,392	3.9	62,956	15,229
2017	[91]	[94]	47,727	2.9	50,591	16,458
2018	[92]	[95]	34,133	1.9	36,181	17,965
2019	[93]	[96]	18,216	0.9	19,309	19,309
					Total	166,245

FIGURE 13.13

NonRoth IRA, Older Spouse Beneficiary Without Election, Owner Dies Before RBD

This figure is an example of a nonRoth IRA where there is an older spouse beneficiary who survives the IRA owner but no spousal election is made, and the IRA owner dies before the required beginning date. The owner is age 65 and died at age 64. The spouse beneficiary is age 70 and dies at age 87. The starting IRA account balance is $100,000.

Distributions were not required in the year of the IRA owner's death because the owner had not reached his required beginning date. In addition, since the spouse is the beneficiary, required minimum distributions are not required until the year the IRA owner would have attained age 70½ (2011). The spouse is age 75 in 2011. Therefore, the RMD Single Life Table factor for the spouse for that year would be 13.4.

The RMD Single Life Table factor for the spouse in the year of the spouse's death would be 6.7. The RMD factor for the spouse in the year after the spouse's death would be 5.7 (6.7 - 1), and the factor is reduced by one for each year thereafter.

FIGURE 13.13 (continued)

IRA Required Minimum Distributions

IRA Type:	NonRoth	Year:	2006
Account Balance:	$100,000	Account Growth Rate:	6%
Beneficiary:	Spouse	Secondary Beneficiary:	NA

IRA Owner (Current Age: 65; Age at Death: 64)

Date of Birth:	6/30/1941	Date of Death:	3/31/2005

Spouse Beneficiary (Current Age: 70; Age at Death: 87)

Date of Birth:	6/30/1936	Date of Death:	3/31/2023
Spousal Election:	No	Spouse Predeceases:	No

Year	Age	Age	Account Balance	RMD Factor	Balance Plus 6%	RMD
2006	[65]	70	100,000	NA	106,000	0
2007	[66]	71	106,000	NA	112,360	0
2008	[67]	72	112,360	NA	119,102	0
2009	[68]	73	119,102	NA	126,248	0
2010	[69]	74	126,248	NA	133,823	0
2011	[70]	75	133,823	13.4	141,852	9,987
2012	[71]	76	131,865	12.7	139,777	10,383
2013	[72]	77	129,394	12.1	137,158	10,694
2014	[73]	78	126,464	11.4	134,052	11,093
2015	[74]	79	122,959	10.8	130,337	11,385
2016	[75]	80	118,952	10.2	126,089	11,662
2017	[76]	81	114,427	9.7	121,293	11,797
2018	[77]	82	109,496	9.1	116,066	12,033
2019	[78]	83	104,033	8.6	110,275	12,097
2020	[79]	84	98,178	8.1	104,069	12,121
2021	[80]	85	91,948	7.6	97,465	12,098
2022	[81]	86	85,367	7.1	90,489	12,024
2023	[82]	87	78,465	6.7	83,173	11,711
2024	[83]	[88]	71,462	5.7	75,750	12,537
2025	[84]	[89]	63,213	4.7	67,006	13,450
2026	[85]	[90]	53,556	3.7	56,769	14,475
2027	[86]	[91]	42,294	2.7	44,832	15,664
2028	[87]	[92]	29,168	1.7	30,918	17,158
2029	[88]	[93]	13,760	0.7	14,586	14,586
					Total	236,951

FIGURE 13.14

NonRoth IRA, Spouse Beneficiary With Election, No Secondary Beneficiary

This figure is an example of a nonRoth IRA where there is a spouse beneficiary who makes the election to treat the IRA as the spouse's own, and there is no secondary beneficiary. The IRA owner is age 80 and dies at age 85. The spouse beneficiary is age 75 and dies at age 88. The starting IRA account balance is $100,000.

The Uniform Lifetime Table factor for an IRA owner 80 equals 18.7. (The RMD Joint and Survivor Table is not used because the spouse is not more than 10 years younger than the IRA owner.)

After the IRA owner dies and the spousal election is made, the spouse is treated as the owner of the IRA. In the year after the death of the IRA owner, the Uniform Lifetime Table factor for the IRA owner/spouse age 81 equals 17.9.

The RMD Single Life Table factor for the spouse in the year of the spouse's death would be 6.3. The RMD factor for the spouse in the year after the spouse's death would be 5.3 (6.3 - 1), and the factor is reduced by one for each year thereafter.

FIGURE 13.14 (continued)

IRA Required Minimum Distributions

IRA Type:	NonRoth	Year:	2006
Account Balance:	$100,000	Account Growth Rate:	6%
Beneficiary:	Spouse	Secondary Beneficiary:	No

IRA Owner (Current Age: 80; Age at Death: 85)

Date of Birth:	6/30/1926	Date of Death:	3/31/2011

Spouse Beneficiary (Current Age: 75; Age at Death: 88)

Date of Birth:	6/30/1931	Date of Death:	3/31/2019
Spousal Election:	Yes	Spouse Predeceases:	NA

Year	Age	Age	Account Balance	RMD Factor	Balance Plus 6%	RMD
2006	80	75	100,000	18.7	106,000	5,348
2007	81	76	100,652	17.9	106,691	5,623
2008	82	77	101,068	17.1	107,132	5,910
2009	83	78	101,222	16.3	107,295	6,210
2010	84	79	101,085	15.5	107,150	6,522
2011	85	80	100,628	14.8	106,666	6,799
2012	<81>	NA	99,867	17.9	105,859	5,579
2013	<82>	NA	100,280	17.1	106,297	5,864
2014	<83>	NA	100,433	16.3	106,459	6,162
2015	<84>	NA	100,297	15.5	106,315	6,471
2016	<85>	NA	99,844	14.8	105,835	6,746
2017	<86>	NA	99,089	14.1	105,034	7,028
2018	<87>	NA	98,006	13.4	103,886	7,314
2019	<88>	NA	96,572	12.7	102,366	7,604
2020	[<89>]	NA	94,762	5.3	100,448	17,880
2021	[<90>]	NA	82,568	4.3	87,522	19,202
2022	[<91>]	NA	68,320	3.3	72,419	20,703
2023	[<92>]	NA	51,716	2.3	54,819	22,485
2024	[<93>]	NA	32,334	1.3	34,274	24,872
2025	[<94>]	NA	9,402	0.3	9,966	9,966
					Total	204,289

FIGURE 13.15

NonRoth IRA, Spouse Beneficiary With Election, Secondary Beneficiary

This figure is an example of a nonRoth IRA where there is a spouse beneficiary who makes the election to treat the IRA as the spouse's own, and the spouse has a beneficiary. The IRA owner is age 80 and dies at age 85. The spouse beneficiary is age 75 and dies at age 88. The spouse's beneficiary is age 50. The starting IRA account balance is $100,000.

The Uniform Lifetime Table factor for an IRA owner 80 equals 18.7. (The RMD Joint and Survivor Table is not used because the spouse is not more than 10 years younger than the IRA owner.)

After the IRA owner dies and the spousal election is made, the spouse is treated as the owner of the IRA. In the year after the death of the IRA owner, the Uniform Lifetime Table factor for the IRA owner/spouse age 81 equals 17.9.

The RMD Single Life Table factor for the spouse in the year of the spouse's death would be 6.3. The RMD factor for the spouse in the year after the spouse's death would be 5.3 (6.3 - 1). The spouse's beneficiary is age 64 in the year after the spouse's death. The RMD Single Life Table factor for age 64 would be 21.8. The RMD factor for the year after the spouse's death equals the higher of the two factors, or 21.8, and the factor is reduced by one for each year thereafter.

FIGURE 13.15 (continued)

IRA Required Minimum Distributions

IRA Type:	NonRoth	Year:	2006
Account Balance:	$100,000	Account Growth Rate:	6%
Beneficiary:	Spouse	Secondary Beneficiary:	Yes

IRA Owner (Current Age: 80; Age at Death: 85)

Date of Birth:	6/30/1926	Date of Death:	3/31/2011

Spouse Beneficiary (Current Age: 75; Age at Death: 88)

Date of Birth:	6/30/1931	Date of Death:	3/31/2019
Spousal Election:	Yes	Spouse Predeceases:	NA

Spouse's Beneficiary (Current Age: 50) Date of Birth: 6/30/1953

Year	Age	Age	Account Balance	RMD Factor	Balance Plus 6%	RMD
2006	80	75	100,000	18.7	106,000	5,348
2007	81	76	100,652	17.9	106,691	5,623
2008	82	77	101,068	17.1	107,132	5,910
2009	83	78	101,222	16.3	107,295	6,210
2010	84	79	101,085	15.5	107,150	6,522
2011	85	80	100,628	14.8	106,666	6,799
2012	<81>	<56>	99,867	17.9	105,859	5,579
2013	<82>	<57>	100,280	17.1	106,297	5,864
2014	<83>	<58>	100,433	16.3	106,459	6,162
2015	<84>	<59>	100,297	15.5	106,315	6,471
2016	<85>	<60>	99,844	14.8	105,835	6,746
2017	<86>	<61>	99,089	14.1	105,034	7,028
2018	<87>	<62>	98,006	13.4	103,886	7,314
2019	<88>	<63>	96,572	12.7	102,366	7,604
2020	[<89>]	<64>	94,762	21.8	100,448	4,347
2021	[<90>]	<65>	96,101	20.8	101,867	4,620
2022	[<91>]	<66>	97,247	19.8	103,082	4,911
2023	[<92>]	<67>	98,171	18.8	104,061	5,222
2024	[<93>]	<68>	98,839	17.8	104,769	5,553
2025	[<94>]	<69>	99,216	16.8	105,169	5,906
2026	[<95>]	<70>	99,263	15.8	105,219	6,282
2027	[<96>]	<71>	98,937	14.8	104,873	6,685
2028	[<97>]	<72>	98,188	13.8	104,079	7,115
2029	[<98>]	<73>	96,964	12.8	102,782	7,575
2030	[<99>]	<74>	95,207	11.8	100,919	8,068
2031	[<100>]	<75>	92,851	10.8	98,422	8,597
2032	[<101>]	<76>	89,825	9.8	95,214	9,166
2033	[<102>]	<77>	86,048	8.8	91,211	9,778
2034	[<103>]	<78>	81,433	7.8	86,319	10,440
2035	[<104>]	<79>	75,879	6.8	80,432	11,159
2036	[<105>]	<80>	69,273	5.8	73,429	11,944
2037	[<106>]	<81>	61,485	4.8	65,174	12,809
2038	[<107>]	<82>	52,365	3.8	55,507	13,780
2039	[<108>]	<83>	41,727	2.8	44,231	14,903
2040	[<109>]	<84>	29,328	1.8	31,088	16,294
2041	[<110>]	<85>	14,795	0.8	15,682	15,682
					Total	290,018

FIGURE 13.16

Roth IRA, No Beneficiary

In the case of a Roth IRA, the required beginning date (RBD) is generally December 31 of the year after the death of the IRA owner. The owner of a Roth IRA is treated as dying before the required beginning date.

If the IRA owner does not have a designated beneficiary at death, the entire account balance must be distributed by the end of the calendar year that contains the fifth anniversary of the owner's death. For example, if an IRA owner aged 65 dies on January 1, 2003, then the entire account must be distributed by the end of 2008.

FIGURE 13.17

Roth IRA, Nonspouse Beneficiary

This figure is an example of a Roth IRA where there is a beneficiary other than the spouse of the IRA owner. The IRA owner would be age 80 and died at age 79. The nonspouse beneficiary is age 50. The starting IRA account balance is $100,000.

No required minimum distributions are required before the death of the Roth IRA owner.

The RMD Single Life Table factor for the beneficiary (age 50) in the year after the death of the IRA owner would be 34.2, and the factor is reduced by one for each year thereafter.

FIGURE 13.17 (continued)

IRA Required Minimum Distributions

IRA Type:	Roth	Year:	2006
Account Balance:	$100,000	Account Growth Rate:	6%
Beneficiary:	Other Than Spouse		

IRA Owner (Current Age: 80; Age at Death: 79)

| Date of Birth: | 6/30/1926 | Date of Death: | 3/31/2005 |

| Owner's Other Beneficiary (Current Age: 50) | | Date of Birth: | 6/30/1956 |

Year	Age	Age	Account Balance	RMD Factor	Balance Plus 6%	RMD
2006	[80]	50	100,000	34.2	106,000	2,924
2007	[81]	51	103,076	33.2	109,261	3,105
2008	[82]	52	106,156	32.2	112,525	3,297
2009	[83]	53	109,228	31.2	115,782	3,501
2010	[84]	54	112,281	30.2	119,018	3,718
2011	[85]	55	115,300	29.2	122,218	3,949
2012	[86]	56	118,269	28.2	125,365	4,194
2013	[87]	57	121,171	27.2	128,441	4,455
2014	[88]	58	123,986	26.2	131,425	4,732
2015	[89]	59	126,693	25.2	134,295	5,027
2016	[90]	60	129,268	24.2	137,024	5,342
2017	[91]	61	131,682	23.2	139,583	5,676
2018	[92]	62	133,907	22.2	141,941	6,032
2019	[93]	63	135,909	21.2	144,064	6,411
2020	[94]	64	137,653	20.2	145,912	6,815
2021	[95]	65	139,097	19.2	147,443	7,245
2022	[96]	66	140,198	18.2	148,610	7,703
2023	[97]	67	140,907	17.2	149,361	8,192
2024	[98]	68	141,169	16.2	149,639	8,714
2025	[99]	69	140,925	15.2	149,380	9,271
2026	[100]	70	140,109	14.2	148,516	9,867
2027	[101]	71	138,649	13.2	146,968	10,504
2028	[102]	72	136,464	12.2	144,652	11,186
2029	[103]	73	133,466	11.2	141,474	11,917
2030	[104]	74	129,557	10.2	137,330	12,702
2031	[105]	75	124,628	9.2	132,106	13,547
2032	[106]	76	118,559	8.2	125,673	14,458
2033	[107]	77	111,215	7.2	117,888	15,447
2034	[108]	78	102,441	6.2	108,587	16,523
2035	[109]	79	92,064	5.2	97,588	17,705
2036	[110]	80	79,883	4.2	84,676	19,020
2037	[111]	81	65,656	3.2	69,595	20,517
2038	[112]	82	49,078	2.2	52,023	22,308
2039	[113]	83	29,715	1.2	31,498	24,762
2040	[114]	84	6,736	0.2	7,140	7,140

Total   337,908

FIGURE 13.18

Roth IRA, Spouse Beneficiary Without Election

This figure is an example of a Roth IRA where there is a beneficiary who is the spouse of the IRA owner, but no spousal election is made. The IRA owner would be age 80 and died at age 79. The spouse beneficiary is age 75 and dies at age 88. The starting IRA account balance is $100,000.

No required minimum distributions are required before the death of the Roth IRA owner. (Nor would distributions be required until after the death of the spouse if the spouse elected to treat the Roth IRA as the spouse's own.)

The RMD Single Life Table factor for the spouse beneficiary (age 75) in the year after the death of the IRA owner would be 13.4.

The RMD Single Life Table factor for the spouse beneficiary (age 88) in the year of the death of the spouse is 6.3, and the factor is reduced by one for each year thereafter.

FIGURE 13.18 (continued)

IRA Required Minimum Distributions

IRA Type:	Roth	Year:	2006
Account Balance:	$100,000	Account Growth Rate:	6%
Beneficiary:	Spouse	Secondary Beneficiary:	NA

IRA Owner (Current Age: 80; Age at Death: 79)

Date of Birth:	6/30/1926	Date of Death:	3/31/2005

Spouse Beneficiary (Current Age: 75; Age at Death: 88)

Date of Birth:	6/30/1931	Date of Death:	3/31/2019
Spousal Election:	No	Spouse Predeceases:	NA

Year	Age	Age	Account Balance	RMD Factor	Balance Plus 6%	RMD
2006	[80]	75	100,000	13.4	106,000	7,463
2007	[81]	76	98,537	12.7	104,449	7,759
2008	[82]	77	96,690	12.1	102,491	7,991
2009	[83]	78	94,500	11.4	100,170	8,289
2010	[84]	79	91,881	10.8	97,394	8,507
2011	[85]	80	88,887	10.2	94,220	8,714
2012	[86]	81	85,506	9.7	90,636	8,815
2013	[87]	82	81,821	9.1	86,730	8,991
2014	[88]	83	77,739	8.6	82,403	9,039
2015	[89]	84	73,364	8.1	77,766	9,057
2016	[90]	85	68,709	7.6	72,832	9,041
2017	[91]	86	63,791	7.1	67,618	8,985
2018	[92]	87	58,633	6.7	62,151	8,751
2019	[93]	88	53,400	6.3	56,604	8,476
2020	[94]	[89]	48,128	5.3	51,016	9,081
2021	[95]	[90]	41,935	4.3	44,451	9,752
2022	[96]	[91]	34,699	3.3	36,781	10,515
2023	[97]	[92]	26,266	2.3	27,842	11,420
2024	[98]	[93]	16,422	1.3	17,407	12,632
2025	[99]	[94]	4,775	0.3	5,061	5,061
					Total	178,341

FIGURE 13.19

Roth IRA, Spouse Beneficiary With Election, Secondary Beneficiary

This figure is an example of a Roth IRA where there is a beneficiary who is the spouse of the IRA owner and the spouse elects to treat the IRA as the spouse's own, and the spouse has a beneficiary. The original IRA owner is dead. The IRA owner/spouse would be age 85 and died at age 84. The secondary beneficiary is age 50. The starting IRA account balance is $100,000.

No required minimum distributions were required before the death of the Roth IRA owner. Nor were distributions required until after the death of the spouse since the spouse elected to treat the Roth IRA as the spouse's own.

Since the original IRA owner is dead and a spousal election was made, the spouse is treated as the IRA owner.

The RMD Single Life Table factor for the secondary beneficiary (age 50) in the year after the death of the IRA owner/spouse is 34.2, and the factor is reduced by one for each year thereafter.

FIGURE 13.19 (continued)

IRA Required Minimum Distributions

IRA Type:	Roth	Year: 2006
Account Balance:	$100,000	Account Growth Rate: 6%
Beneficiary:	Other Than Spouse	

IRA Owner (Current Age: 85; Age at Death: 84)
Date of Birth: 6/30/1921   Date of Death: 3/31/2005

Owner's Other Beneficiary (Current Age: 50)   Date of Birth: 6/30/1956

Year	Age	Age	Account Balance	RMD Factor	Balance Plus 6%	RMD
2006	[85]	50	100,000	34.2	106,000	2,924
2007	[86]	51	103,076	33.2	109,261	3,105
2008	[87]	52	106,156	32.2	112,525	3,297
2009	[88]	53	109,228	31.2	115,782	3,501
2010	[89]	54	112,281	30.2	119,018	3,718
2011	[90]	55	115,300	29.2	122,218	3,949
2012	[91]	56	118,269	28.2	125,365	4,194
2013	[92]	57	121,171	27.2	128,441	4,455
2014	[93]	58	123,986	26.2	131,425	4,732
2015	[94]	59	126,693	25.2	134,295	5,027
2016	[95]	60	129,268	24.2	137,024	5,342
2017	[96]	61	131,682	23.2	139,583	5,676
2018	[97]	62	133,907	22.2	141,941	6,032
2019	[98]	63	135,909	21.2	144,064	6,411
2020	[99]	64	137,653	20.2	145,912	6,815
2021	[100]	65	139,097	19.2	147,443	7,245
2022	[101]	66	140,198	18.2	148,610	7,703
2023	[102]	67	140,907	17.2	149,361	8,192
2024	[103]	68	141,169	16.2	149,639	8,714
2025	[104]	69	140,925	15.2	149,380	9,271
2026	[105]	70	140,109	14.2	148,516	9,867
2027	[106]	71	138,649	13.2	146,968	10,504
2028	[107]	72	136,464	12.2	144,652	11,186
2029	[108]	73	133,466	11.2	141,474	11,917
2030	[109]	74	129,557	10.2	137,330	12,702
2031	[110]	75	124,628	9.2	132,106	13,547
2032	[111]	76	118,559	8.2	125,673	14,458
2033	[112]	77	111,215	7.2	117,888	15,447
2034	[113]	78	102,441	6.2	108,587	16,523
2035	[114]	79	92,064	5.2	97,588	17,705
2036	[115]	80	79,883	4.2	84,676	19,020
2037	[116]	81	65,656	3.2	69,595	20,517
2038	[117]	82	49,078	2.2	52,023	22,308
2039	[118]	83	29,715	1.2	31,498	24,762
2040	[119]	84	6,736	0.2	7,140	7,140

Total   337,908

FIGURE 13.20

Annuitizing Required Minimum Distributions

This figure is an example of using the greater of an annuitized amount or the RMD amount for the IRA owner over the life expectancy of the owner (assumes owner is alive). The owner's starting age is 70 (an owner born in the second half of the year would have a starting age of 71) and the starting IRA account balance is $100,000. The IRA is annuitized over 17 years, the RMD Single Life Table life expectancy for a person age 70.

The Uniform Lifetime Table factor for a person age 70 equals 27.4. (If the spouse of the IRA owner was the sole beneficiary and more than 10 years younger than the owner, the RMD Joint and Survivor Table could be used. However, the annuitized amount would still be the same.) Adding interest at 6 percent to the starting account balance produces a "balance plus 6 percent" equal to $106,000 ($100,000 x 1.06). The required minimum distribution equals $3,650 ($100,000 ÷ 27.4).

The Term Certain Annuity Factor for 17 years at 6 percent interest equals 10.4773 (see Appendix C). Dividing the starting account balance of $100,000 by 10.4773 results in an annual annuity payment of $9,544.

To level distributions from the IRA, the greater of the annuity payment ($9,544) or the required minimum distribution ($3,650), or $9,544, is distributed.

The account balance as of end of the first year is $96,456 ($106,000 - $9,544). The Uniform Lifetime Table factor for the second year for a person age 71 equals 26.5. Adding interest at 6 percent to the account balance produces a "balance plus 6 percent" equal to $102,243 ($96,456 x 1.06). The required minimum distribution equals $3,640 ($96,456 ÷ 26.5). To level distributions from the IRA, the greater of the annuity payment ($9,544) or the required minimum distribution ($3,640), or $9,544, is distributed.

At the end of 17 years, the entire IRA account has been distributed in substantially equal payments that satisfy the required minimum distribution rules.

FIGURE 13.20 (continued)

IRA Required Minimum Distributions

Age	Account Balance	RMD Factor	Balance Plus 6%	RMD	Distribution
70	100,000	27.4	106,000	3,650	9,544
71	96,456	26.5	102,243	3,640	9,544
72	92,699	25.6	98,261	3,621	9,544
73	88,717	24.7	94,040	3,592	9,544
74	84,496	23.8	89,566	3,550	9,544
75	80,022	22.9	84,823	3,494	9,544
76	75,279	22.0	79,796	3,422	9,544
77	70,252	21.2	74,467	3,314	9,544
78	64,923	20.3	68,818	3,198	9,544
79	59,274	19.5	62,830	3,040	9,544
80	53,286	18.7	56,483	2,850	9,544
81	46,939	17.9	49,755	2,622	9,544
82	40,211	17.1	42,624	2,352	9,544
83	33,080	16.3	35,065	2,029	9,544
84	25,521	15.5	27,052	1,647	9,544
85	17,508	14.8	18,558	1,183	9,544
86	9,014	13.4	9,555	673	9,555
				Total	162,249

Endnotes

1. IRC Sec. 72(t), as amended by PPA 2006.

2. Rev. Rul. 2002-62, 2002-42 IRB 710; Notice 89-25(A-12), 1989-1 CB 662.

3. However, Letter Ruling 200432021 permitted annual recalculations under the amortization method using the taxpayer's life expectancy.

4. IRC Sec. 408A(c)(5).

5. IRC Secs. 408(a)(6), 408(b)(3), 401(a)(9), 4974(a).

6. Treas. Reg. §1.401(a)(9)-5(A-4).

7. Treas. Reg. §1.408-8(A-9).

8. IRC Sec. 401(a)(9)(B)(ii); Treas. Reg. §1.401(a)(9)-3(A-2).

9. IRC Sec. 401(a)(9)(B)(iii); Treas. Reg. §1.401(a)(9)-3(A-3).

Chapter 14

Choosing a Beneficiary

I t is important that an IRA owner name a beneficiary or beneficiaries to receive IRA distributions when the IRA owner dies. First, the IRA owner should name a beneficiary so that when the IRA owner dies the IRA goes to the person the IRA owner would most like to benefit. Second, if the IRA owner dies before minimum distributions are required, having a beneficiary named permits distributions to be made for the life expectancy of the beneficiary, rather than requiring that the IRA account be distributed within five years. Third, if the IRA owner dies after minimum distributions are required, having a beneficiary named permits distributions to be made for the life expectancy of the beneficiary, if that is longer than the life expectancy of the IRA owner. Fourth, naming a spouse as beneficiary can be especially useful for required minimum distribution purposes as well as for estate tax purposes. Finally, naming a trust, such as a credit shelter trust or a marital deduction trust, as beneficiary can be important from an estate planning perspective.

An IRA beneficiary may generally be either a specified person, a member of some ascertainable class of persons, a charity, or a trust benefiting one or more of the foregoing. For example, a class of beneficiaries might be the children of the grantor. Note that where there is more than one concurrent beneficiary, the required minimum distribution rules use the age of the oldest beneficiary.

The IRA owner may want to provide for contingent interests as well as succeeding interests. For example, the IRA owner may wish to provide for IRA distributions to

A, only if A is alive when IRA owner dies, otherwise to B. Or the IRA owner may wish to provide for distributions to A while A is alive, and then to B.

Where an estate is subject to estate tax, consider providing that an IRA does not bear the burden of paying estate taxes. If estate taxes are payable from the IRA, the IRA will be required to make a distribution. The distribution reduces the ability to stretch the IRA and the distribution may be partially or fully includable in income for income tax purposes.

In choosing a beneficary of an IRA, the overall estate plan should always be considered. Who does the estate owner/IRA owner wish to benefit, when, and how? The IRA is one part of that estate plan. Tax considerations can be important in choosing the beneficiary of the IRA, and tax savings can provide greater benefits. But choosing the beneficiaries of IRAs must be coordinated with choosing the beneficiaries of the entire estate.

There are a number of implications to choosing an IRA beneficiary based on the type of beneficiary, whether a spouse, other nonfamily members, a charity, or a trust (including a marital trust or a credit shelter bypass trust). There are a couple of other miscellaneous issues that should also be considered when choosing a beneneficary: multiple or separate IRAs, early distributions and substantially equal periodic payments (SEPPs), and income in respect of a decedent (IRD). These are discussed below.

Spouse

A spouse is often the most important beneficiary in the overall estate plan. Naming a spouse as beneficiary can be especially useful for required minimum distribution purposes as well as for estate tax purposes.

One advantage of having a spouse as beneficiary of a traditional IRA, SEP IRA, or SIMPLE IRA is that the minimum distribution incidental benefit (MDIB) rule does not apply where the spouse is the beneficiary. (The MDIB rule does not apply to a Roth IRA.) As part of the required minimum distribution rules, the MDIB rule, is designed to insure that the traditional IRA, SEP IRA, or SIMPLE IRA distributions are primarily for the benefit of the IRA owner (and possibly the spouse of the IRA owner). The rule does this, while the IRA owner is alive, by treating a beneficiary other than the spouse of the IRA owner as no more than 10 years younger than the IRA owner.

Where the spouse of the IRA owner is the sole designated beneficiary of the IRA, after the IRA owner's death the spouse can usually elect to treat the IRA as the spouse's own for income tax purposes. The election is usually made whenever required minimum distributions can be postponed further by making the election. For example, a spouse who elects to treat the IRA owner's account as the spouse's own could postpone distributions from the IRA until after the spouse reaches age 70½, in the case of a traditional IRA, a SEP IRA, or SIMPLE IRA, or until after the spouse's death in the case of a Roth IRA. Furthermore, the life expectancy of the spouse and a beneficiary could be used rather than the life expectancy of the IRA owner and beneficiary.

Additionally, the following considerations, possible disadvantages, should be kept in mind when considering whether the spouse should elect to treat the IRA as the spouse's own.

1. If the election is made, the spouse is treated as the owner of the IRA.

2. If the election is made and the spouse is younger than age 59½, distributions may be subject to the early distribution penalty tax to the extent included in income unless an exception applies (see Chapter 13). The early distribution penalty tax would not apply to distributions after the death of the original IRA owner in the absence of the spouse making the election to be treated as the owner.

3. If the election is made in the case of a traditional IRA, SEP IRA, or SIMPLE IRA and the spouse was older than the original IRA owner, required minimum distributions (see Chapter 13) may or may not be based on a shorter life expectancy while the spouse is alive. The spouse will be able to use the RMD uniform lifetime table, possibly offsetting the spouse's older age. For example, if the original IRA owner was age 60 and the spouse is age 70, the spouse starts with the RMD uniform lifetime table factor of 27.4, whereas the RMD single life factor for the original IRA owner would have started at 25.2 if the election had not been made (a higher RMD factor is better). The greater the difference in age, the more likely it is that there may be a disadvantage if the spouse is older and makes the election. For example, if the original IRA owner was instead age 55, the RMD single life factor for the original IRA owner would have started at 29.6 if the election had not been made.

4. If the election is made in the case of a Roth IRA, whether distributions from the IRA are taxable during the spouse's lifetime generally depends

on whether distributions are considered distributions of contributions or earnings and whether distributions are qualified. If the election had not been made, all distributions after the death of the original Roth IRA owner would have been qualified, and not subject to income tax.

5. If the election is made, the electing spouse (rather than the original IRA owner) must attain age 70½ in order to use the exclusion for qualified charitable distributions (see below).

Where the spouse of the IRA owner is the sole designated beneficiary of the IRA and the IRA owner dies before reaching age 70½, the spouse can postpone receiving required minimum distributions until after the IRA owner would have reached age 70½. This rule can generally be taken advantage of where the IRA owner was younger than the spouse.

Another consideration when naming the spouse as the sole designated beneficiary is that the IRA owner will have no say in who receives the IRA after the spouse dies; the spouse determines who receives the IRA after the spouse's death. With a QTIP (see discussion of trusts, below), the spouse is given an income interest for life and the IRA owner can control who receives the IRA after the spouse dies.

Where the spouse of the IRA owner is named beneficiary of the IRA, the IRA can usually be made to qualify for the estate tax marital deduction. A marital deduction trust could also be the beneficiary of the IRA. See Chapter 18. The effect of using a traditional IRA, SEP IRA, or SIMPLE IRA to fund the marital deduction is generally to create a wasting asset. (Distributions from Roth IRAs are generally not subject to income tax after the death of the IRA owner.) As the traditional IRA, SEP IRA, or SIMPLE IRA is distributed to the spouse, the spouse is required to pay income taxes. Therefore, the amount remaining at the spouse's death that is subject to estate tax has been reduced by the income tax paid by the spouse.

Where a marital deduction trust or a credit shelter trust is named beneficiary of the IRA, the spouse is not given an interest sufficient to allow the spouse to treat the IRA as her own (i.e., the spouse is not the sole designated beneficiary). Therefore, if required minimum distributions did not begin before the IRA owner died, distributions after death must generally be made over the life expectancy of the oldest beneficiary of the marital deduction or credit shelter trust (who is often the spouse). However, if required minimum distributions began before the IRA owner died and the life expectancy of the IRA owner is longer than the life expectancy of the beneficiary, distributions can be made over the life expectancy of the IRA owner. As noted in the discussion of trusts below, if it is important to take advantage of the special required minimum distribution provisions for spouses that often allow greater stretching of the IRA, consider making the spouse the outright beneficiary of the IRA, rather than making a trust the beneficiary.

Other Family Members

Children are also natural beneficiaries. A child as beneficiary generally allows required minimum distributions to be distributed over the life expectancy of the younger child after the death of the IRA owner (including a spouse of the original IRA owner who elects to treat the IRA as the spouse's own).

Often children are also beneficiaries of credit shelter trusts. As noted below, required minimum distributions with a trust as beneficiary use the age of the oldest beneficiary.

Grandchildren can also make great IRA beneficiaries. A grandchild is generally even younger than the spouse or a child, usually allowing required minimum distributions to be spread out even more. Making a grandchild a beneficiary also moves property down two generations, thus skipping possible estate or gift tax at the child's generation. However, naming a grandchild as IRA beneficiary generally results in a generation-skipping transfer subject to the generation-skipping transfer tax unless the IRA owner allocates his generation-skipping transfer tax exemption ($2,000,000 in 2006) to the transfer.

Even though for required minimum distribution purposes children and grand-children generally make good beneficiaries because of their long life expectancies and the ability to stretch out distributions, it must be remembered that, while the IRA owner is alive, the minimum distribution incidental benefit (MDIB) treats a beneficiary other than the spouse of the IRA owner as no more than 10 years younger than the IRA owner. However, the MDIB rule does not apply to a Roth IRA.

At times, older generation family members, such as a parent or brother or sister of the IRA owner, may be a beneficiary of the IRA. The ability to stretch the IRA may be severely limited in such a case. If the beneficiary really needs the IRA funds during the beneficiary's lifetime, stretching the IRA may be of little importance.

Where different generations are all beneficiaries, consider whether it makes sense to have separate IRAs for different generations. If the beneficiaries in a particular generation are all about the same age, using the age of the oldest beneficiary in that generation for required minimum distribution purposes may very well be acceptable. If stretching the IRA is important, consider whether IRAs might be given to younger generations and other assets to older generations. But don't forget that spouses often make special IRA beneficiaries (see above).

Charity

A charity can also make a great IRA beneficiary at death. An estate tax charitable deduction would be available for the transfer to charity. Furthermore, the charity can receive distribution of the IRA without income taxation. This is generally unimportant in the case of a Roth IRA; Roth IRAs can generally be received income tax-free after the IRA owner's death even if received by a noncharitable beneficiary.

For required minimum distribution purposes, if a person other than an individual is designated as beneficiary of an IRA, the IRA will be treated as having no beneficiary, even if an individual is also named beneficiary. A charity is not an individual. Therefore, if a charity is named as a beneficiary of an IRA, or a trust with a charitable beneficiary is named as a beneficiary of an IRA, the IRA will be treated as having no beneficiary and the ability to stretch the IRA will be extremely limited. If it is desired to transfer an interest in an IRA to charity at death, as well as to other beneficiaries, a separate IRA should probably be created for the charity. Furthermore, the transfer to charity of the separate IRA should probabaly be made outright, and not to a charitable trust (unless the charity is the only beneficiary of the trust). Keeping the charitable IRA separate from the IRAs for noncharitable beneficiaries may allow the IRAs for noncharitable beneficiaries to be stretched. (See discussion of multiple IRAs, below.)

Lifetime Gifts to Charity

An IRA owner (or beneficiary) who wishes to make a gift of IRA assets to charity during lifetime must take a distribution from the IRA. Such a distribution may be partially or fully includable in income under the income tax rules for distributions from IRAs (see Chapter 13) unless it is a qualified charitable distribution (see below). The IRA owner (or beneficiary) can then make a gift of the IRA distribution to the charity. The gift would generally qualify for the gift tax charitable deduction. The IRA owner (or beneficiary) can take an income tax deduction for the charitable gift if the IRA owner (or beneficiary) itemizes deductions. The amount of the income tax charitable deduction for the year may be limited to certain percentages (e.g., 50%, 30%, 20%) of adjusted gross income (which is increased to the extent the IRA distribution is included in income – the increase may be favorable here; it may allow higher charitable deduction amounts), with carryover of excess amounts to later years. Also, itemized deductions and personal exemptions might be subject to phaseout based on adjusted gross income (which is increased to the extent the IRA distribution is included in income – the increase may be unfavorable here; it may reduce deductions and personal exemptions allowed).

Thus, where lifetime charitable gifts are made of distributed IRA assets, the amount of the distribution includable in income could be more or less than the amount of the income tax charitable deduction. And, if the charitable dedution must be carried over to a later year, there may be timing differences between when income is recognized and when the income tax charitable deduction is taken. Furthermore, the IRA distribution could lead to reductions in deductions or personal exemptions allowed. Congress has recently been considering legislation to allow direct gifts of IRA and qualified plan assets to charity that avoid these potential problems. PPA 2006 provides a temporary limited solution with qualified charitable distributions.

PPA 2006 provides that certain distributions (**qualified charitable distributions**) from a traditional or Roth IRA made to charity in 2006 or 2007 are not included in income. The provision is not available for SEP and SIMPLE IRAs. The maximum annual amount that can be excluded under this provision is $100,000. The exclusion applies only to amounts otherwise includable in income. The distribution must be made directly from the IRA trustee to a 50% public charity (as described in IRC Section 170(b)(1)(A), other than a support organization or a donor advised fund). The distribution must be made after the IRA owner has attained age 70½. The entire contribution to charity must be otherwise deductible for income tax purposes, disregarding this provision and the charitable deduction percentage limitations based on income for this purpose. Adjustments are made to undistributed nondeductible contributions to reflect the qualified charitable distribution. An income tax charitable deduction is not available for the amount excluded from inome.[1]

For a SEP or SIMPLE IRA, a qualified plan, a tax sheltered annuity, or an eligible Section 457 governmental plan, consider rolling it (or part of it) over to a traditional IRA, and then making a qualified charitable distribution from the traditional IRA. It is not generally recommended to convert to a Roth IRA for purpose of making qualified charitable distribution from the Roth IRA: the conversion to a Roth IRA is a taxable event.

The exclusion for qualified charitable distributions may have little impact on Roth IRAs. Distributions made on or after the date the Roth IRA owner turns age 59½ are generally treated as qualified distributions (see above) that are not includable in income. The exclusion for qualified charitable contributions applies only to amounts includable in income and that are made after the IRA owner has attained age 70½. Distributions from a Roth made after age 70½ are not generally includable in income.

Where the spouse of the IRA owner is the sole designated beneficiary of the IRA, after the IRA owner's death the spouse can usually elect to treat the IRA as the spouse's own for income tax purposes. If the election is made, the exclusion for qualified charitable distributions would depend on the electing spouse attaining age 70½, rather than the age of the original IRA owner.

The entire contribution to charity must otherwise qualify for the charitable deduction. If the deductible amount would be reduced because a benefit is received in return, or would not be allowable because of insufficient substantiation, the exclusion is not available with regard to any part of the contribution. Contributions to charity for fund-raising dinners, auctions, raffle tickets, and other transactions where the donor receives a benefit and the contribution would not fully qualify for a charitable deduction are not qualified charitable distributions.

The exclusion for a qualified charitable distribution is available only after the IRA owner has attained age 70½. What if the IRA owner dies before reaching age 70½? Should the statute be amended to provide for qualified charitable distributions after death or age 70½?

An IRA owner attains age 70½ on the date that is six calendar months after the 70th anniversary of the IRA owner's birth. For example, if an IRA owner's date of birth was June 30, 1936, the 70th anniversary is June 30, 2006, and the IRA owner attains age 70½ on December 30, 2006. It would be helpful if the provision was changed to distributions in the year the IRA owner attained age 70½ and later years (required minimum distributions must generally start in the year a nonRoth IRA owner attains age 70½), rather than distributions on or after attaining age 70½.

The statute provides that for purposes of determining the amount of a qualified charitable distributions, the entire amount of a ditribution is treated as being includable in income "to the extent that such amount does not exceed the aggregate amount which would be so includible if all amounts distributed from all individual retirement accounts were treated as one contract" under IRC Section 408(d)(2)(A). This seems to apply the IRC Section 72 rules to the amount actually distributed. However, the technical explanation to PPA 2006 seems to apply the IRC Section 72 rules as if all amounts were distributed (i.e., a deemed distibution of all amounts) so that, in essence, a distribution would be treated as a distribution of income first for purposes of qualified charitable distributions. A technical correction may be needed.

For example, the technical explanation to PPA 2006 uses the example of an individual with a traditional IRA with a balance of $100,000, with nondeductable contributions of $20,000. The individual has the IRA trustee distribute $80,000 to an appropriate charity. The technical explanation treats the entire $80,000 as a qualified charitable distribution. After the distribution, the individual has $20,000 in the IRA, all of which is treated as undistributed nondeductible contributions. However, if the amount includable in income were based on actual distributions (rather than a deemed distribution of all amounts), $16,000 [$80,000 x ($20,000 / $100,000)] of the distribution would be excludable from income as a distribution of nondeductible contributions, $64,000 [$80,000 - $16,000] would be a qualified charitable distribution excludable from income, and the individual has $20,000 in the IRA but the undistributed nondeductible contributions would be reduced to $4,000.

Trusts

A trust can be useful for a variety of estate planning purposes to provide for flexibility, management of property, accumulation or distributions of income to beneficiaries, distributions of trust corpus to beneficiaries, withdrawal powers in beneficiaries, and other powers of appointment. Such trusts often are designed with estate tax implications in mind. For example, credit shelter bypass trusts (see below) might be designed to take advantage of the unified credit of the decedent and then bypass, or avoid inclusion in, the estates of others. A marital trust (see below) might be used to take advantage of the marital deduction. A trust with spendthrift provisions might be used to provide some additional asset protection for an IRA beneficiary (see Chapter 20).

There are special considerations when a trust is made the beneficiary of an IRA. These considerations should include the implication of who the beneficiaries of the trust are, required minimum distributions, the marital deduction, effective use of the unified credit, and IRAs as a wasting asset.

Technically, a trust cannot be a designated beneficiary of an IRA for required minimum distribution purposes. However, the beneficiaries of a trust will be treated as designated beneficiaries if distributions from the IRA are to be made to the trust and, as of the later of the date on which the trust is named beneficiary or the required beginning date, and for all subsequent periods for which the trust is named beneficiary:

(1)   the trust is valid under state law (or would be but for the lack of corpus);

(2)   the trust is irrevocable, or becomes so upon death of the grantor;

(3)   the trust beneficiaries of the IRA are identifiable;

(4)   the trustee either provides a list of the beneficiaries or a copy of the trust document itself to the IRA administrator (and agrees to provide any later changes in the document to the IRA administrator).

Similar rules apply to a trust that is a beneficiary of another trust.[2]

Generally, the oldest beneficiary of a trust is treated as the designated beneficiary for RMD purposes. It appears that the adverse affect of this rule can be avoided if separate trusts or shares of trusts and separate IRAs or IRA accounts are created for each beneficiary. However, it appears that in this instance, the separate trusts and IRAs would generally have to already exist at the IRA owner's death. If trust shares, or subtrusts, are used, the individual trust shares should be named as beneficiaries on the IRA beneficiary designation form rather than the single trust that holds the trust shares. Furthermore, if the IRA is to go to multiple trusts or subtrusts, the IRA beneficiary designation form should specify how the IRA is to be split. (See discussion of multiple IRAs, below.)

The spouse is not treated as the sole designated beneficiary of an IRA for required minimum distribution purposes if a trust is named the beneficiary of the IRA. If the spouse is not the sole designated beneficiary of the IRA, the spouse cannot elect to be treated as the owner of the IRA or postpone receiving required minimum distributions until after the IRA owner would have reached age 70½. If it is important to take advantage of these special provisions for spouses, which often allow greater stretching of the IRA, consider making the spouse the outright beneficiary of the IRA, rather than making a trust the beneficiary.

Marital Trust

Where it is desired to benefit the surviving spouse of the IRA owner, a marital trust may be useful. Where a marital trust is the beneficiary of the IRA, the estate tax marital deduction and required minimum distributions require special attention. Where a marital trust is the beneficiary of the IRA, a QTIP marital deduction will generally be used for both the IRA and the trust (see below). Where the spouse is not a U.S. citzen, a qualified domestic trust (QDOT) will generally be required (see Chapter 18).

As noted above, if it is important to take advantage of the special required minimum distribution provisions for spouses that often allow greater stretching of the IRA, consider making the spouse the outright beneficiary of the IRA, rather than making a trust the beneficiary. If a trust is the beneficiary of the IRA, required minimum distributions use the life expectancy of the oldest trust beneficiary, which is usually the spouse.

A qualified terminable interest property (QTIP) marital deduction should be available for estate tax purposes if all income from an IRA is distributed at least annually to the surviving spouse, no one has the power to distribute any part of the IRA to anyone other than the surviving spouse, and the executor makes a QTIP election (see Chapter 18).[3] An executor can elect to treat an IRA and a trust as QTIP if (1) the trustee of the trust is the beneficiary of the IRA, (2) the surviving spouse can compel the trustee to withdraw all income earned by the IRA at least annually and distribute that amount to the spouse, and (3) no person has the power to appoint any part of the trust to any person other than the spouse.[4] Allocations between income and principal will be respected if state law provides that reasonable apportionments can be made between income and remainder beneficiaries of the total return of the trust (e.g., a unitrust interest in the range of 3% to 5% could be treated as an income interest).[5]

Revenue Ruling 2006-26[6] provides that the QTIP marital deduction would generally be available for an IRA and a trust with all of the following provisions. While the spouse is alive, the trustee is required to distribute the income of the trust to the spouse annually. The spouse can require the trustee to withdraw from the IRA the greater of the IRA income or the required minimum distribution, and to distribute at least the income of the IRA to the spouse. The IRA is invested in productive assets and the spouse can compel the trustee to invest in assets productive of a reasonable amount of income.

Revenue Ruling 2006-26 also provides that various modern means of determining income under state law are permitted under the QTIP marital deduction. Thus, in certain circumstances, the trustee can make adjustments between income and principal to fulfill the trustee's duty of impartiality between the income and remainder beneficiaries under state laws based on Uniform Principal and Income Act (UPIA) Section 104(a). Also, a state law providing for a unitrust in the range of 3% to 5% could be applied to separately determine the income of the IRA and the trust. And the trustee could separately determine the income of the IRA and the trust under general traditional statutory or common law rules that provide for allocations between income and principal. However, if state law has a provision such as UPIA

Section 409(c), which provides that, under certain circumstances, 10% of a distribution required to be made will be treated as income, and 90% as principal, it may be necessary to make sure that the trust instrument provides that Section 409(c) does not apply (an allocation to income based on a percentage of a distribution is not based on total return, and would not qualify for the QTIP marital deduction).

Where a QTIP marital deduction is used, the IRA owner can control where the property passes after the death of the surviving spouse of the IRA owner. For the purpose of flexibility, it may be useful to give the surviving spouse the power to choose the beneficiary when such spouse dies. If desired, the IRA owner could limit the possible beneficiaries to which the spouse could appoint the IRA (e.g., to one or more children of the IRA owner). Nevertheless, the required minimum distributions after the death of the surviving spouse will generally be based on the remaining life expectancy of the surviving spouse. (If the spouse received the IRA outright, rather than in trust, and elected to be treated as the owner of the IRA, the required minimum distributions after the death of the spouse could be based on the life expectancy of the beneficiary designated by the spouse, usually allowing greater stretching of the IRA.)

Credit Shelter Bypass Trust

A credit shelter trust is generally designed to take advantage of the unifed credit of the decedent and then bypass, or avoid inclusion in, the estates of others (such the estate of a surviving spouse) for estate tax purposes (see Chapter 18). The spouse of the decedent is often given interests in the credit shelter bypass trust, such as an income interest for life or a limited power of appointment, so long as the interest does not cause the trust to be included in the surviving spouse's estate. However, a spouse would not generally be given an interest, such as a general power of appointment, that would cause the trust to be included in the surviving spouse's estate.

As noted above, if it is important to take advantage of the special required minimum distribution provisions for spouses that often allow greater stretching of the IRA, consider making the spouse the outright beneficiary of the IRA, rather than making a trust the beneficiary. If a trust is the beneficiary of the IRA, required minimum distributions use the life expectancy of the oldest trust beneficiary. If the spouse is a beneficiary of the trust, the spouse will usually be the oldest beneficiary.

Children and grandchildren are also often given interests in credit shelter bypass trusts. In general, no beneficiary should be given an interest that would cause the trust to be includable in the beneficiary's estate if the trust is to bypass that beneficiary's estate. However, at times, it may be useful to have property included in the estate of a person (e.g., a child) whose estate is small enough so as to incur no estate tax. This might be a useful alternative to use of generation-skipping transfer tax exemption (see Chapter 19) to protect the trust.

As noted above, if a trust is the beneficiary of the IRA, required minimum distributions use the life expectancy of the oldest trust beneficiary. If the spouse is not a beneficiary of the credit shelter trust and children are, the life expectancy of the oldest child would be used.

At times, older generations, such as a parent or brother or sister of the IRA owner, may be a beneficiary of a credit shelter bypass trust created by the IRA owner at death. However, if the trust is a beneficiary of the IRA, required minimum distributions must use the life expectancy of the oldest beneficiary, and the ability to stretch the IRA may be severely limited.

Whenever there are multiple generations as potential beneficiaries of an IRA, consider whether it makes sense to arrange for separate IRAs and/or trusts with different beneficiaries, or for transfer of IRAs to some beneficiaries and property other than IRAs to other beneficiaries, in order to facilitate stretching the IRA. (See discussion of multiple IRAs, below.)

The effect of using a traditional IRA, SEP IRA, or SIMPLE IRA to fund the credit shelter bypass trust is generally to create a wasting asset. As the IRA is distributed, income taxes must generally be paid. (Distributions from Roth IRAs are generally not subject to income tax after the death of the IRA owner.) Therefore, the amount protected by the unified credit is reduced by the income tax paid. Consider whether it makes sense to have the traditional IRA, SEP IRA, or SIMPLE IRA pass other than to the credit shelter bypass trust, somewhere the unified credit would not be wasted. For example, if the traditional IRA, SEP IRA, or SIMPLE IRA passes to the spouse of the IRA owner, or to a marital trust for the spouse, the effect of the traditional IRA, SEP IRA, or SIMPLE IRA being a wasting asset can reduce the amount included in the spouse's estate at death.

Miscellaneous

Multiple or Separate IRAs

In general, an individual can have multiple IRAs or split up an IRA into separate IRAs. The limitations on contributions still apply to the multiple IRAs as if there was only one IRA. However, the separate IRAs can be given different beneficiaries.

The use of multiple IRAs with different beneficiaries can be useful for a number of reasons. Obviously, having multiple IRAs with different beneficiaries permits the IRA owner to benefit a number of different people. Because the IRAs have different beneficiaries, the required minimum distributions for the IRAs can be different. This can be particularly useful with very young beneficiaries. Also, having multiple IRAs with different beneficiaries can make it easy to qualify certain IRAs for the marital or charitable deduction by eliminating, in essence, split interests in the same property. In addition, having multiple IRAs may help with credit shelter bypass trust/marital trust planning for estates. Furthermore, for generation-skipping transfer tax purposes, the generation-skipping transfer tax exemption could be allocated to IRAs benefiting skip persons (generally, persons two or more generations younger than the transferor – e.g., a grandchild of the IRA owner), but not to IRAs with no skip persons as beneficiary (e.g., spouse or child of IRA owner is beneficiary).

When considering the creation of multiple IRAs or trusts, the potential extra costs that might be incurred with separate IRAs or trusts should be taken into account. Consider also the possible loss of some flexibility to provide for multiple beneficiaries from the same assets. And, of course, consider how the use of multiple IRAs fits into the overall estate plan.

Early Distributions/SEPPs

It should also be noted that the choice of beneficiary can be important while the IRA owner is alive and under age 59½. One exception to the early distribution penalty tax (see Chapter 13) is for substantially equal periodic payments (SEPPs). Calculation of substantially equal periodic payments from an IRA uses the age of the IRA owner or the ages of the IRA owner and a beneficiary. In general, an older beneficiary results in larger payments, a younger beneficiary in smaller payments.

In general, for purpose of calculating SEPPs, the IRA owner can choose to use (1) the IRA owner's age (single life), (2) the IRA owner's age and an age for a deemed beneficiary 10 years younger than the IRA owner (deemed joint and survivor), or (3) the IRA owner's age and the age of a designated beneficiary (joint and survivor). A beneficiary should be chosen carefully; age should be only one consideration. If a beneficiary is named and the IRA owner dies while that beneficiary designation is in effect, the IRA goes to that beneficiary.

Income in Respect of a Decedent (IRD)

A beneficiary who receives a distribution from a traditional IRA, SEP IRA, or SIMPLE IRA that is includable in income can take an income tax deduction for the estate tax attributable to the IRA being includable in the IRA owner's estate (such income would be income in respect of a decedent, or IRD). The deduction against income tax for estate tax attributable to the IRA eliminates potential double taxation of the IRD. However, in many cases, a combination of a credit shelter trust and a marital deduction trust will be designed to produce no estate tax at the death of the first spouse to die and there will be no estate tax to deduct against income tax. Distributions from a Roth IRA are not subject to income tax after the IRA owner's death.

In choosing a beneficiary, consider the effect that paying income tax has on the net amount the beneficiary receives. Also, consider the income tax bracket of the beneficiary. The IRA may be worth more to a beneficiary in a low tax bracket.

Endnotes

1. IRC Sec. 408(d)(8).
2. Treas. Regs. §§1.401(a)(9)-4(Q-5), 1.401(a)(9)-4(Q-6).
3. IRC Sec. 2056(b)(7).
4. Rev. Rul. 2000-2, 2000-1 CB 305.
5. Treas. Reg. §1.643(b)-1.
6. 2006-22 IRB 939.

Chapter 15

IRAs, Time, Money, and Taxes

Individual retirement arrangements generally take advantage of time, money, and taxes to accumulate assets. IRA contributions can accumulate to quite large amounts if permitted to grow for long periods of time. Making regular contributions adds to the growth in value. This is the power of accumulation.

The power of accumulation can be greatly enhanced by stretching the IRA (i.e., by stretching out distributions).

Tax deductions, tax-deferral, and even tax-free distributions can add greatly to the power of accumulations in an IRA. This should be compared to the tax environment for assets held outside an IRA.

The power of accumulation, stretching an IRA, and taxes and IRAs are all discussed below.

The Power of Accumulation

When a contribution is made to an IRA, the contribution will grow tax-deferred (or possibly, tax-free) in the IRA. The affect of taxes on accumulations will be discussed later.

> *Example.* If $1,000 is contributed to an IRA and the IRA grows 6 percent annually, at the end of one year the $1,000 will have grown to $1,060. The next year the $1,060 will have grown to $1,124, and so on. At the end

of 10 years the original $1,000 will have grown to $1,791, and at the end of 30 years the original $1,000 will have grown to $5,743. See Figure 15.1.

Figure 15.1, The Power of Accumulation (One Contribution), shows the amount that a $1,000 contribution will grow to in a given number of years and at a given interest or growth rate. The table can also be used to estimate the future value of multiples of $1,000.

> *Example.* Assume $4,000 is contributed to an IRA and accumulates for 20 years at 8 percent annually. (1) $4,000 divided by $1,000 equals 4. (2) The accumulated value of $1,000 for 20 years at 8 percent (from Figure 15.1) equals 4,661. (3) Multiple 4 by 4,661. The $4,000 will grow to $18,644 in 20 years at 8 percent annual growth.

A quick way to estimate how long it takes a contribution to double is to use the Rule of 72. Under the Rule of 72, if N = 72 ÷ annual interest (or growth) rate, then a given amount will double every N years.

> *Example.* Assuming a 7 percent interest rate, a $4,000 contribution will double in approximately 10 years, double again in 20 years, double again in 30 years, and so on.

The power of accumulation shows why it is much better to make contributions now rather than later.

> *Example.* Ann, age 30, contributes $4,000 to an IRA. Assuming a 6% growth rate, at age 70 the $4,000 will have grown to $41,144 (4 x 10,286 from Figure 15.1) over the 40 years.

> *Example.* Bob, age 50, contributes $4,000 to an IRA. Assuming a 6% growth rate, at age 70 the $4,000 will have grown to $12,828 (4 x 3,207 from Figure 15.1) over the 20 years. This is much less than the amount that Ann accumulated by making the contribution much earlier in life than did Bob.

FIGURE 15.1

The Power of Accumulation
(per $1,000 contribution)

Interest Rate

Years	1%	2%	3%	4%	5%	6%	7%
1	1,010	1,020	1,030	1,040	1,050	1,060	1,070
2	1,020	1,040	1,061	1,082	1,103	1,124	1,145
3	1,030	1,061	1,093	1,125	1,158	1,191	1,225
4	1,041	1,082	1,126	1,170	1,216	1,262	1,311
5	1,051	1,104	1,159	1,217	1,276	1,338	1,403
6	1,062	1,126	1,194	1,265	1,340	1,419	1,501
7	1,072	1,149	1,230	1,316	1,407	1,504	1,606
8	1,083	1,172	1,267	1,369	1,477	1,594	1,718
9	1,094	1,195	1,305	1,423	1,551	1,689	1,838
10	1,105	1,219	1,344	1,480	1,629	1,791	1,967
11	1,116	1,243	1,384	1,539	1,710	1,898	2,105
12	1,127	1,268	1,426	1,601	1,796	2,012	2,252
13	1,138	1,294	1,469	1,665	1,886	2,133	2,410
14	1,149	1,319	1,513	1,732	1,980	2,261	2,579
15	1,161	1,346	1,558	1,801	2,079	2,397	2,759
16	1,173	1,373	1,605	1,873	2,183	2,540	2,952
17	1,184	1,400	1,653	1,948	2,292	2,693	3,159
18	1,196	1,428	1,702	2,026	2,407	2,854	3,380
19	1,208	1,457	1,754	2,107	2,527	3,026	3,617
20	1,220	1,486	1,806	2,191	2,653	3,207	3,870
21	1,232	1,516	1,860	2,279	2,786	3,400	4,141
22	1,245	1,546	1,916	2,370	2,925	3,604	4,430
23	1,257	1,577	1,974	2,465	3,072	3,820	4,741
24	1,270	1,608	2,033	2,563	3,225	4,049	5,072
25	1,282	1,641	2,094	2,666	3,386	4,292	5,427
26	1,295	1,673	2,157	2,772	3,556	4,549	5,807
27	1,308	1,707	2,221	2,883	3,733	4,822	6,214
28	1,321	1,741	2,288	2,999	3,920	5,112	6,649
29	1,335	1,776	2,357	3,119	4,116	5,418	7,114
30	1,348	1,811	2,427	3,243	4,322	5,743	7,612
31	1,361	1,848	2,500	3,373	4,538	6,088	8,145
32	1,375	1,885	2,575	3,508	4,765	6,453	8,715
33	1,389	1,922	2,652	3,648	5,003	6,841	9,325
34	1,403	1,961	2,732	3,794	5,253	7,251	9,978
35	1,417	2,000	2,814	3,946	5,516	7,686	10,677
36	1,431	2,040	2,898	4,104	5,792	8,147	11,424
37	1,445	2,081	2,985	4,268	6,081	8,636	12,224
38	1,460	2,122	3,075	4,439	6,385	9,154	13,079
39	1,474	2,165	3,167	4,616	6,705	9,704	13,995
40	1,489	2,208	3,262	4,801	7,040	10,286	14,974
41	1,504	2,252	3,360	4,993	7,392	10,903	16,023
42	1,519	2,297	3,461	5,193	7,762	11,557	17,144
43	1,534	2,343	3,565	5,400	8,150	12,250	18,344
44	1,549	2,390	3,671	5,617	8,557	12,985	19,628
45	1,565	2,438	3,782	5,841	8,985	13,765	21,002
46	1,580	2,487	3,895	6,075	9,434	14,590	22,473
47	1,596	2,536	4,012	6,318	9,906	15,466	24,046
48	1,612	2,587	4,132	6,571	10,401	16,394	25,729
49	1,628	2,639	4,256	6,833	10,921	17,378	27,530
50	1,645	2,692	4,384	7,107	11,467	18,420	29,457

FIGURE 15.1 (continued)

The Power of Accumulation
(per $1,000 contribution)

Interest Rate

Years	8%	9%	10%	11%	12%	13%	14%
1	1,080	1,090	1,100	1,110	1,120	1,130	1,140
2	1,166	1,188	1,210	1,232	1,254	1,277	1,300
3	1,260	1,295	1,331	1,368	1,405	1,443	1,482
4	1,360	1,412	1,464	1,518	1,574	1,630	1,689
5	1,469	1,539	1,611	1,685	1,762	1,842	1,925
6	1,587	1,677	1,772	1,870	1,974	2,082	2,195
7	1,714	1,828	1,949	2,076	2,211	2,353	2,502
8	1,851	1,993	2,144	2,305	2,476	2,658	2,853
9	1,999	2,172	2,358	2,558	2,773	3,004	3,252
10	2,159	2,367	2,594	2,839	3,106	3,395	3,707
11	2,332	2,580	2,853	3,152	3,479	3,836	4,226
12	2,518	2,813	3,138	3,498	3,896	4,335	4,818
13	2,720	3,066	3,452	3,883	4,363	4,898	5,492
14	2,937	3,342	3,797	4,310	4,887	5,535	6,261
15	3,172	3,642	4,177	4,785	5,474	6,254	7,138
16	3,426	3,970	4,595	5,311	6,130	7,067	8,137
17	3,700	4,328	5,054	5,895	6,866	7,986	9,276
18	3,996	4,717	5,560	6,544	7,690	9,024	10,575
19	4,316	5,142	6,116	7,263	8,613	10,197	12,056
20	4,661	5,604	6,727	8,062	9,646	11,523	13,743
21	5,034	6,109	7,400	8,949	10,804	13,021	15,668
22	5,437	6,659	8,140	9,934	12,100	14,714	17,861
23	5,871	7,258	8,954	11,026	13,552	16,627	20,362
24	6,341	7,911	9,850	12,239	15,179	18,788	23,212
25	6,848	8,623	10,835	13,585	17,000	21,231	26,462
26	7,396	9,399	11,918	15,080	19,040	23,991	30,167
27	7,988	10,245	13,110	16,739	21,325	27,109	34,390
28	8,627	11,167	14,421	18,580	23,884	30,633	39,204
29	9,317	12,172	15,863	20,624	26,750	34,616	44,693
30	10,063	13,268	17,449	22,892	29,960	39,116	50,950
31	10,868	14,462	19,194	25,410	33,555	44,201	58,083
32	11,737	15,763	21,114	28,206	37,582	49,947	66,215
33	12,676	17,182	23,225	31,308	42,092	56,440	75,485
34	13,690	18,728	25,548	34,752	47,143	63,777	86,053
35	14,785	20,414	28,102	38,575	52,800	72,069	98,100
36	15,968	22,251	30,913	42,818	59,136	81,437	111,834
37	17,246	24,254	34,004	47,528	66,232	92,024	127,491
38	18,625	26,437	37,404	52,756	74,180	103,987	145,340
39	20,115	28,816	41,145	58,559	83,081	117,506	165,687
40	21,725	31,409	45,259	65,001	93,051	132,782	188,884
41	23,462	34,236	49,785	72,151	104,217	150,043	215,327
42	25,339	37,318	54,764	80,088	116,723	169,549	245,473
43	27,367	40,676	60,240	88,897	130,730	191,590	279,839
44	29,556	44,337	66,264	98,676	146,418	216,497	319,017
45	31,920	48,327	72,890	109,530	163,988	244,641	363,679
46	34,474	52,677	80,180	121,579	183,666	276,445	414,594
47	37,232	57,418	88,197	134,952	205,706	312,383	472,637
48	40,211	62,585	97,017	149,797	230,391	352,992	538,807
49	43,427	68,218	106,719	166,275	258,038	398,881	614,239
50	46,902	74,358	117,391	184,565	289,002	450,736	700,233

Another way to determine how much a given contribution may grow is to use a future value of a single sum table (see Appendix E).

> *Example.* Assume the same facts as the last example. The future value of a single sum factor for 20 years at 6 percent interest is 3.2071 (see Appendix E). The $4,000 contribution multiplied by 3.2071 equals $12,828.

Up to now, the discussion has focused on the power of accumulation as applied to one contribution to an IRA. However, the power of accumulation can be multiplied by making a series of contributions to IRAs.

> *Example.* Assume $1,000 is contributed to an IRA at the end of year 1. If in year 2 the IRA grows 6 percent, at the end of year 2 the $1,000 will have grown to $1,060. If another $1,000 is contributed at the end of year 2, the IRA will be worth $2,060. The next year the $2,060 will have grown to $2,184, and if another $1,000 is contributed, then the IRA will be worth $3,184, and so on. At the end of 10 years a series of $1,000 contributions will have grown to $13,181, and at the end of 30 years a series of $1,000 contributions will have grown to $79,058. See Figure 15.2.

Figure 15.2, The Power of Accumulation (Series of Contributions), shows the amount that a series of annual contributions of $1,000 (made at the end of the year) will grow to in a given number of years and at a given interest or growth rate. The table can also be used to estimate the future value of multiples of $1,000.

> *Example.* Assume $4,000 is contributed to an IRA each year for 20 years and accumulates at 8 percent annually. (1) $4,000 divided by $1,000 equals 4. (2) The accumulated value of $1,000 for 20 years at 8 percent (from Figure 15.2) equals 45,762. (3) Multiple 4 by 45,762. The series of annual $4,000 contributions will grow to $183,048 in 20 years at 8 percent annual growth.

FIGURE 15.2

The Power of Accumulation
(per $1,000 annual contribution)

Years	Interest Rate 1%	2%	3%	4%	5%	6%	7%
1	1,000	1,000	1,000	1,000	1,000	1,000	1,000
2	2,010	2,020	2,030	2,040	2,050	2,060	2,070
3	3,030	3,060	3,091	3,122	3,153	3,184	3,215
4	4,060	4,122	4,184	4,246	4,310	4,375	4,440
5	5,101	5,204	5,309	5,416	5,526	5,637	5,751
6	6,152	6,308	6,468	6,633	6,802	6,975	7,153
7	7,214	7,434	7,662	7,898	8,142	8,394	8,654
8	8,286	8,583	8,892	9,214	9,549	9,897	10,260
9	9,369	9,755	10,159	10,583	11,027	11,491	11,978
10	10,462	10,950	11,464	12,006	12,578	13,181	13,816
11	11,567	12,169	12,808	13,486	14,207	14,972	15,784
12	12,683	13,412	14,192	15,026	15,917	16,870	17,888
13	13,809	14,680	15,618	16,627	17,713	18,882	20,141
14	14,947	15,974	17,086	18,292	19,599	21,015	22,550
15	16,097	17,293	18,599	20,024	21,579	23,276	25,129
16	17,258	18,639	20,157	21,825	23,657	25,673	27,888
17	18,430	20,012	21,762	23,698	25,840	28,213	30,840
18	19,615	21,412	23,414	25,645	28,132	30,906	33,999
19	20,811	22,841	25,117	27,671	30,539	33,760	37,379
20	22,019	24,297	26,870	29,778	33,066	36,786	40,995
21	23,239	25,783	28,676	31,969	35,719	39,993	44,865
22	24,472	27,299	30,537	34,248	38,505	43,392	49,006
23	25,716	28,845	32,453	36,618	41,430	46,996	53,436
24	26,973	30,422	34,426	39,083	44,502	50,816	58,177
25	28,243	32,030	36,459	41,646	47,727	54,865	63,249
26	29,526	33,671	38,553	44,312	51,113	59,156	68,676
27	30,821	35,344	40,710	47,084	54,669	63,706	74,484
28	32,129	37,051	42,931	49,968	58,403	68,528	80,698
29	33,450	38,792	45,219	52,966	62,323	73,640	87,347
30	34,785	40,568	47,575	56,085	66,439	79,058	94,461
31	36,133	42,379	50,003	59,328	70,761	84,802	102,073
32	37,494	44,227	52,503	62,701	75,299	90,890	110,218
33	38,869	46,112	55,078	66,210	80,064	97,343	118,933
34	40,258	48,034	57,730	69,858	85,067	104,184	128,259
35	41,660	49,994	60,462	73,652	90,320	111,435	138,237
36	43,077	51,994	63,276	77,598	95,836	119,121	148,913
37	44,508	54,034	66,174	81,702	101,628	127,268	160,337
38	45,953	56,115	69,159	85,970	107,710	135,904	172,561
39	47,412	58,237	72,234	90,409	114,095	145,058	185,640
40	48,886	60,402	75,401	95,026	120,800	154,762	199,635
41	50,375	62,610	78,663	99,827	127,840	165,048	214,610
42	51,879	64,862	82,023	104,820	135,232	175,951	230,632
43	53,398	67,159	85,484	110,012	142,993	187,508	247,776
44	54,932	69,503	89,048	115,413	151,143	199,758	266,121
45	56,481	71,893	92,720	121,029	159,700	212,744	285,749
46	58,046	74,331	96,501	126,871	168,685	226,508	306,752
47	59,626	76,817	100,397	132,945	178,119	241,099	329,224
48	61,223	79,354	104,408	139,263	188,025	256,565	353,270
49	62,835	81,941	108,541	145,834	198,427	272,958	378,999
50	64,463	84,579	112,797	152,667	209,348	290,336	406,529

FIGURE 15.2 (continued)

The Power of Accumulation
(per $1,000 annual contribution)

Years	8%	9%	10%	Interest Rate 11%	12%	13%	14%
1	1,000	1,000	1,000	1,000	1,000	1,000	1,000
2	2,080	2,090	2,100	2,110	2,120	2,130	2,140
3	3,246	3,278	3,310	3,342	3,374	3,407	3,440
4	4,506	4,573	4,641	4,710	4,779	4,850	4,921
5	5,867	5,985	6,105	6,228	6,353	6,480	6,610
6	7,336	7,523	7,716	7,913	8,115	8,323	8,536
7	8,923	9,200	9,487	9,783	10,089	10,405	10,730
8	10,637	11,028	11,436	11,859	12,300	12,757	13,233
9	12,488	13,021	13,579	14,164	14,776	15,416	16,085
10	14,487	15,193	15,937	16,722	17,549	18,420	19,337
11	16,645	17,560	18,531	19,561	20,655	21,814	23,045
12	18,977	20,141	21,384	22,713	24,133	25,650	27,271
13	21,495	22,953	24,523	26,212	28,029	29,985	32,089
14	24,215	26,019	27,975	30,095	32,393	34,883	37,581
15	27,152	29,361	31,772	34,405	37,280	40,417	43,842
16	30,324	33,003	35,950	39,190	42,753	46,672	50,980
17	33,750	36,974	40,545	44,501	48,884	53,739	59,118
18	37,450	41,301	45,599	50,396	55,750	61,725	68,394
19	41,446	46,018	51,159	56,939	63,440	70,749	78,969
20	45,762	51,160	57,275	64,203	72,052	80,947	91,025
21	50,423	56,765	64,002	72,265	81,699	92,470	104,768
22	55,457	62,873	71,403	81,214	92,503	105,491	120,436
23	60,893	69,532	79,543	91,148	104,603	120,205	138,297
24	66,765	76,790	88,497	102,174	118,155	136,831	158,659
25	73,106	84,701	98,347	114,413	133,334	155,620	181,871
26	79,954	93,324	109,182	127,999	150,334	176,850	208,333
27	87,351	102,723	121,100	143,079	169,374	200,841	238,499
28	95,339	112,968	134,210	159,817	190,699	227,950	272,889
29	103,966	124,135	148,631	178,397	214,583	258,583	312,094
30	113,283	136,308	164,494	199,021	241,333	293,199	356,787
31	123,346	149,575	181,943	221,913	271,293	332,315	407,737
32	134,214	164,037	201,138	247,324	304,848	376,516	465,820
33	145,951	179,800	222,252	275,529	342,429	426,463	532,035
34	158,627	196,982	245,477	306,837	384,521	482,903	607,520
35	172,317	215,711	271,024	341,590	431,663	546,681	693,573
36	187,102	236,125	299,127	380,164	484,463	618,749	791,673
37	203,070	258,376	330,039	422,982	543,599	700,187	903,507
38	220,316	282,630	364,043	470,511	609,831	792,211	1,030,998
39	238,941	309,066	401,448	523,267	684,010	896,198	1,176,338
40	259,057	337,882	442,593	581,826	767,091	1,013,704	1,342,025
41	280,781	369,292	487,852	646,827	860,142	1,146,486	1,530,909
42	304,244	403,528	537,637	718,978	964,359	1,296,529	1,746,236
43	329,583	440,846	592,401	799,065	1,081,083	1,466,078	1,991,709
44	356,950	481,522	652,641	887,963	1,211,813	1,657,668	2,271,548
45	386,506	525,859	718,905	986,639	1,358,230	1,874,165	2,590,565
46	418,426	574,186	791,795	1,096,169	1,522,218	2,118,806	2,954,244
47	452,900	626,863	871,975	1,217,747	1,705,884	2,395,251	3,368,838
48	490,132	684,280	960,172	1,352,700	1,911,590	2,707,633	3,841,475
49	530,343	746,866	1,057,190	1,502,497	2,141,981	3,060,626	4,380,282
50	573,770	815,084	1,163,909	1,668,771	2,400,018	3,459,507	4,994,521

Once again, the power of accumulation shows why it is much better to make contributions now rather than later.

> *Example.* Ann, age 30, contributes $4,000 annually to an IRA. Assuming a 6% growth rate, at age 70 the IRA will have grown to $619,048 (4 x 154,762 from Figure 15.2) over the 40 years.

> *Example.* Bob, age 50, contributes $4,000 annually to an IRA. Assuming a 6% growth rate, at age 70 the IRA will have grown to $147,144 (4 x 36,786 from Figure 15.2) over the 20 years. This is much less than the amount that Ann accumulated by starting contributions much earlier in life than did Bob.

Another way to determine how much a series of equal contributions may grow is to use a future value of an annuity table (see Appendix E).

> *Example.* Assume the same facts as the last example. The future value of an annuity factor for 20 years at 6 percent interest is 36.7856 (see Appendix E). The $4,000 annual contribution multiplied by 36.7856 equals $147,142. (The slight difference is due to rounding.)

How much could a person age 30 in 2006 accumulate making maximum annual contributions to a traditional or Roth IRA through age 69? For this purpose, indexing of the limits is ignored (an indexing rate of 0 percent is used). A growth rate of 6 percent is used. The IRA will be worth $791,738 at the end of 2045 at age 69. See Figure 15.3.

> However, if the person waits until age 50 in 2026 to start making maximum annual contributions to a traditional or Roth IRA, the IRA will be worth only $220,714 at the end of 2045 at age 69. See Figure 15.4. This is substantially less than if contributions started at age 30. This is so even though all the contributions starting at age 50 were at the $6,000 level, while contributions starting at age 30 started at $4,000.

FIGURE 15.3

IRA Accumulations

IRA Type:	Traditional/Roth	Year:	2006
Owner's Date of Birth (Age 30):	6/30/1976	Account Balance:	$0
Contribution Amount:	Maximum	Target Amount:	Maximum
Target Increase Rate:	NA	Years Until Contributions:	0
Years of Contributions:	40	Years After Contributions:	0
Contributions:	End of Year	Account Growth Rate:	6%
Indexing Rate:	0%	Cumulative Value:	$791,738

1) All Roth IRA and deductible traditional IRA contributions may be subject to phaseout.
2) With a traditional IRA, contributions must stop and distributions must start at age 70½.

Year	Age	Balance	Target	Maximum	Contribution	Balance +
2006	30	0	4,000	4,000	4,000	4,000
2007	31	4,000	4,000	4,000	4,000	8,240
2008	32	8,240	5,000	5,000	5,000	13,734
2009	33	13,734	5,000	5,000	5,000	19,558
2010	34	19,558	5,000	5,000	5,000	25,732
2011	35	25,732	5,000	5,000	5,000	32,276
2012	36	32,276	5,000	5,000	5,000	39,212
2013	37	39,212	5,000	5,000	5,000	46,565
2014	38	46,565	5,000	5,000	5,000	54,359
2015	39	54,359	5,000	5,000	5,000	62,621
2016	40	62,621	5,000	5,000	5,000	71,378
2017	41	71,378	5,000	5,000	5,000	80,661
2018	42	80,661	5,000	5,000	5,000	90,500
2019	43	90,500	5,000	5,000	5,000	100,930
2020	44	100,930	5,000	5,000	5,000	111,986
2021	45	111,986	5,000	5,000	5,000	123,705
2022	46	123,705	5,000	5,000	5,000	136,127
2023	47	136,127	5,000	5,000	5,000	149,295
2024	48	149,295	5,000	5,000	5,000	163,253
2025	49	163,253	5,000	5,000	5,000	178,048
2026	50	178,048	6,000	6,000	6,000	194,731
2027	51	194,731	6,000	6,000	6,000	212,415
2028	52	212,415	6,000	6,000	6,000	231,160
2029	53	231,160	6,000	6,000	6,000	251,029
2030	54	251,029	6,000	6,000	6,000	272,091
2031	55	272,091	6,000	6,000	6,000	294,416
2032	56	294,416	6,000	6,000	6,000	318,081
2033	57	318,081	6,000	6,000	6,000	343,166
2034	58	343,166	6,000	6,000	6,000	369,756
2035	59	369,756	6,000	6,000	6,000	397,942
2036	60	397,942	6,000	6,000	6,000	427,818
2037	61	427,818	6,000	6,000	6,000	459,487
2038	62	459,487	6,000	6,000	6,000	493,056
2039	63	493,056	6,000	6,000	6,000	528,640
2040	64	528,640	6,000	6,000	6,000	566,358
2041	65	566,358	6,000	6,000	6,000	606,340
2042	66	606,340	6,000	6,000	6,000	648,720
2043	67	648,720	6,000	6,000	6,000	693,643
2044	68	693,643	6,000	6,000	6,000	741,262
2045	69	741,262	6,000	6,000	6,000	791,738

FIGURE 15.4

IRA Accumulations

IRA Type:	Traditional/Roth	Year: 2006
Owner's Date of Birth (Age 30):	6/30/1976	Account Balance: $0
Contribution Amount:	Maximum	Target Amount: Maximum
Target Increase Rate:	NA	Years Until Contributions: 20
Years of Contributions:	20	Years After Contributions: 0
Contributions:	End of Year	Account Growth Rate: 6%
Indexing Rate:	0%	Cumulative Value: $220,714

1) All Roth IRA and deductible traditional IRA contributions may be subject to phaseout.
2) With a traditional IRA, contributions must stop and distributions must start at age 70½.

Year	Age	Balance	Target	Maximum	Contribution	Balance +
2006	30	0	0	4,000	0	0
2007	31	0	0	4,000	0	0
2008	32	0	0	5,000	0	0
2009	33	0	0	5,000	0	0
2010	34	0	0	5,000	0	0
2011	35	0	0	5,000	0	0
2012	36	0	0	5,000	0	0
2013	37	0	0	5,000	0	0
2014	38	0	0	5,000	0	0
2015	39	0	0	5,000	0	0
2016	40	0	0	5,000	0	0
2017	41	0	0	5,000	0	0
2018	42	0	0	5,000	0	0
2019	43	0	0	5,000	0	0
2020	44	0	0	5,000	0	0
2021	45	0	0	5,000	0	0
2022	46	0	0	5,000	0	0
2023	47	0	0	5,000	0	0
2024	48	0	0	5,000	0	0
2025	49	0	0	5,000	0	0
2026	50	0	6,000	6,000	6,000	6,000
2027	51	6,000	6,000	6,000	6,000	12,360
2028	52	12,360	6,000	6,000	6,000	19,102
2029	53	19,102	6,000	6,000	6,000	26,248
2030	54	26,248	6,000	6,000	6,000	33,823
2031	55	33,823	6,000	6,000	6,000	41,852
2032	56	41,852	6,000	6,000	6,000	50,363
2033	57	50,363	6,000	6,000	6,000	59,385
2034	58	59,385	6,000	6,000	6,000	68,948
2035	59	68,948	6,000	6,000	6,000	79,085
2036	60	79,085	6,000	6,000	6,000	89,830
2037	61	89,830	6,000	6,000	6,000	101,220
2038	62	101,220	6,000	6,000	6,000	113,293
2039	63	113,293	6,000	6,000	6,000	126,091
2040	64	126,091	6,000	6,000	6,000	139,656
2041	65	139,656	6,000	6,000	6,000	154,035
2042	66	154,035	6,000	6,000	6,000	169,277
2043	67	169,277	6,000	6,000	6,000	185,434
2044	68	185,434	6,000	6,000	6,000	202,560
2045	69	202,560	6,000	6,000	6,000	220,714

Indeed, if a person age 30 contributed only $1,500 annually to IRAs for 40 years, that person would accumulate more (future value of annuity factor of 154.7620 x $1,500 = $232,143) than the person who made maximum annual contributions starting at age 50 for 20 years ($220,714).

Stretching an IRA

If it makes sense to use the power of accumulation in an IRA, it may also make sense to try and keep the money in the IRA as long as possible. This is often referred to as stretching an IRA and an IRA using this technique may be called a stretch IRA. The required minimum distribution (RMD) rules may limit the ability of a person to stretch an IRA.

Of course, if the individual needs payments from the IRA, stretching the IRA may not be possible. If the individual has other property, consider whether the individual's needs can be met from those other assets.

An individual naming a beneficiary of an IRA may wish to consider whether an IRA could be stretched out more if one beneficiary was named rather than another. For example, a spouse beneficiary could make an election to be treated as the owner of the IRA for RMD purposes. The spouse could then essentially spread distributions from a nonRoth IRA over the life expectancy of the spouse and another beneficiary. In general, the younger the other beneficiary, the longer distributions can be stretched.

> Example. Assume a nonRoth IRA owner is age 70 in 2006 and dies at age 87. The spouse is beneficiary and elects to treat the IRA as the spouse's own. The spouse is age 50 and dies at age 84. The spouse has a beneficiary who is age 0 in the year of the spouse's death. Distributions can be stretched out until 2122. Distributions of about $5,521,924 can be made. See Figure 15.5.

FIGURE 15.5

IRA Required Minimum Distributions

IRA Type:	NonRoth	Year:	2006
Account Balance:	$100,000	Account Growth Rate:	6%
Beneficiary:	Spouse	Secondary Beneficiary:	Yes

IRA Owner (Current Age: 70; Age at Death: 87)

Date of Birth:	6/30/1936	Date of Death:	3/31/2023

Spouse Beneficiary (Current Age: 50; Age at Death: 84)

Date of Birth:	6/30/1956	Date of Death:	3/31/2040
Spousal Election:	Yes	Spouse Predeceases:	No

Spouse's Beneficiary (Current Age: -34)		Date of Birth:	1/1/2040

Year	Age	Age	Account Balance	RMD Factor	Balance Plus 6%	RMD
2006	70	50	100,000	35.1	106,000	2,849
2007	71	51	103,151	34.2	109,340	3,016
2008	72	52	106,324	33.2	112,703	3,203
2009	73	53	109,500	32.3	116,070	3,390
2010	74	54	112,680	31.4	119,441	3,589
2011	75	55	115,852	30.4	122,803	3,811
2012	76	56	118,992	29.5	126,132	4,034
2013	77	57	122,098	28.6	129,424	4,269
2014	78	58	125,155	27.7	132,664	4,518
2015	79	59	128,146	26.8	135,835	4,782
2016	80	60	131,053	25.9	138,916	5,060
2017	81	61	133,856	25.0	141,887	5,354
2018	82	62	136,533	24.1	144,725	5,665
2019	83	63	139,060	23.3	147,404	5,968
2020	84	64	141,436	22.4	149,922	6,314
2021	85	65	143,608	21.6	152,224	6,649
2022	86	66	145,575	20.7	154,309	7,033
2023	87	67	147,276	19.9	156,113	7,401
2024	<68>	<-16>	148,712	NA	157,635	0
2025	<69>	<-15>	157,635	NA	167,093	0
2026	<70>	<-14>	167,093	27.4	177,119	6,098
2027	<71>	<-13>	171,021	26.5	181,282	6,454
2028	<72>	<-12>	174,828	25.6	185,318	6,829
2029	<73>	<-11>	178,489	24.7	189,198	7,226
2030	<74>	<-10>	181,972	23.8	192,890	7,646

FIGURE 15.5 (continued)

Year	Age	Age	Account Balance	RMD Factor	Balance Plus 6%	RMD
2031	<75>	<-9>	185,244	22.9	196,359	8,089
2032	<76>	<-8>	188,270	22.0	199,566	8,558
2033	<77>	<-7>	191,008	21.2	202,468	9,010
2034	<78>	<-6>	193,458	20.3	205,065	9,530
2035	<79>	<-5>	195,535	19.5	207,267	10,027
2036	<80>	<-4>	197,240	18.7	209,074	10,548
2037	<81>	<-3>	198,526	17.9	210,438	11,091
2038	<82>	<-2>	199,347	17.1	211,308	11,658
2039	<83>	<-1>	199,650	16.3	211,629	12,248
2040	<84>	<0>	199,381	15.5	211,344	12,863
2041	[<85>]	<1>	198,481	81.6	210,390	2,432
2042	[<86>]	<2>	207,958	80.6	220,435	2,580
2043	[<87>]	<3>	217,855	79.6	230,926	2,737
2044	[<88>]	<4>	228,189	78.6	241,880	2,903
2045	[<89>]	<5>	238,977	77.6	253,316	3,080
2046	[<90>]	<6>	250,236	76.6	265,250	3,267
2047	[<91>]	<7>	261,983	75.6	277,702	3,465
2048	[<92>]	<8>	274,237	74.6	290,691	3,676
2049	[<93>]	<9>	287,015	73.6	304,236	3,900
2050	[<94>]	<10>	300,336	72.6	318,356	4,137
2051	[<95>]	<11>	314,219	71.6	333,072	4,389
2052	[<96>]	<12>	328,683	70.6	348,404	4,656
2053	[<97>]	<13>	343,748	69.6	364,373	4,939
2054	[<98>]	<14>	359,434	68.6	381,000	5,240
2055	[<99>]	<15>	375,760	67.6	398,306	5,559
2056	[<100>]	<16>	392,747	66.6	416,312	5,897
2057	[<101>]	<17>	410,415	65.6	435,040	6,256
2058	[<102>]	<18>	428,784	64.6	454,511	6,638
2059	[<103>]	<19>	447,873	63.6	474,745	7,042
2060	[<104>]	<20>	467,703	62.6	495,765	7,471
2061	[<105>]	<21>	488,294	61.6	517,592	7,927
2062	[<106>]	<22>	509,665	60.6	540,245	8,410
2063	[<107>]	<23>	531,835	59.6	563,745	8,923
2064	[<108>]	<24>	554,822	58.6	588,111	9,468
2065	[<109>]	<25>	578,643	57.6	613,362	10,046
2066	[<110>]	<26>	603,316	56.6	639,515	10,659
2067	[<111>]	<27>	628,856	55.6	666,587	11,310
2068	[<112>]	<28>	655,277	54.6	694,594	12,001
2069	[<113>]	<29>	682,593	53.6	723,549	12,735

FIGURE 15.5 (continued)

Year	Age	Age	Account Balance	RMD Factor	Balance Plus 6%	RMD
2070	[<114>]	<30>	710,814	52.6	753,463	13,514
2071	[<115>]	<31>	739,949	51.6	784,346	14,340
2072	[<116>]	<32>	770,006	50.6	816,206	15,218
2073	[<117>]	<33>	800,988	49.6	849,047	16,149
2074	[<118>]	<34>	832,898	48.6	882,872	17,138
2075	[<119>]	<35>	865,734	47.6	917,678	18,188
2076	[<120>]	<36>	899,490	46.6	953,459	19,302
2077	[<121>]	<37>	934,157	45.6	990,206	20,486
2078	[<122>]	<38>	969,720	44.6	1,027,903	21,743
2079	[<123>]	<39>	1,006,160	43.6	1,066,530	23,077
2080	[<124>]	<40>	1,043,453	42.6	1,106,060	24,494
2081	[<125>]	<41>	1,081,566	41.6	1,146,460	25,999
2082	[<126>]	<42>	1,120,461	40.6	1,187,689	27,598
2083	[<127>]	<43>	1,160,091	39.6	1,229,696	29,295
2084	[<128>]	<44>	1,200,401	38.6	1,272,425	31,098
2085	[<129>]	<45>	1,241,327	37.6	1,315,807	33,014
2086	[<130>]	<46>	1,282,793	36.6	1,359,761	35,049
2087	[<131>]	<47>	1,324,712	35.6	1,404,195	37,211
2088	[<132>]	<48>	1,366,984	34.6	1,449,003	39,508
2089	[<133>]	<49>	1,409,495	33.6	1,494,065	41,949
2090	[<134>]	<50>	1,452,116	32.6	1,539,243	44,543
2091	[<135>]	<51>	1,494,700	31.6	1,584,382	47,301
2092	[<136>]	<52>	1,537,081	30.6	1,629,306	50,231
2093	[<137>]	<53>	1,579,075	29.6	1,673,819	53,347
2094	[<138>]	<54>	1,620,472	28.6	1,717,700	56,660
2095	[<139>]	<55>	1,661,040	27.6	1,760,702	60,183
2096	[<140>]	<56>	1,700,519	26.6	1,802,550	63,929
2097	[<141>]	<57>	1,738,621	25.6	1,842,938	67,915
2098	[<142>]	<58>	1,775,023	24.6	1,881,524	72,155
2099	[<143>]	<59>	1,809,369	23.6	1,917,931	76,668
2100	[<144>]	<60>	1,841,263	22.6	1,951,739	81,472
2101	[<145>]	<61>	1,870,267	21.6	1,982,483	86,586
2102	[<146>]	<62>	1,895,897	20.6	2,009,651	92,034
2103	[<147>]	<63>	1,917,617	19.6	2,032,674	97,838
2104	[<148>]	<64>	1,934,836	18.6	2,050,926	104,023
2105	[<149>]	<65>	1,946,903	17.6	2,063,717	110,619
2106	[<150>]	<66>	1,953,098	16.6	2,070,284	117,657
2107	[<151>]	<67>	1,952,627	15.6	2,069,785	125,168
2108	[<152>]	<68>	1,944,617	14.6	2,061,294	133,193
2109	[<153>]	<69>	1,928,101	13.6	2,043,787	141,772

FIGURE 15.5 (continued)

Year	Age	Age	Account Balance	RMD Factor	Balance Plus 6%	RMD
2110	[<154>]	<70>	1,902,015	12.6	2,016,136	150,954
2111	[<155>]	<71>	1,865,182	11.6	1,977,093	160,792
2112	[<156>]	<72>	1,816,301	10.6	1,925,279	171,349
2113	[<157>]	<73>	1,753,930	9.6	1,859,166	182,701
2114	[<158>]	<74>	1,676,465	8.6	1,777,053	194,938
2115	[<159>]	<75>	1,582,115	7.6	1,677,042	208,173
2116	[<160>]	<76>	1,468,869	6.6	1,557,001	222,556
2117	[<161>]	<77>	1,334,445	5.6	1,414,512	238,294
2118	[<162>]	<78>	1,176,218	4.6	1,246,791	255,700
2119	[<163>]	<79>	991,091	3.6	1,050,556	275,303
2120	[<164>]	<80>	775,253	2.6	821,768	298,174
2121	[<165>]	<81>	523,594	1.6	555,010	327,247
2122	[<166>]	<82>	227,763	0.6	241,429	241,429
					Total	5,521,924

In the case of a Roth IRA using the spousal election, distributions need not begin until after the death of the IRA owner and the spouse. And the younger the next beneficiary is, the longer distributions can be stretched.

> Example. Assume the facts are the same as in the last example except that the IRA is a Roth IRA. Distributions can once again be stretched out until 2122. However, distributions do not even need to start until 2041, the year after the spouse dies. Distributions of about $20,512,583 can be made. See Figure 15.6.

If there are multiple beneficiaries of an IRA, the oldest beneficiary must be used and the ability to stretch the IRA may be reduced. However, separate IRAs or IRA accounts can be created. In general, the required minimum distribution is calculated separately for each IRA. Therefore, separate IRAs or accounts can be created and the accounts can have different beneficiaries so as to stretch out the IRAs.

FIGURE 15.6

IRA Required Minimum Distributions

IRA Type:	Roth	Year:	2006
IRA Type:	Roth	Year:	2006
Account Balance:	$100,000	Account Growth Rate:	6%
Beneficiary:	Spouse	Secondary Beneficiary:	Yes

IRA Owner (Current Age: 70; Age at Death: 87)

| Date of Birth: | 6/30/1936 | Date of Death: | 3/31/2023 |

Spouse Beneficiary (Current Age: 50; Age at Death: 84)

| Date of Birth: | 6/30/1956 | Date of Death: | 3/31/2040 |
| Spousal Election: | Yes | Spouse Predeceases: | No |

Spouse's Beneficiary (Current Age: -34)   Date of Birth: 1/1/2040

Year	Age	Age	Account Balance	RMD Factor	Balance Plus 6%	RMD
2006	70	50	100,000	NA	106,000	0
2007	71	51	106,000	NA	112,360	0
2008	72	52	112,360	NA	119,102	0
2009	73	53	119,102	NA	126,248	0
2010	74	54	126,248	NA	133,823	0
2011	75	55	133,823	NA	141,852	0
2012	76	56	141,852	NA	150,363	0
2013	77	57	150,363	NA	159,385	0
2014	78	58	159,385	NA	168,948	0
2015	79	59	168,948	NA	179,085	0
2016	80	60	179,085	NA	189,830	0
2017	81	61	189,830	NA	201,220	0
2018	82	62	201,220	NA	213,293	0
2019	83	63	213,293	NA	226,091	0
2020	84	64	226,091	NA	239,656	0
2021	85	65	239,656	NA	254,035	0
2022	86	66	254,035	NA	269,277	0
2023	87	67	269,277	NA	285,434	0
2024	<68>	<-16>	285,434	NA	302,560	0
2025	<69>	<-15>	302,560	NA	320,714	0
2026	<70>	<-14>	320,714	NA	339,957	0
2027	<71>	<-13>	339,957	NA	360,354	0
2028	<72>	<-12>	360,354	NA	381,975	0
2029	<73>	<-11>	381,975	NA	404,893	0
2030	<74>	<-10>	404,893	NA	429,187	0

FIGURE 15.6 (continued)

Year	Age	Age	Account Balance	RMD Factor	Balance Plus 6%	RMD
2031	<75>	<-9>	429,187	NA	454,938	0
2032	<76>	<-8>	454,938	NA	482,234	0
2033	<77>	<-7>	482,234	NA	511,168	0
2034	<78>	<-6>	511,168	NA	541,838	0
2035	<79>	<-5>	541,838	NA	574,348	0
2036	<80>	<-4>	574,348	NA	608,809	0
2037	<81>	<-3>	608,809	NA	645,338	0
2038	<82>	<-2>	645,338	NA	684,058	0
2039	<83>	<-1>	684,058	NA	725,101	0
2040	<84>	<0>	725,101	NA	768,607	0
2041	[<85>]	<1>	768,607	81.6	814,723	9,419
2042	[<86>]	<2>	805,304	80.6	853,622	9,991
2043	[<87>]	<3>	843,631	79.6	894,249	10,598
2044	[<88>]	<4>	883,651	78.6	936,670	11,242
2045	[<89>]	<5>	925,428	77.6	980,954	11,926
2046	[<90>]	<6>	969,028	76.6	1,027,170	12,650
2047	[<91>]	<7>	1,014,520	75.6	1,075,391	13,420
2048	[<92>]	<8>	1,061,971	74.6	1,125,689	14,236
2049	[<93>]	<9>	1,111,453	73.6	1,178,140	15,101
2050	[<94>]	<10>	1,163,039	72.6	1,232,821	16,020
2051	[<95>]	<11>	1,216,801	71.6	1,289,809	16,994
2052	[<96>]	<12>	1,272,815	70.6	1,349,184	18,029
2053	[<97>]	<13>	1,331,155	69.6	1,411,024	19,126
2054	[<98>]	<14>	1,391,898	68.6	1,475,412	20,290
2055	[<99>]	<15>	1,455,122	67.6	1,542,429	21,525
2056	[<100>]	<16>	1,520,904	66.6	1,612,158	22,836
2057	[<101>]	<17>	1,589,322	65.6	1,684,681	24,227
2058	[<102>]	<18>	1,660,454	64.6	1,760,081	25,704
2059	[<103>]	<19>	1,734,377	63.6	1,838,440	27,270
2060	[<104>]	<20>	1,811,170	62.6	1,919,840	28,932
2061	[<105>]	<21>	1,890,908	61.6	2,004,362	30,697
2062	[<106>]	<22>	1,973,665	60.6	2,092,085	32,569
2063	[<107>]	<23>	2,059,516	59.6	2,183,087	34,556
2064	[<108>]	<24>	2,148,531	58.6	2,277,443	36,664
2065	[<109>]	<25>	2,240,779	57.6	2,375,226	38,902
2066	[<110>]	<26>	2,336,324	56.6	2,476,503	41,278
2067	[<111>]	<27>	2,435,225	55.6	2,581,338	43,799
2068	[<112>]	<28>	2,537,539	54.6	2,689,791	46,475
2069	[<113>]	<29>	2,643,316	53.6	2,801,915	49,316
2070	[<114>]	<30>	2,752,599	52.6	2,917,755	52,331

FIGURE 15.6 (continued)

Year	Age	Age	Account Balance	RMD Factor	Balance Plus 6%	RMD
2071	[<115>]	<31>	2,865,424	51.6	3,037,349	55,531
2072	[<116>]	<32>	2,981,818	50.6	3,160,727	58,929
2073	[<117>]	<33>	3,101,798	49.6	3,287,906	62,536
2074	[<118>]	<34>	3,225,370	48.6	3,418,892	66,366
2075	[<119>]	<35>	3,352,526	47.6	3,553,678	70,431
2076	[<120>]	<36>	3,483,247	46.6	3,692,242	74,748
2077	[<121>]	<37>	3,617,494	45.6	3,834,544	79,331
2078	[<122>]	<38>	3,755,213	44.6	3,980,526	84,198
2079	[<123>]	<39>	3,896,328	43.6	4,130,108	89,365
2080	[<124>]	<40>	4,040,743	42.6	4,283,188	94,853
2081	[<125>]	<41>	4,188,335	41.6	4,439,635	100,681
2082	[<126>]	<42>	4,338,954	40.6	4,599,291	106,871
2083	[<127>]	<43>	4,492,420	39.6	4,761,965	113,445
2084	[<128>]	<44>	4,648,520	38.6	4,927,431	120,428
2085	[<129>]	<45>	4,807,003	37.6	5,095,423	127,846
2086	[<130>]	<46>	4,967,577	36.6	5,265,632	135,726
2087	[<131>]	<47>	5,129,906	35.6	5,437,700	144,098
2088	[<132>]	<48>	5,293,602	34.6	5,611,218	152,994
2089	[<133>]	<49>	5,458,224	33.6	5,785,717	162,447
2090	[<134>]	<50>	5,623,270	32.6	5,960,666	172,493
2091	[<135>]	<51>	5,788,173	31.6	6,135,463	183,170
2092	[<136>]	<52>	5,952,293	30.6	6,309,431	194,519
2093	[<137>]	<53>	6,114,912	29.6	6,481,807	206,585
2094	[<138>]	<54>	6,275,222	28.6	6,651,735	219,413
2095	[<139>]	<55>	6,432,322	27.6	6,818,261	233,055
2096	[<140>]	<56>	6,585,206	26.6	6,980,318	247,564
2097	[<141>]	<57>	6,732,754	25.6	7,136,719	262,998
2098	[<142>]	<58>	6,873,721	24.6	7,286,144	279,420
2099	[<143>]	<59>	7,006,724	23.6	7,427,127	296,895
2100	[<144>]	<60>	7,130,232	22.6	7,558,046	315,497
2101	[<145>]	<61>	7,242,549	21.6	7,677,102	335,303
2102	[<146>]	<62>	7,341,799	20.6	7,782,307	356,398
2103	[<147>]	<63>	7,425,909	19.6	7,871,464	378,873
2104	[<148>]	<64>	7,492,591	18.6	7,942,146	402,828
2105	[<149>]	<65>	7,539,318	17.6	7,991,677	428,370
2106	[<150>]	<66>	7,563,307	16.6	8,017,105	455,621
2107	[<151>]	<67>	7,561,484	15.6	8,015,173	484,711
2108	[<152>]	<68>	7,530,462	14.6	7,982,290	515,785
2109	[<153>]	<69>	7,466,505	13.6	7,914,495	549,008
2110	[<154>]	<70>	7,365,487	12.6	7,807,416	584,563

FIGURE 15.6 (continued)

Year	Age	Age	Account Balance	RMD Factor	Balance Plus 6%	RMD
2111	[<155>]	<71>	7,222,853	11.6	7,656,224	622,660
2112	[<156>]	<72>	7,033,564	10.6	7,455,578	663,544
2113	[<157>]	<73>	6,792,034	9.6	7,199,556	707,504
2114	[<158>]	<74>	6,492,052	8.6	6,881,575	754,890
2115	[<159>]	<75>	6,126,685	7.6	6,494,286	806,143
2116	[<160>]	<76>	5,688,143	6.6	6,029,432	861,840
2117	[<161>]	<77>	5,167,592	5.6	5,477,648	922,785
2118	[<162>]	<78>	4,554,863	4.6	4,828,155	990,188
2119	[<163>]	<79>	3,837,967	3.6	4,068,245	1,066,102
2120	[<164>]	<80>	3,002,143	2.6	3,182,272	1,154,671
2121	[<165>]	<81>	2,027,601	1.6	2,149,257	1,267,252
2122	[<166>]	<82>	882,005	0.6	934,925	934,925
					Total	20,512,583

Taxes

Taxes and tax rates may be important in the decision to contribute and retain property in an IRA. So how are IRAs taxed? And how does that compare to property held outside an IRA? And how does that affect the power of accumulation and the stretching of an IRA?

General Taxation of IRAs

An income tax deduction may be available for contributions to a traditional IRA. Taking a tax deduction leaves the individual with additional funds to invest. Additionally, nondeductible contributions may be made to a traditional IRA. The assets in the traditional IRA accumulate tax-free until distributed. Upon distribution, the portion of a distribution pro-rated to nondeductible contributions can be excluded; the rest of a distribution is subject to income tax and taxed as ordinary income.

Nondeductible contributions may also be made to a Roth IRA. The assets in the Roth IRA accumulate tax-free until distributed. Upon distribution, contributions are treated as distributed first and contributions are received tax-free. In addition, distributions received after age 59½, death, or disability can generally be received tax-free as qualified distributions. Otherwise, distributions from a Roth IRA are taxed as ordinary income.

Contributions to traditional IRAs and Roth IRAs are subject to common contribution limits. However, contributions cannot be made to a traditional IRA once the IRA owner reaches age 70½. Also, deductible contributions to a traditional IRA and nondeductible contributions to a Roth IRA may be subject to phaseout based on modified adjusted gross income.

It is generally better to make nondeductible contributions to a Roth IRA than to a traditional IRA because of the more favorable taxation of Roth distributions, except to the extent that contributions to a Roth IRA are phased out based on modified adjusted gross income. As to whether it is better to make a deductible contribution to a traditional IRA or a nondeductible contribution to a Roth IRA, see Chapter 9.

Employers with a SEP IRA generally make contributions to the IRA of each covered employee. In the case of the SAR-SEP IRA variety, the employee can elect to defer a portion of salary. In either case, the amount contributed to the IRA is excluded from the employee's income. Thus, it is generally the same as if the employee receives a tax deduction for the contribution. It leaves the individual with additional funds to invest. In addition, traditional IRA type contributions can also be made to SEP IRAs. The assets in the SEP IRA accumulate tax-free until distributed. Distributions from a SEP IRA are taxed the same as distributions from a traditional IRA.

Employees covered by a SIMPLE IRA can make salary reduction contributions. In addition, the employer can make matching contributions or nonelective contributions. All such contributions are excluded from the employee's income. Thus, it is generally the same as if the employee receives a tax deduction for the contribution. It leaves the individual with additional funds to invest. If the employer is making matching contributions, the employee has the advantage of receiving that extra matching contribution if the employee makes salary reduction contributions. The assets in the SIMPLE IRA accumulate tax-free until distributed. Distributions from a SIMPLE IRA are fully subject to income tax as ordinary income.

A traditional IRA, SEP IRA, or a SIMPLE IRA can be converted to a Roth IRA in a taxable event. For the price of the current tax on conversion, it may be possible to obtain later distributions from the Roth IRA that are tax-free. As to whether it makes sense to convert to a Roth IRA, see Chapter 12.

The taxable portion of a distribution from an IRA may be subject to a 10 percent early distribution penalty tax if made before age 59½, death, or disability. Certain other exceptions are available from the penalty tax, including substantially equal periodic payments (SEPPs). See Chapter 13 for more on the early distribution penalty tax.

Qualified charitable distributions from traditional or Roth IRAs are not included in income in 2006 and 2007. See "Lifetime Gifts to Charity" in Chapter 14.

Inside an IRA Versus Outside an IRA

Where tax rates and growth rates are the same for an IRA as for assets outside the IRA, the IRA generally has the advantage of tax-deferral (whether from a deduction for contributions that will not be taxed until distribution or from earnings within the IRA), which allows greater amounts of accumulation. The taxpayer is able to put the tax deferred to work, so accumulations are greater.

Many people anticipate that income will be lower in retirement, so income tax rates will be lower then. If this happens, the IRA has another advantage, deferring taxes until rates are lower.

Indeed, in the case of the Roth IRA, distributions can even be received tax-free. Generally, assets could not be received tax-free outside an IRA without sacrificing some investment return (i.e., the growth rate would be lower).

The general lowering of capital gains and dividends tax rates to 15 percent through 2010 may substantially reduce or even reverse the advantage that IRAs generally have. (However, Roth IRAs can generally be distributed tax-free.) Taxable distributions from IRAs are taxed at ordinary income tax rates. These rates currently range from 10 percent to 35 percent. Therefore, if the assets outside the IRA are invested in stock, the tax deferred inside the IRA would need to grow at a rate sufficient to offset any differential in tax rates.

It may make sense to make investments inside an IRA that are taxed at ordinary income tax rates (but are deferred because of the IRA). Investments outside the IRA could be invested in assets that receive special tax treatment outside an IRA (e.g., stocks, tax-free bonds). In this way, a person might diversify his portfolio while obtaining the best of both tax worlds.

Where taxation outside the IRA is annual, a tax-adjusted growth rate can generally be used for such investments. The growth rate is multiplied by one minus the tax rate. For example, a 6 percent growth rate multiplied by one minus a 28 percent tax rate equals a tax-adjusted growth rate of 4.32 percent.

Where taxation is deferred, whether inside the IRA or outside the IRA, simply use the growth rate until taxation. Then multiply the taxable portion by the tax rate, and subtract the tax from the accumulated value.

At times it may be necessary to factor the early distribution penalty tax into a comparison of IRAs and other investments. Figure 15.7 can be used to determine the number of years that it takes a deductible contribution to an IRA to overcome the early distribution penalty tax (assuming the penalty would apply, see above and Chapter 13) at a given interest rate and a tax rate that stays constant. Figure 15.8 can be used to determine the number of years that it takes a nondeductible contribution to an IRA to overcome the early distribution penalty tax (assuming the penalty would apply, see above and Chapter 13) at a given interest rate and a tax rate that stays constant if growth is taxed upon distribution from the IRA. The early distribution penalty tax could be factored into the examples below by applying the 10 percent tax to taxable distributions from an IRA where appropriate.

The following can be observed about the break even point for overcoming the early distribution penalty.

1.   The higher the regular tax rate, the shorter is the break even point.

2.   The higher the interest rate, the shorter is the break even point.

3.   The break even point is shorter for deductible contributions than for nondeductible contributions.

Examples

A limited number of examples follow. Many more comparisons could be made (e.g., change relative tax rates some more). Sometimes, running the numbers is the only way to know what is better in a particular circumstance.

Due to possible rounding differences (as well as the general nature of projecting future results), insignificant differences between results under different scenarios can essentially be disregarded. Also, future value factors below and in Appendix E are shown rounded to 4 places. However, the future value factors actually used here, and generally throughout the *IRA Calculator* software, are essentially unrounded.

Comparisons of scenarios, while helpful in making the decision of whether to contribute to an IRA and which IRA to contribute to, are generally theoretical. Comparisons are made on an isolated basis as if nothing else happens in the IRA world during the years between contribution and distribution, and as if no other contributions have ever been made to IRAs. However, for purposes of taxation of distributions, generally all nonRoth IRAs are grouped together and all Roth IRAs are grouped together. Other contributions, conversions, and distributions with respect to these or other IRAs could affect taxation of the IRAs being compared.

FIGURE 15.7

Premature Distribution Penalty (10%) - IRA Deductible Contribution - Taxable Distribution (Break Even Point - Years*)

Interest	Constant Tax Rate					
	10%	15%	25%	28%	33%	35%
1%	119	85	58	54	50	49
2%	61	43	30	28	25	25
3%	41	29	20	19	17	17
4%	31	22	15	14	13	13
5%	25	18	12	12	11	10
6%	21	15	11	10	9	9
7%	18	13	9	9	8	8
8%	16	12	8	8	7	7
9%	15	11	7	7	6	6
10%	13	10	7	6	6	6
11%	12	9	6	6	5	5
12%	11	8	6	5	5	5
13%	11	8	5	5	5	5
14%	10	7	5	5	4	4
15%	9	7	5	5	4	4
16%	9	6	5	4	4	4
17%	9	6	4	4	4	4
18%	8	6	4	4	4	4
19%	8	6	4	4	3	3
20%	8	5	4	4	3	3

* Years that it takes a deductible contribution to an IRA to overcome the early distribution penalty tax (see Chapter 13) at a given interest rate and a constant tax rate if the distribution from the IRA is taxable. The deductible contribution is compared to investment of an after-tax equivalent amount outside of an IRA, with the same growth rate but with annual taxation. For example, with a 35 percent tax rate and a 7 percent interest rate, it would take 8 years for a deductible contribution to overcome the early distribution penalty tax and outdo a similar investment outside the IRA. However, if there is less than 8 years until the individual reaches age 59½, death, or disability, or one of the other exceptions to the penalty tax applies, there is no early distribution penalty tax to overcome.

FIGURE 15.8

Premature Distribution Penalty (10%) - IRA Nondeductible Contribution - Taxable Distribution (Break Even Point - Years*)

Interest	Constant Tax Rate					
	10%	15%	25%	28%	33%	35%
1%	187	141	102	96	89	87
2%	95	72	52	49	46	45
3%	64	48	35	33	31	30
4%	49	37	27	26	24	23
5%	40	30	22	21	19	19
6%	33	25	19	18	17	16
7%	29	22	16	16	14	14
8%	26	20	15	14	13	13
9%	23	18	13	13	12	11
10%	21	16	12	11	11	11
11%	20	15	11	11	10	10
12%	18	14	10	10	9	9
13%	17	13	10	9	9	9
14%	16	12	9	9	8	8
15%	15	12	9	8	8	8
16%	14	11	8	8	7	7
17%	14	11	8	8	7	7
18%	13	10	8	7	7	7
19%	12	10	7	7	7	6
20%	12	9	7	7	6	6

* Years that it takes a nondeductible contribution to an IRA to overcome the early distribution penalty tax (see Chapter 13) at a given interest rate and a constant tax rate if growth is taxed upon distribution from the IRA. The nondeductible contribution is compared to investment of an equal amount outside of an IRA, with the same growth rate but with annual taxation. For example, with a 28 percent tax rate and a 6 percent interest rate, it would take 18 years for a nondeductible contribution to overcome the early distribution penalty tax and outdo a similar investment outside the IRA. However, if there is less than 18 years until the individual reaches age 59½, death, or disability, or one of the other exceptions to the penalty tax applies, there is no early distribution penalty tax to overcome.

Example. Traditional IRA, nondeductible contribution, 28 percent tax rate. Ann, age 30 contributes $4,000 to a traditional IRA in a nondeductible contribution. Assuming a 6% growth rate, at age 70 the $4,000 will have grown to $41,144 (4 x 10,286 from Figure 15.1). If the $41,144 is then distributed from the traditional IRA and subject to tax at 28 percent, after tax of $10,400 (($41,144 - $4,000) x 28 percent)), Ann has $30,744 remaining.

Example. Roth IRA, qualified distribution. If Ann contributed the $4,000 to a Roth IRA (in a nondeductible contribution), she would have accumulated the same amount at age 70, $41,144. However, the distribution from the Roth IRA would be a qualified distribution that is received tax-free because Ann is at least age 59½ at distribution. Ann has $41,144 remaining. This is substantially more than with the traditional IRA. (If the distribution were not qualified, the result here would generally be the same as with the nondeductible contribution to a traditional IRA.)

Example. Outside IRA, tax-deferred, 28 percent tax rate. If Ann had not contributed the $4,000 to an IRA and tax on the amount outside the IRA was deferred until age 70, she would have accumulated the same amount at age 70. However, after tax of $10,400 (same 28 percent tax rate), Ann has $30,744 remaining. This is the same as with the traditional IRA but much less than with the Roth IRA.

Example. Outside IRA, tax-deferred, 15 percent tax rate. If Ann had not contributed the $4,000 to an IRA and tax on the amount outside the IRA was deferred until age 70, she would have accumulated the same amount at age 70. However, after tax of $5,572 (15 percent tax rate), Ann has $35,572 remaining. This is the much more than with the traditional IRA but much less than with the Roth IRA.

Example. Outside IRA, taxed annually, 28 percent tax rate. However, if Ann had not contributed the $4,000 to an IRA and the amount outside the IRA was taxed annually at 28 percent, she would have less at age 70. Her tax-adjusted growth rate would be 4.32 percent (6% growth rate x (1 - 28% tax rate). The future value factor for a single sum would be 5.4288 ((1 + 4.32 percent) ^ 40 years). Ann would have $21,715 ($4,000 x 5.4288) remaining. This is much less than with either the traditional IRA or the Roth IRA.

Example. Outside IRA, taxed annually, 15 percent tax rate. Even if Ann had not contributed the $4,000 to an IRA and the amount outside the IRA was taxed annually at 15 percent, she would still have less at age 70. Her tax-adjusted growth rate would be 5.1 percent (6% growth rate x (1 - 15% tax rate). The future value factor for a single sum would be 7.3132 ((1 + 5.1 percent) ^ 40 years). Ann would have $29,253 ($4,000 x 7.3132) remaining. This is still less than with the traditional IRA and much less than with the Roth IRA.

Example. Traditional IRA, nondeductible contribution, 35 percent tax rate. Ann, age 30 contributes $4,000 to a traditional IRA in a nondeductible contribution. Assuming a 6% growth rate, at age 70 the $4,000 will have grown to $41,144 (4 x 10,286 from Figure 15.1). If the $41,144 is then distributed from the traditional IRA and subject to tax at 35 percent, after tax of $13,000 (($41,144 - $4,000) x 35 percent)), Ann has $28,144 remaining. This is less than with outside the IRA with a 15 percent tax rate, but more than with outside the IRA with a 28 percent tax rate (unless the tax outside the IRA is deferred).

Example. Traditional IRA, deductible contribution, 28 percent tax rate. Ann, age 30 contributes $4,000 to a traditional IRA in a deductible contribution. Assuming a 6% growth rate, at age 70 the $4,000 will have grown to $41,144 (4 x 10,286 from Figure 15.1). If the $41,144 is then distributed from the traditional IRA and subject to tax at 28 percent, after tax of $11,520 ($41,144 x 28 percent), Ann has $29,624 remaining from the IRA itself.

In addition, Ann has a $1,120 tax deduction ($4,000 x 28 percent). She puts this tax savings into a side fund. Assuming a 6% growth rate, at age 70 the $1,120 will have grown to $11,520 ($1,120 x 10.2857 future value of single sum factor for 6 percent for 40 years (from Appendix E)). If the side fund were tax-free, Ann has $41,144 remaining when the traditional IRA and the side fund are combined. This is the same as with the Roth IRA.

If, instead, the side fund is then subject to tax at 28 percent, after tax of $2,912 (($11,520 - $1,120) x 28 percent), Ann has $8,608 remaining from the side fund. Ann has $38,232 remaining when the traditional IRA and the side fund are combined. This is less than with the Roth IRA, but more than with the traditional IRA with nondeductible contributions, and more than with outside the IRA.

On the other hand, if the side fund were taxed annually, Ann would have even less. Her tax-adjusted growth rate for the side fund would be 4.32 percent (6% growth rate x (1 - 28% tax rate). The future value factor for a single sum would be 5.4288 ((1 + 4.32 percent) ^ 40 years). Ann would have $6,080 ($1,120 x 5.4288) remaining from the side fund. Ann has $35,704 remaining when the traditional IRA and the side fund are combined. This is more than with some and less than with some of the other examples.

Chapter 16

Multiple Taxes

W hen an IRA owner dies, the IRA is includable in the IRA owner's estate. In the case of a traditional IRA, a SEP IRA, or a SIMPLE IRA, distributions received by a beneficiary will generally be fully includable in income (a pro-rata portion attributable to nondeductible contributions can be excluded from income). Such IRAs are treated as income in respect of a decedent (IRD). IRD items do not receive a step up in basis at the decedent's death. However, for income tax purposes, the beneficiary is permitted to deduct from income the amount of the estate tax attributable to the IRA being includable in the decedent's estate.

· Roth IRAs are likewise includable in the IRA owner's estate. However, distributions received from a Roth IRA are received free of income tax after the IRA owner's death.

The early distribution penalty tax does not apply after the death of the IRA owner. The 50% penalty tax for failing to make required minimum distributions does apply after the death of the IRA owner; required minimum distributions should be made in order to avoid the penalty tax. See Chapter 13.

In addition, generation-skipping transfer tax may be due if the IRA passes to a skip person (generally, a person two or more generations younger than the transferor – e.g., a grandchild). However, for income tax purposes, the beneficiary is permitted to deduct from income the amount of the generation-skipping transfer tax attributable to the IRA being includable in the decedent's estate.

The compound effect of these multiple taxes can be substantial. For example, if in 2006 the IRA owner is in a 46 percent estate tax bracket and the beneficiary is in a 35 percent income tax bracket, only about 35 percent of a traditional IRA remains after estate tax and income tax is paid.

$$
\begin{array}{rl}
\$1.00 & \\
-\ .46 & (\$1 \times 46\% \text{ estate tax}) \\
\hline
.54 & \\
-\ .19 & (.54 \times 35\% \text{ income tax}) \\
\hline
.35 &
\end{array}
$$

If the IRA owner is in a 46 percent estate tax bracket, the transfer is subject to the 46 percent generation-skipping transfer tax, and the beneficiary is in a 35 percent income tax bracket, only about 19 percent of the traditional IRA remains after estate tax, generation-skipping transfer tax, and income tax is paid.

$$
\begin{array}{rl}
\$1.00 & \\
-\ .46 & (\$1 \times 46\% \text{ estate tax}) \\
\hline
.54 & \\
-\ .25 & (.54 \times 46\% \text{ GST tax}) \\
\hline
.29 & \\
-\ .10 & (.29 \times 35\% \text{ income tax}) \\
\hline
.19 &
\end{array}
$$

The examples shown above generally represent a worst case scenario. Many planning techniques are available to reduce the gross estate. The gross estate can be reduced by deductions such as the marital deduction. In general, the estate tax rate is lower than 46% for taxable estates of less than $2 million. The estate tax can be reduced by credits such as the unified credit. Generation-skipping transfers can be reduced by a generation-skipping transfer tax exemption. Roth IRA distributions can often be received income tax-free. Nondeductible contributions can be received income tax-free. And the income tax rate could possibly be reduced by spreading the IRA distributions to the beneficiary over a number of years and thus spreading the beneficiary's taxable income over such years, rather than taking one distribution which may substantially increase the beneficiary's taxable income and income tax tax rate for such year.

This chapter is designed to show the potential cumulative effect of income taxes and transfer taxes on an IRA. The income taxation of distributions is discussed in Chapter 13, as well as elsewhere throughout this book. Gift taxation is discussed in Chapter 17, estate taxation is discussed in Chapter 18, and generation-skipping transfer taxation is discussed in Chapter 19.

Chapter 17

Gift Tax and IRAs

In general, gratuitous transfers of money or other property made during an individual's life are subject to federal gift tax. A lifetime transfer generally cannot be made of an interest in an IRA. Under certain circumstances, a gift can be made to another person for contributions to an IRA. Certain transfers pursuant to divorce are not treated as gifts. Generally, any other attempt to transfer an IRA to another would cause the IRA to cease to qualify as an IRA.

Where there is a gratuitous transfer, the annual exclusion can be used for a gift of a present interest. Also, the marital deduction can generally be used for transfers between spouses. Otherwise, the unified credit can be used to reduce or eliminate the effect of the gift tax on the IRA transfer. Spouses may use the split-gift provisions to, in effect, utilize each other's annual exclusions and unified credit.

If an interest in an IRA is transferred from one spouse to the other in connection with a divorce or separation, a gift may be made. However, a transfer of property to either spouse in settlement for his or her marital or property rights or for child support is usually considered to have been made for full and adequate consideration in money or money's worth if two conditions are satisfied. First, the transfer must be made according to a written agreement between the husband and wife. Second, the divorce must occur within the three-year period beginning on the date one year before the agreement is entered into. Under this statutory provision, it is immaterial whether the agreement is approved by the divorce decree.[1]

Computing the Gift Tax

The gift tax is imposed on the value of gifts made in the calendar year after subtracting allowable exclusions and deductions. A unified credit is available to reduce the tax to the extent the credit has not been used up in a prior year.

An annual exclusion is allowed against gifts to each donee (see "Annual Exclusion," below). There is also an exclusion for "qualified transfers" for educational or medical expenses (see "Exclusion For Qualified Transfers," below).

A married couple may elect to treat a gift made by one of them to a third person as having been made one-half by each spouse. Thus, if only one spouse makes all gifts, his annual exclusions are, in effect, doubled (see "Split-Gifts," below). However, in the case of community property, each spouse is automatically treated as making a gift of one-half of property given to a third person.

A gift tax marital deduction may be available for a gift by a husband to his wife, or by a wife to her husband (see "Marital Deduction," below). A deduction may generally be taken for the full value of gifts made to charitable organizations (see "Charitable Deductions," below).

Because the gift tax is cumulative in effect, gifts in previous years (since June 6, 1932) must be taken into account in figuring the tax on gifts in the current calendar year. Consequently, taxable gifts in past years boost later gifts into higher brackets (reductions in tax rates in later years could offset this effect). [Note that the cumulative effect may also apply to calculation of the federal estate tax (see Chapter 18) due to unification of the gift and estate tax systems.] The gift tax is based on taxable gifts (the balance after subtracting allowable exclusions and deductions). In general, the steps are:

(1)   Compute the tax on total taxable gifts for all years, including those made in the current calendar year. Use the gift tax rate schedule for the year of the gift (see Figure 17.1). EGTRRA 2001 reduces the top gift tax rate in steps over the years 2002 to 2010, after which rates return to 2001 levels.

(2)   Compute the tax on gifts made in previous years, leaving out gifts in the current calendar year (use same rate schedule).

(3) Subtract (2) from (1). The difference is the gross gift tax for the current calendar year.[2]

Any available unified credit (i.e., not used in a previous year) can be subtracted from the gross gift tax to arrive at the gift tax payable (see "Unified Credit," below).

In years before 2002 and after 2010, the unified tax rates are increased by a 5 percent surtax (built into the tables) in the case of certain large cumulative taxable transfers.

For example, assume John Smith made $200,000 of gifts during 2006 and $50,000 of the gifts qualified for the annual exclusion. John made $100,000 of taxable gifts in previous years. Figure 17.2 illustrates calculation of the gift tax.

FIGURE 17.1

2006 Gift and Estate Tax Table

Taxable Gift/Estate		Tax on	Rate on
From	To	Col. 1	Excess
$ 0	$ 10,000	$ 0	18%
10,000	20,000	1,800	20%
20,000	40,000	3,800	22%
40,000	60,000	8,200	24%
60,000	80,000	13,000	26%
80,000	10,0000	18,200	28%
100,000	150,000	23,800	30%
150,000	250,000	38,800	32%
250,000	500,000	70,800	34%
500,000	750,000	155,800	37%
750,000	1,000,000	248,300	39%
1,000,000	1,250,000	345,800	41%
1,250,000	1,500,000	448,300	43%
1,500,000	2,000,000	555,800	45%
2,000,000	....	780,800	46%

Reduction in Top Gift Tax Rate

2005	47%
2006	46%
2007-2009	45%
2010	35%
2011	55%

See Appendix A for complete gift tax tables.

FIGURE 17.2

Federal Gift Tax

Year of Gift(s)		2006
Gifts Made During Year		$200,000
Less: Annual Exclusion(s)	$50,000	
Exclusions for Qualified Transfers	$0	
Charitable Deduction	$0	
Marital Deduction	$0	($50,000)
Taxable Gifts Made During Current Year		$150,000
Taxable Gifts Made During Earlier Years		$100,000
Total Taxable Gifts		$250,000
Tax on Total Taxable Gifts		$70,800
Tax on Gifts Made During Earlier Years		($23,800)
Gross Gift Tax		$47,000
Allowable Unified Credit		($47,000)
Gift Tax Payable		$0

Gifts

In general, gratuitous transfers of money or other property made during an individual's life are subject to federal gift tax.[3] The gift tax is an excise tax on an individual's right to transfer property by gift rather than a tax on the property itself. Thus, transfers of certain bonds, notes or certificates of indebtedness of the government and income thereon which are exempt from income tax (i.e., tax-exempt obligations) are nevertheless subject to gift tax.

A lifetime transfer generally cannot be made of an interest in an IRA. A designation of an IRA beneficiary would not be irrevocable until death. A gift can be made to another person for contributions to an IRA; however, the donee must qualify to make contributions to such IRA (e.g., compensation is required for contributions for all IRAs). Certain transfers pursuant to divorce are not treated as gifts. Any other attempt to transfer an IRA to another would cause the IRA to cease to qualify as an IRA (the IRA would be treated as distributed and subject to the income tax rules on distributions, including the early distribution penalty tax if applicable – see Chapter 13), in addition to being treated as a gift for gift tax purposes. A person could take distributions from an IRA, and then make a gift of the distributed amount (or, perhaps, the amount remaining after payment of income tax on the distribution) to another person.

If an IRA is transferred in connection with a divorce or separation, the IRA owner may be treated as making a gift to the other spouse to the extent that the owner spouse does not receive full and adequate consideration.

However, a transfer of property to either spouse in settlement for his or her marital or property rights or for child support shall be considered as made for full and adequate consideration in money or money's worth if certain conditions are met. First, the transfer must be made according to a written agreement between the husband and wife. Second, the divorce must occur within the three-year period beginning on the date one year before the agreement is entered into. Under this statutory provision, it is immaterial whether the agreement is approved by the divorce decree.[4]

Also, if the transfer is made pursuant to a divorce decree and the transfer is made in exchange for a release or promised release of marital or property rights or support rights, the transfer will not be considered a gift.

Otherwise, the relinquishment or promised relinquishment of dower or curtesy, or of a statutory estate created in lieu of dower or curtesy, or of other marital rights in the spouse's property or estate, is not deemed a consideration in money or money's worth. Consequently, such transfer would be considered a gift. However, a surrender of support rights is not a surrender of "other marital rights," as that phrase is used in the regulations. Therefore, to the extent of the value of any support rights released by the transferee spouse in a separation agreement, consideration in money or money's worth will be deemed to have been given.

Split-Gifts

A husband and wife may elect to have all gifts made by either spouse to third persons during a year treated as having been made one-half by each spouse.[5] If the election is made, then gifts made by either spouse to a third person during the year are simply split down the middle and each spouse calculates his or her separate gift tax on his or her one-half. Thus, each spouse uses his or her own annual exclusions, graduated tax rates, and unified credits.

The split-gifts provision is a useful way to assure that each spouse's annual exclusions, graduated tax rates, and unified credit are used to reduce the overall gift tax burden on the spouses, especially where one spouse owns all the property and makes all the gifts.

With regard to community property, each spouse is already treated as making a gift of one-half of the property. Thus, the split-gifts provision essentially permits gifts of non-community property to receive the same treatment accorded gifts of community property.

Annual Exclusion

Each donor has a $10,000 as indexed ($12,000 in 2006) per donee annual exclusion for gifts of a present interest.[6] A donor who splits gifts with his spouse, as discussed above, can effectively double the annual exclusion to $24,000 (in 2006) per donee.

For example, a donor who makes a gift of $24,000 in 2006 to a donee which qualifies for the annual exclusion has made a taxable gift of $12,000 ($24,000 gift minus $12,000 annual exclusion). However, if the donor splits the $24,000 gift with his spouse, each spouse is treated as making a gift of $12,000, and no taxable gift has been made ($12,000 gift per spouse minus $12,000 annual exclusion of each spouse).

If the spouse of the donor is not a United States citizen, the annual exclusion for a transfer from the donor spouse to the non-citizen spouse is increased from $12,000 to $120,000 (as indexed for 2006) (provided the transfer would otherwise qualify for the marital deduction if the donee spouse were a United States citizen). However, the marital deduction is not available for a transfer to a spouse who is not a United States citizen, as discussed below.[7]

Exclusion for Qualified Transfers

An exclusion from gift tax is provided for certain qualified transfers for educational expenses or medical expenses. In order to qualify for the exclusion, the gift must be paid on behalf of an individual as tuition to an educational organization for the education or training of such individual, or as payment for medical care to a person providing medical care to such individual.[8]

Charitable Deduction

Gifts to qualified charitable organizations are not subject to the federal gift tax.[9] However, in order to insure that a charity actually receives the amount for which a charitable deduction is claimed, gifts of partial interests in trust must meet certain requirements.

A charitable deduction is allowed for the full amount of gifts made to or for the use of:

- the United States, any State, or any political subdivision thereof, or the District of Columbia, for exclusively public purposes;

- a corporation, or trust, or community chest, fund, or foundation, orga-nized and operated exclusively for religious, charitable, scientific, literary, or educational purposes, or to foster national or international amateur sports competition (but only if no part of its activities involve the provi-sion of athletic facilities or equipment), including the encouragement of art and the prevention of cruelty to children or animals, no part of the net earnings of which inures to the benefit of any private shareholder or individual, which is not disqualified for tax exemption under IRC Section 501(c)(3) by attempting to influence legislation, and which does not par-ticipate or intervene in political campaigns;

- a fraternal society, order, or association, operating under the lodge system, but only if such gifts are to be used exclusively for religious, charitable, scientific, literary or educational purposes, including the encouragement of art and the prevention of cruelty to children or animals;

- posts or organizations of war veterans, or auxiliary units, or societies of any such posts or organizations, if such posts, organizations, units, or societies are organized in the United States or any of its possessions, and if no part of their earnings inures to the benefit of any private shareholder or individual.[10]

The IRS maintains lists of charities for which a taxpayer can take a charitable deduction.

Where a donor makes a gift of an interest in property (other than a remainder interest in a personal residence or farm or an undivided portion of the donor's entire interest in property or certain gifts of property interests exclusively for conservation purposes) to a qualified charity, and an interest in the same property is retained by the donor or is given to a donee other than a qualified charity, no charitable deduc-tion is allowed for the interest given the charity unless:

(1)   in the case of a remainder interest, such interest is in a trust which is a charitable remainder annuity trust (CRAT), a charitable remainder uni-trust (CRUT), or a pooled income fund (PIF); or

(2)   in the case of any other interest (such as an interest in the income from a short term trust), such interest is in the form of a guaranteed annuity or is a fixed percentage distributed yearly of the fair market value of the property (to be determined yearly) (e.g., a charitable lead annuity trust (CLAT) or a charitable lead unitrust (CLUT)).[11]

Marital Deduction

In general, an unlimited gift tax marital deduction is available for transfers between spouses.[12] Technically, the amount of the gift tax marital deduction would be reduced by the amount of the transfer which qualifies for the annual exclusion [up to $10,000 as indexed ($12,000 in 2006), see above]. Thus, if a husband transfers $50,000 to his wife in 2006 and $12,000 of the transfer qualifies for the annual exclusion, the marital deduction would be limited to $38,000 ($50,000 transfer minus $12,000 annual exclusion).

If the spouse of the donor is not a United States citizen, the marital deduction is no longer available. However, in such a case, the annual exclusion (see above) for the transfer from the donor spouse to the noncitizen spouse is increased from $12,000 to $120,000 (as indexed for 2006) (provided the transfer would otherwise qualify for the marital deduction if the donee spouse were a United States citizen).[13]

The marital deduction is generally not available for gifts of terminable interests. A "terminable interest" in property is an interest which will terminate or fail on the lapse of time or on the occurrence or failure to occur of some contingency. For example, an interest in trust income for life would ordinarily be a terminable interest.

With respect to transfers in trust, the following interests will not be treated as nondeductible terminable interests for purposes of the marital deduction:

- an income interest for life with a general power of appointment over trust corpus;

- a qualified terminable interest property (QTIP) trust;

- an estate trust; and

- a special rule charitable remainder trust.

A brief summary of these types of marital deduction trusts follows.

Life Estate with General Power of Appointment

It is provided by statute that if the donee spouse is given a right to trust income payable at least annually, the donee spouse has the power to appoint the trust corpus to herself or her estate (a general power of appointment), and no one has the power to appoint property to anyone other than the donee spouse, the marital deduction will be allowed. The life estate with power of appointment marital deduction can apply to a specific portion of a trust, but only if the specific portion is determined on a fractional or percentage basis. Property subject to the general power of appointment at the donee spouse's death will generally be includable in the donee spouse's estate for estate tax purposes. Property which the donee spouse transfers to others during the donee spouse's lifetime will generally be subject to gift tax.

Qualified Terminable Interest Property (QTIP) Trust

A donee spouse in a QTIP trust must be given a right to trust income payable at least annually. Also, no one can be given a power to appoint property to anyone other than the donee spouse. However, in a QTIP trust, the donee spouse need not be given any power of appointment (perhaps, enabling the donor spouse to control who receives the property after the donee spouse dies). The QTIP marital deduction can apply to a specific portion of a trust, but only if the specific portion is determined on a fractional or percentage basis. An election is made as to the amount of the transfer as to which the QTIP marital deduction is to apply. QTIP property is subject to gift tax when given away by a donee spouse or included in the donee spouse's estate if retained until death.

Estate Trust

An estate trust is a trust in which the donee spouse is the only permissible income beneficiary and trust corpus is payable to the donee spouse's estate at death. Since the spouse holds all interests in the trust, an estate trust is not a terminable interest. In an estate trust, the donee spouse need not be given a right to trust income payable at least annually. The estate trust is includable in the donee spouse's estate for estate tax purposes.

Special Rule Charitable Trust

If the donee spouse is the only noncharitable beneficiary (other than possibly the donor) of a "qualified charitable remainder trust" created by the donor spouse, the donee spouse's interest is not considered a nondeductible terminable interest and the value of such interest will qualify for the marital deduction. A "qualified charitable remainder trust" means a charitable remainder annuity trust (CRAT) or a charitable remainder unitrust (CRUT). Thus, the donee spouse would receive an annuity or unitrust interest for life or for a term of years not to exceed 20 years, and the charity would receive a remainder interest. A part of such a trust should qualify for the charitable deduction, and the balance of the trust for the marital deduction.

Unified Credit

The unified credit is a dollar amount (the gift tax amount is currently $345,800, see Figure 17.3) which can be applied against the gift tax and the estate tax (see Chapter 18 for the estate tax amounts).[14] Actually, use of the credit (to the extent available) is mandatory when the donor makes a taxable gift. Application of the unified credit for gift tax purposes reduces the amount of the credit which is available for gifts in future years, as well as the amount available for estate tax purposes. The unified credit is also reduced by 20 percent of the amount of the lifetime exemption a donor elected to use against gifts made after September 8, 1976 and before January 1, 1977.

The unified credit can protect up to $1,000,000 of transfers from the gift tax (see Chapter 18 for the estate tax amounts). This $1,000,000 unified credit equivalent (or applicable exclusion) is equal to the amount of taxable transfers which would produce a gift or estate tax equal to $345,800. Note, however, that gift or estate tax is first calculated and then the unified credit is used to reduce the amount of tax, rather than by reducing the amount of taxable transfers by the unified credit equivalent and then calculating the tax (see "Computing the Gift Tax," above).

FIGURE 17.3

Gift Tax Unified Credit

Year	Exclusion Equivalent	Unified Credit
1977 (1-1 to 6-30)	$30,000	$6,000
1977 (7-1 to 12-31)	120,667	30,000
1978	134,000	34,000
1979	147,333	38,000
1980	161,563	42,500
1981	175,625	47,000
1982	225,000	62,800
1983	275,000	79,300
1984	325,000	96,300
1985	400,000	121,800
1986	500,000	155,800
1987-1997	600,000	192,800
1998	625,000	202,050
1999	650,000	211,300
2000-2001	675,000	220,550
2002-2009	1,000,000	345,800
2010	1,000,000	330,800
2011-	1,000,000	345,800

Endnotes

1. IRC Sec. 2516.
2. IRC Sec. 2502.
3. IRC Sec. 2501.
4. IRC Sec. 2516.
5. IRC Sec. 2513.
6. IRC Sec. 2503(b).
7. IRC Sec. 2523(i).
8. IRC Sec. 2503(e).
9. IRC Sec. 2522.
10. IRC Sec. 2522(a).
11. IRC Sec. 2522(c)(2).
12. IRC Sec. 2523.
13. IRC Sec. 2523(i).
14. IRC Sec. 2505.

Chapter 18

Estate Tax and IRAs

T he estate tax is a tax on a decedent's right to transfer property at death. The Economic Growth and Tax Relief Reconciliation Act of 2001 (EGTRRA 2001) repeals the estate tax for one year for decedents dying in 2010.

Various deductions can often be used to reduce or eliminate the effect of the estate tax on IRA transfers. In particular, an unlimited marital deduction is generally available for transfers to a surviving spouse. Also, an unlimited charitable deduction is available for transfers to charity. A deduction may be available for state death taxes.

A number of credits can also be used to reduce or eliminate the effect of the estate tax on IRA transfers. In particular, each person has a unified credit which can be used to shelter gift tax during life or estate tax at death. In addition, a credit may be allowed against federal estate tax for some or all of the death taxes paid to a state.

A traditional IRA, Roth IRA, SEP IRA, or SIMPLE IRA will generally be fully includable in the estate of the original IRA owner. A decedent's estate includes the value of an annuity or other payment receivable by reason of surviving the decedent where the decedent held certain interests in the property while alive. The amount includable is proportionate to the part of the purchase price contributed by the decedent. Any contribution by the employer of the decedent to the traditional IRA, Roth IRA, SEP IRA, or SIMPLE IRA is treated as made by the employee for this purpose.[1] Thus, the original IRA owner will generally have contributed 100 percent of the contributions to the traditional IRA, Roth IRA, SEP IRA, or SIMPLE IRA and the full value of the IRA will be includable in the original owner's estate.

If upon the original owner's death the traditional IRA, Roth IRA, SEP IRA, or SIMPLE IRA passes to the spouse of the original IRA owner, the transfer will generally qualify for the marital deduction. If the transfer to the surviving spouse qualifies for the marital deduction, any amount still left in the IRA at the surviving spouse's death will be includable in the surviving spouse's estate.

A traditional IRA, Roth IRA, SEP IRA, or SIMPLE IRA is not ordinarily includable in the estate of a beneficiary for estate tax purposes because the beneficiary did not contribute to the IRA. (However, note the comments in the preceding paragraph regarding spouses and the marital deduction.) However, if the beneficiary did contribute to the IRA, the IRA would be includable in the beneficiary's estate at the beneficiary's death in the same manner as described for an owner of the IRA above. Also, if the IRA were payable to the beneficiary's estate at the beneficiary's death, the IRA would be includable in the beneficiary's estate. Additionally, if the beneficiary is given a general power of appointment over the IRA, the IRA would be includable in the beneficiary's estate. And if the beneficiary gave away his interest in the IRA while retaining certain interests in the IRA, the IRA could be includable in the beneficiary's estate. See "Gross Estate," below.

The value of an IRA includable in the the gross estate is not discounted for income tax payable by the beneficiary or for lack of marketability. However, an income tax deduction may be available for the estate tax attributable to the IRA as the beneficiary receives distributions from the IRA.

Computing the Estate Tax

The estate tax is imposed on the transfer of the taxable estate. The taxable estate is the gross estate less allowable deductions, as discussed below. The estate tax rates (see Figure 18.1) are applied to the sum of the amount of the taxable estate and the amount of "adjusted taxable gifts."

Adjusted taxable gifts are taxable gifts (the balance after subtracting allowable exclusions and deductions) made by the decedent after 1976 other than gifts includable in the decedent's gross estate. The term generally includes one-half the amount of any gift the decedent or his spouse made to a third party that was consented to by the donor's spouse (i.e., a split gift – see Chapter 17). This produces a "tentative tax" from which is deducted the aggregate amount of gift tax which would have been payable by the decedent or his estate with respect to gifts made by the decedent after 1976 if the tax rate schedule (see Figure 18.1) as in effect at the decedent's death had been applicable at the time of such gifts. The result of this computation is the estate tax, against which allowable credits, discussed below, are applied to determine the final tax payable.[2]

For decedents dying before 2002 and after 2010, the benefit of the graduated tax rates is phased out for cumulative taxable transfers in excess of $10 million through imposition of a 5 percent surtax. Thus, in 2011, the tentative estate tax is calculated at a 60 percent rate on cumulative taxable transfers from $10 million to $17,184,000.

FIGURE 18.1

2006 Gift and Estate Tax Table

Taxable Gift/Estate		Tax on	Rate on
From	To	Col. 1	Excess
$ 0	$ 10,000	$ 0	18%
10,000	20,000	1,800	20%
20,000	40,000	3,800	22%
40,000	60,000	8,200	24%
60,000	80,000	13,000	26%
80,000	10,0000	18,200	28%
100,000	150,000	23,800	30%
150,000	250,000	38,800	32%
250,000	500,000	70,800	34%
500,000	750,000	155,800	37%
750,000	1,000,000	248,300	39%
1,000,000	1,250,000	345,800	41%
1,250,000	1,500,000	448,300	43%
1,500,000	2,000,000	555,800	45%
2,000,000	....	780,800	46%

Reduction in Top Estate Tax Rate

2005	47%
2006	46%
2007-2009	45%
2010	NA
2011	55%

See Appendix A for complete estate tax tables.

FIGURE 18.2

Federal Estate Tax

Year of Death		2006
Gross Estate		$4,000,000
Less: Funeral and Administration Expenses	20,000	
Claims Against Estate and Certain Debt	0	
Uncompensated Losses During Administration	0	($20,000)
Adjusted Gross Estate		$3,980,000
Less: Charitable Deduction	$40,000	
Marital Deduction	$1,000,000	
State Death Tax	$190,000	($1,230,000)
Taxable Estate		$2,750,000
Adjusted Taxable Gifts		$100,000
Computation Base		$2,850,000
Tentative Tax on Computation Base		$1,171,800
Gift Tax Payable on Post-1976 Gifts		($0)
Gross Regular Federal Estate Tax		$1,171,800
Less: Unified Credit	$780,800	
Credit for State Death Taxes	NA	
Credit for Certain Pre-1977 Gift Taxes	$0	
Credit for Foreign Death Taxes	$0	
Credit for Tax on Prior Transfers	$0	($780,800)
Federal Estate Tax		$391,000

For example, assume a decedent died in 2006 with a $4,000,000 gross estate. In 1990, the decedent made only one taxable gift of $100,000 (after utilizing the annual exclusion). The decedent paid no gift tax because $23,800 of the decedent's unified credit was applied to offset the $23,800 gift tax liability. The decedent's estate had funeral and administration expenses of $20,000. The decedent left $40,000 to charity and $1,000,000 to his wife. State death taxes of $190,000 were paid. Figure 18.2 illustrates calculation of the estate tax.

Gross Estate

Property may be includable in a decedent's estate where:

(1)   the decedent owns the property at death (IRC Section 2033);

(2)   the decedent retains a life estate in the property (IRC Section 2036);

(3)   the decedent retains a reversionary interest in the property (IRC Section 2037);

(4)   the decedent retains or holds certain rights to change beneficial interests in the property (IRC Section 2038);

(5)   the decedent holds the right to certain annuity payments (IRC Section 2039);

(6)   life insurance on the decedent's life is payable to the decedent's estate or the decedent holds incidents of ownership in the life insurance (IRC Section 2042);

(7)   the decedent gives away interests described in (2), (3), (4), or (6) within three years of death (IRC Section 2035);

(8)   the decedent holds a general power of appointment (generally, the power to appoint property to the powerholder or the powerholder's estate, or the creditors of either – IRC Section 2041); and

(9)   a QTIP marital deduction election has been made, the QTIP is includable in the surviving spouse's estate (IRC Section 2044).

Transfers under IRC Sections 2036, 2037, 2038, or 2041 which are made for insufficient consideration are generally includable in a decedent's estate to the extent that the transfer exceeds the consideration furnished by other persons.[3] A qualified disclaimer of interests in property which would otherwise pass to a disclaimant can also be used to remove property which would otherwise be includable in the disclaimant's estate.[4]

Deductions

Deductions against the gross estate are available for funeral and administration expenses, claims against the estate and debt on property includable in the estate, and uncompensated losses during administration arising from fires, storms, shipwrecks, or other casualties, or from theft.[5] For decedents dying before 2004 or after 2010, a deduction may also be available for qualified family-owned business interests.[6] For decedents dying in 2005 to 2009, a deduction may be available for state death taxes.[7] A substantial amount of estate planning revolves around the charitable deduction and the marital deduction discussed below.

Charitable Deduction

Bequests to qualified charitable organizations are not subject to the federal estate tax.[8] However, in order to insure that a charity actually receives the amount for which a charitable deduction is claimed, bequests of partial interests in property must meet certain requirements.

If any death taxes are, by the terms of the will, by the law of the jurisdiction under which the estate is administered, or by the law of the jurisdiction imposing the particular tax, payable in whole or in part out of the bequests otherwise deductible as charitable contributions, then the amount deductible is the amount of such bequests reduced by the amount of such taxes.

A charitable deduction is allowed for the full amount of bequests made to or for the use of:

- the United States, any State, or any political subdivision thereof, or the District of Columbia, for exclusively public purposes;

- a corporation, or trust, or community chest, fund, or foundation, organized and operated exclusively for religious, charitable, scientific, literary, or educational purposes, or to foster national or international amateur sports competition (but only if no part of its activities involve the provision of athletic facilities or equipment), including the encouragement of art and the prevention of cruelty to children or animals, no part of the net earnings of which inures to the benefit of any private shareholder or individual, which is not disqualified for tax exemption under IRC Section 501(c)(3) by attempting to influence legislation, and which does not participate or intervene in political campaigns;

- a fraternal society, order, or association, operating under the lodge system, but only if such gifts are to be used exclusively for religious, charitable, scientific, literary or educational purposes, including the prevention of cruelty to children or animals which is not disqualified for tax exemption under IRC Section 501(c)(3) by attempting to influence legislation, and which does not participate or intervene in political campaigns;

- organizations of war veterans incorporated by Act of Congress, or departments, chapters, or posts of such organizations, if no part of their earnings inures to the benefit of any private shareholder or individual.[9]

The IRS maintains lists of charities for which a taxpayer can take a charitable deduction.

Where a decedent makes a bequest of an interest in property (other than a remainder interest in a personal residence or farm or an undivided portion of the donor's entire interest in property or certain gifts of property interests exclusively for conservation purposes) to a qualified charity, and an interest in the same property is given to a donee other than a qualified charity (or retained by the donor in the case of a charitable trust created by a donor during the donor's lifetime and includable in the donor's estate at death), no charitable deduction is allowed for the interest given the charity unless:

(1)   in the case of a remainder interest, such interest is in a trust which is a charitable remainder annuity trust (CRAT), a charitable remainder unitrust (CRUT), or a pooled income fund (PIF); or

(2)   in the case of any other interest (such as an interest in the income from a short term trust), such interest is in the form of a guaranteed annuity or is a fixed percentage distributed yearly of the fair market value of the property (to be determined yearly) (e.g., a charitable lead annuity trust (CLAT) or a charitable lead unitrust (CLUT)).[10]

Note. For required minimum distribution purposes, if it is desired to transfer an interest in an IRA to charity at death, as well as to other beneficiaries, a separate IRA should probably be created for the charity. Furthermore, the transfer to charity of the separate IRA should probabaly be made outright, and not to a charitable trust (unless the charity is the only beneficiary of the trust). Keeping the charitable IRA separate from the IRAs for noncharitable beneficiaries may allow the IRAs for noncharitable beneficiaries to be stretched. See Chapter 13 regarding required minimum distributions and Chapter 14 on choosing a beneficiary.

Marital Deduction

In general, an unlimited estate tax marital deduction is available for transfers to the surviving spouse of the decedent.[11] However, if the spouse of the decedent is not a United States citizen, the marital deduction is generally available only for transfers to a qualified domestic trust (QDOT), as discussed below.

The marital deduction is limited to the net value of qualifying property interests passing to the surviving spouse. Thus, the value of such interests must be reduced by federal and state death taxes payable out of those interests, by encumbrances on those interests, and by any obligation imposed by the decedent upon the surviving spouse with respect to the passing of such interests. The decedent spouse can generally specify to what extent the marital deduction portion bears the burden of payment of taxes or other obligations.

The marital deduction is generally not available for bequests of terminable interests. A "terminable interest" in property is an interest which will terminate or fail on the lapse of time or on the occurrence or failure to occur of some contingency. For example, an interest in trust income for life would ordinarily be a terminable interest.

Decedents often use common disaster and time clauses to prevent property from falling into the estate of a beneficiary who dies at approximately the same time as the decedent. The decedent may have good reasons for not wanting his property to pass through two estates in quick succession:

(1)   he may want to avoid duplicate probate costs, administration expenses, and inheritance taxes;

(2)   he may want his heirs, not his beneficiary's heirs, to have the property if his beneficiary does not survive a sufficient length of time to enjoy it.

The marital deduction will be allowed for a common disaster or a time clause (which would otherwise be terminable interests) if the only condition under which the surviving spouse's interest will terminate is the death of the surviving spouse within six months after decedent's death or as a result of a common disaster, and the condition does not occur.

With respect to transfers in trust, the following interests will not be treated as nondeductible terminable interests for purposes of the marital deduction:

- an income interest for life with a general power of appointment over trust corpus;

- a qualified terminable interest property (QTIP) trust;

- an estate trust;

- a special rule charitable remainder trust; and

- a qualified domestic trust (QDOT).

Where a marital trust is the beneficiary of the IRA, a QTIP marital deduction will generally be used for both the IRA and the trust. Where the spouse is not a U.S. citizen, a qualified domestic trust (QDOT) will generally be required.

Note. If it is important to take advantage of the special required minimum distribution provisions for spouses which often allow greater stretching of the IRA, consider making the spouse the outright beneficiary of the IRA, rather than making a trust the beneficiary. If a trust is the beneficiary of the IRA, required minimum distributions use the life expectancy of the oldest trust beneficiary, which is usually the spouse. See Chapter 13 regarding required minimum distributions and Chapter 14 on choosing a beneficiary.

Life Estate with General Power of Appointment

It is provided by statute that if the surviving spouse is given a right to trust income payable at least annually, the surviving spouse has the power to appoint the trust corpus to herself or her estate (a general power of appointment), and no one has the power to appoint property to anyone other than the surviving spouse, the marital deduction will be allowed. The life estate with power of appointment marital deduction can apply to a specific portion of a trust, but only if the specific portion is determined on a fractional or percentage basis. Property subject to the general power of appointment at the surviving spouse's death will generally be includable in the surviving spouse's estate for estate tax purposes. Property which the surviving spouse transfers to others during the surviving spouse's lifetime will generally be subject to gift tax.

Qualified Terminable Interest Property (QTIP) Trust

A surviving spouse in a QTIP trust must be given a right to trust income payable at least annually. Also, no one can be given a power to appoint property to anyone other than the surviving spouse. However, in a QTIP trust, the surviving spouse need not be given any power of appointment (perhaps, enabling the donor spouse to control who receives the property after the donee spouse dies). The QTIP marital deduction can apply to a specific portion of a trust, but only if the specific portion is determined on a fractional or percentage basis. An election is made as to the amount of the transfer as to which the QTIP marital deduction is to apply. QTIP property is subject to gift tax when given away by a surviving spouse or included in the surviving spouse's estate if retained until death.

A qualified terminable interest property (QTIP) marital deduction should be available for estate tax purposes if all income from an IRA is distributed at least annually to the surviving spouse, no one has the power to distribute any part of the IRA to anyone other than the surviving spouse, and the executor makes a QTIP election.[12] An executor can elect to treat an IRA and a trust as QTIP if (1) the trustee of the trust is the beneficiary of the IRA, (2) the surviving spouse can compel the trustee to withdraw all income earned by the IRA at least annually and distribute that amount to the spouse, and (3) no person has the power to appoint any part of the trust to any person other than the spouse.[13] Allocations between income and principal will be respected if state law provides that reasonable apportionments can be made between income and remainder beneficiaries of the total return of the trust (e.g., a unitrust interest in the range of 3% to 5% could be treated as an income interest).[14]

Revenue Ruling 2006-26[15] provides that the QTIP marital deduction would generally be available for an IRA and a trust with all of the following provisions. While the spouse is alive, the trustee is required to distribute the income of the trust to the spouse annually. The spouse can require the trustee to withdraw from the IRA the greater of the IRA income or the required minimum distribution, and to distribute at least the income of the IRA to the spouse. The IRA is invested in productive assets and the spouse can compel the trustee to invest in assets productive of a reasonable amount of income.

Revenue Ruling 2006-26 also provides that various modern means of determining income under state law are permitted under the QTIP marital deduction. Thus, in certain circumstances, the trustee can make adjustments between income and principal to fulfill the trustee's duty of impartiality between the income and remainder beneficiaries under state laws based on Uniform Principal and Income Act (UPIA) Section 104(a). Also, a state law providing for a unitrust in the range of 3% to 5% could be applied to separately determine the income of the IRA and the trust. And the trustee could separately determine the income of the IRA and the trust under general traditional statutory or common law rules that provide for allocations between income and principal. However, if state law has a provision such as UPIA Section 409(c), which provides that, under certain circumstances, 10% of a distribution required to be made will be treated as income, and 90% as principal, it may be necessary to make sure that the trust instrument provides that Section 409(c) does not apply (an allocation as income based on a percentage of a distribution is not based on total return, and would not qualify for the QTIP marital deduction).

Estate Trust

An estate trust is a trust in which the surviving spouse is the only permissible income beneficiary and trust corpus is payable to the surviving spouse's estate at death. Since the spouse holds all interests in the trust, an estate trust is not a terminable interest. In an estate trust, the surviving spouse need not be given a right to trust income payable at least annually. The estate trust is includable in the surviving spouse's estate for estate tax purposes.

Special Rule Charitable Trust

If the surviving spouse is the only noncharitable beneficiary of a "qualified charitable remainder trust" created by the decedent (or donor) spouse, the surviving spouse's interest is not considered a nondeductible terminable interest and the value of such interest will qualify for the marital deduction. A "qualified charitable remainder trust" means a charitable remainder annuity trust (CRAT) or a charitable remainder unitrust (CRUT). Thus, the surviving spouse would receive an annuity or unitrust interest for life or for a term of years not to exceed 20 years, and the charity would receive a remainder interest. A part of such a trust should qualify for the charitable deduction, and the balance of the trust for the marital deduction.

Qualified Domestic Trust (QDOT)

Where the surviving spouse is not a United States citizen, a qualified domestic trust (QDOT) must generally be used to qualify bequests to the surviving spouse for the estate tax marital deduction. (In order to qualify for the marital deduction, the transfer to the non-citizen must meet the QDOT requirements, as well as the marital deduction requirements of one of the other marital deduction trusts discussed above.)

At least one trustee of the QDOT must be a United States citizen or a domestic corporation and no distribution (other than a distribution of income) may be made from the trust unless that trustee has the right to withhold any additional gift or estate tax imposed on the trust. Additional gift tax is due on any distribution while the surviving spouse is still alive (other than a distribution to the surviving spouse of income or on account of hardship). Additional estate tax is due on any property remaining in the QDOT at the death of the surviving spouse (or at the time the trust ceases to qualify as a QDOT, if earlier). The additional gift or estate tax is calculated as if any property subject to the tax had been included in the taxable estate of the first spouse to die.[16]

Credits

The following credits are allowed against the federal estate tax:

- the unified credit;

- the state death tax credit (decedents dying before 2005 or after 2010);

- the credit for certain pre-1976 gift tax (IRC Section 2012);

- the credit for tax on prior transfers (IRC Section 2013); and

- the credit for foreign death taxes (IRC Section 2014).

Unified Credit

The unified credit is a dollar amount (currently $780,800 for estate tax purposes) which can be applied against the gift tax (see Chapter 17 for the gift tax amounts) and the estate tax.[17] Actually, use of the credit (to the extent available) is mandatory when the donor makes a taxable gift. Application of the unified credit for gift tax purposes reduces the amount of the credit which is available for gifts in future years, as well as the amount available for estate tax purposes. The unified credit is also reduced by 20 percent of the amount of the lifetime exemption a donor elected to use against gifts made after September 8, 1976 and before January 1, 1977.

The unified credit can currently protect up to $2,000,000 of transfers from the estate tax (see Chapter 17 for the gift tax amounts). This $2,000,000 unified credit equivalent (or applicable exclusion) is equal to the amount of taxable transfers which would produce an estate tax equal to $780,800. Note, however, that gift or estate tax is first calculated and then the unified credit is used to reduce the amount of tax, rather than by reducing the amount of taxable transfers by the unified credit equivalent and then calculating the tax (see "Computing the Estate Tax," above). Note, also, that when calculating estate tax the reduction for gift taxes payable on post-1976 gifts is equal to the gift taxes payable after reduction for the unified credit available at the time of the gift, as discussed above.

For example, assume a taxable estate of $2,750,000 in 2006 and one lifetime taxable gift of $100,000. If the gift of $100,000 produced $23,800 of gift tax which was offset by $23,800 of unified credit, the estate tax reduction for gift taxes payable on that post-1976 gift is equal to $0. The unified credit of $780,800 is then subtracted from the $1,171,800 of estate tax otherwise payable to produce an estate tax of $391,000.

Federal Estate Tax

FIGURE 18.3

Year of Death	2006
Taxable Estate	$2,750,000
Adjusted Taxable Gifts	$100,000
Computation Base	$3,750,000
Tentative Tax on Computation Base	$1,171,800
Gift Tax Payable on Post-1976 Gifts	($ 0)
Gross Regular Federal Estate Tax	$1,171,800
Less: Unified Credit	$780,800
Federal Estate Tax	$391,000

EGTRRA 2001 increases the estate tax (but not the gift tax, see Chapter 17) unified credit as follows.

Estate Tax Unified Credit

Year of Death	Unified Credit	Exclusion Equivalent
2004-2005	$555,800	$1,500,000
2006-2008	$780,800	$2,000,000
2009	$1,455,800	$3,500,000
2010	NA	NA
2011-	$345,800	$1,000,000

A great deal of estate planning revolves around using the unified credit separately, or using the unified credit in a credit shelter bypass trust in conjunction with a marital deduction trust.

State Death Tax Credit

For decedents dying before 2005 or after 2010, a credit is allowed against the federal estate tax for state death taxes – inheritance, legacy, estate and succession taxes – paid to any state of the United States or the District of Columbia with respect to property included in the gross estate.[18] The credit is limited to specified percentages of the "adjusted taxable estate" in excess of $40,000. The "adjusted taxable estate" is the taxable estate (see above) reduced by $60,000. If the decedent's adjusted taxable estate is $40,000 or less (i.e., a taxable estate of $100,000 or less), the credit for state death taxes is zero.

EGTRRA 2001 reduced the maximum amount for which a credit could be taken by 25 percent in 2002, 50 percent in 2003, and 75 percent in 2004. The credit is replaced by a deduction for state death taxes in 2005 to 2009.

Figure 18.4 sets out the amount of the state death tax credit.

FIGURE 18.4

State Death Tax Credit (SDTC) Table

Value of Adjusted Taxable Estate*		Credit on Col. 1	Credit Rate on Excess
From	To		
$40,000	$90,000	$0	0.8%
$90,000	$140,000	$400	1.6%
$140,000	$240,000	$1,200	2.4%
$240,000	$440,000	$3,600	3.2%
$440,000	$640,000	$10,000	4.0%
$640,000	$840,000	$18,000	4.8%
$840,000	$1,040,000	$27,600	5.6%
$1,040,000	$1,540,000	$38,800	6.4%
$1,540,000	$2,040,000	$70,800	7.2%
$2,040,000	$2,540,000	$106,800	8.0%
$2,540,000	$3,040,000	$146,800	8.8%
$3,040,000	$3,540,000	$190,800	9.6%
$3,540,000	$4,040,000	$238,800	10.4%
$4,040,000	$5,040,000	$290,800	11.2%
$5,040,000	$6,040,000	$402,800	12.0%
$6,040,000	$7,040,000	$522,800	12.8%
$7,040,000	$8,040,000	$650,800	13.6%
$8,040,000	$9,040,000	$786,800	14.4%
$9,040,000	$10,040,000	$930,800	15.2%
$10,040,000	......	$1,082,800	16.0%

*   Adjusted taxable estate reduced by $60,000.
    Multiply maximum SDTC by 75% in 2002, 50% in 2003, and 25% in 2004.

Endnotes

1. IRC Sec. 2039.
2. IRC Sec. 2001.
3. IRC Sec. 2043.
4. IRC Sec. 2046.
5. IRC Secs. 2053, 2054.
6. IRC Sec. 2057.
7. IRC Section 2058.
8. IRC Sec. 2055.
9. IRC Sec. 2055(a).
10. IRC Sec. 2055(e)(2).
11. IRC Sec. 2056.
12. IRC Sec. 2056(b)(7).
13. Rev. Rul. 2000-2, 2000-1 CB 305.
14. Treas. Reg. §1.643(b)-1.
15. 2006-22 IRB 939.
16. IRC Sec. 2056A.
17. IRC Sec. 2010.
18. IRC Sec. 2011.

Chapter 19

Generation-Skipping Transfer Tax and IRAs

The generation-skipping transfer (GST) tax applies to transfers to a skip person (generally, a person two or more generations younger than the transferor). The GST tax rate is a flat rate. Each transferor has a GST tax exemption. The Economic Growth and Tax Relief Reconciliation Act of 2001 (EGTRRA 2001) repeals the generation-skipping transfer tax for one year in 2010.[1]

When the original IRA owner dies, a transfer of the IRA to a skip person would be a generation-skipping transfer. A transfer to a skip person at death by a spouse, who received the IRA by marital deduction from the original IRA owner, would also generally be a generation-skipping transfer. However, if the original IRA owner made a reverse QTIP marital deduction election, the original IRA owner would be treated as the transferor with respect to the amount for which the reverse QTIP marital deduction was elected. In the case of a generation-skipping transfer, the transferor can allocate the GST tax exemption to the transfer.

Where a spouse or a child is named as beneficiary, the generation-skipping transfer tax generally does not apply. However, who gets the IRA if the spouse or child dies or disclaims the IRA? If the IRA passes to a beneficiary (e.g., a grandchild) who is two generations younger than the IRA owner, the GST tax may apply.

For required minimum distribution purposes grandchildren generally make good IRA beneficiaries because of their long life expectancies and the ability to stretch out distributions. However, the GST tax must be considered whenever the beneficiary (e.g., a grandchild) is two or more generations younger than the transferor (e.g., a grandparent).

Whenever a trust is named as a beneficiary of an IRA, it is necessary to examine who the beneficiaries of the trust are. If any potential beneficiaries of the trust are two or more generations younger than the transferor (generally the IRA owner who named the trust as beneficiary), the GST tax may apply.

Generation-Skipping Transfers

In general, generation-skipping transfers are transfers to persons two or more generations younger than the transferor (skip persons). Generation-skipping transfers are either:

- direct skips;

- taxable distributions; or

- taxable terminations.[2]

In order to determine whether a generation-skipping transfer has occurred, it is necessary to know who is the transferor and it is often necessary to know who has an interest in property held in trust, as discussed below.

The following are not considered generation-skipping transfers:

- Any transfer which, if made during life by an individual, would be a nontaxable gift because of the "annual exclusion" or because it is a "qualified transfer" (amounts not subject to federal gift tax paid on behalf of an individual for his education or medical care). However, with respect to transfers after March 31, 1988, a nontaxable gift which is a direct skip to a trust for the benefit of an individual has an inclusion ratio of zero (i.e., nontaxable) only if (1) during the life of such individual no portion of the trust corpus or income may be distributed to or for the benefit of any other person, and (2) the trust would be included in such individual's estate if the trust did not terminate before such individual died.

- Any transfer to the extent (1) the property transferred was subject to a prior GST tax, (2) the transferee in the prior transfer was in the same generation as the current transferee or a younger generation, and (3) the transfers do not have the effect of avoiding the GST tax.[3]

> *Example.* A transfers property to his great-grandchild, B, in a generation-skipping transfer. B transfers the property to his grandfather, C. (This is not a transfer to a skip person.) C transfers the property to his grandchild, D, who is in B's generation. The transfer from C to D is not a generation-skipping transfer.

In general, irrevocable trusts created prior to October 23, 1986, are grandfathered from the GST tax (except to the extent of corpus added to the trust after October 22, 1986 or income thereon). The GST tax applies generally to any generation-skipping transfer made after October 22, 1986. Also, any lifetime transfer after September 25, 1985, and on or before October 22, 1986, is treated as if made on October 23, 1986.

Transferor

Property which is subject to GST tax may also be subject to gift or estate tax at the same time it is subject to GST tax. A "transferor" for GST tax purposes, in the case of any property subject to the federal estate tax, is the decedent. In the case of any property subject to the federal gift tax, the transferor for GST tax purposes is the donor.[4] Thus, to the extent that a lapse of a general power of appointment (including a right of withdrawal) is subject to gift or estate tax, the powerholder becomes the transferor with respect to such lapsed amount.[5]

If there is a generation-skipping transfer of any property and immediately after such transfer such property is held in trust, a different rule (the "multiple skip" rule) applies to subsequent transfers from such trust. In such case, the trust is treated as if the transferor (for purposes of subsequent transfers) were assigned to the first generation above the highest generation of any person having an "interest" (see below) in such trust immediately after such transfer.[6] If no person holds an interest immediately after the GST, then the transferor is assigned to the first generation above the highest generation of any person in existence at the time of the GST who may subsequently hold an interest in the trust.[7]

> *Example.* Grandfather transfers property to a trust benefiting his grandchildren and great-grandchildren in a generation-skipping transfer. Immediately after the transfer, the transferor is treated as being one generation above the grandchildren (the highest generation having an interest in the trust after the transfer). The grandchildren are no longer skip persons, but the great-grandchildren are.

If an election is made to split gifts between spouses for gift tax purposes, each spouse may be treated as a transferor of one-half of the property transferred (assuming the general rule treating donors as transferors applies).[8] Such an election would generally allow a spouse who owns most of the property to take advantage of the other spouse's annual exclusion and GST exemption, as discussed below.

A reverse QTIP election may be made for property under the GST tax.[9] The effect of making the reverse QTIP election is to have the decedent or the donor (rather than the surviving or donee spouse) treated as the transferor for generation-skipping purposes. Such an election would generally be used to insure that a decedent's GST exemption, discussed below, was not wasted.

> *Example.* In 2006, decedent (who has made $500,000 of taxable gifts protected by the unified credit) with a $4,000,000 estate leaves $1,500,000 in a credit shelter trust and $2,500,000 to his surviving spouse in a QTIP trust, reducing his taxable estate to zero. (Assume each trust would be subject to GST tax to the extent that the $2,000,000 GST exemption is not allocated to such trust.) The executor allocates $1,500,000 of the decedent's $2,000,000 GST tax exemption to the credit shelter trust and makes a reverse QTIP election as to $500,000 of the QTIP property so that the decedent's full $2,000,000 exemption can be used. The surviving spouse's $2,000,000 exemption amount may then be used to protect the remaining $2,000,000 of property, and the entire $4,000,000 has escaped GST tax (assuming separate QTIP trusts of $2,000,000 and $500,000 are created).

Assignment To Generations

An individual (and his spouse or former spouse) who is a lineal descendant of a grandparent of the transferor (or the transferor's spouse) is assigned to that generation which results from comparing the number of generations between the grandparent and such individual with the number of generations between the grandparent and the transferor (or the transferor's spouse). A relationship by legal adoption is treated as a relationship by blood, and a relationship by the half-blood is treated as a relationship of the whole blood. A person married to the transferor or a lineal descendant of a grandparent of the transferor (or the transferor's spouse) is assigned to the generation of the person to whom the person is married.[10]

However, with respect to terminations, distributions, and transfers occurring after 1997, where an individual's parent is dead at the time of a transfer subject to gift or estate tax upon which the individual's interest is established or derived, such individual will be treated as being one generation below the lower of (1) the transferor's generation or (2) the generation of the youngest living ancestor of the individual who is also a descendant of the parents of the transferor or the transferor's spouse. This predeceased parent rule applies to collateral relatives (e.g., nieces and nephews) only if there are no living lineal descendants of the transferor at the time of the transfer.[11]

An individual who cannot be assigned to a generation under the foregoing rules is assigned to a generation on the basis of his date of birth. An individual born not more than 12½ years after the date of birth of the transferor is assigned to the transferor's generation. An individual born more than 12½ years but not more than 37½ years after the date of birth of the transferor is assigned to the first generation younger than the transferor. There are similar rules for a new generation every 25 years.[12]

Interest In Property

In determining whether a generation-skipping transfer has occurred, it is often necessary to know who has an interest in the property. A person has an "interest in property" held in trust if (at the time the determination is made) such person:

(1) has a present right to receive income or corpus from the trust (e.g., a life income interest);

(2) is a permissible current recipient of income or corpus from the trust (e.g., a beneficiary entitled to distribution of income or corpus, but only in the discretion of the trustee) and is not a charitable organization as determined for gift tax purposes; or

(3) is such a charitable organization and the trust is a charitable remainder annuity trust, a charitable remainder unitrust, or a pooled income fund).

In determining whether a person has an interest in property, the fact that income or corpus may be used to satisfy a support obligation is disregarded if such use is discretionary or made pursuant to the Uniform Gifts to Minors Act (or a similar state statute). An interest may be disregarded if it is used primarily to postpone or avoid the generation-skipping tax.[13]

Direct Skip

A direct skip is a transfer subject to federal gift or estate tax to a skip person.[14]

Generally, some examples of direct skips include (among others):

- G transfers property to his grandchildren;

- G transfers property to a trust for his grandchildren;

- G transfers in trust property to his grandchild for life, remainder to grandchild's children;

- P is given a general power of appointment (exercisable during life or at death) in a trust and appoints the property subject to the power (either in trust or outright) to a skip person; and

- at G's death, property included in G's estate passes in trust to G's grand-children, or to G's grandchildren and great-grandchildren.

In the case of a direct skip, the taxable amount is the value of the property received by the transferee.[15] In the case of a direct skip from a trust, the tax is paid by the trustee. In the case of a direct skip (other than a direct skip from a trust), the tax is paid by the transferor. Unless the governing instrument of transfer otherwise directs, the GST tax is charged to the property constituting the transfer.[16]

Taxable Termination

A taxable termination occurs when an "interest in property" held in trust is terminated by an individual's death, lapse of time, release of a power, or otherwise, unless either:

(1) a non-skip person has an interest in the trust immediately after such termination; or

(2) at no time after the termination may a distribution be made from the trust to a skip person other than a distribution the probability of which occurring is so remote as to be negligible (i.e., less than a five percent actuarial probability).

If upon the termination of an interest in a trust by reason of the death of a lineal descendant of the transferor, a portion of the trust is distributed to skip persons (or to trusts for such persons), such partial termination is treated as taxable. If a transfer subject to estate or gift tax occurs at the time of the termination, the transfer is not a taxable termination (but it may be a direct skip, as discussed above).[17]

> *Example.* G transfers property in trust to his wife for life, then to children for life, then to grandchildren for life, and finally to great-grand-

children. If separate shares are created for each child and each grandchild, generally, a taxable termination would occur with respect to each such share at each child's or grandchild's death. If the interest of a generation does not terminate until the last person in such generation dies, generally, a taxable termination would occur at the death of the last child to die and at the death of the last grandchild to die.

In the case of a taxable termination, the taxable amount is the value of all property with respect to which the taxable termination has occurred, reduced by the expenses, similar to those allowed as a deduction under IRC Section 2053 in determining the taxable estate for estate tax purposes, with respect to which the taxable termination has occurred.[18] In the case of a taxable termination, the tax is paid by the trustee. Unless the governing instrument of transfer otherwise directs, the GST tax is charged to the property constituting the transfer.[19]

Taxable Distribution

A taxable distribution is any distribution from a trust to a skip person (other than a taxable termination or a direct skip).[20] When property is held in trust immediately following a generation-skipping transfer, the "multiple skip" rule (see "transferor," above) places the transferor one generation above the highest generation with an interest in the trust. Therefore, once there has been a direct skip or taxable termination to a generation, generally, such generation will no longer be a skip person and distributions to such generation will not be taxable distributions.

> *Example.* G transfers property in trust to his wife for life, then to children for life, then to grandchildren for life, and finally to great-grandchildren. The trustee is given certain powers to sprinkle income or corpus. If separate shares are created for each child, generally, any distribution from the trust to a grandchild prior to the termination of the interest of the grandmother and the parent of such grandchild is treated as a taxable distribution. If the interest of the children's generation does not terminate until the last person in such generation dies, generally, any distribution from the trust to a grandchild prior to the termination of the interest of G's wife and of the last child to die is treated as a taxable distribution. Similarly, any distribution from the trust to a great-grandchild prior to the termination of the interest of the grandmother, the children, and the grandchildren is generally treated as a taxable distribution.

> *Example.* G transfers property in trust to his grandchildren for life, and then to great-grandchildren. The trustee is given certain pow-

ers to sprinkle income or corpus. When G transferred the property to the trust there was a direct skip to the trust. Distributions to the grandchildren would not be taxable distributions because the trust would be treated as the transferor (see "multiple skip" rule, above) and assigned to the children's generation (first generation above grandchildren's) immediately after the direct skip. However, any distribution from the trust to a great-grandchild prior to the termination of the interest of the grandchildren would generally be treated as a taxable distribution. Also, when the grandchildren's interests end there would be a taxable termination.

In the case of a taxable distribution, the taxable amount is the value of the property received by the transferee reduced by any expense incurred by the transferee with respect to the GST tax imposed on the distribution. If any portion of the GST tax with respect to a taxable distribution is paid out of the trust, the taxable distribution is increased by such an amount.[21] In the case of a taxable distribution, the tax is paid by the transferee.[22]

Calculation of GST Tax

Each transferor has a GST tax exemption, discussed below. Allocations of the GST exemption can be made to transferred property. In order to determine how much of a trust is exempt and how much is nonexempt when a taxable termination or a taxable distribution occurs for GST tax purposes, an inclusion ratio, discussed below, is determined for the trust based upon allocations of the GST exemption to the trust.

The inclusion ratio may change as additional transfers are made to the trust. An inclusion ratio is also used for direct skips. In general, a trust which is totally exempt has an inclusion ratio of zero and a trust which is totally nonexempt has an inclusion ratio of one. The inclusion ratio is multiplied by the GST tax rate and then multiplied by the amount of the GST (see above).[23] The result is the GST tax imposed on the trust transfer.

The GST tax rate is a flat rate equal to the top estate tax rate. The GST tax rate is as follows:[24]

GST Tax Rate

Year	Rate
2005	47%
2006	46%
2007-2009	45%
2010	NA
2011-	55%

For generation-skipping transfers occuring before 2005 or after 2010, if the transfer (other than a direct skip) occurs at the same time as and as a result of the death of an individual, a credit against the GST tax imposed is allowed in an amount equal to the GST tax actually paid to any state with respect to any property included in the GST, but the amount cannot exceed five percent of the GST tax. EGTRRA 2001 eliminates the credit from 2005 to 2010.[25]

GST Exemption

Every individual is allowed a GST exemption which may be allocated irrevocably by him (or his executor) to any property with respect to which he is the transferor.[26] The amount of the GST exemption is as follows:

GST Tax Exemption

Year	Exemption
2004-2005	$1,500,000
2006-2008	$2,000,000
2009	$3,500,000
2010	NA
2011-	$1,120,000*

* plus indexing for inflation

From 2004 to 2010, the GST exemption and the estate tax unified credit exemption equivalent are equal.

In general, an individual or the individual's executor may allocate the GST exemption at any time from the date of the transfer until the time for filing the individual's federal estate tax return (including extensions actually granted), regardless of whether a return is required.[27]

The GST exemption is automatically allocated to lifetime direct skips unless otherwise elected on a timely filed federal gift tax return.[28]

In addition, any unused GST exemption is automatically allocated to indirect skips to a GST trust, effective 2001 to 2009.[29] An indirect skip is a transfer (other than a direct skip) subject to gift tax to a GST trust. A transferor can elect to have the automatic allocation not apply to (1) an indirect skip, or (2) to any or all transfers made by the individual to a particular trust. The transferor can also elect to treat a trust as a GST trust with respect to any or all transfers made by the individual to the trust. Nevertheless, an allocation still cannot be made until the end of any estate tax inclusion period (see below).

A GST trust is a trust that could have a generation-skipping transfer with respect to the transferor unless:

1.   The trust provides that more than 25 percent of the trust corpus must be distributed to, or may be withdrawn by, one or more individuals who are non-skip persons, either (a) before the individual's 46th birthday, (b) on or before a date prior to such birthday, or (c) an event that may reasonably be expected to occur before such birthday.

2.   The trust provides that more than 25 percent of the trust corpus must be distributed to, or may be withdrawn by, one or more individuals who are non-skip persons and who are living on the date of death of an individual identified in the trust (by name or class) who is more than 10 years older than such individuals.

3.   The trust provides that, if one or more individuals who are non-skip persons die before a date or event described in (1) or (2), more than 25 percent of the trust corpus must either (a) be distributed to the estate(s) of one or more of such individuals, or (b) be subject to a general power of appointment exercisable by one or more of such individuals.

4.   Any portion of the trust would be included in the gross estate of a non-skip person (other than the transferor) if such person died immediately after the transfer.

5.   The trust is a charitable lead annuity trust (CLAT), charitable remainder annuity trust (CRAT), charitable remainder unitrust (CRUT), or a charitable lead unitrust (CLUT) with a non-skip remainder person.

For purposes of these GST trust rules, the value of transferred property is not treated as includable in the gross estate of a non-skip person nor subject to a power of withdrawal if the withdrawal right does not exceed the amount of the gift tax annual exclusion (see Chapter 17) with respect to the transfer. It is also assumed that a power of appointment held by a non-skip person will not be exercised.

The statutory definitions of a GST trust for purposes of automatic allocation of GST exemption to indirect skips are purely arbitrary (and can be difficult to apply). They represent trusts to which Congress thought taxpayers might want to allocate GST exemption. While the automatic allocation provisions may be useful in some circumstances, it is probably better not to rely on the default provisions (at least not the indirect skip provisions).

It probably makes sense for grantors to make elections to allocate or not allocate GST exemption with respect to all transfers to a particular trust. GST exemption can be allocated to trusts benefiting skip persons; while allocations are not made to trusts benefiting non-skip persons. If need be, the election could be changed later, for future transfers.

A retroactive allocation of the GST exemption can be made when certain non-skip beneficiaries of a trust predecease the transferor, effective 2001 to 2009. The non-skip beneficiary must (1) have an interest or a future interest (for this purpose, a future interest means the trust may permit income or corpus to be paid to such person on a date or dates in the future) in the trust to which any transfer has been made, (2) be a lineal descendant of a grandparent of the transferor or of a grandparent of the transferor's spouse or former spouse, (3) be assigned to a generation lower than that of the transferor, and (4) predecease the transferor. In such a case, an allocation of the transferor's unused GST exemption (determined immediately before the non-skip person's death) can be made to any previous transfer or transfers to the trust (value of transfer is its gift tax value at the time of the transfer) on a chronological order. The allocation is made by the transferor on the gift tax return for the year of the non-skip person's death. The allocation is treated as effective immediately before the non-skip person's death.[30]

> *Example.* Grandparent creates a trust for the primary benefit of Child, with Grandchild as contingent remainder beneficiary. Grandparent doesn't expect Grandchild will receive anything, or that the trust will be generation-skipping; so he doesn't allocate GST exemption to the trust. (Or, perhaps, allocation of the GST exemption was simply overlooked.) Child dies unexpectedly before Grandparent. There is a GST taxable ter-

mination (see above) at Child's death. Grandparent can make a retroactive allocation of GST exemption to the trust to reduce or eliminate the GST tax on the taxable termination.

With regard to lifetime transfers other than a direct skip, an allocation is made on the federal gift tax return. An allocation can use a formula (e.g., the amount necessary to produce an inclusion ratio of zero). An allocation on a timely filed gift tax return is generally effective as of the date of the transfer. An allocation on an untimely filed gift tax return is generally effective as of the date the return is filed and is deemed to precede any taxable event occurring on such date. An allocation of the GST exemption is irrevocable after the due date. Except with respect to the special rules for charitable lead annuity trusts, discussed below, an allocation of GST exemption to a trust is void to the extent the allocation exceeds the amount necessary to obtain a zero inclusion ratio, discussed below, with respect to the trust.[31]

An executor can make an allocation of the transferor's unused GST exemption on the transferor's federal estate tax return. An allocation with respect to property included in the transferor's estate is effective as of the date of death. A late allocation of the GST with respect to a lifetime transfer can be made by the executor on the estate tax return and is effective as of the date the allocation is filed. A decedent's unused GST exemption is automatically and irrevocably allocated on the due date for the federal estate tax return to the extent not otherwise allocated by the executor. The automatic allocation is made to nonexempt property: first to direct skips occurring at death, and then to trusts with potential taxable distributions or taxable terminations.[32]

With respect to late allocations of the GST exemption to a trust, the transferor may elect (solely for purpose of determining the fair market value of trust assets) to treat the allocation as made on the first day of the month in which the allocation is made. This election is not effective with respect to a trust holding a life insurance policy, if the insured individual has died.[33]

Charitable Lead Annuity Trusts

Special rules apply to allocations of the GST exemption to charitable lead annuity trusts. With respect to property transferred after October 13, 1987, the GST tax exemption inclusion ratio for any charitable lead annuity trust is to be determined by dividing the amount of exemption allocated to the trust by the value of the property in the trust following the charitable term. For this purpose, the exemption allocated to the trust is increased by interest determined at the interest rate used in determining the amount of the estate or gift tax charitable deduction with respect to such a trust over the charitable term. With respect to a late allocation of the GST exemption, as discussed above, interest accrues only from the date of the late allocation. The amount of GST exemption allocated to the trust is not reduced even though it is determined at a later time that a lesser amount of GST exemption would have produced a zero inclusion ratio.[34]

Estate Tax Inclusion Period (ETIP)

In general, allocations of the GST tax exemption are postponed during the period in which property would be includable in the estate of the transferor or the spouse of the transferor for estate tax purposes. With respect to inter vivos transfers subject at some point in time to the GST tax, the allocation of any portion of the GST exemption to such a transfer is postponed until the earlier of:

(1)   the expiration of the period (not to extend beyond the transferor's death) during which the property being transferred would be included in the transferor's estate (other than by reason of the gifts within three years of death rule of IRC Section 2035) if he died; or

(2)   the GST.

For purposes of determining the inclusion ratio, discussed below, with respect to such exemption, the value of such property is:

(1)   its estate tax value if it is included in the transferor's estate (other than by reason of the three year rule of IRC Section 2035); or

(2)   its value determined at the end of the ETIP.

However, if the allocation of the exemption under the second valuation method is not made on a timely filed gift tax return for the year in which the ETIP ends, determination of value is postponed until such allocation is filed.[35]

> *Example.* Grantor sets up an irrevocable trust under which income is retained for 10 years. Then, a life estate for the children is provided for, followed by remainder to the grandchildren. The valuation of property for purpose of the inclusion rule is delayed until the earlier of the expiration of the 10-year period or the transferor's death. If the grantor were to die during such time the property would be included in the grantor's estate under IRC Section 2036(a) as a retained life estate. However, if the grantor survived the 10-year period and failed to make an allocation of the exemption on a timely filed gift tax return, the determination of value is postponed until the earlier of the time an allocation is filed or death.

Except as provided in regulations, for purpose of the GST exemption allocation rules, any reference to an individual or a transferor is generally treated as including the spouse of such individual or transferor.[36] Thus, an ETIP includes the period during which, if death occurred, the property being transferred would be included in the estate (other than by reason of the gifts within three years of death rule of IRC Section 2035) of the transferor or the spouse of the transferor. However, the property is not considered as includable in the estate of the transferor or the spouse of the transferor if the possibility of inclusion is so remote as to be negligible (i.e., less than a five percent actuarial probability).

The property is not considered as includable in the estate of the spouse of the transferor by reason of a withdrawal power limited to the greater of $5,000 or five percent of the trust corpus if the withdrawal power terminates no later than 60 days after the transfer to trust.

Apparently, the ETIP rules do not apply if a reverse QTIP election is made.

The ETIP terminates on the earlier of:

(1)   the death of the transferor;

(2)   the time at which no portion would be includable in the transferor's estate (other than by reason of IRC Section 2035) or, in the case of the spouse who consents to a split-gift, the time at which no portion would be includable in the other spouse's estate;

(3)   the time of the GST (but only with respect to property involved in the GST); or

(4)   in the case of an ETIP arising because of an interest or power held by the transferor's spouse, at the earlier of (a) the death of the spouse, or (b) the time at which no portion would be includable in the spouse's estate (other than by reason of IRC Section 2035).[37]

Example. Grantor sets up an irrevocable trust under which income is retained for the shorter of nine years or life, with the remainder to a grandchild. Grantor and spouse elect to split the gift. If the spouse dies during trust term, the spouse's executor can allocate GST exemption to the spouse's deemed one-half of the trust. However, the allocation is not effective until the earlier of the expiration of grantor's income interest or grantor's death.

Inclusion Ratio

In general, the inclusion ratio with respect to any property transferred in a generation-skipping transfer is the excess of 1 minus (a) the "applicable fraction" for the trust from which the transfer is made, or (b) in the case of a direct skip to a trust, the applicable fraction determined for the skip.[38]

The "applicable fraction" is a fraction (a) the *numerator* of which is the amount of the GST exemption allocated to the trust (or to the property transferred, if a direct skip), and (b) the *denominator* of which is the value of the property transferred reduced by (i) the sum of any federal estate or state death tax actually recovered from the trust attributable to such property, (ii) any federal gift tax or estate tax charitable deduction allowed with respect to such property, and (iii) with respect to a direct skip, the portion that is a nontaxable gift, as discussed below. The fraction should be rounded to the nearest one-thousandth, with 5 rounded up (i.e., .2345 is rounded to .235). If the denominator of the applicable fraction is zero, the inclusion ratio is zero.[39]

> *Example.* In the year 2006, G transfers irrevocably in trust for his grandchildren $6 million and allocates all his $2,000,000 GST exemption to the transfer. The applicable fraction is 2,000,000/6,000,000, or .333. The inclusion ratio is 1 minus .333, or .667. The maximum estate tax rate, 46 percent, is applied against the inclusion ratio, .667. The resulting percentage, 30.7 percent, is applied against the value of the property transferred, $6,000,000, to produce a GST tax of $1,842,000. The tax is paid by G, the transferor, because this is a direct skip (other than a direct skip from a trust).

> *Example.* Assume the same facts as in preceding example, except that for federal gift tax purposes G's wife consented to a split gift of the $6 million. Thus, for GST tax purposes as well, the gift is considered split between the spouses. They both elect to have their respective GST exemptions allocated to the transfer. For each of them, the applicable fraction is 2,000,000/3,000,000, or .667. The inclusion ratio is one minus .667, or .333. The maximum estate tax rate, 46 percent, is applied against the inclusion ratio, .333. The resulting percentage, 15.3 percent, is applied against the value of the property transferred, $3,000,000, to produce a GST tax of $459,000 for each spouse (or a total GST tax of $918,000 on the $6 million transfer).

If there is more than one transfer in trust the applicable fraction must be recomputed at the time of each transfer. Thus, if property is transferred to a preexisting trust, the "recomputed applicable fraction" is determined as follows: The *numerator* of such fraction is the sum of (1) the amount of the GST exemption allocated to the property involved in such transfer and (2) the nontax portion of the trust immediately before the transfer. (The nontax portion of the trust is the value of the trust immediately before the transfer multiplied by the applicable fraction in effect before such transfer.) The *denominator* of such fraction is the value of the trust immediately after the transfer reduced by (1) the sum of any federal estate or state death tax actually recovered from the trust attributable to such property, (2) any federal gift tax or estate tax charitable deduction allowed with respect to such property, and (3) with respect to a direct skip, the portion that is a nontaxable gift.[40]

> *Example.* In the year 1995, G transfers irrevocably in trust for his children and grandchildren $4 million and allocates all his $1 million GST exemption to the transfer. The applicable fraction is 1,000,000/4,000,000, or .250. The inclusion ratio is 1 minus .250, or .750.
>
> In 2001, the trust makes a taxable distribution to the grandchildren of $100,000. The maximum estate tax rate, 55 percent in 2001, is applied against the inclusion ratio, .750. The resulting percentage, 41.3 percent, is multiplied by the $100,000 transfer, resulting in a GST tax of $41,300. GST taxes in this example are paid by the grandchildren, the transferees, because the transfers are taxable distributions (see above).
>
> In 2006, the trust makes a taxable distribution to the grandchildren of $100,000. The maximum estate tax rate, 46 percent in 2006, is applied against the inclusion ratio, .750. The resulting percentage, 34.5 percent, is multiplied by the $100,000 transfer, resulting in a GST tax of $34,500.
>
> Later in 2006, when the trust property has grown to $6 million, G transfers an additional $3 million to the trust. An additional $1,000,000 of GST exemption is available to G in 2006 ($2,000,000 GST exemption in 2006 minus $1,000,000 exemption already used). The numerator of the recomputed fraction is the value of the nontax portion of the trust immediately before the transfer, or $1.5 million (value of the trust, $6 million, multiplied by the applicable fraction of .250), plus $1,000,000 additional exemption, or $2,500,000. The denominator of the recomputed fraction is $9 million (the sum of the transferred property, $3 million, and the value of all the property in the trust immediately before the transfer, $6 million). The applicable fraction is 2,500,000/9,000,000, or .278. The inclusion ratio is 1 minus .278, or .722.

Later in 2006, the trust makes a taxable distribution to the grand-children of $100,000. The maximum estate tax rate, 46 percent in 2006, is applied against the inclusion ratio, .722. The resulting percentage, 33.2 percent, is multiplied by the $100,000 transfer, resulting in a GST tax of $33,200.

Generally, planners strive for trusts (or portions of trust treated as separate trusts) with inclusion ratios of zero (totally GST tax exempt) and one (totally GST tax nonexempt) rather than for intermediate ratios. Then, a trustee may be able to make distributions from a trust with a zero inclusion ratio if distributions are to a skip person (thus avoiding GST tax), while distributions from a trust with an inclusion ratio of one are made to non-skip persons (thus reducing the amount of property remaining which may later be subject to generation-skipping tax). It also makes for much easier math.

Endnotes

1. IRC Sec. 2664; EGTRRA 2001 Sec. 901.

2. IRC Secs. 2611(a), 2613.

3. IRC Secs. 2611(b), 2642(c).

4. IRC Sec. 2652(a)(1).

5. Treas. Reg. §26.2652-1(a).

6. IRC Sec. 2653(a).

7. Treas. Reg. §26.2653-1.

8. IRC Sec. 2652(a)(2).

9. IRC Sec. 2652(a)(3).

10. IRC Secs. 2651(a), 2651(b), 2651(c).

11. IRC Sec. 2651(e).

12. IRC Sec. 2651(d).

13. IRC Sec. 2652(c).

14. IRC Sec. 2612(c).

15. IRC Sec. 2623.

16. IRC Secs. 2603(a)(3), 2603(b).

17. IRC Sec. 2612(a); Treas. Reg. §26.2612-1(b).

18. IRC Sec. 2622.

19. IRC Secs. 2603(a)(2), 2603(b).

20. IRC Sec. 2612(b).

21. IRC Sec. 2621.

22. IRC Secs. 2603(a)(1), 2603(b).

23. IRC Secs. 2602, 2642.

24. IRC Secs. 2641, 2001(c).

25. IRC Sec. 2604.

26. IRC Sec. 2631.

27. IRC Sec. 2632.

28. IRC Sec. 2632(b).

29. IRC Sec. 2632(c).

30. IRC Sec. 2632(d).

31. Treas. Reg. §26.2632-1(b).

32. IRC Sec. 2632(c); Treas. Reg. §26.2632-1(d).

33. IRC Sec. 2642(b)(2)(A); Treas. Reg. §26.2642-2(a)(2).

34. IRC Sec. 2642(e); Treas. Reg. §26.2642-3.

35. IRC Sec. 2642(f).

36. IRC Sec. 2642(f)(4).

37. Treas. Reg. §26.2632-1(c).

38. IRC Sec. 2642(a)(1).

39. IRC Sec. 2642(a)(2); Treas. Reg. §26.2642-1.

40. IRC Sec. 2642(d); Treas. Reg. §26.2642-4.

Chapter 20

Bankruptcy, Asset Protection, and IRAs

C ertain protections are provided for IRAs in bankruptcy (see detailed discussion below). In general, these protections have been strengthened by the Bankruptcy Abuse Prevention and Consumer Protection Act of 2005 despite the sweeping changes made by the Act designed generally to make it harder for a debtor to get relief through bankruptcy. In addition, a number of other protections have been provided for IRA owners and beneficiaries against creditors and other claimants under a number of other laws.

States have various laws protecting certain IRAs (or portions thereof) from the claims of creditors, bankruptcy or insolvency laws, attachment, execution, seizure for debts, levy, sale under execution, garnishment, setoff, or other process or court proceedings. The laws vary widely from state to state. A survey of state creditor exemptions and IRAs is available on the Ultimate IRA Resource CD.

Some references under state law are made to plans under certain listed Internal Revenue Code sections. IRC Section 408 covers traditional IRAs, SEPs (including SAR-SEPs), and SIMPLE IRAs. IRC Section 408A covers Roth IRAs. IRC Section 402A covers elective deferral Roths (but, depending on the type of elective deferral Roth, income tax exemption for the retirement fund may be based on either IRC Section 401(a), 403(b), or 501(a), and distributions may be taxable under a combination of IRC Section 402A, 408A, or 72). After Roth IRAs were added under federal law, many state statutes were slowly amended over time to add references to

IRC Section 408A. Some amendments to state statutes may also be needed now for elective deferral Roths.

The amount of an IRA protected under state law varies widely. Some common provisions include protection for: unlimited amounts, amounts limited to certain contribution levels, amounts limited to a specific dollar amount of assets, amounts limited to assets that would generate specific amounts of distributions, amounts limited to that needed for support, amounts limited to extent contributions were made during some recent period of time (e.g., during preceding one year), or amounts limited to extent transfers were fraudulent.

To the extent that a state statute attempts to protect or reach a retirement plan that is subject to ERISA, the provision may be preempted by ERISA. If the state provision is preempted by ERISA, the state provision may not be effective. For example, ERISA requires generally that retirement plans must contain an anti-alienation provision. SEPs, SIMPLE IRAs, and elective deferral Roths are generally subject to ERISA; traditional and Roth IRAs are not.

There are a couple of super creditors against which federal or state protection may be limited. Interests in an IRA can generally be reached by the federal or state government for the failure of the IRA owner or beneficiary to pay taxes or to satisfy other claims of the government. Interests in IRAs may also be reached to satisfy the claims of a spouse (or former spouse) for alimony or support, or for the support of dependents.

The effect of a successful claim by a creditor or other person against IRA assets would generally be to cause the claimed amount to be distributed from the IRA. The distribution would generally be subject to income tax, possibly including the early distribution penalty tax, under the rules for distributions from IRAs (see Chapter 13). The IRA owner, during lifetime, or the IRA beneficiary, after the death of the IRA owner, would generally be the person subject to income tax. However, a transfer of an IRA by one spouse to the other in connection with divorce or separation is generally not considered a taxable transfer for income tax purposes. The spouse to whom the IRA is transferred is thereafter treated as the IRA owner.

Once assets are distributed from an IRA, any protections provided specifically to IRAs cease to apply at some point. A beneficiary will generally have to take required minimum distributions from an IRA. Furthermore, the beneficiary could withdraw more than the required minimum distributions. Transferring a beneficiary's interest in an IRA to a trust with spendthrift provisions (see below) may offer some addititional protection for the IRA after the death of the IRA owner and peace of mind for the IRA owner.

Bankruptcy

The Bankruptcy Code is contained in Title 11 of the United States Code. Bankruptcy Code Section 541 generally defines property included or excluded in the bankruptcy estate. Bankruptcy Code Section 522 provides for certain exemptions from the bankruptcy estate.

Section 541(a) broadly includes in the bankruptcy estate all legal interests of the debtor as of, or after, the commencement of the bankruptcy case, including earnings and proceeds from property included in the bankruptcy estate. Absent other provisions, this would generally be sufficient to bring all IRAs into the bankruptcy estate of the IRA owner/debtor, while alive, or an IRA beneficiary/debtor, after the death of the original owner.

However, a number of provisions provide certain protections for IRAs in bankruptcy. Section 541(b) provides that certain items are not included in the bankruptcy estate (i.e., exclusions). Also, Section 541(c)(2) provides that a restriction on the transfer of an interest of the debtor that is enforceable under applicable nonbankruptcy law is enforceable in a bankrupcy case (in effect, creating an excluson). In addition, as noted, Section 522 provides for certain exemptions. These provisions are discussed below as they apply to IRAs.

The Bankruptcy Abuse Prevention and Consumer Protection Act of 2005 (BAPCPA 2005) made sweeping changes to bankruptcy law. In general, the changes were designed to make it harder for a debtor to get relief through bankruptcy. However, certain changes were intended to provide protections for certain qualified plans and IRAs in bankruptcy. Changes affecting IRAs are discussed below.

Note. Some references under bankruptcy law are made to Internal Revenue Code sections. IRC Section 408 covers traditional IRAs, SEPs (including SAR-SEPs), and SIMPLE IRAs. IRC Section 408A covers Roth IRAs. IRC Section 402A covers elective deferral Roths (but, depending on the type of elective deferral Roth, income tax exemption for the retirement fund may be based on either IRC Section 401(a), 403(b), or 501(a)).

Overview

A couple of exclusions are provided for certain retirement plans from the bankruptcy estate. These exclusions should apply to SEPs, SIMPLE IRAs, and elective deferral Roths, but not to traditional and Roth IRAs. But even if an exclusion is not available, an exemption may be available.

A debtor can choose to exempt property from the bankruptcy estate under either one of two alternative methods: the list method or the nonlist method. If the nonlist method is chosen, IRAs are exempt from the bankruptcy estate. If the list method is chosen, an exemption is available for IRAs, unless applicable state law specifically does not so authorize. The exemptions for traditional IRAs and Roth IRAs are generally limited in the aggregate to $1,000,000 (as indexed).

A person choosing between the list and nonlist methods should examine all of the debtor's assets, not just the IRA provisions, to determine which method would be more beneficial for the debtor in bankruptcy. However, the discussion below is limited to IRAs in bankruptcy.

Exclusions

A couple of exclusions are, in effect, provided for certain retirement plans from the bankruptcy estate under Section 541(b)(7) and Section 541(c)(2). These exclusions should apply to SEPs, SIMPLE IRAs, and elective deferral Roths, but not to traditional and Roth IRAs. But even if an exclusion is not available, an exemption (see below) may be available.

Section 541(b)(7) Exclusion

Section 541(b) provides that certain items are not included in the bankruptcy estate. BAPCPA 2005 added a new Section 541(b)(7), which provides that certain contributions to certain retirement plans are not included in the bankruptcy estate. For this purpose, contributions include amounts withheld by an employer from the wages of employees, as well as amounts received by an employer from employees. For this purpose, retirement plans include an employee benefit plan that is subject to ERISA Title I, as well as certain listed retirement plans.

IRAs are not listed under Section 541(b). However, SEPs, SIMPLE IRAs, and elective deferral Roths are generally plans subject to ERISA Title I (unless the plan has no employees, just owners and their spouses). Therefore, contributions to SEPs, SIMPLE IRAs, and elective deferral Roths should generally be excluded from the bankruptcy estate under Section 541(b); contributions to traditional and Roth IRAs should not.

The language used in Section 541(b) does raise some questions. Note that Section 541(b) seems to apply to elective deferral contributions (amounts withheld from the wages of employees) and employee contributions. Does it not apply to employer contributions? Employer contributions are not generally regarded as withheld from the wages of employees, nor as employee contributions.

Section 541(b) provides an exclusion for contributions. Does that mean the exclusion applies to the actual contribution to the retirement plan, to contributions once they are in the retirement plan, to contributions plus earnings on those contributions, to the entire rerirement plan? *Rousey v. Jacoway*, see below, applied an exemption tied to the right to payments (i.e., distributions) under Section 522(d)(10)(E) to the entire retirement plan assets. Perhaps the use of the terms contributions, distributions, and retirement assets is meaningless here and the exclusion applies to the entire retirement fund assets of the debtor.

Section 541(c)(2) Exclusion

Section 541(c)(2) provides that a restriction on transfer that is enforceable under applicable nonbankruptcy law is enforceable under bankruptcy law. In *Patterson v. Shumate*, 504 U.S. 773 (1992), the Supreme Court ruled that the ERISA anti-alienation provisions that generally apply to qualified plans are a restriction on transfer that is enforceable under applicable nonbankruptcy law as described under Section 541(c)(2). Therefore, a debtor may exclude an interest in a qualified plans with such an anti-alienation provision from the bankruptcy estate.

SEPs, SIMPLE IRAs, and elective deferral Roths should generally be eligible for exclusion under Section 541(c)(2) (unless the plan has no employees, just owners and their spouses). Traditional and Roth IRAs are not subject to ERISA and are not required to have an anti-alienation provision. Therefore, traditional and Roth IRAs are not eligible for exclusion from the bankruptcy estate under Section 541(c)(2).

Exemptions

Bankruptcy Code Section 522 provides for certain exemptions from the bankruptcy estate. Under BAPCPA 2005, Section 522 has been somewhat reorganized and some new provisions added, including some relating to IRAs.

Section 522(b)(1) provides that a debtor can choose to exempt property from the bankruptcy estate under either one of two alternative methods: the list method or the nonlist method. If the nonlist method is chosen, IRAs are exempt from the bankruptcy estate. If the list method is chosen, an exemption is available for IRAs, unless applicable state law specifically does not so authorize. Property exempted under one of these methods would be in addition to any property already excluded under Section 541 (see above). The nonlist method, the list method, some common rules for retirement funds under both methods, and the determination and effect of applicable state law for purposes of these two methods are discussed below.

New Section 522(n) provides that any exemption under Section 522 for traditional IRAs and Roth IRAs is generally limited in the aggregate to $1,000,000. The $1,000,000 amount is periodically adjusted for inflation under Bankruptcy Code Section 104. The dollar amount can be increased if the interests of justice so require (presumably, a case by case approach with the burden of proof on the debtor). The dollar limitation does not apply to SEPs, SIMPLE IRAs, and elective deferral Roths (or qualified plans), including amounts (and the earnings thereon) rolled over from such accounts to a traditional IRA or Roth IRA. Consider maintaining a rollover in a separate traditional or Roth IRA to facilitate accounting for the rollover and earnings thereon.

Nonlist Method

Under Section 522(b)(2), the debtor has exemptions for (1) property exempt under federal law (other than property listed in Section 522(d) (see below)) or applicable state (or local) law (see below); (2) certain jointly owned property to the extent exempt under applicable nonbankruptcy law; and (3) retirement funds in accounts exempt from income tax under IRC Sections 401, 403, 408, 408A, 414, 457, or 501(a). Exemption (3) was added by BAPCPA 2005. If the nonlist method is chosen, IRAs are exempt from the bankruptcy estate.

List Method

Under Section 522(b)(1), the debtor can exclude property that is listed in Section 522(d), unless applicable state law (see below) specifically does not so authorize. Two items are of interest regarding IRAs under the Section 522(d) list.

Section 522(d)(10)(E) provides, under certain circumstances (see below), for an exemption from the bankruptcy estate for the debtor's right to receive a payment under a stock bonus, pension, profit sharing, annuity, or similar plan on account of a number of reasons (including age) to the extent reasonably necessary for the support of the debtor and dependents of the debtor. However, this exemption does not apply if (1) the plan was established by an insider that employed the debtor at the time the debtor received rights under the plan; (2) the payment is on account of age or service; and (3) the plan does not qualify under IRC Section 401(a), 403(a),

403(b), or 408. [It appears that the statute needs to be amended to add IRC Section 408A (Roth IRAs).]

In *Patterson v. Shumate*, see above, the court stated that it expressed no opinion on the separate question of whether Section 522(d)(10)(E) applies only to distributions that a debtor has an immediate and present right to receive, or the entire undistributed corpus of the qualified plan.

In *Rousey v. Jacoway*, 544 U.S. ___ (2005), the Supreme Court ruled that IRAs are a similar plan as those listed in Section 522(d)(10)(E) and confer a right to payment based on age. Therefore, assets in an IRA are eligible for the exemption under Section 522(d)(10)(E) (assuming the exemption is available, see below). Furthermore, use of the term "IRA assets" in *Rousey v. Jacoway* suggests that Section 522(d)(10)(E) is applied to the entire undistributed corpus of the plan.

In determining the amount of the exempton under Section 522(d)(10)(E), a determination must be made as to the needs of the debtor and dependents of the debtor for support. The exemption is limited to those needs for support; presumably, calculated using present value concepts.

New Section 522(d)(12) provides an exemption from the bankruptcy estate for retirement funds in accounts exempt from income tax under IRC Sections 401, 403, 408, 408A, 414, 457, or 501(a). This exemption includes IRAs. This exemption is not limited to the amount needed for support of the debtor and dependents.

Thus, under the list method, an exemption is available for IRAs, unless applicable state law specifically does not so authorize.

Common Rules Under Both Methods

New Section 522(b)(4) provides special rules for the exemptions for retirement funds under Section 522(b)(3)(C) (part of the nonlist method) and Section 522(d)(12) (part of the list method). Section 522(b)(4) provides that for purpose of those sections:

1. If the retirement funds are in a fund that received a favorable determination letter under IRC Section 7805 that is in effect on the date of filing the bankruptcy petition, the funds are presumed to be exempt from the bankruptcy estate.

2. If the retirement funds are in a fund that has not received a favorable determination letter under IRC Section 7805, funds are exempt if the

debtor demonstrates that either (a) no prior determination to the contrary has been made by a court or the IRS and the retirement fund is in substantial compliance with the Internal Revenue Code; or (b) the retirement fund is not in substantial compliance with the Internal Revenue Code and the debtor is not materially responsible for that failure.

3.   A direct transfer (in general, a form of rollover) of retirement funds exempt from tax under IRC Sections 401, 403, 408, 408A, 414, 457, or 501(a) does not cease to qualify for bankruptcy exemption under Section 522(b)(3)(C) or Section 522(d)(12) by reason of the direct transfer.

4.   A distribution from a retirement fund exempt from tax under IRC Sections 401, 403, 408, 408A, 414, 457, or 501(a) that qualifies for rollover treatment does not cease to qualify for bankruptcy exemption under Section 522(b)(3)(C) or Section 522(d)(12) by reason of the rollover.

Thus, retirement assets in IRAs (and qualified plans) are generally exempt under Section 522(b)(3)(C) or Section 522(d)(12) (unless applicable state provides otherwise for this section). Direct transfers and rollovers generally do not affect this treatment.

State Law

State law can provide variations in the exemptions available under federal bankruptcy law. Therefore, state law should be reviewed whenever bankruptcy protection is being considered. A person may consider moving to a state with more favorable exemptions in order to obtain greater protection in bankruptcy. However, a two year (730 day) domicillary requirement may limit a person's ability to effectively do so for bankruptcy purposes.

Under either the list or nonlist exemption method, applicable state (or local) law (as defined in Section 522 (b)(3)) generally means the law of the place where the debtor was domiciled for the 730 days (i.e., 2 years) preceding the date for filing the bankruptcy petition. However, if the debtor was not domiciled in a single state during the 730-day period, applicable state law means the law of the place in which the debtor was domiciled for the longest time during the 180-day period preceding the 730-day period. If the effect of the domicillary requirement renders the debtor ineligible for any exemption, the debtor can exempt property listed in Section 522(d).

> *Example.* A debtor was domiciled in Florida for the last 2 years (730 days) preceding the date for filing for bankruptcy. The 730-day domiciliary test is met. Applicable state law means Florida law.

Example. A debtor was domiciled in Florida for the last year preceding the date for filing for bankruptcy. Prior to moving to Florida, the debtor was domiciled in Ohio for 25 years. Thus, the debtor was not domiciled in one state for the entire 730-day period. The debtor was domiciled in Ohio for all of the 180-day period preceding the 730-day period. Applicable state law means Ohio law.

Under the nonlist method, a debtor can use the bankruptcy exemptions provided under state law (as well as federal exemptions other than those listed in Section 522(d)), plus the exemption for IRAs (and qualified plans).

Under the list method, an exemption is available for IRAs (as well as other listed items, including qualified plans), unless applicable state law specifically does not so authorize. About two thirds of the states provide that the federal list exemptions are not available.

The following states permit debtors to apply the federal exemptions listed in Section 522(d): Alaska, Arkansas, Connecticut, District of Columbia, Hawaii, Massachusetts, Michigan Minnesota, New Hampshire, New Jersey, New Mexico, Pennsylvania, Rhode Island, Texas, Vermont, Washington, and Wisconsin.

The following states do not permit debtors to apply the federal exemptions listed in Section 522(d). Arizona, California, Colorado, Delaware, Florida, Georgia, Idaho, Illinois, Indiana, Iowa, Kansas, Kentucky, Louisiana, Maine, Maryland, Mississippi, Missouri, Montana, Nebraska, Nevada, New York, North Carolina, North Dakota, Ohio, Oklahoma, Oregon, South Carolina, South Dakota, Tennessee, Utah, Virginia, West Virginia, and Wyoming. Nevertheless, state law exemptions for IRAs may still be available in federal bankruptcy.

Spendthrift Trusts for Beneficiaries

Transferring a beneficiary's interest in an IRA to a trust with spendthrift provisions may offer some addititional protection for the IRA after the death of the IRA owner and peace of mind for the IRA owner. Some states define certain retirement plans as being spendthrift trusts (for purposes of certain protections provided specifically to IRA, see general discussion above). The discussion in this section is focused on use of a separate spendthrift trust that is the beneficiary of an IRA, rather than on an IRA that is treated as a spendthrift trust under state law.

In the case of a spouse beneficiary, a trust with a spendthrift provision cannot be used if the IRA owner is planning to use the estate tax marital deduction (see Chapter 18) for the IRA. Property subject to a spendthrift provision would not qualify for the marital deduction. Also, a spouse is not treated as the sole designated beneficiary for required minimum distribution purposes if a trust is the beneficiary of the IRA. In addition, a trust with a spendthrift provision is less likely to provide asset protection if the surviving spouse of the IRA owner is treated as the owner of the IRA rather than as a beneficiary of the IRA.

Once assets are distributed from an IRA, any protections provided specifically to IRAs cease to apply at some point. A beneficiary will generally have to take required minimum distributions from an IRA. (Distributions are not required during the lifetime of a surviving spouse who elects to be treated as the owner of a Roth IRA.) Furthermore, the beneficiary could withdraw more than the required minimum distributions. In addition, the protection provided to a spendthrift trust could be greater than the protection provided to an IRA in some cases. This is where transferring a beneficiary's interest in an IRA to a trust with spendthrift provisions may offer some addititional protection for the IRA after the death of the IRA owner.

Spendthrift Provisions

In a broad sense, a spendthrift provision is a provision in a trust in which the grantor attempts to provide funds to a beneficiary while limiting the ability of the beneficiary to squander the funds or creditors of the beneficiary from reaching the funds. Spendthrift provisions might include any of the following: (1) prohibition of beneficiary transferring the beneficiary's interest; (2) forfeiture of beneficiary's interest if beneficiary attempts to transfer interest; (3) distributions of income or principal to a beneficiary limited to support of the beneficiary (possibly, limited to distributions on behalf of beneficiary for support rather than distributions directly to beneficiary); (4) distributions to a beneficiary at the trustee's discretion; (5) prohibition against creditors reaching beneficiary's interest.

There is a considerable amount of diversity among the states as to when a creditor of a beneficiary can reach the beneficiary's trust interest. Unless the trust document or state law provides otherwise, a creditor of a beneficiary can generally reach the beneficiary's trust interest.

State laws generally attempt to restrict the ability of a grantor to prevent creditors from reaching a beneficiary's interest in one of the following ways: (1) no restriction, creditor can reach trust interest; (2) creditor can reach amount not needed by beneficiary for support; (3) creditor can reach amount above some dollar amount; or (4) creditor cannot reach trust property.

Where a special power of appointment (in general, a power that cannot be exercised in favor of the powerholder) is received by a beneficiary from the grantor, a creditor generally cannot reach property subject to the power unless the power is actually exercised. Where the beneficiary has a general power of appointment (in general, a power that can be exercised in favor of the powerholder), a creditor of the beneficiary can reach property subject to the power if the power is actually exercised. Generally, a creditor cannot reach an unexercised power held by a trust beneficiary unless a state statute provides otherwise or a beneficiary is in bankruptcy. A general power of appointment retained by a grantor can be reached by a creditor of the grantor whether or not the power is exercised. Whether and under what circumstances a special power of appointment retained by a grantor can be reached by a creditor varies greatly among the states.

Even if the beneficiary's interest in the trust itself is not protected from creditors of a beneficiary (including a grantor who is a beneficiary of the trust), protections provided to certain types of property (e.g., prohibitions against alienation of certain interests in retirement plans) under state or federal law may still be available for property in the trust.

Appendices

Appendix A

Gift and Estate Tax Tables

2005 Gift and Estate Tax Table

Taxable Gift/Estate		Tax on	Rate on
From	To	Col. 1	Excess
$ 0	$ 10,000	$ 0	18%
10,000	20,000	1,800	20%
20,000	40,000	3,800	22%
40,000	60,000	8,200	24%
60,000	80,000	13,000	26%
80,000	10,0000	18,200	28%
100,000	150,000	23,800	30%
150,000	250,000	38,800	32%
250,000	500,000	70,800	34%
500,000	750,000	155,800	37%
750,000	1,000,000	248,300	39%
1,000,000	1,250,000	345,800	41%
1,250,000	1,500,000	448,300	43%
1,500,000	2,000,000	555,800	45%
2,000,000	....	780,800	47%

2006 Gift and Estate Tax Table

Taxable Gift/Estate		Tax on	Rate on
From	To	Col. 1	Excess
$ 0	$ 10,000	$ 0	18%
10,000	20,000	1,800	20%
20,000	40,000	3,800	22%
40,000	60,000	8,200	24%
60,000	80,000	13,000	26%
80,000	10,0000	18,200	28%
100,000	150,000	23,800	30%
150,000	250,000	38,800	32%
250,000	500,000	70,800	34%
500,000	750,000	155,800	37%
750,000	1,000,000	248,300	39%
1,000,000	1,250,000	345,800	41%
1,250,000	1,500,000	448,300	43%
1,500,000	2,000,000	555,800	45%
2,000,000	....	780,800	46%

2007-2009 Gift and Estate Tax Table

Taxable Gift/Estate		Tax on	Rate on
From	To	Col. 1	Excess
$ 0	$ 10,000	$ 0	18%
10,000	20,000	1,800	20%
20,000	40,000	3,800	22%
40,000	60,000	8,200	24%
60,000	80,000	13,000	26%
80,000	10,0000	18,200	28%
100,000	150,000	23,800	30%
150,000	250,000	38,800	32%
250,000	500,000	70,800	34%
500,000	750,000	155,800	37%
750,000	1,000,000	248,300	39%
1,000,000	1,250,000	345,800	41%
1,250,000	1,500,000	448,300	43%
1,500,000	....	555,800	45%

2010 Gift Tax Only Table

Taxable Gift/Estate		Tax on	Rate on
From	To	Col. 1	Excess
$ 0	$ 10,000	$ 0	18%
10,000	20,000	1,800	20%
20,000	40,000	3,800	22%
40,000	60,000	8,200	24%
60,000	80,000	13,000	26%
80,000	10,0000	18,200	28%
100,000	150,000	23,800	30%
150,000	250,000	38,800	32%
250,000	500,000	70,800	34%
500,000	....	155,800	35%

2011- Gift and Estate Tax Table

Taxable Gift/Estate		Tax on	Rate on
From	To	Col. 1	Excess
$ 0	$ 10,000	$ 0	18%
10,000	20,000	1,800	20%
20,000	40,000	3,800	22%
40,000	60,000	8,200	24%
60,000	80,000	13,000	26%
80,000	10,0000	18,200	28%
100,000	150,000	23,800	30%
150,000	250,000	38,800	32%
250,000	500,000	70,800	34%
500,000	750,000	155,800	37%
750,000	1,000,000	248,300	39%
1,000,000	1,250,000	345,800	41%
1,250,000	1,500,000	448,300	43%
1,500,000	2,000,000	555,800	45%
2,000,000	2,500,000	780,800	49%
2,500,000	3,000,000	1,025,800	53%
3,000,000	10,000,000	1,290,800	55%
10,000,000	17,184,000	5,140,800	60%
17,184,000	....	9,451,200	55%

Appendix B

IRA Contribution Phaseout Tables

Deductible contributions to traditional IRAs (see Chapter 4) and SEP IRAs (see Chapter 6) and contributions to Roth IRAs (see Chapter 5) may be subject to phaseout based on modified adjusted gross income (MAGI). The IRA contribution phaseout tables can be used to estimate the allowable contribution after phaseout.

First, determine whether the phaseout range is $10,000, $15,000, or $20,000 for the particular type and year of contribution. Use the corresponding IRA contribution phaseout table.

Second, determine the total contribution limit for the year of contribution. This includes catchup contributions if the IRA owner is age 50 or more. Go to the corresponding column for maximum contributions in the appropriate IRA contribution phaseout table.

Third, determine the amount of MAGI in excess of the applicable dollar amount for the particular type and year of contribution. Go to the corresponding row for MAGI in excess of the applicable dollar amount in the IRA contribution phaseout table.

The amount at the intersection of the column and row in the table is the phased out IRA contribution limit.

Figure 4.1 in Chapter 4 provides a phaseout table method worksheet for estimating the amount of deductible contributions that can be made to a traditional IRA where there is active participation. See Figure 4.2 in Chapter 4 for an example of using this method.

Figure 5.1 in Chapter 5 provides a phaseout table method worksheet for estimating the amount of contributions that can be made to a Roth IRA. See Figure 5.2 in Chapter 5 for an example of using this method.

IRA Contribution Phaseout Table
(Phaseout Range: $10,000)

MAGI in Excess of Applicable Dollar Amount	Maximum Contribution					
	$3,000	$3,500	$4,000	$4,500	$5,000	$6,000
$0	$3,000	$3,500	$4,000	$4,500	$5,000	$6,000
$100	$2,970	$3,470	$3,960	$4,460	$4,950	$5,940
$200	$2,940	$3,430	$3,920	$4,410	$4,900	$5,880
$300	$2,910	$3,400	$3,880	$4,370	$4,850	$5,820
$400	$2,880	$3,360	$3,840	$4,320	$4,800	$5,760
$500	$2,850	$3,330	$3,800	$4,280	$4,750	$5,700
$600	$2,820	$3,290	$3,760	$4,230	$4,700	$5,640
$700	$2,790	$3,260	$3,720	$4,190	$4,650	$5,580
$800	$2,760	$3,220	$3,680	$4,140	$4,600	$5,520
$900	$2,730	$3,190	$3,640	$4,100	$4,550	$5,460
$1,000	$2,700	$3,150	$3,600	$4,050	$4,500	$5,400
$1,100	$2,670	$3,120	$3,560	$4,010	$4,450	$5,340
$1,200	$2,640	$3,080	$3,520	$3,960	$4,400	$5,280
$1,300	$2,610	$3,050	$3,480	$3,920	$4,350	$5,220
$1,400	$2,580	$3,010	$3,440	$3,870	$4,300	$5,160
$1,500	$2,550	$2,980	$3,400	$3,830	$4,250	$5,100
$1,600	$2,520	$2,940	$3,360	$3,780	$4,200	$5,040
$1,700	$2,490	$2,910	$3,320	$3,740	$4,150	$4,980
$1,800	$2,460	$2,870	$3,280	$3,690	$4,100	$4,920
$1,900	$2,430	$2,840	$3,240	$3,650	$4,050	$4,860
$2,000	$2,400	$2,800	$3,200	$3,600	$4,000	$4,800
$2,100	$2,370	$2,770	$3,160	$3,560	$3,950	$4,740
$2,200	$2,340	$2,730	$3,120	$3,510	$3,900	$4,680
$2,300	$2,310	$2,700	$3,080	$3,470	$3,850	$4,620
$2,400	$2,280	$2,660	$3,040	$3,420	$3,800	$4,560
$2,500	$2,250	$2,630	$3,000	$3,380	$3,750	$4,500
$2,600	$2,220	$2,590	$2,960	$3,330	$3,700	$4,440
$2,700	$2,190	$2,560	$2,920	$3,290	$3,650	$4,380
$2,800	$2,160	$2,520	$2,880	$3,240	$3,600	$4,320
$2,900	$2,130	$2,490	$2,840	$3,200	$3,550	$4,260
$3,000	$2,100	$2,450	$2,800	$3,150	$3,500	$4,200
$3,100	$2,070	$2,420	$2,760	$3,110	$3,450	$4,140
$3,200	$2,040	$2,380	$2,720	$3,060	$3,400	$4,080
$3,300	$2,010	$2,350	$2,680	$3,020	$3,350	$4,020
$3,400	$1,980	$2,310	$2,640	$2,970	$3,300	$3,960
$3,500	$1,950	$2,280	$2,600	$2,930	$3,250	$3,900
$3,600	$1,920	$2,240	$2,560	$2,880	$3,200	$3,840
$3,700	$1,890	$2,210	$2,520	$2,840	$3,150	$3,780
$3,800	$1,860	$2,170	$2,480	$2,790	$3,100	$3,720
$3,900	$1,830	$2,140	$2,440	$2,750	$3,050	$3,660
$4,000	$1,800	$2,100	$2,400	$2,700	$3,000	$3,600
$4,100	$1,770	$2,070	$2,360	$2,660	$2,950	$3,540
$4,200	$1,740	$2,030	$2,320	$2,610	$2,900	$3,480
$4,300	$1,710	$2,000	$2,280	$2,570	$2,850	$3,420

IRA Contribution Phaseout Table
(Phaseout Range: $10,000)

MAGI in Excess of Applicable Dollar Amount	Maximum Contribution					
	$3,000	$3,500	$4,000	$4,500	$5,000	$6,000
$4,400	$1,680	$1,960	$2,240	$2,520	$2,800	$3,360
$4,500	$1,650	$1,930	$2,200	$2,480	$2,750	$3,300
$4,600	$1,620	$1,890	$2,160	$2,430	$2,700	$3,240
$4,700	$1,590	$1,860	$2,120	$2,390	$2,650	$3,180
$4,800	$1,560	$1,820	$2,080	$2,340	$2,600	$3,120
$4,900	$1,530	$1,790	$2,040	$2,300	$2,550	$3,060
$5,000	$1,500	$1,750	$2,000	$2,250	$2,500	$3,000
$5,100	$1,470	$1,720	$1,960	$2,210	$2,450	$2,940
$5,200	$1,440	$1,680	$1,920	$2,160	$2,400	$2,880
$5,300	$1,410	$1,650	$1,880	$2,120	$2,350	$2,820
$5,400	$1,380	$1,610	$1,840	$2,070	$2,300	$2,760
$5,500	$1,350	$1,580	$1,800	$2,030	$2,250	$2,700
$5,600	$1,320	$1,540	$1,760	$1,980	$2,200	$2,640
$5,700	$1,290	$1,510	$1,720	$1,940	$2,150	$2,580
$5,800	$1,260	$1,470	$1,680	$1,890	$2,100	$2,520
$5,900	$1,230	$1,440	$1,640	$1,850	$2,050	$2,460
$6,000	$1,200	$1,400	$1,600	$1,800	$2,000	$2,400
$6,100	$1,170	$1,370	$1,560	$1,760	$1,950	$2,340
$6,200	$1,140	$1,330	$1,520	$1,710	$1,900	$2,280
$6,300	$1,110	$1,300	$1,480	$1,670	$1,850	$2,220
$6,400	$1,080	$1,260	$1,440	$1,620	$1,800	$2,160
$6,500	$1,050	$1,230	$1,400	$1,580	$1,750	$2,100
$6,600	$1,020	$1,190	$1,360	$1,530	$1,700	$2,040
$6,700	$990	$1,160	$1,320	$1,490	$1,650	$1,980
$6,800	$960	$1,120	$1,280	$1,440	$1,600	$1,920
$6,900	$930	$1,090	$1,240	$1,400	$1,550	$1,860
$7,000	$900	$1,050	$1,200	$1,350	$1,500	$1,800
$7,100	$870	$1,020	$1,160	$1,310	$1,450	$1,740
$7,200	$840	$980	$1,120	$1,260	$1,400	$1,680
$7,300	$810	$950	$1,080	$1,220	$1,350	$1,620
$7,400	$780	$910	$1,040	$1,170	$1,300	$1,560
$7,500	$750	$880	$1,000	$1,130	$1,250	$1,500
$7,600	$720	$840	$960	$1,080	$1,200	$1,440
$7,700	$690	$810	$920	$1,040	$1,150	$1,380
$7,800	$660	$770	$880	$990	$1,100	$1,320
$7,900	$630	$740	$840	$950	$1,050	$1,260
$8,000	$600	$700	$800	$900	$1,000	$1,200
$8,100	$570	$670	$760	$860	$950	$1,140
$8,200	$540	$630	$720	$810	$900	$1,080
$8,300	$510	$600	$680	$770	$850	$1,020
$8,400	$480	$560	$640	$720	$800	$960
$8,500	$450	$530	$600	$680	$750	$900
$8,600	$420	$490	$560	$630	$700	$840
$8,700	$390	$460	$520	$590	$650	$780
$8,800	$360	$420	$480	$540	$600	$720
$8,900	$330	$390	$440	$500	$550	$660
$9,000	$300	$350	$400	$450	$500	$600
$9,100	$270	$320	$360	$410	$450	$540
$9,200	$240	$280	$320	$360	$400	$480
$9,300	$210	$250	$280	$320	$350	$420
$9,400	$200	$210	$240	$270	$300	$360
$9,500	$200	$200	$200	$230	$250	$300
$9,600	$200	$200	$200	$200	$200	$240
$9,700	$200	$200	$200	$200	$200	$200
$9,800	$200	$200	$200	$200	$200	$200
$9,900	$200	$200	$200	$200	$200	$200
$10,000	$0	$0	$0	$0	$0	$0

IRA Contribution Phaseout Table
(Phaseout Range: $15,000)

MAGI in Excess of Applicable Dollar Amount	Maximum Contribution					
	$3,000	$3,500	$4,000	$4,500	$5,000	$6,000
$0	$3,000	$3,500	$4,000	$4,500	$5,000	$6,000
$100	$2,980	$3,480	$3,980	$4,470	$4,970	$5,960
$200	$2,960	$3,460	$3,950	$4,440	$4,940	$5,920
$300	$2,940	$3,430	$3,920	$4,410	$4,900	$5,880
$400	$2,920	$3,410	$3,900	$4,380	$4,870	$5,840
$500	$2,900	$3,390	$3,870	$4,350	$4,840	$5,800
$600	$2,880	$3,360	$3,840	$4,320	$4,800	$5,760
$700	$2,860	$3,340	$3,820	$4,290	$4,770	$5,720
$800	$2,840	$3,320	$3,790	$4,260	$4,740	$5,680
$900	$2,820	$3,290	$3,760	$4,230	$4,700	$5,640
$1,000	$2,800	$3,270	$3,740	$4,200	$4,670	$5,600
$1,100	$2,780	$3,250	$3,710	$4,170	$4,640	$5,560
$1,200	$2,760	$3,220	$3,680	$4,140	$4,600	$5,520
$1,300	$2,740	$3,200	$3,660	$4,110	$4,570	$5,480
$1,400	$2,720	$3,180	$3,630	$4,080	$4,540	$5,440
$1,500	$2,700	$3,150	$3,600	$4,050	$4,500	$5,400
$1,600	$2,680	$3,130	$3,580	$4,020	$4,470	$5,360
$1,700	$2,660	$3,110	$3,550	$3,990	$4,440	$5,320
$1,800	$2,640	$3,080	$3,520	$3,960	$4,400	$5,280
$1,900	$2,620	$3,060	$3,500	$3,930	$4,370	$5,240
$2,000	$2,600	$3,040	$3,470	$3,900	$4,340	$5,200
$2,100	$2,580	$3,010	$3,440	$3,870	$4,300	$5,160
$2,200	$2,560	$2,990	$3,420	$3,840	$4,270	$5,120
$2,300	$2,540	$2,970	$3,390	$3,810	$4,240	$5,080
$2,400	$2,520	$2,940	$3,360	$3,780	$4,200	$5,040
$2,500	$2,500	$2,920	$3,340	$3,750	$4,170	$5,000
$2,600	$2,480	$2,900	$3,310	$3,720	$4,140	$4,960
$2,700	$2,460	$2,870	$3,280	$3,690	$4,100	$4,920
$2,800	$2,440	$2,850	$3,260	$3,660	$4,070	$4,880
$2,900	$2,420	$2,830	$3,230	$3,630	$4,040	$4,840
$3,000	$2,400	$2,800	$3,200	$3,600	$4,000	$4,800
$3,100	$2,380	$2,780	$3,180	$3,570	$3,970	$4,760
$3,200	$2,360	$2,760	$3,150	$3,540	$3,940	$4,720
$3,300	$2,340	$2,730	$3,120	$3,510	$3,900	$4,680
$3,400	$2,320	$2,710	$3,100	$3,480	$3,870	$4,640
$3,500	$2,300	$2,690	$3,070	$3,450	$3,840	$4,600
$3,600	$2,280	$2,660	$3,040	$3,420	$3,800	$4,560
$3,700	$2,260	$2,640	$3,020	$3,390	$3,770	$4,520
$3,800	$2,240	$2,620	$2,990	$3,360	$3,740	$4,480
$3,900	$2,220	$2,590	$2,960	$3,330	$3,700	$4,440
$4,000	$2,200	$2,570	$2,940	$3,300	$3,670	$4,400
$4,100	$2,180	$2,550	$2,910	$3,270	$3,640	$4,360
$4,200	$2,160	$2,520	$2,880	$3,240	$3,600	$4,320
$4,300	$2,140	$2,500	$2,860	$3,210	$3,570	$4,280
$4,400	$2,120	$2,480	$2,830	$3,180	$3,540	$4,240
$4,500	$2,100	$2,450	$2,800	$3,150	$3,500	$4,200
$4,600	$2,080	$2,430	$2,780	$3,120	$3,470	$4,160
$4,700	$2,060	$2,410	$2,750	$3,090	$3,440	$4,120
$4,800	$2,040	$2,380	$2,720	$3,060	$3,400	$4,080
$4,900	$2,020	$2,360	$2,700	$3,030	$3,370	$4,040
$5,000	$2,000	$2,340	$2,670	$3,000	$3,340	$4,000
$5,100	$1,980	$2,310	$2,640	$2,970	$3,300	$3,960
$5,200	$1,960	$2,290	$2,620	$2,940	$3,270	$3,920
$5,300	$1,940	$2,270	$2,590	$2,910	$3,240	$3,880
$5,400	$1,920	$2,240	$2,560	$2,880	$3,200	$3,840
$5,500	$1,900	$2,220	$2,540	$2,850	$3,170	$3,800
$5,600	$1,880	$2,200	$2,510	$2,820	$3,140	$3,760
$5,700	$1,860	$2,170	$2,480	$2,790	$3,100	$3,720
$5,800	$1,840	$2,150	$2,460	$2,760	$3,070	$3,680

IRA Contribution Phaseout Table
(Phaseout Range: $15,000)

MAGI in Excess of Applicable Dollar Amount	$3,000	$3,500	$4,000	$4,500	$5,000	$6,000
			Maximum Contribution			
$5,900	$1,820	$2,130	$2,430	$2,730	$3,040	$3,640
$6,000	$1,800	$2,100	$2,400	$2,700	$3,000	$3,600
$6,100	$1,780	$2,080	$2,380	$2,670	$2,970	$3,560
$6,200	$1,760	$2,060	$2,350	$2,640	$2,940	$3,520
$6,300	$1,740	$2,030	$2,320	$2,610	$2,900	$3,480
$6,400	$1,720	$2,010	$2,300	$2,580	$2,870	$3,440
$6,500	$1,700	$1,990	$2,270	$2,550	$2,840	$3,400
$6,600	$1,680	$1,960	$2,240	$2,520	$2,800	$3,360
$6,700	$1,660	$1,940	$2,220	$2,490	$2,770	$3,320
$6,800	$1,640	$1,920	$2,190	$2,460	$2,740	$3,280
$6,900	$1,620	$1,890	$2,160	$2,430	$2,700	$3,240
$7,000	$1,600	$1,870	$2,140	$2,400	$2,670	$3,200
$7,100	$1,580	$1,850	$2,110	$2,370	$2,640	$3,160
$7,200	$1,560	$1,820	$2,080	$2,340	$2,600	$3,120
$7,300	$1,540	$1,800	$2,060	$2,310	$2,570	$3,080
$7,400	$1,520	$1,780	$2,030	$2,280	$2,540	$3,040
$7,500	$1,500	$1,750	$2,000	$2,250	$2,500	$3,000
$7,600	$1,480	$1,730	$1,980	$2,220	$2,470	$2,960
$7,700	$1,460	$1,710	$1,950	$2,190	$2,440	$2,920
$7,800	$1,440	$1,680	$1,920	$2,160	$2,400	$2,880
$7,900	$1,420	$1,660	$1,900	$2,130	$2,370	$2,840
$8,000	$1,400	$1,640	$1,870	$2,100	$2,340	$2,800
$8,100	$1,380	$1,610	$1,840	$2,070	$2,300	$2,760
$8,200	$1,360	$1,590	$1,820	$2,040	$2,270	$2,720
$8,300	$1,340	$1,570	$1,790	$2,010	$2,240	$2,680
$8,400	$1,320	$1,540	$1,760	$1,980	$2,200	$2,640
$8,500	$1,300	$1,520	$1,740	$1,950	$2,170	$2,600
$8,600	$1,280	$1,500	$1,710	$1,920	$2,140	$2,560
$8,700	$1,260	$1,470	$1,680	$1,890	$2,100	$2,520
$8,800	$1,240	$1,450	$1,660	$1,860	$2,070	$2,480
$8,900	$1,220	$1,430	$1,630	$1,830	$2,040	$2,440
$9,000	$1,200	$1,400	$1,600	$1,800	$2,000	$2,400
$9,100	$1,180	$1,380	$1,580	$1,770	$1,970	$2,360
$9,200	$1,160	$1,360	$1,550	$1,740	$1,940	$2,320
$9,300	$1,140	$1,330	$1,520	$1,710	$1,900	$2,280
$9,400	$1,120	$1,310	$1,500	$1,680	$1,870	$2,240
$9,500	$1,100	$1,290	$1,470	$1,650	$1,840	$2,200
$9,600	$1,080	$1,260	$1,440	$1,620	$1,800	$2,160
$9,700	$1,060	$1,240	$1,420	$1,590	$1,770	$2,120
$9,800	$1,040	$1,220	$1,390	$1,560	$1,740	$2,080
$9,900	$1,020	$1,190	$1,360	$1,530	$1,700	$2,040
$10,000	$1,000	$1,170	$1,340	$1,500	$1,670	$2,000
$10,100	$980	$1,150	$1,310	$1,470	$1,640	$1,960
$10,200	$960	$1,120	$1,280	$1,440	$1,600	$1,920
$10,300	$940	$1,100	$1,260	$1,410	$1,570	$1,880
$10,400	$920	$1,080	$1,230	$1,380	$1,540	$1,840
$10,500	$900	$1,050	$1,200	$1,350	$1,500	$1,800
$10,600	$880	$1,030	$1,180	$1,320	$1,470	$1,760
$10,700	$860	$1,010	$1,150	$1,290	$1,440	$1,720
$10,800	$840	$980	$1,120	$1,260	$1,400	$1,680
$10,900	$820	$960	$1,100	$1,230	$1,370	$1,640
$11,000	$800	$940	$1,070	$1,200	$1,340	$1,600
$11,100	$780	$910	$1,040	$1,170	$1,300	$1,560
$11,200	$760	$890	$1,020	$1,140	$1,270	$1,520
$11,300	$740	$870	$990	$1,110	$1,240	$1,480
$11,400	$720	$840	$960	$1,080	$1,200	$1,440
$11,500	$700	$820	$940	$1,050	$1,170	$1,400
$11,600	$680	$800	$910	$1,020	$1,140	$1,360
$11,700	$660	$770	$880	$990	$1,100	$1,320

IRA Contribution Phaseout Table
(Phaseout Range: $15,000)

MAGI in Excess of Applicable Dollar Amount	Maximum Contribution					
	$3,000	$3,500	$4,000	$4,500	$5,000	$6,000
$11,800	$640	$750	$860	$960	$1,070	$1,280
$11,900	$620	$730	$830	$930	$1,040	$1,240
$12,000	$600	$700	$800	$900	$1,000	$1,200
$12,100	$580	$680	$780	$870	$970	$1,160
$12,200	$560	$660	$750	$840	$940	$1,120
$12,300	$540	$630	$720	$810	$900	$1,080
$12,400	$520	$610	$700	$780	$870	$1,040
$12,500	$500	$590	$670	$750	$840	$1,000
$12,600	$480	$560	$640	$720	$800	$960
$12,700	$460	$540	$620	$690	$770	$920
$12,800	$440	$520	$590	$660	$740	$880
$12,900	$420	$490	$560	$630	$700	$840
$13,000	$400	$470	$540	$600	$670	$800
$13,100	$380	$450	$510	$570	$640	$760
$13,200	$360	$420	$480	$540	$600	$720
$13,300	$340	$400	$460	$510	$570	$680
$13,400	$320	$380	$430	$480	$540	$640
$13,500	$300	$350	$400	$450	$500	$600
$13,600	$280	$330	$380	$420	$470	$560
$13,700	$260	$310	$350	$390	$440	$520
$13,800	$240	$280	$320	$360	$400	$480
$13,900	$220	$260	$300	$330	$370	$440
$14,000	$200	$240	$270	$300	$340	$400
$14,100	$200	$210	$240	$270	$300	$360
$14,200	$200	$200	$220	$240	$270	$320
$14,300	$200	$200	$200	$210	$240	$280
$14,400	$200	$200	$200	$200	$200	$240
$14,500	$200	$200	$200	$200	$200	$200
$14,600	$200	$200	$200	$200	$200	$200
$14,700	$200	$200	$200	$200	$200	$200
$14,800	$200	$200	$200	$200	$200	$200
$14,900	$200	$200	$200	$200	$200	$200
$15,000	$0	$0	$0	$0	$0	$0

IRA Contribution Phaseout Table
(Phaseout Range: $20,000)

MAGI in Excess of Applicable Dollar Amount	\$3,000	\$3,500	\$4,000	\$4,500	\$5,000	\$6,000
\$0	\$3,000	\$3,500	\$4,000	\$4,500	\$5,000	\$6,000
\$100	\$2,990	\$3,490	\$3,980	\$4,480	\$4,980	\$5,970
\$200	\$2,970	\$3,470	\$3,960	\$4,460	\$4,950	\$5,940
\$300	\$2,960	\$3,450	\$3,940	\$4,440	\$4,930	\$5,910
\$400	\$2,940	\$3,430	\$3,920	\$4,410	\$4,900	\$5,880
\$500	\$2,930	\$3,420	\$3,900	\$4,390	\$4,880	\$5,850
\$600	\$2,910	\$3,400	\$3,880	\$4,370	\$4,850	\$5,820
\$700	\$2,900	\$3,380	\$3,860	\$4,350	\$4,830	\$5,790
\$800	\$2,880	\$3,360	\$3,840	\$4,320	\$4,800	\$5,760
\$900	\$2,870	\$3,350	\$3,820	\$4,300	\$4,780	\$5,730
\$1,000	\$2,850	\$3,330	\$3,800	\$4,280	\$4,750	\$5,700
\$1,100	\$2,840	\$3,310	\$3,780	\$4,260	\$4,730	\$5,670
\$1,200	\$2,820	\$3,290	\$3,760	\$4,230	\$4,700	\$5,640
\$1,300	\$2,810	\$3,280	\$3,740	\$4,210	\$4,680	\$5,610
\$1,400	\$2,790	\$3,260	\$3,720	\$4,190	\$4,650	\$5,580
\$1,500	\$2,780	\$3,240	\$3,700	\$4,170	\$4,630	\$5,550
\$1,600	\$2,760	\$3,220	\$3,680	\$4,140	\$4,600	\$5,520
\$1,700	\$2,750	\$3,210	\$3,660	\$4,120	\$4,580	\$5,490
\$1,800	\$2,730	\$3,190	\$3,640	\$4,100	\$4,550	\$5,460
\$1,900	\$2,720	\$3,170	\$3,620	\$4,080	\$4,530	\$5,430
\$2,000	\$2,700	\$3,150	\$3,600	\$4,050	\$4,500	\$5,400
\$2,100	\$2,690	\$3,140	\$3,580	\$4,030	\$4,480	\$5,370
\$2,200	\$2,670	\$3,120	\$3,560	\$4,010	\$4,450	\$5,340
\$2,300	\$2,660	\$3,100	\$3,540	\$3,990	\$4,430	\$5,310
\$2,400	\$2,640	\$3,080	\$3,520	\$3,960	\$4,400	\$5,280
\$2,500	\$2,630	\$3,070	\$3,500	\$3,940	\$4,380	\$5,250
\$2,600	\$2,610	\$3,050	\$3,480	\$3,920	\$4,350	\$5,220
\$2,700	\$2,600	\$3,030	\$3,460	\$3,900	\$4,330	\$5,190
\$2,800	\$2,580	\$3,010	\$3,440	\$3,870	\$4,300	\$5,160
\$2,900	\$2,570	\$3,000	\$3,420	\$3,850	\$4,280	\$5,130
\$3,000	\$2,550	\$2,980	\$3,400	\$3,830	\$4,250	\$5,100
\$3,100	\$2,540	\$2,960	\$3,380	\$3,810	\$4,230	\$5,070
\$3,200	\$2,520	\$2,940	\$3,360	\$3,780	\$4,200	\$5,040
\$3,300	\$2,510	\$2,930	\$3,340	\$3,760	\$4,180	\$5,010
\$3,400	\$2,490	\$2,910	\$3,320	\$3,740	\$4,150	\$4,980
\$3,500	\$2,480	\$2,890	\$3,300	\$3,720	\$4,130	\$4,950
\$3,600	\$2,460	\$2,870	\$3,280	\$3,690	\$4,100	\$4,920
\$3,700	\$2,450	\$2,860	\$3,260	\$3,670	\$4,080	\$4,890
\$3,800	\$2,430	\$2,840	\$3,240	\$3,650	\$4,050	\$4,860
\$3,900	\$2,420	\$2,820	\$3,220	\$3,630	\$4,030	\$4,830
\$4,000	\$2,400	\$2,800	\$3,200	\$3,600	\$4,000	\$4,800
\$4,100	\$2,390	\$2,790	\$3,180	\$3,580	\$3,980	\$4,770
\$4,200	\$2,370	\$2,770	\$3,160	\$3,560	\$3,950	\$4,740
\$4,300	\$2,360	\$2,750	\$3,140	\$3,540	\$3,930	\$4,710
\$4,400	\$2,340	\$2,730	\$3,120	\$3,510	\$3,900	\$4,680
\$4,500	\$2,330	\$2,720	\$3,100	\$3,490	\$3,880	\$4,650
\$4,600	\$2,310	\$2,700	\$3,080	\$3,470	\$3,850	\$4,620
\$4,700	\$2,300	\$2,680	\$3,060	\$3,450	\$3,830	\$4,590
\$4,800	\$2,280	\$2,660	\$3,040	\$3,420	\$3,800	\$4,560
\$4,900	\$2,270	\$2,650	\$3,020	\$3,400	\$3,780	\$4,530
\$5,000	\$2,250	\$2,630	\$3,000	\$3,380	\$3,750	\$4,500
\$5,100	\$2,240	\$2,610	\$2,980	\$3,360	\$3,730	\$4,470
\$5,200	\$2,220	\$2,590	\$2,960	\$3,330	\$3,700	\$4,440
\$5,300	\$2,210	\$2,580	\$2,940	\$3,310	\$3,680	\$4,410
\$5,400	\$2,190	\$2,560	\$2,920	\$3,290	\$3,650	\$4,380
\$5,500	\$2,180	\$2,540	\$2,900	\$3,270	\$3,630	\$4,350
\$5,600	\$2,160	\$2,520	\$2,880	\$3,240	\$3,600	\$4,320
\$5,700	\$2,150	\$2,510	\$2,860	\$3,220	\$3,580	\$4,290
\$5,800	\$2,130	\$2,490	\$2,840	\$3,200	\$3,550	\$4,260
\$5,900	\$2,120	\$2,470	\$2,820	\$3,180	\$3,530	\$4,230

IRA Contribution Phaseout Table
(Phaseout Range: $20,000)

MAGI in Excess of Applicable Dollar Amount	Maximum Contribution					
	$3,000	$3,500	$4,000	$4,500	$5,000	$6,000
$6,000	$2,100	$2,450	$2,800	$3,150	$3,500	$4,200
$6,100	$2,090	$2,440	$2,780	$3,130	$3,480	$4,170
$6,200	$2,070	$2,420	$2,760	$3,110	$3,450	$4,140
$6,300	$2,060	$2,400	$2,740	$3,090	$3,430	$4,110
$6,400	$2,040	$2,380	$2,720	$3,060	$3,400	$4,080
$6,500	$2,030	$2,370	$2,700	$3,040	$3,380	$4,050
$6,600	$2,010	$2,350	$2,680	$3,020	$3,350	$4,020
$6,700	$2,000	$2,330	$2,660	$3,000	$3,330	$3,990
$6,800	$1,980	$2,310	$2,640	$2,970	$3,300	$3,960
$6,900	$1,970	$2,300	$2,620	$2,950	$3,280	$3,930
$7,000	$1,950	$2,280	$2,600	$2,930	$3,250	$3,900
$7,100	$1,940	$2,260	$2,580	$2,910	$3,230	$3,870
$7,200	$1,920	$2,240	$2,560	$2,880	$3,200	$3,840
$7,300	$1,910	$2,230	$2,540	$2,860	$3,180	$3,810
$7,400	$1,890	$2,210	$2,520	$2,840	$3,150	$3,780
$7,500	$1,880	$2,190	$2,500	$2,820	$3,130	$3,750
$7,600	$1,860	$2,170	$2,480	$2,790	$3,100	$3,720
$7,700	$1,850	$2,160	$2,460	$2,770	$3,080	$3,690
$7,800	$1,830	$2,140	$2,440	$2,750	$3,050	$3,660
$7,900	$1,820	$2,120	$2,420	$2,730	$3,030	$3,630
$8,000	$1,800	$2,100	$2,400	$2,700	$3,000	$3,600
$8,100	$1,790	$2,090	$2,380	$2,680	$2,980	$3,570
$8,200	$1,770	$2,070	$2,360	$2,660	$2,950	$3,540
$8,300	$1,760	$2,050	$2,340	$2,640	$2,930	$3,510
$8,400	$1,740	$2,030	$2,320	$2,610	$2,900	$3,480
$8,500	$1,730	$2,020	$2,300	$2,590	$2,880	$3,450
$8,600	$1,710	$2,000	$2,280	$2,570	$2,850	$3,420
$8,700	$1,700	$1,980	$2,260	$2,550	$2,830	$3,390
$8,800	$1,680	$1,960	$2,240	$2,520	$2,800	$3,360
$8,900	$1,670	$1,950	$2,220	$2,500	$2,780	$3,330
$9,000	$1,650	$1,930	$2,200	$2,480	$2,750	$3,300
$9,100	$1,640	$1,910	$2,180	$2,460	$2,730	$3,270
$9,200	$1,620	$1,890	$2,160	$2,430	$2,700	$3,240
$9,300	$1,610	$1,880	$2,140	$2,410	$2,680	$3,210
$9,400	$1,590	$1,860	$2,120	$2,390	$2,650	$3,180
$9,500	$1,580	$1,840	$2,100	$2,370	$2,630	$3,150
$9,600	$1,560	$1,820	$2,080	$2,340	$2,600	$3,120
$9,700	$1,550	$1,810	$2,060	$2,320	$2,580	$3,090
$9,800	$1,530	$1,790	$2,040	$2,300	$2,550	$3,060
$9,900	$1,520	$1,770	$2,020	$2,280	$2,530	$3,030
$10,000	$1,500	$1,750	$2,000	$2,250	$2,500	$3,000
$10,100	$1,490	$1,740	$1,980	$2,230	$2,480	$2,970
$10,200	$1,470	$1,720	$1,960	$2,210	$2,450	$2,940
$10,300	$1,460	$1,700	$1,940	$2,190	$2,430	$2,910
$10,400	$1,440	$1,680	$1,920	$2,160	$2,400	$2,880
$10,500	$1,430	$1,670	$1,900	$2,140	$2,380	$2,850
$10,600	$1,410	$1,650	$1,880	$2,120	$2,350	$2,820
$10,700	$1,400	$1,630	$1,860	$2,100	$2,330	$2,790
$10,800	$1,380	$1,610	$1,840	$2,070	$2,300	$2,760
$10,900	$1,370	$1,600	$1,820	$2,050	$2,280	$2,730
$11,000	$1,350	$1,580	$1,800	$2,030	$2,250	$2,700
$11,100	$1,340	$1,560	$1,780	$2,010	$2,230	$2,670
$11,200	$1,320	$1,540	$1,760	$1,980	$2,200	$2,640
$11,300	$1,310	$1,530	$1,740	$1,960	$2,180	$2,610
$11,400	$1,290	$1,510	$1,720	$1,940	$2,150	$2,580
$11,500	$1,280	$1,490	$1,700	$1,920	$2,130	$2,550
$11,600	$1,260	$1,470	$1,680	$1,890	$2,100	$2,520
$11,700	$1,250	$1,460	$1,660	$1,870	$2,080	$2,490
$11,800	$1,230	$1,440	$1,640	$1,850	$2,050	$2,460

IRA Contribution Phaseout Table
(Phaseout Range: $20,000)

MAGI in Excess of Applicable Dollar Amount	Maximum Contribution					
	$3,000	$3,500	$4,000	$4,500	$5,000	$6,000
$11,900	$1,220	$1,420	$1,620	$1,830	$2,030	$2,430
$12,000	$1,200	$1,400	$1,600	$1,800	$2,000	$2,400
$12,100	$1,190	$1,390	$1,580	$1,780	$1,980	$2,370
$12,200	$1,170	$1,370	$1,560	$1,760	$1,950	$2,340
$12,300	$1,160	$1,350	$1,540	$1,740	$1,930	$2,310
$12,400	$1,140	$1,330	$1,520	$1,710	$1,900	$2,280
$12,500	$1,130	$1,320	$1,500	$1,690	$1,880	$2,250
$12,600	$1,110	$1,300	$1,480	$1,670	$1,850	$2,220
$12,700	$1,100	$1,280	$1,460	$1,650	$1,830	$2,190
$12,800	$1,080	$1,260	$1,440	$1,620	$1,800	$2,160
$12,900	$1,070	$1,250	$1,420	$1,600	$1,780	$2,130
$13,000	$1,050	$1,230	$1,400	$1,580	$1,750	$2,100
$13,100	$1,040	$1,210	$1,380	$1,560	$1,730	$2,070
$13,200	$1,020	$1,190	$1,360	$1,530	$1,700	$2,040
$13,300	$1,010	$1,180	$1,340	$1,510	$1,680	$2,010
$13,400	$990	$1,160	$1,320	$1,490	$1,650	$1,980
$13,500	$980	$1,140	$1,300	$1,470	$1,630	$1,950
$13,600	$960	$1,120	$1,280	$1,440	$1,600	$1,920
$13,700	$950	$1,110	$1,260	$1,420	$1,580	$1,890
$13,800	$930	$1,090	$1,240	$1,400	$1,550	$1,860
$13,900	$920	$1,070	$1,220	$1,380	$1,530	$1,830
$14,000	$900	$1,050	$1,200	$1,350	$1,500	$1,800
$14,100	$890	$1,040	$1,180	$1,330	$1,480	$1,770
$14,200	$870	$1,020	$1,160	$1,310	$1,450	$1,740
$14,300	$860	$1,000	$1,140	$1,290	$1,430	$1,710
$14,400	$840	$980	$1,120	$1,260	$1,400	$1,680
$14,500	$830	$970	$1,100	$1,240	$1,380	$1,650
$14,600	$810	$950	$1,080	$1,220	$1,350	$1,620
$14,700	$800	$930	$1,060	$1,200	$1,330	$1,590
$14,800	$780	$910	$1,040	$1,170	$1,300	$1,560
$14,900	$770	$900	$1,020	$1,150	$1,280	$1,530
$15,000	$750	$880	$1,000	$1,130	$1,250	$1,500
$15,100	$740	$860	$980	$1,110	$1,230	$1,470
$15,200	$720	$840	$960	$1,080	$1,200	$1,440
$15,300	$710	$830	$940	$1,060	$1,180	$1,410
$15,400	$690	$810	$920	$1,040	$1,150	$1,380
$15,500	$680	$790	$900	$1,020	$1,130	$1,350
$15,600	$660	$770	$880	$990	$1,100	$1,320
$15,700	$650	$760	$860	$970	$1,080	$1,290
$15,800	$630	$740	$840	$950	$1,050	$1,260
$15,900	$620	$720	$820	$930	$1,030	$1,230
$16,000	$600	$700	$800	$900	$1,000	$1,200
$16,100	$590	$690	$780	$880	$980	$1,170
$16,200	$570	$670	$760	$860	$950	$1,140
$16,300	$560	$650	$740	$840	$930	$1,110
$16,400	$540	$630	$720	$810	$900	$1,080
$16,500	$530	$620	$700	$790	$880	$1,050
$16,600	$510	$600	$680	$770	$850	$1,020
$16,700	$500	$580	$660	$750	$830	$990
$16,800	$480	$560	$640	$720	$800	$960
$16,900	$470	$550	$620	$700	$780	$930
$17,000	$450	$530	$600	$680	$750	$900
$17,100	$440	$510	$580	$660	$730	$870
$17,200	$420	$490	$560	$630	$700	$840
$17,300	$410	$480	$540	$610	$680	$810
$17,400	$390	$460	$520	$590	$650	$780
$17,500	$380	$440	$500	$570	$630	$750
$17,600	$360	$420	$480	$540	$600	$720
$17,700	$350	$410	$460	$520	$580	$690

IRA Contribution Phaseout Table
(Phaseout Range: $20,000)

MAGI in Excess of Applicable Dollar Amount	Maximum Contribution					
	$3,000	$3,500	$4,000	$4,500	$5,000	$6,000
$17,800	$330	$390	$440	$500	$550	$660
$17,900	$320	$370	$420	$480	$530	$630
$18,000	$300	$350	$400	$450	$500	$600
$18,100	$290	$340	$380	$430	$480	$570
$18,200	$270	$320	$360	$410	$450	$540
$18,300	$260	$300	$340	$390	$430	$510
$18,400	$240	$280	$320	$360	$400	$480
$18,500	$230	$270	$300	$340	$380	$450
$18,600	$210	$250	$280	$320	$350	$420
$18,700	$200	$230	$260	$300	$330	$390
$18,800	$200	$210	$240	$270	$300	$360
$18,900	$200	$200	$220	$250	$280	$330
$19,000	$200	$200	$200	$230	$250	$300
$19,100	$200	$200	$200	$210	$230	$270
$19,200	$200	$200	$200	$200	$200	$240
$19,300	$200	$200	$200	$200	$200	$210
$19,400	$200	$200	$200	$200	$200	$200
$19,500	$200	$200	$200	$200	$200	$200
$19,600	$200	$200	$200	$200	$200	$200
$19,700	$200	$200	$200	$200	$200	$200
$19,800	$200	$200	$200	$200	$200	$200
$19,900	$200	$200	$200	$200	$200	$200
$20,000	$0	$0	$0	$0	$0	$0

Appendix C

RMD Tables

The required minimum distribution (RMD) tables are tables for life expectancy. The RMD tables are used in this book primarily for calculating substantially equal periodic payments (SEPPs) under the early distributions penalty tax and for calculating required minimum distributions.

The RMD Single Life Table is used for a single life. The RMD Joint and Survivor Table is used for joint and survivor two lives (i.e., second to die). The Uniform Lifetime Table is a joint and survivor table that treats the beneficiary as being 10 years younger than the IRA owner.

In general, a single life expectancy table can be used to show how long a person a certain age can generally be expected to live. For example, using the RMD Single Life Table, a person age 70 can be expected to live another 17 years. A joint and survivor table can be used to project how long it will be until two persons are both dead. For example, using the RMD Joint and Survivor Table, it can be expected that a person age 70 and a person age 60 will both be dead in 27.4 years.

A single life expected return multiple can be used to show how much a person receiving a series of payments for life would generally receive over his lifetime. For example, using the RMD Single Life Table, a person age 60 receiving $1,000 a year for life could expect to receive $25,200 over his lifetime ($1,000 x 25.2). Similarly, a joint and survivor expected return multiple table can be used to project how much two persons would receive while either person is alive. For example, using the RMD

Joint and Survivor Table, it can be expected that a person age 70 and a person age 60 receiving $1,000 a year until both persons are dead can be expected to receive $27,400 while either is alive ($1,000 x 27.4).

There is an exception to the early distribution penalty tax for substantially equal periodic payments (SEPPs) under IRC Section 72(t) (see Chapter 13). The required minimum distributions method and the amortization method (see Appendix D) for calculating substantially equal periodic payments use the RMD tables.

In general, certain required minimum distributions must be made from an IRA or a 50 percent penalty tax applies (see Chapter 13). Required minimum distributions are calculated using the RMD tables. In addition, when making projections of future required minimum distributions, it may be helpful to use a person's life expectancy (RMD Single Life Table) to project when death may occur.

In determining whether to convert a traditional IRA, SEP IRA, or SIMPLE IRA to a Roth IRA (see Chapter 12), or whether to make deductible contributions to a traditional or SEP IRA or nondeductible contributions to a Roth IRA (see Chapter 9), it is useful to make projections of future distributions. It may be helpful to use a person's life expectancy (RMD Single Life Table) to project when death may occur.

Uniform Lifetime Table - Distribution Period

Age	Factor	Age	Factor	Age	Factor
10	86.2	45	51.5	80	18.7
11	85.2	46	50.5	81	17.9
12	84.2	47	49.5	82	17.1
13	83.2	48	48.5	83	16.3
14	82.2	49	47.5	84	15.5
15	81.2	50	46.5	85	14.8
16	80.2	51	45.5	86	14.1
17	79.2	52	44.6	87	13.4
18	78.2	53	43.6	88	12.7
19	77.3	54	42.6	89	12.0
20	76.3	55	41.6	90	11.4
21	75.3	56	40.7	91	10.8
22	74.3	57	39.7	92	10.2
23	73.3	58	38.7	93	9.6
24	72.3	59	37.8	94	9.1
25	71.3	60	36.8	95	8.6
26	70.3	61	35.8	96	8.1
27	69.3	62	34.9	97	7.6
28	68.3	63	33.9	98	7.1
29	67.3	64	33.0	99	6.7
30	66.3	65	32.0	100	6.3
31	65.3	66	31.1	101	5.9
32	64.3	67	30.2	102	5.5
33	63.3	68	29.2	103	5.2
34	62.3	69	28.3	104	4.9
35	61.4	70	27.4	105	4.5
36	60.4	71	26.5	106	4.2
37	59.4	72	25.6	107	3.9
38	58.4	73	24.7	108	3.7
39	57.4	74	23.8	109	3.4
40	56.4	75	22.9	110	3.1
41	55.4	76	22.0	111	2.9
42	54.4	77	21.2	112	2.6
43	53.4	78	20.3	113	2.4
44	52.4	79	19.5	114	2.1
				115+	1.9

RMD Single Life Table - Life Expectancy

Age	Factor	Age	Factor	Age	Factor
0	82.4	38	45.6	76	12.7
1	81.6	39	44.6	77	12.1
2	80.6	40	43.6	78	11.4
3	79.7	41	42.7	79	10.8
4	78.7	42	41.7	80	10.2
5	77.7	43	40.7	81	9.7
6	76.7	44	39.8	82	9.1
7	75.8	45	38.8	83	8.6
8	74.8	46	37.9	84	8.1
9	73.8	47	37.0	85	7.6
10	72.8	48	36.0	86	7.1
11	71.8	49	35.1	87	6.7
12	70.8	50	34.2	88	6.3
13	69.9	51	33.3	89	5.9
14	68.9	52	32.3	90	5.5
15	67.9	53	31.4	91	5.2
16	66.9	54	30.5	92	4.9
17	66.0	55	29.6	93	4.6
18	65.0	56	28.7	94	4.3
19	64.0	57	27.9	95	4.1
20	63.0	58	27.0	96	3.8
21	62.1	59	26.1	97	3.6
22	61.1	60	25.2	98	3.4
23	60.1	61	24.4	99	3.1
24	59.1	62	23.5	100	2.9
25	58.2	63	22.7	101	2.7
26	57.2	64	21.8	102	2.5
27	56.2	65	21.0	103	2.3
28	55.3	66	20.2	104	2.1
29	54.3	67	19.4	105	1.9
30	53.3	68	18.6	106	1.7
31	52.4	69	17.8	107	1.5
32	51.4	70	17.0	108	1.4
33	50.4	71	16.3	109	1.2
34	49.4	72	15.5	110	1.1
35	48.5	73	14.8	111+	1.0
36	47.5	74	14.1		
37	46.5	75	13.4		

RMD Joint and Survivor Table - Life Expectancy

Ages	20	21	22	23	24	25	26	27	28	29
20	70.1	69.6	69.1	68.7	68.3	67.9	67.5	67.2	66.9	66.6
21	69.6	69.1	68.6	68.2	67.7	67.3	66.9	66.6	66.2	65.9
22	69.1	68.6	68.1	67.6	67.2	66.7	66.3	65.9	65.6	65.2
23	68.7	68.2	67.9	67.1	66.6	66.2	65.7	65.3	64.9	64.6
24	68.3	67.7	67.2	66.6	66.1	65.6	65.2	64.7	64.3	63.9
25	67.9	67.3	66.7	66.2	65.6	65.1	64.6	64.2	63.7	63.3
26	67.5	66.9	66.3	65.7	65.2	64.6	64.1	63.6	63.2	62.8
27	67.2	66.6	65.9	65.3	64.7	64.2	63.6	63.1	62.7	62.2
28	66.9	66.2	65.6	64.9	64.3	63.7	63.2	62.7	62.1	61.7
29	66.6	65.9	65.2	64.6	63.9	63.3	62.8	62.2	61.7	61.2
30	66.3	65.6	64.9	64.2	63.6	62.9	62.3	61.8	61.2	60.7
31	66.1	65.3	64.6	63.9	63.2	62.6	62.0	61.4	60.8	60.2
32	65.8	65.1	64.3	63.6	62.9	62.2	61.6	61.0	60.4	59.8
33	65.6	64.8	64.1	63.3	62.6	61.9	61.3	60.6	60.0	59.4
34	65.4	64.6	63.8	63.1	62.3	61.6	60.9	60.3	59.6	59.0
35	65.2	64.4	63.6	62.8	62.1	61.4	60.6	59.9	59.3	58.6
36	65.0	64.2	63.4	62.6	61.9	61.1	60.4	59.6	69.0	58.3
37	64.9	64.0	63.2	62.4	61.6	60.9	60.1	59.4	58.7	58.0
38	64.7	63.9	63.0	62.2	61.4	60.6	59.9	59.1	58.4	57.7
39	64.6	63.7	62.9	62.1	61.2	60.4	59.6	58.9	58.1	57.4
40	64.4	63.6	62.7	61.9	61.1	60.2	59.4	58.7	57.9	57.1
41	64.3	63.5	62.6	61.7	60.9	60.1	59.3	58.5	57.7	56.9
42	64.2	63.3	62.5	61.6	60.8	59.9	59.1	58.3	57.5	56.7
43	64.1	63.2	62.4	61.5	60.6	59.8	58.9	58.1	57.3	56.5
44	64.0	63.1	62.2	61.4	60.5	59.6	58.8	57.9	57.1	56.3
45	64.0	63.0	62.2	61.3	60.4	59.5	58.6	57.8	56.9	56.1
46	63.9	63.0	62.1	61.2	60.3	59.4	58.5	57.7	56.8	56.0
47	63.8	62.9	62.0	61.1	60.2	59.3	58.4	57.5	56.7	55.8
48	63.7	62.8	61.9	61.0	60.1	59.2	58.3	57.4	56.5	55.7
49	63.7	62.8	61.8	60.9	60.0	59.1	58.2	57.3	56.4	55.6
50	63.6	62.7	61.8	60.8	59.9	59.0	58.1	57.2	56.3	55.4
51	63.6	62.6	61.7	60.8	59.9	58.9	58.0	57.1	56.2	55.3
52	63.5	62.6	61.7	60.7	59.8	58.9	58.0	57.1	56.1	55.2
53	63.5	62.5	61.6	60.7	59.7	58.8	57.9	57.0	56.1	55.2
54	63.5	62.5	61.6	60.6	59.7	58.8	57.8	56.9	56.0	55.1
55	63.4	62.5	61.5	60.6	59.6	58.7	57.8	56.8	55.9	55.0
56	63.4	62.4	61.5	60.5	59.6	58.7	57.7	56.8	55.9	54.9
57	63.4	62.4	61.5	60.5	59.6	58.6	57.7	56.7	55.8	54.9
58	63.3	62.4	61.4	60.5	59.5	58.6	57.6	56.7	55.8	54.8
59	63.3	62.3	61.4	60.4	59.5	58.5	57.6	56.7	55.7	54.8
60	63.3	62.3	61.4	60.4	59.5	58.5	57.6	56.6	55.7	54.7
61	63.3	62.3	61.3	60.4	59.4	58.5	57.5	56.6	55.6	54.7
62	63.2	62.3	61.3	60.4	59.4	58.4	57.5	56.5	55.6	54.7
63	63.2	62.3	61.3	60.3	59.4	58.4	57.5	56.5	55.6	54.6
64	63.2	62.2	61.3	60.3	59.4	58.4	57.4	56.5	55.5	54.6
65	63.2	62.2	61.3	60.3	59.3	58.4	57.4	56.5	55.5	54.6
66	63.2	62.2	61.2	60.3	59.3	58.4	57.4	56.4	55.5	54.5
67	63.2	62.2	61.2	60.3	59.3	58.3	57.4	56.4	55.5	54.5
68	63.1	62.2	61.2	60.2	59.3	58.3	57.4	56.4	55.4	54.5
69	63.1	62.2	61.2	60.2	59.3	58.3	57.3	56.4	55.4	54.5
70	63.1	62.2	61.2	60.2	59.3	58.3	57.3	56.4	55.4	54.4
71	63.1	62.1	61.2	60.2	59.2	58.3	57.3	56.4	55.4	54.4
72	63.1	62.1	61.2	60.2	59.2	58.3	57.3	56.3	55.4	54.4
73	63.1	62.1	61.2	60.2	59.2	58.3	57.3	56.3	55.4	54.4
74	63.1	62.1	61.2	60.2	59.2	58.2	57.3	56.3	55.4	54.4
75	63.1	62.1	61.1	60.2	59.2	58.2	57.3	56.3	55.3	54.4
76	63.1	62.1	61.1	60.2	59.2	58.2	57.3	56.3	55.3	54.4
77	63.1	62.1	61.1	60.2	59.2	58.2	57.3	56.3	55.3	54.4
78	63.1	62.1	61.1	60.2	59.2	58.2	57.3	56.3	55.3	54.4

RMD Joint and Survivor Table - Life Expectancy

Ages	20	21	22	23	24	25	26	27	28	29
79	63.1	62.1	61.1	60.2	59.2	58.2	57.2	56.3	55.3	54.3
80	63.1	62.1	61.1	60.1	59.2	58.2	57.2	56.3	55.3	54.3
81	63.1	62.1	61.1	60.1	59.2	58.2	57.2	56.3	55.3	54.3
82	63.1	62.1	61.1	60.1	59.2	58.2	57.2	56.3	55.3	54.3
83	63.1	62.1	61.1	60.1	59.2	58.2	57.2	56.3	55.3	54.3
84	63.0	62.1	61.1	60.1	59.2	58.2	57.2	56.3	55.3	54.3
85	63.0	62.1	61.1	60.1	59.2	58.2	57.2	56.3	55.3	54.3
86	63.0	62.1	61.1	60.1	59.2	58.2	57.2	56.2	55.3	54.3
87	63.0	62.1	61.1	60.1	59.2	58.2	57.2	56.2	55.3	54.3
88	63.0	62.1	61.1	60.1	59.2	58.2	57.2	56.2	55.3	54.3
89	63.0	62.1	61.1	60.1	59.1	58.2	57.2	56.2	55.3	54.3
90	63.0	62.1	61.1	60.1	59.1	58.2	57.2	56.2	55.3	54.3
91	63.0	62.1	61.1	60.1	59.1	58.2	57.2	56.2	55.3	54.3
92	63.0	62.1	61.1	60.1	59.1	58.2	57.2	56.2	55.3	54.3
93	63.0	62.1	61.1	60.1	59.1	58.2	57.2	56.2	55.3	54.3
94	63.0	62.1	61.1	60.1	59.1	58.2	57.2	56.2	55.3	54.3
95	63.0	62.1	61.1	60.1	59.1	58.2	57.2	56.2	55.3	54.3
96	63.0	62.1	61.1	60.1	59.1	58.2	57.2	56.2	55.3	54.3
97	60.3	62.1	61.1	60.1	59.1	58.2	57.2	56.2	55.3	54.3
98	63.0	62.1	61.1	60.1	59.1	58.2	57.2	56.2	55.3	54.3
99	63.0	62.1	61.1	60.1	59.1	58.2	57.2	56.2	55.3	54.3
100	63.0	62.1	61.1	60.1	59.1	58.2	57.2	56.2	55.3	54.3
101	63.0	62.1	61.1	60.1	59.1	58.2	57.2	56.2	55.3	54.3
102	63.0	62.1	61.1	60.1	59.1	58.2	57.2	56.2	55.3	54.3
103	63.0	62.1	61.1	60.1	59.1	58.2	57.2	56.2	55.3	54.3
104	63.0	62.1	61.1	60.1	59.1	58.2	57.2	56.2	55.3	54.3
105	63.0	62.1	61.1	60.1	59.1	58.2	57.2	56.2	55.3	54.3
106	63.0	62.1	61.1	60.1	59.1	58.2	57.2	56.2	55.3	54.3
107	63.0	62.1	61.1	60.1	59.1	58.2	57.2	56.2	55.3	54.3
108	63.0	62.1	61.1	60.1	59.1	58.2	57.2	56.2	55.3	54.3
109	63.0	62.1	61.1	60.1	59.1	58.2	57.2	56.2	55.3	54.3
110	63.0	62.1	61.1	60.1	59.1	58.2	57.2	56.2	55.3	54.3
111	63.0	62.1	61.1	60.1	59.1	58.2	57.2	56.2	55.3	54.3
112	63.0	62.1	61.1	60.1	59.1	58.2	57.2	56.2	55.3	54.3
113	63.0	62.1	61.1	60.1	59.1	58.2	57.2	56.2	55.3	54.3
114	63.0	62.1	61.1	60.1	59.1	58.2	57.2	56.2	55.3	54.3
115+	63.0	62.1	61.1	60.1	59.1	58.2	57.2	56.2	55.3	54.3

RMD Joint and Survivor Table - Life Expectancy

Ages	30	31	32	33	34	35	36	37	38	39
30	60.2	59.7	59.2	58.8	58.4	58.0	57.6	57.3	57.0	56.7
31	59.7	59.2	58.7	58.2	57.8	57.4	57.0	56.6	56.3	56.0
32	59.2	58.7	58.2	57.7	57.2	56.8	56.4	56.0	55.6	55.3
33	58.8	58.2	57.7	57.2	56.7	56.2	55.8	55.4	55.0	54.7
34	58.4	57.8	57.2	56.7	56.2	55.7	55.3	54.8	54.4	54.0
35	58.0	57.4	56.8	56.2	55.7	55.2	54.7	54.3	53.8	53.4
36	57.6	57.0	56.4	55.8	55.3	54.7	54.2	53.7	53.3	52.8
37	57.3	56.6	56.0	55.4	54.8	54.3	53.7	53.2	52.7	52.3
38	57.0	56.3	55.6	55.0	54.4	53.8	53.3	52.7	52.2	51.7
39	56.7	56.0	55.3	54.7	54.0	53.4	52.8	52.3	51.7	51.2
40	56.4	55.7	55.0	54.3	53.7	53.0	52.4	51.8	51.3	50.8
41	56.1	55.4	54.7	54.0	53.3	52.7	52.0	51.4	50.9	50.3
42	55.9	55.2	54.4	53.7	53.0	52.3	51.7	51.1	50.4	49.9
43	55.7	54.9	54.2	53.4	52.7	52.0	51.3	50.7	50.1	49.5
44	55.5	54.7	53.9	53.2	52.4	51.7	51.0	50.4	49.7	49.1
45	55.3	54.5	53.7	52.9	52.2	51.5	50.7	50.0	49.4	48.7
46	55.1	54.3	53.5	52.7	52.0	51.2	50.5	49.8	49.1	48.4
47	55.0	54.1	53.3	52.5	51.7	51.0	50.2	49.5	48.8	48.1
48	54.8	54.0	53.2	52.3	51.5	50.8	50.0	49.2	48.5	47.8
49	54.7	53.8	53.0	52.2	51.4	50.6	49.8	49.0	48.2	47.5
50	54.6	53.7	52.9	52.0	51.2	50.4	49.6	48.8	48.0	47.3
51	54.5	53.6	52.7	51.9	51.0	50.2	49.4	48.6	47.8	47.0
52	54.4	53.5	52.6	51.7	50.9	50.0	49.2	48.4	47.6	46.8
53	54.3	53.4	52.5	51.6	50.8	49.9	49.1	48.2	47.4	46.6
54	54.2	53.3	52.4	51.5	50.6	49.8	48.9	48.1	47.2	46.4
55	54.1	53.2	52.3	51.4	50.5	49.7	48.8	47.9	47.1	46.3
56	54.0	53.1	52.2	51.3	50.4	49.5	48.7	47.8	47.0	46.1
57	54.0	53.0	52.1	51.2	50.3	49.4	48.6	47.7	46.8	46.0
58	53.9	53.0	52.1	51.2	50.3	49.4	48.5	47.6	46.7	45.8
59	53.8	52.9	52.0	51.1	50.2	49.3	48.4	47.5	46.6	45.7
60	53.8	52.9	51.9	51.0	50.1	49.2	48.3	47.4	46.5	45.6
61	53.8	52.8	51.9	51.0	50.0	49.1	48.2	47.3	46.4	45.5
62	53.7	52.8	51.8	50.9	50.0	49.1	48.1	47.2	46.3	45.4
63	53.7	52.7	51.8	50.9	49.9	49.0	48.1	47.2	46.3	45.3
64	53.6	52.7	51.8	50.8	49.9	48.9	48.0	47.1	46.2	45.3
65	53.6	52.7	51.7	50.8	49.8	48.9	48.0	47.0	46.1	45.2
66	53.6	52.6	51.7	50.7	49.8	48.9	47.9	47.0	46.1	45.1
67	53.6	52.6	51.7	50.7	49.8	48.8	47.9	46.9	46.0	45.1
68	53.5	52.6	51.6	50.7	49.7	48.8	47.8	46.9	46.0	45.0
69	53.5	52.6	51.6	50.6	49.7	48.7	47.8	46.9	45.9	45.0
70	53.5	52.5	51.6	50.6	49.7	48.7	47.8	46.8	45.9	44.9
71	53.5	52.5	51.6	50.6	49.6	48.7	47.7	46.8	45.9	44.9
72	53.5	52.5	51.5	50.6	49.6	48.7	47.7	46.8	45.8	44.9
73	53.4	52.5	51.5	50.6	49.6	48.6	47.7	46.7	45.8	44.8
74	53.4	52.5	51.5	50.5	49.6	48.6	47.7	46.7	45.8	44.8
75	53.4	52.5	51.5	50.5	49.6	48.6	47.7	46.7	45.7	44.8
76	53.4	52.4	51.5	50.5	49.6	48.6	47.6	46.7	45.7	44.8
77	53.4	52.4	51.5	50.5	49.5	48.6	47.6	46.7	45.7	44.8
78	53.4	52.4	51.5	50.5	49.5	48.6	47.6	46.6	45.7	44.7
79	53.4	52.4	51.5	50.5	49.5	48.6	47.6	46.6	45.7	44.7
80	53.4	52.4	51.4	50.5	49.5	48.5	47.6	46.6	45.7	44.7
81	53.4	52.4	51.4	50.5	49.5	48.5	47.6	46.6	45.7	44.7
82	53.4	52.4	51.4	50.5	49.5	48.5	47.6	46.6	45.6	44.7
83	53.4	52.4	51.4	50.5	49.5	48.5	47.6	46.6	45.6	44.7
84	53.4	52.4	51.4	50.5	49.5	48.5	47.6	46.6	45.6	44.7
85	53.3	52.4	51.4	50.4	49.5	48.5	47.5	46.6	45.6	44.7
86	53.3	52.4	51.4	50.4	49.5	48.5	47.5	46.6	45.6	44.6
87	53.3	52.4	51.4	50.4	49.5	48.5	47.5	46.6	45.6	44.6
88	53.3	52.4	51.4	50.4	49.5	48.5	47.5	46.6	45.6	44.6

RMD Joint and Survivor Table - Life Expectancy

Ages	40	41	42	43	44	45	46	47	48	49
40	50.2	49.8	49.3	48.9	48.5	48.1	47.7	47.4	47.1	46.8
41	49.8	49.3	48.8	48.3	47.9	47.5	47.1	46.7	46.4	46.1
42	49.3	48.8	48.3	47.8	47.3	46.9	46.5	46.1	45.8	45.4
43	48.9	48.3	47.8	47.3	46.8	46.3	45.9	45.5	45.1	44.8
44	48.5	47.9	47.3	46.8	46.3	45.8	45.4	44.9	44.5	44.2
45	48.1	47.5	46.9	46.3	45.8	45.3	44.8	44.4	44.0	43.6
46	47.7	47.1	46.5	45.9	45.4	44.8	44.3	43.9	43.4	43.0
47	47.4	46.7	46.1	45.5	44.9	44.4	43.9	43.4	42.9	42.4
48	47.1	46.4	45.8	45.1	44.5	44.0	.43.4	42.9	42.4	41.9
49	46.8	46.1	45.4	44.8	44.2	43.6	43.0	42.4	41.9	41.4
50	46.5	45.8	45.1	44.4	43.8	43.2	42.6	42.0	41.5	40.9
51	46.3	45.5	44.8	44.1	43.5	42.8	42.2	41.6	41.0	40.5
52	46.0	45.3	44.6	43.8	43.2	42.5	41.8	41.2	40.6	40.1
53	45.8	45.1	44.3	43.6	42.9	42.2	41.5	40.9	40.3	39.7
54	45.6	44.8	44.1	43.3	42.6	41.9	41.2	40.5	39.9	39.3
55	45.5	44.7	43.9	43.1	42.4	41.6	40.9	40.2	39.6	38.9
56	45.3	44.5	43.7	42.9	42.1	41.4	40.7	40.0	39.3	38.6
57	45.1	44.3	43.5	42.7	41.9	41.2	40.4	39.7	39.0	38.3
58	45.0	44.2	43.3	42.5	41.7	40.9	40.2	39.4	38.7	38.0
59	44.9	44.0	43.2	42.4	41.5	40.7	40.0	39.2	38.5	37.8
60	44.7	43.9	43.0	42.2	41.4	40.6	39.8	39.0	38.2	37.5
61	44.6	43.8	42.9	42.1	41.2	40.4	39.6	38.8	38.0	37.3
62	44.5	43.7	42.8	41.9	41.1	40.3	39.4	38.6	37.8	37.1
63	44.5	43.6	42.7	41.8	41.0	40.1	39.3	38.5	37.7	36.9
64	44.4	43.5	42.6	41.7	40.8	40.0	39.2	38.3	37.5	36.7
65	44.3	43.4	42.5	41.6	40.7	39.9	39.0	38.2	37.4	36.6
66	44.2	43.3	42.4	41.5	40.6	39.8	38.9	38.1	37.2	36.4
67	44.2	43.3	42.3	41.4	40.6	39.7	38.8	38.0	37.1	36.3
68	44.1	43.2	42.3	41.4	40.5	39.6	38.7	37.9	37.0	36.2
69	44.1	43.1	42.2	41.3	40.4	39.5	38.6	37.8	36.9	36.0
70	44.0	43.1	42.2	41.3	40.3	39.4	38.6	37.7	36.8	35.9
71	44.0	43.0	42.1	41.2	40.3	39.4	38.5	37.6	36.7	35.9
72	43.9	43.0	42.1	41.1	40.2	39.3	38.4	37.5	36.6	35.8
73	43.9	43.0	42.0	41.1	40.2	39.3	38.4	37.5	36.6	35.7
74	43.9	42.9	42.0	41.1	40.1	39.2	38.3	37.4	36.5	35.6
75	43.8	42.9	42.0	41.0	40.1	39.2	38.3	37.4	36.5	35.6
76	43.8	42.9	41.9	41.0	40.1	39.1	38.2	37.3	36.4	35.5
77	43.8	42.9	41.9	41.0	40.0	39.1	38.2	37.3	36.4	35.5
78	43.8	42.8	41.9	40.9	40.0	39.1	38.2	37.2	36.3	35.4
79	43.8	42.8	41.9	40.9	40.0	39.1	38.1	37.2	36.3	35.4
80	43.7	42.8	41.8	40.9	40.0	39.0	38.1	37.2	36.3	35.4
81	43.7	42.8	41.8	40.9	39.9	39.0	38.1	37.2	36.2	35.3
82	43.7	42.8	41.8	40.9	39.9	39.0	38.1	37.1	36.2	35.3
83	43.7	42.8	41.8	40.9	39.9	39.0	38.0	37.1	36.2	35.3
84	43.7	42.7	41.8	40.8	39.9	39.0	38.0	37.1	36.2	35.3
85	43.7	42.7	41.8	40.8	39.9	38.9	38.0	37.1	36.2	35.2
86	43.7	42.7	41.8	40.8	39.9	38.9	38.0	37.1	36.1	35.2
87	43.7	42.7	41.8	40.8	39.9	38.9	38.0	37.0	36.1	35.2
88	43.7	42.7	41.8	40.8	39.9	38.9	38.0	37.0	36.1	35.2
89	43.7	42.7	41.7	40.8	39.8	38.9	38.0	37.0	36.1	35.2
90	43.7	42.7	41.7	40.8	39.8	38.9	38.0	37.0	36.1	35.2
91	43.7	42.7	41.7	40.8	39.8	38.9	37.9	37.0	36.1	35.2
92	43.7	42.7	41.7	40.8	39.8	38.9	37.9	37.0	36.1	35.1
93	43.7	42.7	41.7	40.8	39.8	38.9	37.9	37.0	36.1	35.1
94	43.7	42.7	41.7	40.8	39.8	38.9	37.9	37.0	36.1	35.1
95	43.6	42.7	41.7	40.8	39.8	38.9	37.9	37.0	36.1	35.1
96	43.6	42.7	41.7	40.8	39.8	38.9	37.9	37.0	36.1	35.1
97	43.6	42.7	41.7	40.8	39.8	38.9	37.9	37.0	36.1	35.1
98	43.6	42.7	41.7	40.8	39.8	38.9	37.9	37.0	36.0	35.1

RMD Joint and Survivor Table - Life Expectancy

Ages	50	51	52	53	54	55	56	57	58	59
50	40.4	40.0	39.5	39.1	38.7	38.3	38.0	37.6	37.3	37.1
51	40.0	39.5	39.0	38.5	38.1	37.7	37.4	37.0	36.7	36.4
52	39.5	39.0	38.5	38.0	37.6	37.2	36.8	36.4	36.0	35.7
53	39.1	38.5	38.0	37.5	37.1	36.6	36.2	35.8	35.4	35.1
54	38.7	38.1	37.6	37.1	36.6	36.1	35.7	35.2	34.8	34.5
55	38.3	37.7	37.2	36.6	36.1	35.6	35.1	34.7	34.3	33.9
56	38.0	37.4	36.8	36.2	35.7	35.1	34.7	34.2	33.7	33.3
57	37.6	37.0	36.4	35.8	35.2	34.7	34.2	33.7	33.2	32.8
58	37.3	36.7	36.0	35.4	34.8	34.3	33.7	33.2	32.8	32.3
59	37.1	36.4	35.7	35.1	34.5	33.9	33.3	32.8	32.3	31.8
60	36.8	36.1	35.4	34.8	34.1	33.5	32.9	32.4	31.9	31.3
61	36.6	35.8	35.1	34.5	33.8	33.2	32.6	32.0	31.4	30.9
62	36.3	35.6	34.9	34.2	33.5	32.9	32.2	31.6	31.1	30.5
63	36.1	35.4	34.6	33.9	33.2	32.6	31.9	31.3	30.7	30.1
64	35.9	35.2	34.4	33.7	33.0	32.3	31.6	31.0	30.4	29.8
65	35.8	35.0	34.2	33.5	32.7	32.0	31.4	30.7	30.0	29.4
66	35.6	34.8	34.0	33.3	32.5	31.8	31.1	30.4	29.8	29.1
67	35.5	34.7	33.9	33.1	32.3	31.6	30.9	30.2	29.5	28.8
68	35.3	34.5	33.7	32.9	32.1	31.4	30.7	29.9	29.2	28.6
69	35.2	34.4	33.6	32.8	32.0	31.2	30.5	29.7	29.0	28.3
70	35.1	34.3	33.4	32.6	31.8	31.1	30.3	29.5	28.8	28.1
71	35.0	34.2	33.3	32.5	31.7	30.9	30.1	29.4	28.6	27.9
72	34.9	34.1	33.2	32.4	31.6	30.8	30.0	29.2	28.4	27.7
73	34.8	34.0	33.1	32.3	31.5	30.6	29.8	29.1	28.3	27.5
74	34.8	33.9	33.0	32.2	31.4	30.5	29.7	28.9	28.1	27.4
75	34.7	33.8	33.0	32.1	31.3	30.4	29.6	28.8	28.0	27.2
76	34.6	33.8	32.9	32.0	31.2	30.3	29.5	28.7	27.9	27.1
77	34.6	33.7	32.8	32.0	31.1	30.3	29.4	28.6	27.8	27.0
78	34.5	33.6	32.8	31.9	31.0	30.2	29.3	28.5	27.7	26.9
79	34.5	33.6	32.7	31.8	31.0	30.1	29.3	28.4	27.6	26.8
80	34.5	33.6	32.7	31.8	30.9	30.1	29.2	28.4	27.5	26.7
81	34.4	33.5	32.6	31.8	30.9	30.0	29.2	28.3	27.5	26.6
82	34.4	33.5	32.6	31.7	30.8	30.0	29.1	28.3	27.4	26.6
83	34.4	33.5	32.6	31.7	30.8	29.9	29.1	28.2	27.4	26.5
84	34.3	33.4	32.5	31.7	30.8	29.9	29.0	28.2	27.3	26.5
85	34.3	33.4	32.5	31.6	30.7	29.9	29.0	28.1	27.3	26.4
86	34.3	33.4	32.5	31.6	30.7	29.8	29.0	28.1	27.2	26.4
87	34.3	33.4	32.5	31.6	30.7	29.8	28.9	28.1	27.2	26.4
88	34.3	33.4	32.5	31.6	30.7	29.8	28.9	28.0	27.2	26.3
89	34.3	33.3	32.4	31.5	30.7	29.8	28.9	28.0	27.2	26.3
90	34.2	33.3	32.4	31.5	30.6	29.8	28.9	28.0	27.1	26.3
91	34.2	33.3	32.4	31.5	30.6	29.7	28.9	28.0	27.1	26.3
92	34.2	33.3	32.4	31.5	30.6	29.7	28.8	28.0	27.1	26.2
93	34.2	33.3	32.4	31.5	30.6	29.7	28.8	28.0	27.1	26.2
94	34.2	33.3	32.4	31.5	30.6	29.7	28.8	27.9	27.1	26.2
95	34.2	33.3	32.4	31.5	30.6	29.7	28.8	27.9	27.1	26.2
96	34.2	33.3	32.4	31.5	30.6	29.7	28.8	27.9	27.0	26.2
97	34.2	33.3	32.4	31.5	30.6	29.7	28.8	27.9	27.0	26.2
98	34.2	33.3	32.4	31.5	30.6	29.7	28.8	27.9	27.0	26.2
99	34.2	33.3	32.4	31.5	30.6	29.7	28.8	27.9	27.0	26.2
100	34.2	33.3	32.4	31.5	30.6	29.7	28.8	27.9	27.0	26.1
101	34.2	33.3	32.4	31.5	30.6	29.7	28.8	27.9	27.0	26.1
102	34.2	33.3	32.4	31.4	30.5	29.7	28.8	27.9	27.0	26.1
103	34.2	33.3	32.4	31.4	30.5	29.7	28.8	27.9	27.0	26.1
104	34.2	33.3	32.4	31.4	30.5	29.6	28.8	27.9	27.0	26.1
105	34.2	33.3	32.3	31.4	30.5	29.6	28.8	27.9	27.0	26.1
106	34.2	33.3	32.3	31.4	30.5	29.6	28.8	27.9	27.0	26.1
107	34.2	33.3	32.3	31.4	30.5	29.6	28.8	27.9	27.0	26.1
108	34.2	33.3	32.3	31.4	30.5	29.6	28.8	27.9	27.0	26.1

RMD Joint and Survivor Table - Life Expectancy

Ages	60	61	62	63	64	65	66	67	68	69
60	30.9	30.4	30.0	29.6	29.2	28.8	28.5	28.2	27.9	27.6
61	30.4	29.9	29.5	29.0	28.6	28.3	27.9	27.6	27.3	27.0
62	30.0	29.5	29.0	28.5	28.1	27.7	27.3	27.0	26.7	26.4
63	29.6	29.0	28.5	28.1	27.6	27.2	26.8	26.4	26.1	25.7
64	29.2	28.6	28.1	27.6	27.1	26.7	26.3	25.9	25.5	25.2
65	28.8	28.3	27.7	27.2	26.7	26.2	25.8	25.4	25.0	24.6
66	28.5	27.9	27.3	26.8	26.3	25.8	25.3	24.9	24.5	24.1
67	28.2	27.6	27.0	26.4	25.9	25.4	24.9	24.4	24.0	23.6
68	27.9	27.3	26.7	26.1	25.5	25.0	24.5	24.0	23.5	23.1
69	27.6	27.0	26.4	25.7	25.2	24.6	24.1	23.6	23.1	22.6
70	27.4	26.7	26.1	25.4	24.8	24.3	23.7	23.2	22.7	22.2
71	27.2	26.5	25.8	25.2	24.5	23.9	23.4	22.8	22.3	21.8
72	27.0	26.3	25.6	24.9	24.3	23.7	23.1	22.5	22.0	21.4
73	26.8	26.1	25.4	24.7	24.0	23.4	22.8	22.2	21.6	21.1
74	26.6	25.9	25.2	24.5	23.8	23.1	22.5	21.9	21.3	20.8
75	26.5	25.7	25.0	24.3	23.6	22.9	22.3	21.6	21.0	20.5
76	26.3	25.6	24.8	24.1	23.4	22.7	22.0	21.4	20.8	20.2
77	26.2	25.4	24.7	23.9	23.2	22.5	21.8	21.2	20.6	19.9
78	26.1	25.3	24.6	23.8	23.1	22.4	21.7	21.0	20.3	19.7
79	26.0	25.2	24.4	23.7	22.9	22.2	21.5	20.8	20.1	19.5
80	25.9	25.1	24.3	23.6	22.8	22.1	21.3	20.6	20.0	19.3
81	25.8	25.0	24.2	23.4	22.7	21.9	21.2	20.5	19.8	19.1
82	25.8	24.9	24.1	23.4	22.6	21.8	21.1	20.4	19.7	19.0
83	25.7	24.9	24.1	23.3	22.5	21.7	21.0	20.2	19.5	18.8
84	25.6	24.8	24.0	23.2	22.4	21.6	20.9	20.1	19.4	18.7
85	25.6	24.8	23.9	23.1	22.3	21.6	20.8	20.1	19.3	18.6
86	25.5	24.7	23.9	23.1	22.3	21.5	20.7	20.0	19.2	18.5
87	25.5	24.7	23.8	23.0	22.2	21.4	20.7	19.9	19.2	18.4
88	25.5	24.6	23.8	23.0	22.2	21.4	20.6	19.8	19.1	18.3
89	25.4	24.6	23.8	22.9	22.1	21.3	20.5	19.8	19.0	18.3
90	25.4	24.6	23.7	22.9	22.1	21.3	20.5	19.7	19.0	18.2
91	25.4	24.5	23.7	22.9	22.1	21.3	20.5	19.7	18.9	18.2
92	25.4	24.5	23.7	22.9	22.0	21.2	20.4	19.6	18.9	18.1
93	25.4	24.5	23.7	22.8	22.0	21.2	20.4	19.6	18.8	18.1
94	25.3	24.5	23.6	22.8	22.0	21.2	20.4	19.6	18.8	18.0
95	25.3	24.5	23.6	22.8	22.0	21.1	20.3	19.6	18.8	18.0
96	25.3	24.5	23.6	22.8	21.9	21.1	20.3	19.5	18.8	18.0
97	25.3	24.5	23.6	22.8	21.9	21.1	20.3	19.5	18.7	18.0
98	25.3	24.4	23.6	22.8	21.9	21.1	20.3	19.5	18.7	17.9
99	25.3	24.4	23.6	22.7	21.9	21.1	20.3	19.5	18.7	17.9
100	25.3	24.4	23.6	22.7	21.9	21.1	20.3	19.5	18.7	17.9
101	25.3	24.4	23.6	22.7	21.9	21.1	20.2	19.4	18.7	17.9
102	25.3	24.4	23.6	22.7	21.9	21.1	20.2	19.4	18.6	17.9
103	25.3	24.4	23.6	22.7	21.9	21.0	20.2	19.4	18.6	17.9
104	25.3	24.4	23.5	22.7	21.9	21.0	20.2	19.4	18.6	17.8
105	25.3	24.4	23.5	22.7	21.9	21.0	20.2	19.4	18.6	17.8
106	25.3	24.4	23.5	22.7	21.9	21.0	20.2	19.4	18.6	17.8
107	25.2	24.4	23.5	22.7	21.8	21.0	20.2	19.4	18.6	17.8
108	25.2	24.4	23.5	22.7	21.8	21.0	20.2	19.4	18.6	17.8
109	25.2	24.4	23.5	22.7	21.8	21.0	20.2	19.4	18.6	17.8
110	25.2	24.4	23.5	22.7	21.8	21.0	20.2	19.4	18.6	17.8
111	25.2	24.4	23.5	22.7	21.8	21.0	20.2	19.4	18.6	17.8
112	25.2	24.4	23.5	22.7	21.8	21.0	20.2	19.4	18.6	17.8
113	25.2	24.4	23.5	22.7	21.8	21.0	20.2	19.4	18.6	17.8
114	25.2	24.4	23.5	22.7	21.8	21.0	20.2	19.4	18.6	17.8
115+	25.2	24.4	23.5	22.7	21.8	21.0	20.2	19.4	18.6	17.8

RMD Joint and Survivor Table - Life Expectancy

Ages	70	71	72	73	74	75	76	77	78	79
70	21.8	21.3	20.9	20.6	20.2	19.9	19.6	19.4	19.1	18.9
71	21.3	20.9	20.5	20.1	19.7	19.4	19.1	18.8	18.5	18.3
72	20.9	20.5	20.0	19.6	19.3	18.9	18.6	18.3	18.0	17.7
73	20.6	20.1	19.6	19.2	18.8	18.4	18.1	17.8	17.5	17.2
74	20.2	19.7	19.3	18.8	18.4	18.0	17.6	17.3	17.0	16.7
75	19.9	19.4	18.9	18.4	18.0	17.6	17.2	16.8	16.5	16.2
76	19.6	19.1	18.6	18.1	17.6	17.2	16.8	16.4	16.0	15.7
77	19.4	18.8	18.3	17.8	17.3	16.8	16.4	16.0	15.6	15.3
78	19.1	18.5	18.0	17.5	17.0	16.5	16.0	15.6	15.2	14.9
79	18.9	18.3	17.7	17.2	16.7	16.2	15.7	15.3	14.9	14.5
80	18.7	18.1	17.5	16.9	16.4	15.9	15.4	15.0	14.5	14.1
81	18.5	17.9	17.3	16.7	16.2	15.6	15.1	14.7	14.2	13.8
82	18.3	17.7	17.1	16.5	15.9	15.4	14.9	14.4	13.9	13.5
83	18.2	17.5	16.9	16.3	15.7	15.2	14.7	14.2	13.7	13.2
84	18.0	17.4	16.7	16.1	15.5	15.0	14.4	13.9	13.4	13.0
85	17.9	17.3	16.6	16.0	15.4	14.8	14.3	13.7	13.2	12.8
86	17.8	17.1	16.5	15.8	15.2	14.6	14.1	13.5	13.0	12.5
87	17.7	17.0	16.4	15.7	15.1	14.5	13.9	13.4	12.9	12.4
88	17.6	16.9	16.3	15.6	15.0	14.4	13.8	13.2	12.7	12.2
89	17.6	16.9	16.2	15.5	14.9	14.3	13.7	13.1	12.6	12.0
90	17.5	16.8	16.1	15.4	14.8	14.2	13.6	13.0	12.4	11.9
91	17.4	16.7	16.0	15.4	14.7	14.1	13.5	12.9	12.3	11.8
92	17.4	16.7	16.0	15.3	14.6	14.0	13.4	12.8	12.2	11.7
93	17.3	16.6	15.9	15.2	14.6	13.9	13.3	12.7	12.1	11.6
94	17.3	16.6	15.9	15.2	14.5	13.9	13.2	12.6	12.0	11.5
95	17.3	16.5	15.8	15.1	14.5	13.8	13.2	12.6	12.0	11.4
96	17.2	16.5	15.8	15.1	14.4	13.8	13.1	12.5	11.9	11.3
97	17.2	16.5	15.8	15.1	14.4	13.7	13.1	12.5	11.9	11.3
98	17.2	16.4	15.7	15.0	14.3	13.7	13.0	12.4	11.8	11.2
99	17.2	16.4	15.7	15.0	14.3	13.6	13.0	12.4	11.8	11.2
100	17.1	16.4	15.7	15.0	14.3	13.6	12.9	12.3	11.7	11.1
101	17.1	16.4	15.6	14.9	14.2	13.6	12.9	12.3	11.7	11.1
102	17.1	16.4	15.6	14.9	14.2	13.5	12.9	12.2	11.6	11.0
103	17.1	16.3	15.6	14.9	14.2	13.5	12.9	12.2	11.6	11.0
104	17.1	16.3	15.6	14.9	14.2	13.5	12.8	12.2	11.6	11.0
105	17.1	16.3	15.6	14.9	14.2	13.5	12.8	12.2	11.5	10.9
106	17.1	16.3	15.6	14.8	14.1	13.5	12.8	12.2	11.5	10.9
107	17.0	16.3	15.6	14.8	14.1	13.4	12.8	12.1	11.5	10.9
108	17.0	16.3	15.5	14.8	14.1	13.4	12.8	12.1	11.5	10.9
109	17.0	16.3	15.5	14.8	14.1	13.4	12.8	12.1	11.5	10.9
110	17.0	16.3	15.5	14.8	14.1	13.4	12.7	12.1	11.5	10.9
111	17.0	16.3	15.5	14.8	14.1	13.4	12.7	12.1	11.5	10.8
112	17.0	16.3	15.5	14.8	14.1	13.4	12.7	12.1	11.5	10.8
113	17.0	16.3	15.5	14.8	14.1	13.4	12.7	12.1	11.4	10.8
114	17.0	16.3	15.5	14.8	14.1	13.4	12.7	12.1	11.4	10.8
115+	17.0	16.3	15.5	14.8	14.1	13.4	12.7	12.1	11.4	10.8

RMD Joint and Survivor Table - Life Expectancy

Ages	80	81	82	83	84	85	86	87	88	89
80	13.8	13.4	13.1	12.8	12.6	12.3	12.1	11.9	11.7	11.5
81	13.4	13.1	12.7	12.4	12.2	11.9	11.7	11.4	11.3	11.1
82	13.1	12.7	12.4	12.1	11.8	11.5	11.3	11.0	10.8	10.6
83	12.8	12.4	12.1	11.7	11.4	11.1	10.9	10.6	10.4	10.2
84	12.6	12.2	11.8	11.4	11.1	10.8	10.5	10.3	10.1	9.9
85	12.3	11.9	11.5	11.1	10.8	10.5	10.2	9.9	9.7	9.5
86	12.1	11.7	11.3	10.9	10.5	10.2	9.9	9.6	9.4	9.2
87	11.9	11.4	11.0	10.6	10.3	9.9	9.6	9.4	9.1	8.9
88	11.7	11.3	10.8	10.4	10.1	9.7	9.4	9.1	8.8	8.6
89	11.5	11.1	10.6	10.2	9.9	9.5	9.2	8.9	8.6	8.3
90	11.4	10.9	10.5	10.1	9.7	9.3	9.0	8.6	8.3	8.1
91	11.3	10.8	10.3	9.9	9.5	9.1	8.8	8.4	8.1	7.9
92	11.2	10.7	10.2	9.8	9.3	9.0	8.6	8.3	8.0	7.7
93	11.1	10.6	10.1	9.6	9.2	8.8	8.5	8.1	7.8	7.5
94	11.0	10.5	10.0	9.5	9.1	8.7	8.3	8.0	7.6	7.3
95	10.9	10.4	9.9	9.4	9.0	8.6	8.2	7.8	7.5	7.2
96	10.8	10.3	9.8	9.3	8.9	8.5	8.1	7.7	7.4	7.1
97	10.7	10.2	9.7	9.2	8.8	8.4	8.0	7.6	7.3	6.9
98	10.7	10.1	9.6	9.2	8.7	8.3	7.9	7.5	7.1	6.8
99	10.6	10.1	9.6	9.1	8.6	8.2	7.8	7.4	7.0	6.7
100	10.6	10.0	9.5	9.0	8.5	8.1	7.7	7.3	6.9	6.6
101	10.5	10.0	9.4	9.0	8.5	8.0	7.6	7.2	6.9	6.5
102	10.5	9.9	9.4	8.9	8.4	8.0	7.5	7.1	6.8	6.4
103	10.4	9.9	9.4	8.8	8.4	7.9	7.5	7.1	6.7	6.3
104	10.4	9.8	9.3	8.8	8.3	7.9	7.4	7.0	6.6	6.3
105	10.4	9.8	9.3	8.8	8.3	7.8	7.4	7.0	6.6	6.2
106	10.3	9.8	9.2	8.7	8.2	7.8	7.3	6.9	6.5	6.2
107	10.3	9.8	9.2	8.7	8.2	7.7	7.3	6.9	6.5	6.1
108	10.3	9.7	9.2	8.7	8.2	7.7	7.3	6.8	6.4	6.1
109	10.3	9.7	9.2	8.7	8.2	7.7	7.2	6.8	6.4	6.0
110	10.3	9.7	9.2	8.6	8.1	7.7	7.2	6.8	6.4	6.0
111	10.3	9.7	9.1	8.6	8.1	7.6	7.2	6.8	6.3	6.0
112	10.2	9.7	9.1	8.6	8.1	7.6	7.2	6.7	6.3	5.9
113	10.2	9.7	9.1	8.6	8.1	7.6	7.2	6.7	6.3	5.9
114	10.2	9.7	9.1	8.6	8.1	7.6	7.1	6.7	6.3	5.9
115+	10.2	9.7	9.1	8.6	8.1	7.6	7.1	6.7	6.3	5.9

Appendix D

Substantially Equal Periodic Payments (Present Value Tables)

There is an exception to the early distribution penalty tax for substantially equal periodic payments (SEPPs) under IRC Section 72(t) (see Chapter 13). The amortization and annuitization methods for calculating substantially equal periodic payments use present value annuity tables. RMD factors in Appendix C are used under the required minimum distribution method for calculating substantially equal periodic payments.

A present value annuity factor table is used to show what a series of regular contributions or payments (an annuity) to be received for a given number of years in the future is worth today.

Term certain annuity factors are used to value an annuity for a given number of years (e.g., 10 years). The amortization method for calculating substantially equal periodic payments uses the life expectancy of the IRA owner (or the IRA owner and beneficiary) under the RMD tables (see Appendix C) as the term certain with these factors.

Single life annuity factors are used to value an annuity for a person's life (e.g., for the rest of the life of a person age 40). The single life annuity factors in this appendix are based on the mortality table underlying required minimum distributions. The annuitization method for calculating substantially equal periodic payments uses these single life annuity factors where there is one measuring life.

A present value annuity factor table is used to show what a stream of payments to be received in the future for a given number of years, or for life, is worth today assuming a given interest rate. For example, at 7% interest, payments of $1,000 per year for 10 years are worth $7,024 today ($1,000 x 7.0236 term certain annuity factor). On the other hand, at 7% interest, payments of $1,000 per year for life for a person age 40 are worth $13,165 today ($1,000 x 13.1651 single life annuity factor).

For term certain periodic contributions other than annually at the end of the year, a factor from either Annuity Adjustment Factor Table A (if payments are at end of period) or Annuity Adjustment Factor Table B (if payments are at beginning of period) could be multiplied by the present value annuity factor to produce a factor that is adjusted for frequency of payments.

For periodic contributions for a single life other than annually at the end of the year, a factor from Annuity Adjustment Factor Table A could be multiplied by the present value annuity factor to produce a factor that is adjusted for frequency of payments. If the payments are at the beginning of each period, the frequency adjusted annuity factor could be increased by 1 ÷ the number of payments per year. For example if payments are quarterly at the beginning of each period, the frequency adjusted annuity factor would be increased by .25 (1 ÷ 4).

In general, dividing a given fund (or IRA account balance) by a present value annuity factor (with appropriate adjustments for frequency of payments) produces the payment amount which will exhaust the fund in a given number of years or over the life of the annuitant. This is generally known as amortizing or annuitizing the fund. Such an amount would also be a substantially equal periodic payment.

Annuity Adjustment Factors Table A*

INTEREST RATE	ANNUALLY	SEMI ANNUALLY	FREQUENCY OF PAYMENTS QUARTERLY	MONTHLY	WEEKLY
0.5%	1.0000	1.0012	1.0019	1.0023	1.0024
1.0%	1.0000	1.0025	1.0037	1.0046	1.0049
1.5%	1.0000	1.0037	1.0056	1.0069	1.0073
2.0%	1.0000	1.0050	1.0075	1.0091	1.0098
2.5%	1.0000	1.0062	1.0093	1.0114	1.0122
3.0%	1.0000	1.0074	1.0112	1.0137	1.0146
3.5%	1.0000	1.0087	1.0130	1.0159	1.0171
4.0%	1.0000	1.0099	1.0149	1.0182	1.0195
4.5%	1.0000	1.0111	1.0167	1.0205	1.0219
5.0%	1.0000	1.0123	1.0186	1.0227	1.0243
5.5%	1.0000	1.0136	1.0204	1.0250	1.0267
6.0%	1.0000	1.0148	1.0222	1.0272	1.0291
6.5%	1.0000	1.0160	1.0241	1.0295	1.0315
7.0%	1.0000	1.0172	1.0259	1.0317	1.0339
7.5%	1.0000	1.0184	1.0277	1.0339	1.0363
8.0%	1.0000	1.0196	1.0295	1.0362	1.0387
8.5%	1.0000	1.0208	1.0313	1.0384	1.0411
9.0%	1.0000	1.0220	1.0331	1.0406	1.0435
9.5%	1.0000	1.0232	1.0350	1.0428	1.0459
10.0%	1.0000	1.0244	1.0368	1.0450	1.0482
10.5%	1.0000	1.0256	1.0386	1.0473	1.0506
11.0%	1.0000	1.0268	1.0404	1.0495	1.0530
11.5%	1.0000	1.0280	1.0421	1.0517	1.0554
12.0%	1.0000	1.0292	1.0439	1.0539	1.0577
12.5%	1.0000	1.0303	1.0457	1.0561	1.0601
13.0%	1.0000	1.0315	1.0475	1.0583	1.0624
13.5%	1.0000	1.0327	1.0493	1.0605	1.0648
14.0%	1.0000	1.0339	1.0511	1.0626	1.0671
14.5%	1.0000	1.0350	1.0528	1.0648	1.0695
15.0%	1.0000	1.0362	1.0546	1.0670	1.0718

*For use in calculating the value of an annuity payable at the end of each period or, if the term of the annuity is determined with respect to one or more lives, an annuity payable at the beginning of each period.

Annuity Adjustment Factors Table B*

FREQUENCY OF PAYMENTS

INTEREST RATE	ANNUALLY	SEMI ANNUALLY	QUARTERLY	MONTHLY	WEEKLY
0.5%	1.0050	1.0037	1.0031	1.0027	1.0025
1.0%	1.0100	1.0075	1.0062	1.0054	1.0051
1.5%	1.0150	1.0112	1.0094	1.0081	1.0076
2.0%	1.0200	1.0150	1.0125	1.0108	1.0102
2.5%	1.0250	1.0187	1.0156	1.0135	1.0127
3.0%	1.0300	1.0224	1.0187	1.0162	1.0152
3.5%	1.0350	1.0262	1.0218	1.0189	1.0177
4.0%	1.0400	1.0299	1.0249	1.0215	1.0203
4.5%	1.0450	1.0336	1.0280	1.0242	1.0228
5.0%	1.0500	1.0373	1.0311	1.0269	1.0253
5.5%	1.0550	1.0411	1.0341	1.0295	1.0278
6.0%	1.0600	1.0448	1.0372	1.0322	1.0303
6.5%	1.0650	1.0485	1.0403	1.0349	1.0328
7.0%	1.0700	1.0522	1.0434	1.0375	1.0353
7.5%	1.0750	1.0559	1.0465	1.0402	1.0378
8.0%	1.0800	1.0596	1.0495	1.0428	1.0403
8.5%	1.0850	1.0633	1.0526	1.0455	1.0427
9.0%	1.0900	1.0670	1.0556	1.0481	1.0452
9.5%	1.0950	1.0707	1.0587	1.0507	1.0477
10.0%	1.1000	1.0744	1.0618	1.0534	1.0502
10.5%	1.1050	1.0781	1.0648	1.0560	1.0526
11.0%	1.1100	1.0818	1.0679	1.0586	1.0551
11.5%	1.1150	1.0855	1.0709	1.0613	1.0576
12.0%	1.1200	1.0892	1.0739	1.0639	1.0600
12.5%	1.1250	1.0928	1.0770	1.0665	1.0625
13.0%	1.1300	1.0965	1.0800	1.0691	1.0649
13.5%	1.1350	1.1002	1.0830	1.0717	1.0674
14.0%	1.1400	1.1039	1.0861	1.0743	1.0698
14.5%	1.1450	1.1075	1.0891	1.0769	1.0723
15.0%	1.1500	1.1112	1.0921	1.0795	1.0747

*For use in calculating the value of a term certain annuity payable at the beginning of each period.

Term Certain Annuity Factors

INTEREST RATE

YEARS	0.5%	1.0%	1.5%	2.0%	2.5%	3.0%	3.5%	4.0%	4.5%
1	0.9950	0.9901	0.9852	0.9804	0.9756	0.9709	0.9662	0.9615	0.9569
2	1.9851	1.9704	1.9559	1.9416	1.9274	1.9135	1.8997	1.8861	1.8727
3	2.9702	2.9410	2.9122	2.8839	2.8560	2.8286	2.8016	2.7751	2.7490
4	3.9505	3.9020	3.8544	3.8077	3.7620	3.7171	3.6731	3.6299	3.5875
5	4.9259	4.8534	4.7826	4.7135	4.6458	4.5797	4.5151	4.4518	4.3900
6	5.8964	5.7955	5.6972	5.6014	5.5081	5.4172	5.3286	5.2421	5.1579
7	6.8621	6.7282	6.5982	6.4720	6.3494	6.2303	6.1145	6.0021	5.8927
8	7.8230	7.6517	7.4859	7.3255	7.1701	7.0197	6.8740	6.7327	6.5959
9	8.7791	8.5660	8.3605	8.1622	7.9709	7.7861	7.6077	7.4353	7.2688
10	9.7304	9.4713	9.2222	8.9826	8.7521	8.5302	8.3166	8.1109	7.9127
11	10.6770	10.3676	10.0711	9.7868	9.5142	9.2526	9.0016	8.7605	8.5289
12	11.6189	11.2551	10.9075	10.5753	10.2578	9.9540	9.6633	9.3851	9.1186
13	12.5562	12.1337	11.7315	11.3484	10.9832	10.6350	10.3027	9.9856	9.6829
14	13.4887	13.0037	12.5434	12.1062	11.6909	11.2961	10.9205	10.5631	10.2228
15	14.4166	13.8651	13.3432	12.8493	12.3814	11.9379	11.5174	11.1184	10.7395
16	15.3399	14.7179	14.1313	13.5777	13.0550	12.5611	12.0941	11.6523	11.2340
17	16.2586	15.5623	14.9076	14.2919	13.7122	13.1661	12.6513	12.1657	11.7072
18	17.1728	16.3983	15.6726	14.9920	14.3534	13.7535	13.1897	12.6593	12.1600
19	18.0824	17.2260	16.4262	15.6785	14.9789	14.3238	13.7098	13.1339	12.5933
20	18.9874	18.0456	17.1686	16.3514	15.5892	14.8775	14.2124	13.5903	13.0079
21	19.8880	18.8570	17.9001	17.0112	16.1845	15.4150	14.6980	14.0292	13.4047
22	20.7841	19.6604	18.6208	17.6580	16.7654	15.9369	15.1671	14.4511	13.7844
23	21.6757	20.4558	19.3309	18.2922	17.3321	16.4436	15.6204	14.8568	14.1478
24	22.5629	21.2434	20.0304	18.9139	17.8850	16.9355	16.0584	15.2470	14.4955
25	23.4456	22.0232	20.7196	19.5235	18.4244	17.4131	16.4815	15.6221	14.8282
26	24.3240	22.7952	21.3986	20.1210	18.9506	17.8768	16.8904	15.9828	15.1466
27	25.1980	23.5596	22.0676	20.7069	19.4640	18.3270	17.2854	16.3296	15.4513
28	26.0677	24.3164	22.7267	21.2813	19.9649	18.7641	17.6670	16.6631	15.7429
29	26.9330	25.0658	23.3761	21.8444	20.4536	19.1885	18.0358	16.9837	16.0219
30	27.7941	25.8077	24.0158	22.3965	20.9303	19.6004	18.3920	17.2920	16.2889
31	28.6508	26.5423	24.6461	22.9377	21.3954	20.0004	18.7363	17.5885	16.5444
32	29.5033	27.2696	25.2671	23.4683	21.8492	20.3888	19.0689	17.8736	16.7889
33	30.3515	27.9897	25.8790	23.9886	22.2919	20.7658	19.3902	18.1476	17.0229
34	31.1955	28.7027	26.4817	24.4986	22.7238	21.1318	19.7007	18.4112	17.2468
35	32.0354	29.4086	27.0756	24.9986	23.1452	21.4872	20.0007	18.6646	17.4610
36	32.8710	30.1075	27.6607	25.4888	23.5563	21.8323	20.2905	18.9083	17.6660
37	33.7025	30.7995	28.2371	25.9695	23.9573	22.1672	20.5705	19.1426	17.8622
38	34.5299	31.4847	28.8051	26.4406	24.3486	22.4925	20.8411	19.3679	18.0500
39	35.3531	32.1630	29.3646	26.9026	24.7303	22.8082	21.1025	19.5845	18.2297
40	36.1722	32.8347	29.9158	27.3555	25.1028	23.1148	21.3551	19.7928	18.4016
41	36.9873	33.4997	30.4590	27.7995	25.4661	23.4124	21.5991	19.9931	18.5661
42	37.7983	34.1581	30.9941	28.2348	25.8206	23.7014	21.8349	20.1856	18.7235
43	38.6053	34.8100	31.5212	28.6616	26.1664	23.9819	22.0627	20.3708	18.8742
44	39.4082	35.4555	32.0406	29.0800	26.5038	24.2543	22.2828	20.5488	19.0184
45	40.2072	36.0945	32.5523	29.4902	26.8330	24.5187	22.4955	20.7200	19.1563
46	41.0022	36.7272	33.0565	29.8923	27.1542	24.7754	22.7009	20.8847	19.2884
47	41.7932	37.3537	33.5532	30.2866	27.4675	25.0247	22.8994	21.0429	19.4147
48	42.5803	37.9740	34.0426	30.6731	27.7732	25.2667	23.0912	21.1951	19.5356
49	43.3635	38.5881	34.5247	31.0521	28.0714	25.5017	23.2766	21.3415	19.6513
50	44.1428	39.1961	34.9997	31.4236	28.3623	25.7298	23.4556	21.4822	19.7620
51	44.9182	39.7981	35.4677	31.7878	28.6462	25.9512	23.6286	21.6175	19.8679
52	45.6897	40.3942	35.9287	32.1450	28.9231	26.1662	23.7958	21.7476	19.9693
53	46.4575	40.9844	36.3830	32.4950	29.1932	26.3750	23.9573	21.8727	20.0663
54	47.2214	41.5687	36.8305	32.8383	29.4568	26.5777	24.1133	21.9930	20.1592
55	47.9814	42.1472	37.2715	33.1748	29.7140	26.7744	24.2641	22.1086	20.2480

Term Certain Annuity Factors

INTEREST RATE

YEARS	5.0%	5.5%	6.0%	6.5%	7.0%	7.5%	8.0%	8.5%	9.0%
1	0.9524	0.9479	0.9434	0.9390	0.9346	0.9302	0.9259	0.9217	0.9174
2	1.8594	1.8463	1.8334	1.8206	1.8080	1.7956	1.7833	1.7711	1.7591
3	2.7232	2.6979	2.6730	2.6485	2.6243	2.6005	2.5771	2.5540	2.5313
4	3.5460	3.5052	3.4651	3.4258	3.3872	3.3493	3.3121	3.2756	3.2397
5	4.3295	4.2703	4.2124	4.1557	4.1002	4.0459	3.9927	3.9406	3.8897
6	5.0757	4.9955	4.9173	4.8410	4.7665	4.6938	4.6229	4.5536	4.4859
7	5.7864	5.6830	5.5824	5.4845	5.3893	5.2966	5.2064	5.1185	5.0330
8	6.4632	6.3346	6.2098	6.0888	5.9713	5.8573	5.7466	5.6392	5.5348
9	7.1078	6.9522	6.8017	6.6561	6.5152	6.3789	6.2469	6.1191	5.9952
10	7.7217	7.5376	7.3601	7.1888	7.0236	6.8641	6.7101	6.5613	6.4177
11	8.3064	8.0925	7.8869	7.6890	7.4987	7.3154	7.1390	6.9690	6.8052
12	8.8633	8.6185	8.3838	8.1587	7.9427	7.7353	7.5361	7.3447	7.1607
13	9.3936	9.1171	8.8527	8.5997	8.3577	8.1258	7.9038	7.6910	7.4869
14	9.8986	9.5896	9.2950	9.0138	8.7455	8.4892	8.2442	8.0101	7.7862
15	10.3797	10.0376	9.7122	9.4027	9.1079	8.8271	8.5595	8.3042	8.0607
16	10.8378	10.4622	10.1059	9.7678	9.4466	9.1415	8.8514	8.5753	8.3126
17	11.2741	10.8646	10.4773	10.1106	9.7632	9.4340	9.1216	8.8252	8.5436
18	11.6896	11.2461	10.8276	10.4325	10.0591	9.7060	9.3719	9.0555	8.7556
19	12.0853	11.6077	11.1581	10.7347	10.3356	9.9591	9.6036	9.2677	8.9501
20	12.4622	11.9504	11.4699	11.0185	10.5940	10.1945	9.8181	9.4633	9.1285
21	12.8212	12.2752	11.7641	11.2850	10.8355	10.4135	10.0168	9.6436	9.2922
22	13.1630	12.5832	12.0416	11.5352	11.0612	10.6172	10.2007	9.8098	9.4424
23	13.4886	12.8750	12.3034	11.7701	11.2722	10.8067	10.3711	9.9629	9.5802
24	13.7986	13.1517	12.5504	11.9907	11.4693	10.9830	10.5288	10.1041	9.7066
25	14.0939	13.4139	12.7834	12.1979	11.6536	11.1469	10.6748	10.2342	9.8226
26	14.3752	13.6625	13.0032	12.3924	11.8258	11.2995	10.8100	10.3541	9.9290
27	14.6430	13.8981	13.2105	12.5750	11.9867	11.4414	10.9352	10.4646	10.0266
28	14.8981	14.1214	13.4062	12.7465	12.1371	11.5734	11.0511	10.5665	10.1161
29	15.1411	14.3331	13.5907	12.9075	12.2777	11.6962	11.1584	10.6603	10.1983
30	15.3725	14.5337	13.7648	13.0587	12.4090	11.8104	11.2578	10.7468	10.2737
31	15.5928	14.7239	13.9291	13.2006	12.5318	11.9166	11.3498	10.8266	10.3428
32	15.8027	14.9042	14.0840	13.3339	12.6466	12.0155	11.4350	10.9001	10.4062
33	16.0025	15.0751	14.2302	13.4591	12.7538	12.1074	11.5139	10.9678	10.4644
34	16.1929	15.2370	14.3681	13.5766	12.8540	12.1929	11.5869	11.0302	10.5178
35	16.3742	15.3906	14.4982	13.6870	12.9477	12.2725	11.6546	11.0878	10.5668
36	16.5469	15.5361	14.6210	13.7906	13.0352	12.3465	11.7172	11.1408	10.6118
37	16.7113	15.6740	14.7368	13.8879	13.1170	12.4154	11.7752	11.1897	10.6530
38	16.8679	15.8047	14.8460	13.9792	13.1935	12.4794	11.8289	11.2347	10.6908
39	17.0170	15.9287	14.9491	14.0650	13.2649	12.5390	11.8786	11.2763	10.7255
40	17.1591	16.0461	15.0463	14.1455	13.3317	12.5944	11.9246	11.3145	10.7574
41	17.2944	16.1575	15.1380	14.2212	13.3941	12.6460	11.9672	11.3498	10.7866
42	17.4232	16.2630	15.2245	14.2922	13.4524	12.6939	12.0067	11.3823	10.8134
43	17.5459	16.3630	15.3062	14.3588	13.5070	12.7385	12.0432	11.4123	10.8380
44	17.6628	16.4579	15.3832	14.4214	13.5579	12.7800	12.0771	11.4399	10.8605
45	17.7741	16.5477	15.4558	14.4802	13.6055	12.8186	12.1084	11.4653	10.8812
46	17.8801	16.6329	15.5244	14.5354	13.6500	12.8545	12.1374	11.4888	10.9002
47	17.9810	16.7137	15.5890	14.5873	13.6916	12.8879	12.1643	11.5104	10.9176
48	18.0772	16.7902	15.6500	14.6359	13.7305	12.9190	12.1891	11.5303	10.9336
49	18.1687	16.8628	15.7076	14.6816	13.7668	12.9479	12.2122	11.5487	10.9482
50	18.2559	16.9315	15.7619	14.7245	13.8007	12.9748	12.2335	11.5656	10.9617
51	18.3390	16.9967	15.8131	14.7648	13.8325	12.9998	12.2532	11.5812	10.9740
52	18.4181	17.0585	15.8614	14.8026	13.8621	13.0231	12.2715	11.5956	10.9853
53	18.4934	17.1170	15.9070	14.8382	13.8898	13.0447	12.2884	11.6088	10.9957
54	18.5651	17.1726	15.9500	14.8715	13.9157	13.0649	12.3041	11.6210	11.0053
55	18.6335	17.2252	15.9905	14.9028	13.9399	13.0836	12.3186	11.6323	11.0140

Term Certain Annuity Factors

INTEREST RATE

YEARS	9.5%	10.0%	10.5%	11.0%	11.5%	12.0%	12.5%	13.0%	13.5%
1	0.9132	0.9091	0.9050	0.9009	0.8969	0.8929	0.8889	0.8850	0.8811
2	1.7473	1.7355	1.7240	1.7125	1.7012	1.6901	1.6790	1.6681	1.6573
3	2.5089	2.4869	2.4651	2.4437	2.4226	2.4018	2.3813	2.3612	2.3413
4	3.2045	3.1699	3.1359	3.1024	3.0696	3.0373	3.0056	2.9745	2.9438
5	3.8397	3.7908	3.7429	3.6959	3.6499	3.6048	3.5606	3.5172	3.4747
6	4.4198	4.3553	4.2922	4.2305	4.1703	4.1114	4.0538	3.9975	3.9425
7	4.9496	4.8684	4.7893	4.7122	4.6370	4.5638	4.4923	4.4226	4.3546
8	5.4334	5.3349	5.2392	5.1461	5.0556	4.9676	4.8820	4.7988	4.7177
9	5.8753	5.7590	5.6463	5.5370	5.4311	5.3282	5.2285	5.1317	5.0377
10	6.2788	6.1446	6.0148	5.8892	5.7678	5.6502	5.5364	5.4262	5.3195
11	6.6473	6.4951	6.3482	6.2065	6.0697	5.9377	5.8102	5.6869	5.5679
12	6.9838	6.8137	6.6500	6.4924	6.3406	6.1944	6.0535	5.9176	5.7867
13	7.2912	7.1034	6.9230	6.7499	6.5835	6.4235	6.2698	6.1218	5.9794
14	7.5719	7.3667	7.1702	6.9819	6.8013	6.6282	6.4620	6.3025	6.1493
15	7.8282	7.6061	7.3938	7.1909	6.9967	6.8109	6.6329	6.4624	6.2989
16	8.0623	7.8237	7.5962	7.3792	7.1719	6.9740	6.7848	6.6039	6.4308
17	8.2760	8.0216	7.7794	7.5488	7.3291	7.1196	6.9198	6.7291	6.5469
18	8.4713	8.2014	7.9451	7.7016	7.4700	7.2497	7.0398	6.8399	6.6493
19	8.6496	8.3649	8.0952	7.8393	7.5964	7.3658	7.1465	6.9380	6.7395
20	8.8124	8.5136	8.2309	7.9633	7.7098	7.4694	7.2414	7.0248	6.8189
21	8.9611	8.6487	8.3538	8.0751	7.8115	7.5620	7.3256	7.1016	6.8889
22	9.0969	8.7715	8.4649	8.1757	7.9027	7.6446	7.4006	7.1695	6.9506
23	9.2209	8.8832	8.5656	8.2664	7.9845	7.7184	7.4672	7.2297	7.0049
24	9.3341	8.9847	8.6566	8.3481	8.0578	7.7843	7.5264	7.2829	7.0528
25	9.4376	9.0770	8.7390	8.4217	8.1236	7.8431	7.5790	7.3300	7.0950
26	9.5320	9.1609	8.8136	8.4881	8.1826	7.8957	7.6258	7.3717	7.1321
27	9.6183	9.2372	8.8811	8.5478	8.2355	7.9426	7.6674	7.4086	7.1649
28	9.6971	9.3066	8.9422	8.6016	8.2830	7.9844	7.7043	7.4412	7.1937
29	9.7690	9.3696	8.9974	8.6501	8.3255	8.0218	7.7372	7.4701	7.2191
30	9.8347	9.4269	9.0474	8.6938	8.3637	8.0552	7.7664	7.4957	7.2415
31	9.8947	9.4790	9.0927	8.7331	8.3980	8.0850	7.7923	7.5183	7.2613
32	9.9495	9.5264	9.1337	8.7686	8.4287	8.1116	7.8154	7.5383	7.2786
33	9.9996	9.5694	9.1707	8.8005	8.4562	8.1354	7.8359	7.5560	7.2940
34	10.0453	9.6086	9.2043	8.8293	8.4809	8.1566	7.8542	7.5717	7.3075
35	10.0870	9.6442	9.2347	8.8552	8.5030	8.1755	7.8704	7.5856	7.3193
36	10.1251	9.6765	9.2621	8.8786	8.5229	8.1924	7.8848	7.5979	7.3298
37	10.1599	9.7059	9.2870	8.8996	8.5407	8.2075	7.8976	7.6087	7.3390
38	10.1917	9.7327	9.3095	8.9186	8.5567	8.2210	7.9089	7.6183	7.3472
39	10.2207	9.7570	9.3299	8.9357	8.5710	8.2330	7.9191	7.6268	7.3543
40	10.2472	9.7791	9.3483	8.9511	8.5839	8.2438	7.9281	7.6344	7.3607
41	10.2715	9.7991	9.3650	8.9649	8.5954	8.2534	7.9361	7.6410	7.3662
42	10.2936	9.8174	9.3801	8.9774	8.6058	8.2619	7.9432	7.6469	7.3711
43	10.3138	9.8340	9.3937	8.9886	8.6150	8.2696	7.9495	7.6522	7.3754
44	10.3322	9.8491	9.4061	8.9988	8.6233	8.2764	7.9551	7.6568	7.3792
45	10.3490	9.8628	9.4173	9.0079	8.6308	8.2825	7.9601	7.6609	7.3826
46	10.3644	9.8753	9.4274	9.0161	8.6375	8.2880	7.9645	7.6645	7.3855
47	10.3785	9.8866	9.4366	9.0235	8.6435	8.2928	7.9685	7.6677	7.3881
48	10.3913	9.8969	9.4448	9.0302	8.6489	8.2972	7.9720	7.6705	7.3904
49	10.4030	9.9063	9.4524	9.0362	8.6537	8.3010	7.9751	7.6730	7.3924
50	10.4137	9.9148	9.4591	9.0417	8.6580	8.3045	7.9778	7.6752	7.3942
51	10.4235	9.9226	9.4653	9.0465	8.6619	8.3076	7.9803	7.6772	7.3958
52	10.4324	9.9296	9.4708	9.0509	8.6654	8.3103	7.9825	7.6789	7.3972
53	10.4405	9.9360	9.4759	9.0549	8.6685	8.3128	7.9844	7.6805	7.3984
54	10.4480	9.9418	9.4804	9.0585	8.6713	8.3150	7.9862	7.6818	7.3995
55	10.4548	9.9471	9.4846	9.0617	8.6738	8.3170	7.9877	7.6830	7.4004

RMD Single Life Annuity Factors

INTEREST RATE

AGE	0.5%	1.0%	1.5%	2.0%	2.5%	3.0%	3.5%	4.0%	4.5%
0	67.0520	55.4440	46.5720	39.6980	34.3000	30.0033	26.5394	23.7120	21.3760
1	66.5200	55.1080	46.3633	39.5715	34.2260	29.9640	26.5220	23.7085	21.3813
2	65.9060	54.7040	46.0960	39.3950	34.1096	29.8873	26.4720	23.6760	21.3611
3	65.2640	54.2740	45.8073	39.2000	33.9772	29.7970	26.4100	23.6335	21.3318
4	64.6120	53.8350	45.5100	38.9975	33.8384	29.7010	26.3434	23.5870	21.2991
5	63.9540	53.3890	45.2060	38.7885	33.6940	29.6007	26.2731	23.5372	21.2638
6	63.2900	52.9360	44.8953	38.5740	33.5448	29.4960	26.1991	23.4848	21.2260
7	62.6200	52.4770	44.5787	38.3540	33.3908	29.3877	26.1220	23.4295	21.1860
8	61.9460	52.0130	44.2560	38.1290	33.2324	29.2750	26.0417	23.3715	21.1436
9	61.2680	51.5440	43.9300	37.9000	33.0708	29.1600	25.9591	23.3115	21.1000
10	60.5900	51.0720	43.5993	37.6670	32.9056	29.0420	25.8740	23.2498	21.0547
11	59.9080	50.5960	43.2647	37.4305	32.7368	28.9207	25.7863	23.1860	21.0076
12	59.2240	50.1160	42.9260	37.1895	32.5644	28.7967	25.6963	23.1200	20.9589
13	58.5380	49.6320	42.5827	36.9440	32.3880	28.6690	25.6031	23.0515	20.9082
14	57.8480	49.1430	42.2340	36.6945	32.2076	28.5380	25.5071	22.9808	20.8558
15	57.1560	48.6500	41.8813	36.4400	32.0232	28.4033	25.4083	22.9075	20.8009
16	56.4600	48.1530	41.5233	36.1810	31.8344	28.2650	25.3060	22.8315	20.7440
17	55.7620	47.6510	41.1607	35.9170	31.6416	28.1227	25.2006	22.7528	20.6849
18	55.0600	47.1450	40.7927	35.6485	31.4440	27.9767	25.0917	22.6712	20.6233
19	54.3560	46.6340	40.4200	35.3750	31.2420	27.8263	24.9797	22.5868	20.5591
20	53.6500	46.1180	40.0420	35.0960	31.0352	27.6723	24.8637	22.4992	20.4927
21	52.9400	45.5990	39.6593	34.8125	30.8240	27.5140	24.7446	22.4085	20.4233
22	52.2280	45.0740	39.2713	34.5240	30.6080	27.3513	24.6214	22.3148	20.3513
23	51.5120	44.5450	38.8780	34.2305	30.3872	27.1847	24.4946	22.2178	20.2767
24	50.7940	44.0120	38.4800	33.9315	30.1616	27.0133	24.3634	22.1172	20.1989
25	50.0740	43.4740	38.0767	33.6270	29.9308	26.8373	24.2286	22.0132	20.1182
26	49.3500	42.9320	37.6673	33.3175	29.6952	26.6567	24.0897	21.9055	20.0342
27	48.6240	42.3850	37.2533	33.0020	29.4536	26.4710	23.9460	21.7938	19.9471
28	47.8940	41.8320	36.8333	32.6810	29.2068	26.2803	23.7980	21.6782	19.8562
29	47.1620	41.2750	36.4073	32.3535	28.9544	26.0843	23.6449	21.5582	19.7616
30	46.4260	40.7120	35.9753	32.0200	28.6956	25.8827	23.4869	21.4335	19.6629
31	45.6860	40.1440	35.5367	31.6800	28.4308	25.6750	23.3234	21.3042	19.5598
32	44.9420	39.5700	35.0920	31.3335	28.1588	25.4613	23.1543	21.1698	19.4524
33	44.1940	38.9900	34.6400	30.9795	27.8804	25.2410	22.9791	21.0298	19.3400
34	43.4420	38.4050	34.1813	30.6185	27.5952	25.0140	22.7980	20.8842	19.2224
35	42.6860	37.8130	33.7153	30.2500	27.3024	24.7803	22.6103	20.7330	19.0998
36	41.9260	37.2140	33.2420	29.8740	27.0020	24.5393	22.4160	20.5755	18.9716
37	41.1640	36.6100	32.7620	29.4905	26.6944	24.2913	22.2151	20.4118	18.8376
38	40.3960	36.0000	32.2747	29.1000	26.3796	24.0363	22.0074	20.2420	18.6978
39	39.6260	35.3850	31.7813	28.7020	26.0576	23.7743	21.7931	20.0658	18.5524
40	38.8540	34.7650	31.2820	28.2980	25.7284	23.5053	21.5726	19.8838	18.4016
41	38.0800	34.1410	30.7767	27.8870	25.3928	23.2300	21.3454	19.6958	18.2449
42	37.3040	33.5140	30.2660	27.4700	25.0508	22.9480	21.1120	19.5015	18.0829
43	36.5280	32.8820	29.7507	27.0470	24.7024	22.6600	20.8726	19.3015	17.9151
44	35.7520	32.2480	29.2307	26.6185	24.3480	22.3657	20.6269	19.0958	17.7418
45	34.9740	31.6120	28.7060	26.1850	23.9880	22.0653	20.3754	18.8842	17.5631
46	34.2000	30.9730	28.1773	25.7460	23.6220	21.7590	20.1180	18.6670	17.3791
47	33.4240	30.3310	27.6453	25.3020	23.2504	21.4467	19.8546	18.4438	17.1893
48	32.6500	29.6890	27.1093	24.8535	22.8736	21.1287	19.5851	18.2150	16.9940
49	31.8780	29.0440	26.5693	24.4000	22.4908	20.8047	19.3100	17.9803	16.7929
50	31.1060	28.3980	26.0260	23.9415	22.1024	20.4747	19.0286	17.7392	16.5860
51	30.3360	27.7500	25.4787	23.4780	21.7084	20.1387	18.7409	17.4922	16.3731
52	29.5680	27.1000	24.9280	23.0095	21.3092	19.7967	18.4469	17.2388	16.1540
53	28.8000	26.4490	24.3740	22.5365	20.9036	19.4483	18.1466	16.9790	15.9284
54	28.0340	25.7970	23.8167	22.0585	20.4928	19.0937	17.8397	16.7128	15.6964
55	27.2700	25.1440	23.2560	21.5760	20.0760	18.7330	17.5263	16.4395	15.4580
56	26.5080	24.4890	22.6920	21.0885	19.6536	18.3657	17.2063	16.1598	15.2124
57	25.7480	23.8330	22.1247	20.5965	19.2252	17.9920	16.8791	15.8728	14.9600

RMD Single Life Annuity Factors

AGE	0.5%	1.0%	1.5%	2.0%	INTEREST RATE 2.5%	3.0%	3.5%	4.0%	4.5%
58	24.9880	23.1750	21.5533	20.0990	18.7908	17.6113	16.5449	15.5785	14.7000
59	24.2300	22.5160	20.9780	19.5960	18.3500	17.2237	16.2031	15.2763	14.4322
60	23.4740	21.8550	20.3993	19.0880	17.9024	16.8287	15.8537	14.9662	14.1564
61	22.7200	21.1930	19.8173	18.5745	17.4488	16.4270	15.4966	14.6482	13.8727
62	21.9680	20.5310	19.2327	18.0570	16.9896	16.0183	15.1326	14.3228	13.5811
63	21.2180	19.8690	18.6460	17.5355	16.5252	15.6037	14.7614	13.9900	13.2820
64	20.4740	19.2080	18.0580	17.0115	16.0564	15.1837	14.3843	13.6508	12.9758
65	19.7360	18.5500	17.4700	16.4850	15.5844	14.7593	14.0017	13.3050	12.6631
66	19.0040	17.8950	16.8827	15.9575	15.1092	14.3307	13.6143	12.9540	12.3444
67	18.2780	17.2440	16.2973	15.4290	14.6320	13.8987	13.2223	12.5978	12.0200
68	17.5620	16.5980	15.7140	14.9015	14.1536	13.4637	12.8266	12.2370	11.6902
69	16.8540	15.9580	15.1333	14.3745	13.6744	13.0270	12.4277	11.8720	11.3560
70	16.1560	15.3240	14.5573	13.8495	13.1952	12.5890	12.0266	11.5040	11.0176
71	15.4680	14.6980	13.9860	13.3275	12.7168	12.1503	11.6234	11.1330	10.6756
72	14.7920	14.0800	13.4207	12.8090	12.2404	11.7120	11.2194	10.7600	10.3309
73	14.1300	13.4720	12.8620	12.2945	11.7668	11.2747	10.8151	10.3858	9.9840
74	13.4780	12.8730	12.3107	11.7855	11.2964	10.8390	10.4114	10.0110	9.6356
75	12.8420	12.2860	11.7673	11.2830	10.8304	10.4063	10.0091	9.6365	9.2862
76	12.2200	11.7100	11.2333	10.7875	10.3696	9.9773	9.6091	9.2630	8.9373
77	11.6140	11.1480	10.7100	10.3000	9.9148	9.5530	9.2126	8.8918	8.5893
78	11.0260	10.5990	10.1980	9.8215	9.4676	9.1343	8.8200	8.5233	8.2431
79	10.4540	10.0640	9.6980	9.3530	9.0284	8.7220	8.4326	8.1588	7.8998
80	9.8980	9.5440	9.2107	8.8955	8.5980	8.3170	8.0509	7.7988	7.5600
81	9.3620	9.0410	8.7367	8.4495	8.1776	7.9200	7.6760	7.4445	7.2247
82	8.8460	8.5530	8.2773	8.0155	7.7676	7.5323	7.3091	7.0968	6.8949
83	8.3480	8.0830	7.8327	7.5950	7.3692	7.1547	6.9506	6.7562	6.5711
84	7.8700	7.6310	7.4040	7.1880	6.9828	6.7877	6.6014	6.4240	6.2544
85	7.4120	7.1960	6.9913	6.7960	6.6096	6.4320	6.2626	6.1005	5.9458
86	6.9760	6.7810	6.5953	6.4185	6.2500	6.0887	5.9346	5.7872	5.6460
87	6.5600	6.3850	6.2180	6.0580	5.9052	5.7590	5.6189	5.4848	5.3562
88	6.1660	6.0090	5.8587	5.7145	5.5760	5.4437	5.3166	5.1948	5.0776
89	5.7980	5.6560	5.5200	5.3895	5.2644	5.1443	5.0291	4.9185	4.8120
90	5.4520	5.3240	5.2013	5.0840	4.9708	4.8623	4.7577	4.6570	4.5602
91	5.1300	5.0140	4.9040	4.7975	4.6952	4.5970	4.5020	4.4105	4.3224
92	4.8300	4.7250	4.6260	4.5300	4.4372	4.3480	4.2620	4.1788	4.0987
93	4.5500	4.4560	4.3660	4.2795	4.1956	4.1147	4.0366	3.9610	3.8880
94	4.2880	4.2030	4.1220	4.0440	3.9680	3.8947	3.8240	3.7552	3.6889
95	4.0400	3.9650	3.8920	3.8210	3.7528	3.6863	3.6223	3.5600	3.4996
96	3.8060	3.7380	3.6727	3.6085	3.5468	3.4870	3.4289	3.3725	3.3178
97	3.5800	3.5190	3.4600	3.4030	3.3472	3.2933	3.2411	3.1900	3.1407
98	3.3580	3.3030	3.2507	3.1995	3.1496	3.1013	3.0543	3.0088	2.9642
99	3.1400	3.0920	3.0453	2.9995	2.9552	2.9120	2.8703	2.8292	2.7893
100	2.9260	2.8840	2.8427	2.8020	2.7628	2.7247	2.6874	2.6510	2.6156
101	2.7160	2.6790	2.6427	2.6070	2.5724	2.5387	2.5057	2.4738	2.4424
102	2.5100	2.4780	2.4460	2.4150	2.3848	2.3553	2.3266	2.2985	2.2709
103	2.3100	2.2830	2.2553	2.2285	2.2020	2.1763	2.1514	2.1268	2.1027
104	2.1140	2.0910	2.0673	2.0440	2.0216	1.9993	1.9777	1.9565	1.9356
105	1.9240	1.9040	1.8833	1.8640	1.8444	1.8257	1.8071	1.7887	1.7709
106	1.7400	1.7220	1.7053	1.6890	1.6724	1.6563	1.6409	1.6252	1.6100
107	1.5620	1.5480	1.5340	1.5205	1.5068	1.4933	1.4800	1.4670	1.4542
108	1.3940	1.3830	1.3713	1.3595	1.3480	1.3370	1.3260	1.3150	1.3044
109	1.2360	1.2260	1.2167	1.2070	1.1980	1.1887	1.1794	1.1705	1.1618
110	1.0880	1.0800	1.0720	1.0640	1.0564	1.0487	1.0414	1.0340	1.0267
111	0.9500	0.9430	0.9367	0.9305	0.9240	0.9180	0.9120	0.9060	0.9000
112	0.8220	0.8160	0.8113	0.8065	0.8012	0.7963	0.7914	0.7868	0.7820
113	0.7040	0.7000	0.6960	0.6915	0.6876	0.6840	0.6800	0.6762	0.6724
114	0.5960	0.5930	0.5893	0.5865	0.5832	0.5803	0.5774	0.5743	0.5713
115	0.4980	0.4950	0.4927	0.4900	0.4880	0.4853	0.4831	0.4808	0.4784

RMD Single Life Annuity Factors

INTEREST RATE

AGE	5.0%	5.5%	6.0%	6.5%	7.0%	7.5%	8.0%	8.5%	9.0%
0	19.4248	17.7773	16.3725	15.1635	14.1144	13.1967	12.3881	11.6708	11.0308
1	19.4354	17.7913	16.3883	15.1803	14.1314	13.2136	12.4048	11.6871	11.0464
2	19.4232	17.7844	16.3852	15.1795	14.1324	13.2156	12.4074	11.6902	11.0499
3	19.4030	17.7705	16.3755	15.1731	14.1280	13.2128	12.4056	11.6892	11.0493
4	19.3798	17.7540	16.3637	15.1646	14.1219	13.2083	12.4024	11.6868	11.0477
5	19.3546	17.7356	16.3503	15.1548	14.1146	13.2028	12.3982	11.6836	11.0452
6	19.3272	17.7156	16.3355	15.1437	14.1061	13.1964	12.3932	11.6798	11.0422
7	19.2978	17.6940	16.3193	15.1314	14.0969	13.1892	12.3876	11.6753	11.0386
8	19.2668	17.6707	16.3020	15.1182	14.0866	13.1812	12.3812	11.6701	11.0343
9	19.2344	17.6467	16.2838	15.1043	14.0759	13.1728	12.3746	11.6647	11.0300
10	19.2010	17.6216	16.2648	15.0898	14.0647	13.1640	12.3676	11.6592	11.0254
11	19.1660	17.5956	16.2450	15.0748	14.0530	13.1548	12.3604	11.6534	11.0208
12	19.1298	17.5684	16.2245	15.0589	14.0407	13.1453	12.3528	11.6473	11.0158
13	19.0920	17.5398	16.2028	15.0423	14.0279	13.1352	12.3448	11.6408	11.0106
14	19.0526	17.5100	16.1800	15.0248	14.0141	13.1244	12.3362	11.6340	11.0050
15	19.0114	17.4789	16.1562	15.0063	13.9997	13.1131	12.3272	11.6268	10.9991
16	18.9684	17.4462	16.1310	14.9868	13.9846	13.1011	12.3176	11.6191	10.9929
17	18.9236	17.4118	16.1045	14.9663	13.9684	13.0884	12.3075	11.6108	10.9862
18	18.8766	17.3758	16.0768	14.9446	13.9514	13.0748	12.2966	11.6021	10.9790
19	18.8278	17.3382	16.0477	14.9218	13.9334	13.0605	12.2852	11.5928	10.9714
20	18.7768	17.2987	16.0170	14.8977	13.9144	13.0453	12.2730	11.5829	10.9634
21	18.7234	17.2575	15.9847	14.8725	13.8944	13.0293	12.2601	11.5725	10.9548
22	18.6680	17.2144	15.9508	14.8457	13.8731	13.0124	12.2464	11.5613	10.9457
23	18.6100	17.1691	15.9155	14.8177	13.8509	12.9944	12.2319	11.5495	10.9360
24	18.5496	17.1218	15.8782	14.7882	13.8271	12.9755	12.2165	11.5369	10.9257
25	18.4866	17.0724	15.8390	14.7569	13.8023	12.9553	12.2000	11.5236	10.9147
26	18.4208	17.0205	15.7978	14.7242	13.7759	12.9340	12.1829	11.5094	10.9030
27	18.3522	16.9662	15.7547	14.6895	13.7480	12.9115	12.1644	11.4944	10.8904
28	18.2804	16.9093	15.7092	14.6529	13.7184	12.8873	12.1448	11.4781	10.8771
29	18.2054	16.8493	15.6612	14.6142	13.6870	12.8617	12.1238	11.4607	10.8627
30	18.1268	16.7864	15.6103	14.5731	13.6536	12.8343	12.1011	11.4420	10.8471
31	18.0444	16.7202	15.5568	14.5295	13.6179	12.8049	12.0769	11.4219	10.8302
32	17.9578	16.6502	15.5000	14.4832	13.5797	12.7735	12.0508	11.4000	10.8119
33	17.8672	16.5765	15.4398	14.4338	13.5390	12.7397	12.0225	11.3764	10.7919
34	17.7718	16.4989	15.3762	14.3812	13.4954	12.7035	11.9921	11.3507	10.7702
35	17.6718	16.4169	15.3087	14.3252	13.4489	12.6644	11.9592	11.3229	10.7466
36	17.5668	16.3304	15.2370	14.2657	13.3990	12.6225	11.9238	11.2928	10.7208
37	17.4566	16.2393	15.1612	14.2023	13.3459	12.5775	11.8856	11.2601	10.6928
38	17.3410	16.1433	15.0812	14.1351	13.2890	12.5293	11.8445	11.2249	10.6624
39	17.2204	16.0427	14.9968	14.0640	13.2289	12.4781	11.8006	11.1872	10.6299
40	17.0946	15.9373	14.9082	13.9891	13.1651	12.4236	11.7539	11.1468	10.5949
41	16.9636	15.8273	14.8152	13.9102	13.0977	12.3659	11.7042	11.1039	10.5574
42	16.8276	15.7124	14.7178	13.8272	13.0269	12.3049	11.6515	11.0581	10.5176
43	16.6862	15.5929	14.6162	13.7403	12.9523	12.2407	11.5959	11.0096	10.4752
44	16.5398	15.4685	14.5100	13.6495	12.8740	12.1731	11.5371	10.9585	10.4303
45	16.3882	15.3393	14.3995	13.5546	12.7921	12.1020	11.4752	10.9044	10.3829
46	16.2316	15.2055	14.2847	13.4555	12.7064	12.0275	11.4102	10.8474	10.3328
47	16.0696	15.0665	14.1652	13.3522	12.6169	11.9495	11.3420	10.7875	10.2799
48	15.9022	14.9227	14.0410	13.2446	12.5231	11.8677	11.2704	10.7245	10.2242
49	15.7294	14.7736	13.9120	13.1325	12.4254	11.7821	11.1951	10.6581	10.1656
50	15.5510	14.6193	13.7778	13.0157	12.3233	11.6924	11.1161	10.5884	10.1036
51	15.3668	14.4595	13.6387	12.8940	12.2164	11.5985	11.0332	10.5148	10.0383
52	15.1766	14.2938	13.4940	12.7672	12.1050	11.5001	10.9461	10.4375	9.9694
53	14.9804	14.1224	13.3437	12.6351	11.9886	11.3971	10.8548	10.3561	9.8968
54	14.7778	13.9449	13.1877	12.4975	11.8669	11.2892	10.7588	10.2706	9.8202
55	14.5686	13.7611	13.0257	12.3543	11.7399	11.1763	10.6580	10.1805	9.7394
56	14.3528	13.5707	12.8573	12.2049	11.6070	11.0579	10.5521	10.0855	9.6541
57	14.1300	13.3736	12.6823	12.0494	11.4683	10.9337	10.4408	9.9854	9.5639

RMD Single Life Annuity Factors

AGE	5.0%	5.5%	6.0%	6.5%	INTEREST RATE 7.0%	7.5%	8.0%	8.5%	9.0%
58	13.8998	13.1693	12.5005	11.8871	11.3230	10.8035	10.3236	9.8799	9.4684
59	13.6620	12.9573	12.3112	11.7175	11.1709	10.6665	10.2003	9.7682	9.3673
60	13.4160	12.7375	12.1142	11.5406	11.0116	10.5228	10.0701	9.6504	9.2602
61	13.1620	12.5096	11.9095	11.3560	10.8449	10.3719	9.9332	9.5259	9.1468
62	12.9002	12.2740	11.6968	11.1638	10.6709	10.2137	9.7894	9.3947	9.0269
63	12.6308	12.0307	11.4767	10.9642	10.4893	10.0485	9.6386	9.2568	8.9006
64	12.3540	11.7800	11.2492	10.7572	10.3007	9.8763	9.4809	9.1122	8.7678
65	12.0704	11.5224	11.0145	10.5432	10.1050	9.6971	9.3165	8.9611	8.6286
66	11.7804	11.2580	10.7732	10.3223	9.9026	9.5111	9.1454	8.8034	8.4830
67	11.4844	10.9875	10.5252	10.0949	9.6934	9.3185	8.9679	8.6393	8.3312
68	11.1828	10.7107	10.2712	9.8611	9.4780	9.1196	8.7839	8.4689	8.1731
69	10.8758	10.4285	10.0112	9.6212	9.2564	8.9145	8.5938	8.2924	8.0089
70	10.5642	10.1413	9.7458	9.3757	9.0289	8.7033	8.3975	8.1098	7.8387
71	10.2486	9.8493	9.4753	9.1249	8.7959	8.4867	8.1956	7.9214	7.6627
72	9.9294	9.5533	9.2005	8.8692	8.5577	8.2645	7.9883	7.7274	7.4811
73	9.6072	9.2538	8.9217	8.6092	8.3150	8.0376	7.7759	7.5284	7.2943
74	9.2828	8.9513	8.6393	8.3454	8.0681	7.8063	7.5588	7.3245	7.1026
75	8.9568	8.6467	8.3543	8.0783	7.8174	7.5709	7.3374	7.1161	6.9062
76	8.6302	8.3405	8.0672	7.8086	7.5639	7.3321	7.1124	6.9039	6.7058
77	8.3038	8.0338	7.7787	7.5371	7.3080	7.0907	6.8844	6.6882	6.5018
78	7.9782	7.7275	7.4897	7.2643	7.0504	6.8472	6.6539	6.4699	6.2947
79	7.6544	7.4218	7.2010	6.9914	6.7920	6.6023	6.4216	6.2494	6.0851
80	7.3332	7.1180	6.9133	6.7186	6.5333	6.3567	6.1881	6.0274	5.8738
81	7.0156	6.8169	6.6277	6.4472	6.2753	6.1111	5.9544	5.8046	5.6612
82	6.7024	6.5193	6.3445	6.1778	6.0186	5.8665	5.7210	5.5816	5.4483
83	6.3946	6.2260	6.0652	5.9112	5.7643	5.6235	5.4886	5.3594	5.2356
84	6.0926	5.9380	5.7900	5.6485	5.5129	5.3828	5.2582	5.1386	5.0238
85	5.7976	5.6560	5.5202	5.3900	5.2653	5.1455	5.0305	4.9200	4.8138
86	5.5106	5.3811	5.2567	5.1372	5.0226	4.9124	4.8065	4.7046	4.6064
87	5.2328	5.1144	5.0005	4.8911	4.7860	4.6847	4.5872	4.4934	4.4030
88	4.9650	4.8569	4.7530	4.6528	4.5564	4.4636	4.3740	4.2878	4.2044
89	4.7094	4.6109	4.5158	4.4242	4.3360	4.2508	4.1686	4.0893	4.0126
90	4.4668	4.3767	4.2900	4.2063	4.1254	4.0473	3.9720	3.8991	3.8286
91	4.2374	4.1553	4.0760	3.9995	3.9254	3.8539	3.7846	3.7176	3.6528
92	4.0212	3.9462	3.8738	3.8038	3.7360	3.6704	3.6069	3.5453	3.4857
93	3.8174	3.7491	3.6830	3.6189	3.5569	3.4968	3.4385	3.3819	3.3270
94	3.6246	3.5624	3.5020	3.4434	3.3866	3.3315	3.2780	3.2261	3.1757
95	3.4410	3.3844	3.3293	3.2758	3.2239	3.1735	3.1245	3.0768	3.0306
96	3.2646	3.2131	3.1630	3.1143	3.0669	3.0208	2.9760	2.9325	2.8900
97	3.0926	3.0458	3.0003	2.9560	2.9130	2.8711	2.8302	2.7905	2.7517
98	2.9208	2.8787	2.8375	2.7975	2.7586	2.7205	2.6835	2.6474	2.6122
99	2.7506	2.7127	2.6758	2.6398	2.6047	2.5705	2.5370	2.5044	2.4726
100	2.5808	2.5471	2.5142	2.4820	2.4506	2.4199	2.3898	2.3605	2.3319
101	2.4116	2.3818	2.3525	2.3238	2.2959	2.2685	2.2419	2.2156	2.1900
102	2.2438	2.2175	2.1917	2.1665	2.1417	2.1175	2.0939	2.0706	2.0479
103	2.0792	2.0560	2.0335	2.0112	1.9896	1.9684	1.9475	1.9271	1.9070
104	1.9152	1.8953	1.8757	1.8563	1.8374	1.8189	1.8008	1.7829	1.7654
105	1.7534	1.7362	1.7193	1.7028	1.6864	1.6705	1.6548	1.6394	1.6242
106	1.5952	1.5805	1.5662	1.5518	1.5380	1.5243	1.5109	1.4976	1.4846
107	1.4416	1.4293	1.4170	1.4051	1.3933	1.3816	1.3702	1.3589	1.3479
108	1.2938	1.2835	1.2733	1.2632	1.2533	1.2436	1.2340	1.2245	1.2152
109	1.1530	1.1444	1.1358	1.1275	1.1193	1.1112	1.1031	1.0953	1.0874
110	1.0196	1.0125	1.0055	0.9988	0.9919	0.9852	0.9786	0.9721	0.9657
111	0.8942	0.8885	0.8828	0.8772	0.8717	0.8663	0.8609	0.8555	0.8502
112	0.7772	0.7727	0.7680	0.7635	0.7591	0.7547	0.7503	0.7460	0.7417
113	0.6686	0.6649	0.6613	0.6577	0.6541	0.6507	0.6471	0.6436	0.6402
114	0.5684	0.5655	0.5627	0.5598	0.5570	0.5541	0.5514	0.5487	0.5460
115	0.4762	0.4740	0.4717	0.4695	0.4673	0.4651	0.4630	0.4608	0.4587

RMD Single Life Annuity Factors

AGE	9.5%	10.0%	10.5%	11.0%	INTEREST RATE 11.5%	12.0%	12.5%	13.0%	13.5%
0	10.4563	9.9381	9.4684	9.0408	8.6499	8.2912	7.9610	7.6561	7.3735
1	10.4715	9.9526	9.4824	9.0542	8.6628	8.3037	7.9730	7.6675	7.3846
2	10.4751	9.9563	9.4860	9.0578	8.6663	8.3072	7.9764	7.6708	7.3878
3	10.4748	9.9565	9.4864	9.0584	8.6670	8.3078	7.9771	7.6716	7.3886
4	10.4737	9.9556	9.4858	9.0580	8.6668	8.3078	7.9771	7.6717	7.3887
5	10.4718	9.9542	9.4847	9.0571	8.6660	8.3072	7.9766	7.6713	7.3884
6	10.4694	9.9522	9.4830	9.0557	8.6649	8.3062	7.9758	7.6706	7.3878
7	10.4664	9.9497	9.4810	9.0539	8.6634	8.3048	7.9746	7.6696	7.3869
8	10.4628	9.9468	9.4785	9.0518	8.6615	8.3032	7.9732	7.6683	7.3857
9	10.4593	9.9437	9.4759	9.0496	8.6596	8.3016	7.9718	7.6670	7.3845
10	10.4556	9.9406	9.4733	9.0474	8.6577	8.2998	7.9702	7.6656	7.3833
11	10.4517	9.9374	9.4706	9.0450	8.6557	8.2982	7.9687	7.6643	7.3821
12	10.4476	9.9340	9.4677	9.0426	8.6537	8.2963	7.9672	7.6629	7.3809
13	10.4434	9.9305	9.4648	9.0401	8.6515	8.2945	7.9655	7.6615	7.3796
14	10.4388	9.9267	9.4616	9.0375	8.6491	8.2925	7.9638	7.6599	7.3783
15	10.4340	9.9227	9.4583	9.0346	8.6467	8.2904	7.9620	7.6583	7.3768
16	10.4288	9.9184	9.4547	9.0315	8.6442	8.2882	7.9600	7.6566	7.3753
17	10.4234	9.9139	9.4509	9.0283	8.6414	8.2858	7.9579	7.6548	7.3737
18	10.4175	9.9090	9.4468	9.0248	8.6383	8.2832	7.9557	7.6528	7.3720
19	10.4112	9.9038	9.4424	9.0211	8.6352	8.2805	7.9534	7.6508	7.3701
20	10.4045	9.8982	9.4377	9.0172	8.6318	8.2776	7.9508	7.6485	7.3682
21	10.3975	9.8923	9.4328	9.0130	8.6283	8.2745	7.9482	7.6462	7.3661
22	10.3899	9.8861	9.4274	9.0085	8.6244	8.2713	7.9453	7.6438	7.3640
23	10.3819	9.8794	9.4219	9.0038	8.6204	8.2678	7.9423	7.6412	7.3617
24	10.3734	9.8722	9.4159	8.9987	8.6161	8.2640	7.9391	7.6384	7.3593
25	10.3642	9.8647	9.4095	8.9934	8.6115	8.2601	7.9357	7.6354	7.3567
26	10.3545	9.8566	9.4027	8.9875	8.6066	8.2559	7.9321	7.6323	7.3539
27	10.3441	9.8479	9.3954	8.9814	8.6014	8.2514	7.9282	7.6289	7.3510
28	10.3329	9.8385	9.3875	8.9747	8.5957	8.2465	7.9240	7.6253	7.3479
29	10.3209	9.8284	9.3790	8.9675	8.5895	8.2412	7.9194	7.6213	7.3444
30	10.3079	9.8174	9.3696	8.9595	8.5827	8.2354	7.9144	7.6169	7.3406
31	10.2937	9.8054	9.3594	8.9508	8.5752	8.2289	7.9088	7.6121	7.3364
32	10.2782	9.7923	9.3483	8.9413	8.5670	8.2218	7.9026	7.6066	7.3316
33	10.2614	9.7779	9.3359	8.9306	8.5577	8.2138	7.8956	7.6005	7.3261
34	10.2428	9.7620	9.3223	8.9188	8.5476	8.2048	7.8878	7.5936	7.3201
35	10.2226	9.7447	9.3072	8.9058	8.5362	8.1948	7.8790	7.5858	7.3132
36	10.2005	9.7256	9.2907	8.8914	8.5235	8.1838	7.8691	7.5771	7.3053
37	10.1763	9.7046	9.2725	8.8754	8.5094	8.1713	7.8581	7.5672	7.2965
38	10.1500	9.6817	9.2525	8.8577	8.4939	8.1575	7.8458	7.5562	7.2867
39	10.1217	9.6570	9.2308	8.8386	8.4770	8.1424	7.8323	7.5442	7.2758
40	10.0912	9.6303	9.2072	8.8178	8.4584	8.1260	7.8176	7.5309	7.2639
41	10.0585	9.6016	9.1819	8.7954	8.4385	8.1082	7.8016	7.5165	7.2508
42	10.0236	9.5708	9.1548	8.7713	8.4170	8.0889	7.7843	7.5009	7.2367
43	9.9863	9.5380	9.1257	8.7455	8.3939	8.0682	7.7657	7.4841	7.2214
44	9.9468	9.5031	9.0947	8.7178	8.3692	8.0460	7.7457	7.4660	7.2050
45	9.9051	9.4661	9.0618	8.6885	8.3430	8.0224	7.7243	7.4466	7.1874
46	9.8608	9.4269	9.0269	8.6573	8.3150	7.9972	7.7016	7.4260	7.1687
47	9.8140	9.3853	8.9898	8.6241	8.2852	7.9703	7.6774	7.4040	7.1486
48	9.7646	9.3414	8.9507	8.5890	8.2536	7.9418	7.6515	7.3806	7.1273
49	9.7125	9.2949	8.9090	8.5517	8.2200	7.9115	7.6241	7.3556	7.1045
50	9.6575	9.2457	8.8650	8.5121	8.1843	7.8793	7.5947	7.3290	7.0802
51	9.5993	9.1937	8.8183	8.4700	8.1463	7.8448	7.5635	7.3005	7.0542
52	9.5377	9.1385	8.7687	8.4254	8.1059	7.8083	7.5302	7.2702	7.0264
53	9.4726	9.0801	8.7161	8.3778	8.0630	7.7692	7.4946	7.2377	6.9967
54	9.4039	9.0183	8.6603	8.3274	8.0171	7.7275	7.4566	7.2030	6.9650
55	9.3313	8.9528	8.6010	8.2736	7.9683	7.6831	7.4161	7.1658	6.9308
56	9.2543	8.8833	8.5381	8.2165	7.9163	7.6356	7.3726	7.1260	6.8943
57	9.1728	8.8095	8.4711	8.1555	7.8607	7.5848	7.3261	7.0832	6.8550

RMD Single Life Annuity Factors

AGE	9.5%	10.0%	10.5%	11.0%	11.5%	12.0%	12.5%	13.0%	13.5%
58	9.0864	8.7310	8.3997	8.0905	7.8012	7.5303	7.2761	7.0372	6.8125
59	8.9946	8.6474	8.3235	8.0207	7.7373	7.4716	7.2222	6.9875	6.7666
60	8.8971	8.5584	8.2420	7.9461	7.6688	7.4086	7.1640	6.9338	6.7169
61	8.7935	8.4636	8.1551	7.8663	7.5953	7.3408	7.1014	6.8758	6.6632
62	8.6837	8.3629	8.0626	7.7810	7.5167	7.2681	7.0341	6.8134	6.6051
63	8.5677	8.2562	7.9643	7.6903	7.4327	7.1903	6.9619	6.7464	6.5427
64	8.4455	8.1435	7.8602	7.5940	7.3435	7.1075	6.8849	6.6746	6.4758
65	8.3171	8.0249	7.7503	7.4921	7.2489	7.0194	6.8028	6.5980	6.4042
66	8.1824	7.9002	7.6347	7.3845	7.1488	6.9262	6.7157	6.5166	6.3280
67	8.0417	7.7695	7.5131	7.2714	7.0432	6.8276	6.6235	6.4302	6.2470
68	7.8948	7.6328	7.3857	7.1525	6.9321	6.7236	6.5261	6.3388	6.1610
69	7.7419	7.4902	7.2526	7.0280	6.8155	6.6142	6.4234	6.2422	6.0701
70	7.5831	7.3417	7.1136	6.8977	6.6933	6.4994	6.3154	6.1405	5.9742
71	7.4184	7.1875	6.9690	6.7619	6.5656	6.3792	6.2021	6.0337	5.8733
72	7.2482	7.0278	6.8189	6.6206	6.4325	6.2538	6.0836	5.9217	5.7673
73	7.0727	6.8627	6.6634	6.4742	6.2943	6.1231	5.9600	5.8047	5.6564
74	6.8922	6.6925	6.5029	6.3225	6.1508	5.9872	5.8314	5.6827	5.5407
75	6.7069	6.5176	6.3374	6.1659	6.0025	5.8467	5.6979	5.5558	5.4201
76	6.5175	6.3382	6.1675	6.0048	5.8496	5.7014	5.5598	5.4245	5.2949
77	6.3241	6.1549	5.9936	5.8395	5.6925	5.5519	5.4174	5.2887	5.1654
78	6.1276	5.9682	5.8161	5.6706	5.5316	5.3985	5.2711	5.1490	5.0319
79	5.9284	5.7786	5.6354	5.4985	5.3673	5.2416	5.1212	5.0056	4.8947
80	5.7269	5.5866	5.4522	5.3235	5.2000	5.0817	4.9681	4.8589	4.7541
81	5.5241	5.3928	5.2670	5.1462	5.0303	4.9191	4.8122	4.7095	4.6106
82	5.3204	5.1979	5.0803	4.9674	4.8588	4.7545	4.6542	4.5576	4.4647
83	5.1166	5.0025	4.8929	4.7875	4.6861	4.5885	4.4945	4.4040	4.3167
84	4.9135	4.8074	4.7053	4.6072	4.5126	4.4216	4.3338	4.2491	4.1673
85	4.7116	4.6132	4.5185	4.4273	4.3393	4.2544	4.1726	4.0935	4.0172
86	4.5120	4.4210	4.3332	4.2485	4.1669	4.0879	4.0118	3.9381	3.8669
87	4.3158	4.2316	4.1504	4.0720	3.9963	3.9230	3.8522	3.7837	3.7174
88	4.1240	4.0463	3.9713	3.8987	3.8286	3.7608	3.6950	3.6314	3.5698
89	3.9385	3.8669	3.7976	3.7305	3.6657	3.6028	3.5418	3.4828	3.4256
90	3.7603	3.6942	3.6303	3.5684	3.5083	3.4502	3.3937	3.3389	3.2858
91	3.5900	3.5291	3.4701	3.4129	3.3574	3.3035	3.2513	3.2005	3.1512
92	3.4278	3.3717	3.3173	3.2645	3.2131	3.1633	3.1149	3.0678	3.0221
93	3.2738	3.2221	3.1719	3.1231	3.0757	3.0296	2.9847	2.9411	2.8987
94	3.1267	3.0791	3.0328	2.9877	2.9439	2.9013	2.8598	2.8194	2.7801
95	2.9855	2.9417	2.8990	2.8575	2.8171	2.7778	2.7394	2.7020	2.6656
96	2.8487	2.8085	2.7692	2.7311	2.6938	2.6576	2.6222	2.5876	2.5539
97	2.7139	2.6771	2.6412	2.6062	2.5720	2.5387	2.5061	2.4743	2.4433
98	2.5778	2.5443	2.5115	2.4795	2.4483	2.4178	2.3881	2.3590	2.3305
99	2.4414	2.4110	2.3813	2.3523	2.3239	2.2962	2.2690	2.2425	2.2165
100	2.3038	2.2764	2.2496	2.2235	2.1977	2.1727	2.1481	2.1241	2.1005
101	2.1649	2.1405	2.1165	2.0929	2.0699	2.0473	2.0252	2.0036	1.9824
102	2.0257	2.0038	1.9825	1.9615	1.9410	1.9208	1.9010	1.8817	1.8627
103	1.8874	1.8681	1.8492	1.8307	1.8125	1.7947	1.7771	1.7599	1.7430
104	1.7482	1.7314	1.7148	1.6985	1.6825	1.6668	1.6514	1.6362	1.6213
105	1.6093	1.5947	1.5803	1.5661	1.5522	1.5385	1.5250	1.5118	1.4988
106	1.4718	1.4592	1.4469	1.4346	1.4226	1.4108	1.3992	1.3878	1.3765
107	1.3369	1.3263	1.3157	1.3053	1.2950	1.2849	1.2750	1.2652	1.2556
108	1.2060	1.1969	1.1880	1.1792	1.1705	1.1620	1.1535	1.1452	1.1370
109	1.0798	1.0722	1.0648	1.0574	1.0501	1.0429	1.0358	1.0288	1.0219
110	0.9593	0.9530	0.9469	0.9407	0.9347	0.9287	0.9228	0.9170	0.9113
111	0.8451	0.8399	0.8348	0.8298	0.8248	0.8199	0.8150	0.8102	0.8055
112	0.7375	0.7333	0.7291	0.7251	0.7210	0.7171	0.7131	0.7092	0.7053
113	0.6368	0.6335	0.6302	0.6269	0.6237	0.6204	0.6173	0.6141	0.6110
114	0.5433	0.5406	0.5380	0.5354	0.5328	0.5302	0.5277	0.5252	0.5227
115	0.4566	0.4545	0.4525	0.4505	0.4484	0.4464	0.4445	0.4425	0.4405

INTEREST RATE

Appendix E

Future Value Tables

A future value table is used to show what a single sum or a series of regular contributions or payments (an annuity) will grow to, or be worth, at some point in the future. Future value tables are used in this book primarily in making projections with regard to determining whether to convert a traditional IRA, SEP IRA, or SIMPLE IRA to a Roth IRA, or whether to make deductible contributions to a traditional or SEP IRA or nondeductible contributions to a Roth IRA.

A future value of a single sum table is used to show what a single sum will grow to at some point in the future if it grows at a given interest rate. For example, at 10% interest, $100,000 can be expected to grow to $259,370 in 10 years ($100,000 x 2.5937).

A future value of an annuity table is used to show what a fund will grow to at some point in the future if regular contributions are made to the fund and the fund grows at a given interest rate. For example, at 10% interest, contributions of $1,000 per year can be expected to grow to $15,937 in 10 years ($1,000 x 15.9374).

For periodic contributions other than annually at the end of the year, a factor from either Annuity Adjustment Factor Table A or Annuity Adjustment Factor Table B (see Appendix D) could be multiplied by the future value of an annuity factor to produce a factor that is adjusted for frequency of payments.

In determining whether to convert a traditional IRA, SEP IRA, or SIMPLE IRA to a Roth IRA (see Chapter 12), or whether to make deductible contributions to a traditional or SEP IRA or nondeductible contributions to a Roth IRA (see Chapter 9), it is useful to make projections of the future value of the two IRAs (and a side fund for tax savings) for comparison purposes. Future value tables are used in those projections.

In addition, future value tables can be used for the sole purpose of showing the amount that may be accumulated in an IRA (see Chapter 15). It may be useful to show what amount may accumulate in an IRA and be available in the future for some purpose such as retirement. It may also be useful to show what amount may accumulate in an IRA and be subject to estate tax when a person dies.

Future Value Single Sum Factors

YEAR	0.5%	1.0%	1.5%	INTEREST RATE 2.0%	2.5%	3.0%	3.5%
1	1.0050	1.0100	1.0150	1.0200	1.0250	1.0300	1.0350
2	1.0100	1.0201	1.0302	1.0404	1.0506	1.0609	1.0712
3	1.0151	1.0303	1.0457	1.0612	1.0769	1.0927	1.1087
4	1.0202	1.0406	1.0614	1.0824	1.1038	1.1255	1.1475
5	1.0253	1.0510	1.0773	1.1041	1.1314	1.1593	1.1877
6	1.0304	1.0615	1.0934	1.1262	1.1597	1.1941	1.2293
7	1.0355	1.0721	1.1098	1.1487	1.1887	1.2299	1.2723
8	1.0407	1.0829	1.1265	1.1717	1.2184	1.2668	1.3168
9	1.0459	1.0937	1.1434	1.1951	1.2489	1.3048	1.3629
10	1.0511	1.1046	1.1605	1.2190	1.2801	1.3439	1.4106
11	1.0564	1.1157	1.1779	1.2434	1.3121	1.3842	1.4600
12	1.0617	1.1268	1.1956	1.2682	1.3449	1.4258	1.5111
13	1.0670	1.1381	1.2136	1.2936	1.3785	1.4685	1.5640
14	1.0723	1.1495	1.2318	1.3195	1.4130	1.5126	1.6187
15	1.0777	1.1610	1.2502	1.3459	1.4483	1.5580	1.6753
16	1.0831	1.1726	1.2690	1.3728	1.4845	1.6047	1.7340
17	1.0885	1.1843	1.2880	1.4002	1.5216	1.6528	1.7947
18	1.0939	1.1961	1.3073	1.4282	1.5597	1.7024	1.8575
19	1.0994	1.2081	1.3270	1.4568	1.5987	1.7535	1.9225
20	1.1049	1.2202	1.3469	1.4859	1.6386	1.8061	1.9898
21	1.1104	1.2324	1.3671	1.5157	1.6796	1.8603	2.0594
22	1.1160	1.2447	1.3876	1.5460	1.7216	1.9161	2.1315
23	1.1216	1.2572	1.4084	1.5769	1.7646	1.9736	2.2061
24	1.1272	1.2697	1.4295	1.6084	1.8087	2.0328	2.2833
25	1.1328	1.2824	1.4509	1.6406	1.8539	2.0938	2.3632
26	1.1385	1.2953	1.4727	1.6734	1.9003	2.1566	2.4460
27	1.1442	1.3082	1.4948	1.7069	1.9478	2.2213	2.5316
28	1.1499	1.3213	1.5172	1.7410	1.9965	2.2879	2.6202
29	1.1556	1.3345	1.5400	1.7758	2.0464	2.3566	2.7119
30	1.1614	1.3478	1.5631	1.8114	2.0976	2.4273	2.8068
31	1.1672	1.3613	1.5865	1.8476	2.1500	2.5001	2.9050
32	1.1730	1.3749	1.6103	1.8845	2.2038	2.5751	3.0067
33	1.1789	1.3887	1.6345	1.9222	2.2589	2.6523	3.1119
34	1.1848	1.4026	1.6590	1.9607	2.3153	2.7319	3.2209
35	1.1907	1.4166	1.6839	1.9999	2.3732	2.8139	3.3336
36	1.1967	1.4308	1.7091	2.0399	2.4325	2.8983	3.4503
37	1.2027	1.4451	1.7348	2.0807	2.4933	2.9852	3.5710
38	1.2087	1.4595	1.7608	2.1223	2.5557	3.0748	3.6960
39	1.2147	1.4741	1.7872	2.1647	2.6196	3.1670	3.8254
40	1.2208	1.4889	1.8140	2.2080	2.6851	3.2620	3.9593
41	1.2269	1.5038	1.8412	2.2522	2.7522	3.3599	4.0978
42	1.2330	1.5188	1.8688	2.2972	2.8210	3.4607	4.2413
43	1.2392	1.5340	1.8969	2.3432	2.8915	3.5645	4.3897
44	1.2454	1.5493	1.9253	2.3901	2.9638	3.6715	4.5433
45	1.2516	1.5648	1.9542	2.4379	3.0379	3.7816	4.7024
46	1.2579	1.5805	1.9835	2.4866	3.1139	3.8950	4.8669
47	1.2642	1.5963	2.0133	2.5363	3.1917	4.0119	5.0373
48	1.2705	1.6122	2.0435	2.5871	3.2715	4.1323	5.2136
49	1.2768	1.6283	2.0741	2.6388	3.3533	4.2562	5.3961
50	1.2832	1.6446	2.1052	2.6916	3.4371	4.3839	5.5849

Future Value Single Sum Factors

YEAR	4.0%	4.5%	5.0%	INTEREST RATE 5.5%	6.0%	6.5%	7.0%
1	1.0400	1.0450	1.0500	1.0550	1.0600	1.0650	1.0700
2	1.0816	1.0920	1.1025	1.1130	1.1236	1.1342	1.1449
3	1.1249	1.1412	1.1576	1.1742	1.1910	1.2079	1.2250
4	1.1699	1.1925	1.2155	1.2388	1.2625	1.2865	1.3108
5	1.2167	1.2462	1.2763	1.3070	1.3382	1.3701	1.4026
6	1.2653	1.3023	1.3401	1.3788	1.4185	1.4591	1.5007
7	1.3159	1.3609	1.4071	1.4547	1.5036	1.5540	1.6058
8	1.3686	1.4221	1.4775	1.5347	1.5938	1.6550	1.7182
9	1.4233	1.4861	1.5513	1.6191	1.6895	1.7626	1.8385
10	1.4802	1.5530	1.6289	1.7081	1.7908	1.8771	1.9672
11	1.5395	1.6229	1.7103	1.8021	1.8983	1.9992	2.1049
12	1.6010	1.6959	1.7959	1.9012	2.0122	2.1291	2.2522
13	1.6651	1.7722	1.8856	2.0058	2.1329	2.2675	2.4098
14	1.7317	1.8519	1.9799	2.1161	2.2609	2.4149	2.5785
15	1.8009	1.9353	2.0789	2.2325	2.3966	2.5718	2.7590
16	1.8730	2.0224	2.1829	2.3553	2.5404	2.7390	2.9522
17	1.9479	2.1134	2.2920	2.4848	2.6928	2.9170	3.1588
18	2.0258	2.2085	2.4066	2.6215	2.8543	3.1067	3.3799
19	2.1068	2.3079	2.5270	2.7656	3.0256	3.3086	3.6165
20	2.1911	2.4117	2.6533	2.9178	3.2071	3.5236	3.8697
21	2.2788	2.5202	2.7860	3.0782	3.3996	3.7527	4.1406
22	2.3699	2.6337	2.9253	3.2475	3.6035	3.9966	4.4304
23	2.4647	2.7522	3.0715	3.4262	3.8197	4.2564	4.7405
24	2.5633	2.8760	3.2251	3.6146	4.0489	4.5331	5.0724
25	2.6658	3.0054	3.3864	3.8134	4.2919	4.8277	5.4274
26	2.7725	3.1407	3.5557	4.0231	4.5494	5.1415	5.8074
27	2.8834	3.2820	3.7335	4.2444	4.8223	5.4757	6.2139
28	2.9987	3.4297	3.9201	4.4778	5.1117	5.8316	6.6488
29	3.1187	3.5840	4.1161	4.7241	5.4184	6.2107	7.1143
30	3.2434	3.7453	4.3219	4.9840	5.7435	6.6144	7.6123
31	3.3731	3.9139	4.5380	5.2581	6.0881	7.0443	8.1451
32	3.5081	4.0900	4.7649	5.5473	6.4534	7.5022	8.7153
33	3.6484	4.2740	5.0032	5.8524	6.8406	7.9898	9.3253
34	3.7943	4.4664	5.2533	6.1742	7.2510	8.5092	9.9781
35	3.9461	4.6673	5.5160	6.5138	7.6861	9.0623	10.6766
36	4.1039	4.8774	5.7918	6.8721	8.1473	9.6513	11.4239
37	4.2681	5.0969	6.0814	7.2500	8.6361	10.2786	12.2236
38	4.4388	5.3262	6.3855	7.6488	9.1543	10.9467	13.0793
39	4.6164	5.5659	6.7048	8.0695	9.7035	11.6583	13.9948
40	4.8010	5.8164	7.0400	8.5133	10.2857	12.4161	14.9745
41	4.9931	6.0781	7.3920	8.9815	10.9029	13.2231	16.0227
42	5.1928	6.3516	7.7616	9.4755	11.5570	14.0826	17.1443
43	5.4005	6.6374	8.1497	9.9967	12.2505	14.9980	18.3444
44	5.6165	6.9361	8.5571	10.5465	12.9855	15.9729	19.6285
45	5.8412	7.2482	8.9850	11.1266	13.7646	17.0111	21.0025
46	6.0748	7.5744	9.4343	11.7385	14.5905	18.1168	22.4726
47	6.3178	7.9153	9.9060	12.3841	15.4659	19.2944	24.0457
48	6.5705	8.2715	10.4013	13.0653	16.3939	20.5485	25.7289
49	6.8333	8.6437	10.9213	13.7838	17.3775	21.8842	27.5299
50	7.1067	9.0326	11.4674	14.5420	18.4201	23.3067	29.4570

Future Value Single Sum Factors

INTEREST RATE

YEAR	7.5%	8.0%	8.5%	9.0%	9.5%	10.0%	10.5%
1	1.0750	1.0800	1.0850	1.0900	1.0950	1.1000	1.1050
2	1.1556	1.1664	1.1772	1.1881	1.1990	1.2100	1.2210
3	1.2423	1.2597	1.2773	1.2950	1.3129	1.3310	1.3492
4	1.3355	1.3605	1.3859	1.4116	1.4377	1.4641	1.4909
5	1.4356	1.4693	1.5037	1.5386	1.5742	1.6105	1.6474
6	1.5433	1.5869	1.6315	1.6771	1.7238	1.7716	1.8204
7	1.6590	1.7138	1.7701	1.8280	1.8876	1.9487	2.0116
8	1.7835	1.8509	1.9206	1.9926	2.0669	2.1436	2.2228
9	1.9172	1.9990	2.0839	2.1719	2.2632	2.3579	2.4562
10	2.0610	2.1589	2.2610	2.3674	2.4782	2.5937	2.7141
11	2.2156	2.3316	2.4532	2.5804	2.7137	2.8531	2.9991
12	2.3818	2.5182	2.6617	2.8127	2.9715	3.1384	3.3140
13	2.5604	2.7196	2.8879	3.0658	3.2537	3.4523	3.6619
14	2.7524	2.9372	3.1334	3.3417	3.5629	3.7975	4.0464
15	2.9589	3.1722	3.3997	3.6425	3.9013	4.1772	4.4713
16	3.1808	3.4259	3.6887	3.9703	4.2719	4.5950	4.9408
17	3.4194	3.7000	4.0023	4.3276	4.6778	5.0545	5.4596
18	3.6758	3.9960	4.3425	4.7171	5.1222	5.5599	6.0328
19	3.9515	4.3157	4.7116	5.1417	5.6088	6.1159	6.6663
20	4.2479	4.6610	5.1120	5.6044	6.1416	6.7275	7.3662
21	4.5664	5.0338	5.5466	6.1088	6.7251	7.4003	8.1397
22	4.9089	5.4365	6.0180	6.6586	7.3639	8.1403	8.9944
23	5.2771	5.8715	6.5296	7.2579	8.0635	8.9543	9.9388
24	5.6729	6.3412	7.0846	7.9111	8.8296	9.8497	10.9823
25	6.0983	6.8485	7.6868	8.6231	9.6684	10.8347	12.1355
26	6.5557	7.3964	8.3401	9.3992	10.5869	11.9182	13.4097
27	7.0474	7.9881	9.0491	10.2451	11.5926	13.1100	14.8177
28	7.5759	8.6271	9.8182	11.1671	12.6939	14.4210	16.3736
29	8.1441	9.3173	10.6528	12.1722	13.8998	15.8631	18.0928
30	8.7550	10.0627	11.5583	13.2677	15.2203	17.4494	19.9926
31	9.4116	10.8677	12.5407	14.4618	16.6662	19.1944	22.0918
32	10.1174	11.7371	13.6067	15.7633	18.2495	21.1138	24.4114
33	10.8763	12.6761	14.7632	17.1820	19.9832	23.2252	26.9746
34	11.6920	13.6901	16.0181	18.7284	21.8817	25.5477	29.8070
35	12.5689	14.7853	17.3796	20.4140	23.9604	28.1025	32.9367
36	13.5115	15.9682	18.8569	22.2512	26.2367	30.9127	36.3950
37	14.5249	17.2456	20.4598	24.2538	28.7291	34.0040	40.2165
38	15.6143	18.6253	22.1988	26.4367	31.4584	37.4044	44.4393
39	16.7853	20.1153	24.0857	28.8160	34.4470	41.1448	49.1054
40	18.0442	21.7245	26.1330	31.4094	37.7194	45.2593	54.2615
41	19.3976	23.4625	28.3543	34.2363	41.3028	49.7852	59.9589
42	20.8524	25.3395	30.7644	37.3175	45.2265	54.7637	66.2546
43	22.4163	27.3666	33.3794	40.6761	49.5230	60.2401	73.2113
44	24.0975	29.5560	36.2167	44.3370	54.2277	66.2641	80.8985
45	25.9048	31.9205	39.2951	48.3273	59.3794	72.8905	89.3929
46	27.8477	34.4741	42.6352	52.6768	65.0204	80.1796	98.7791
47	29.9363	37.2320	46.2592	57.4177	71.1974	88.1975	109.1509
48	32.1815	40.2106	50.1912	62.5853	77.9611	97.0173	120.6118
49	34.5951	43.4274	54.4575	68.2179	85.3674	106.7190	133.2760
50	37.1898	46.9016	59.0863	74.3576	93.4773	117.3909	147.2700

Future Value Single Sum Factors

INTEREST RATE

YEAR	11.0%	11.5%	12.0%	12.5%	13.0%	13.5%	14.0%
1	1.1100	1.1150	1.1200	1.1250	1.1300	1.1350	1.1400
2	1.2321	1.2432	1.2544	1.2656	1.2769	1.2882	1.2996
3	1.3676	1.3862	1.4049	1.4238	1.4429	1.4621	1.4815
4	1.5181	1.5456	1.5735	1.6018	1.6305	1.6595	1.6890
5	1.6851	1.7234	1.7623	1.8020	1.8424	1.8836	1.9254
6	1.8704	1.9215	1.9738	2.0273	2.0820	2.1378	2.1950
7	2.0762	2.1425	2.2107	2.2807	2.3526	2.4264	2.5023
8	2.3045	2.3889	2.4760	2.5658	2.6584	2.7540	2.8526
9	2.5580	2.6636	2.7731	2.8865	3.0040	3.1258	3.2519
10	2.8394	2.9699	3.1058	3.2473	3.3946	3.5478	3.7072
11	3.1518	3.3115	3.4786	3.6532	3.8359	4.0267	4.2262
12	3.4985	3.6923	3.8960	4.1099	4.3345	4.5704	4.8179
13	3.8833	4.1169	4.3635	4.6236	4.8980	5.1874	5.4924
14	4.3104	4.5904	4.8871	5.2016	5.5348	5.8877	6.2613
15	4.7846	5.1183	5.4736	5.8518	6.2543	6.6825	7.1379
16	5.3109	5.7069	6.1304	6.5833	7.0673	7.5846	8.1372
17	5.8951	6.3632	6.8660	7.4062	7.9861	8.6085	9.2765
18	6.5436	7.0949	7.6900	8.3319	9.0243	9.7707	10.5752
19	7.2633	7.9108	8.6128	9.3734	10.1974	11.0897	12.0557
20	8.0623	8.8206	9.6463	10.5451	11.5231	12.5869	13.7435
21	8.9492	9.8350	10.8038	11.8632	13.0211	14.2861	15.6676
22	9.9336	10.9660	12.1003	13.3461	14.7138	16.2147	17.8610
23	11.0263	12.2271	13.5523	15.0144	16.6266	18.4037	20.3616
24	12.2392	13.6332	15.1786	16.8912	18.7881	20.8882	23.2122
25	13.5855	15.2010	17.0001	19.0026	21.2305	23.7081	26.4619
26	15.0799	16.9491	19.0401	21.3779	23.9905	26.9087	30.1666
27	16.7386	18.8982	21.3249	24.0502	27.1093	30.5413	34.3899
28	18.5799	21.0715	23.8839	27.0564	30.6335	34.6644	39.2045
29	20.6237	23.4948	26.7499	30.4385	34.6158	39.3441	44.6931
30	22.8923	26.1967	29.9599	34.2433	39.1159	44.6556	50.9501
31	25.4104	29.2093	33.5551	38.5237	44.2010	50.6841	58.0832
32	28.2056	32.5684	37.5817	43.3392	49.9471	57.5264	66.2148
33	31.3082	36.3137	42.0915	48.7566	56.4402	65.2925	75.4849
34	34.7521	40.4898	47.1425	54.8512	63.7774	74.1070	86.0528
35	38.5749	45.1461	52.7996	61.7075	72.0685	84.1114	98.1001
36	42.8181	50.3379	59.1356	69.4210	81.4374	95.4665	111.8342
37	47.5281	56.1268	66.2319	78.0986	92.0243	108.3544	127.4909
38	52.7562	62.5814	74.1797	87.8609	103.9874	122.9823	145.3397
39	58.5593	69.7782	83.0812	98.8436	117.5058	139.5849	165.6872
40	65.0009	77.8027	93.0510	111.1990	132.7815	158.4289	188.8834
41	72.1510	86.7500	104.2171	125.0989	150.0431	179.8168	215.3271
42	80.0878	96.7263	116.7232	140.7362	169.5487	204.0920	245.4729
43	88.8972	107.8498	130.7299	158.3283	191.5901	231.6444	279.8391
44	98.6759	120.2525	146.4175	178.1193	216.4968	262.9164	319.0166
45	109.5302	134.0816	163.9876	200.3842	244.6414	298.4102	363.6789
46	121.5786	149.5009	183.6662	225.4322	276.4447	338.6955	414.5939
47	134.9522	166.6936	205.7061	253.6113	312.3825	384.4194	472.6370
48	149.7969	185.8633	230.3908	285.3127	352.9923	436.3160	538.8062
49	166.2746	207.2376	258.0377	320.9768	398.8813	495.2187	614.2391
50	184.5648	231.0699	289.0023	361.0989	450.7358	562.0732	700.2325

Future Value Annuity Factors

YEAR	0.5%	1.0%	1.5%	INTEREST RATE 2.0%	2.5%	3.0%	3.5%
1	1.0000	1.0000	1.0000	1.0000	1.0000	1.0000	1.0000
2	2.0050	2.0100	2.0150	2.0200	2.0250	2.0300	2.0350
3	3.0150	3.0301	3.0452	3.0604	3.0756	3.0909	3.1062
4	4.0301	4.0604	4.0909	4.1216	4.1525	4.1836	4.2149
5	5.0503	5.1010	5.1523	5.2040	5.2563	5.3091	5.3625
6	6.0755	6.1520	6.2296	6.3081	6.3877	6.4684	6.5502
7	7.1059	7.2135	7.3230	7.4343	7.5474	7.6625	7.7794
8	8.1414	8.2857	8.4328	8.5830	8.7361	8.8923	9.0517
9	9.1821	9.3685	9.5593	9.7546	9.9545	10.1591	10.3685
10	10.2280	10.4622	10.7027	10.9497	11.2034	11.4639	11.7314
11	11.2792	11.5668	11.8633	12.1687	12.4835	12.8078	13.1420
12	12.3356	12.6825	13.0412	13.4121	13.7956	14.1920	14.6020
13	13.3972	13.8093	14.2368	14.6803	15.1404	15.6178	16.1130
14	14.4642	14.9474	15.4504	15.9739	16.5190	17.0863	17.6770
15	15.5365	16.0969	16.6821	17.2934	17.9319	18.5989	19.2957
16	16.6142	17.2579	17.9324	18.6393	19.3802	20.1569	20.9710
17	17.6973	18.4304	19.2014	20.0121	20.8647	21.7616	22.7050
18	18.7858	19.6147	20.4894	21.4123	22.3863	23.4144	24.4997
19	19.8797	20.8109	21.7967	22.8406	23.9460	25.1169	26.3572
20	20.9791	22.0190	23.1237	24.2974	25.5447	26.8704	28.2797
21	22.0840	23.2392	24.4705	25.7833	27.1833	28.6765	30.2695
22	23.1944	24.4716	25.8376	27.2990	28.8629	30.5368	32.3289
23	24.3104	25.7163	27.2251	28.8450	30.5844	32.4529	34.4604
24	25.4320	26.9735	28.6335	30.4219	32.3490	34.4265	36.6665
25	26.5591	28.2432	30.0630	32.0303	34.1578	36.4593	38.9499
26	27.6919	29.5256	31.5140	33.6709	36.0117	38.5530	41.3131
27	28.8304	30.8209	32.9867	35.3443	37.9120	40.7096	43.7591
28	29.9745	32.1291	34.4815	37.0512	39.8598	42.9309	46.2906
29	31.1244	33.4504	35.9987	38.7922	41.8563	45.2188	48.9108
30	32.2800	34.7849	37.5387	40.5681	43.9027	47.5754	51.6227
31	33.4414	36.1327	39.1018	42.3794	46.0003	50.0027	54.4295
32	34.6086	37.4941	40.6883	44.2270	48.1503	52.5028	57.3345
33	35.7817	38.8690	42.2986	46.1116	50.3540	55.0778	60.3412
34	36.9606	40.2577	43.9331	48.0338	52.6129	57.7302	63.4531
35	38.1454	41.6603	45.5921	49.9945	54.9282	60.4621	66.6740
36	39.3361	43.0769	47.2760	51.9944	57.3014	63.2759	70.0076
37	40.5328	44.5076	48.9851	54.0343	59.7339	66.1742	73.4579
38	41.7354	45.9527	50.7199	56.1149	62.2273	69.1594	77.0289
39	42.9441	47.4123	52.4807	58.2372	64.7830	72.2342	80.7249
40	44.1588	48.8864	54.2679	60.4020	67.4026	75.4013	84.5503
41	45.3796	50.3752	56.0819	62.6100	70.0876	78.6633	88.5095
42	46.6065	51.8790	57.9231	64.8622	72.8398	82.0232	92.6074
43	47.8396	53.3978	59.7920	67.1595	75.6608	85.4839	96.8486
44	49.0788	54.9318	61.6889	69.5027	78.5523	89.0484	101.2383
45	50.3242	56.4811	63.6142	71.8927	81.5161	92.7199	105.7817
46	51.5758	58.0459	65.5684	74.3306	84.5540	96.5015	110.4840
47	52.8337	59.6263	67.5519	76.8172	87.6679	100.3965	115.3510
48	54.0978	61.2226	69.5652	79.3535	90.8596	104.4084	120.3882
49	55.3683	62.8348	71.6087	81.9406	94.1311	108.5406	125.6018
50	56.6452	64.4632	73.6828	84.5794	97.4843	112.7969	130.9979

Future Value Annuity Factors

YEAR	4.0%	4.5%	5.0%	INTEREST RATE 5.5%	6.0%	6.5%	7.0%
1	1.0000	1.0000	1.0000	1.0000	1.0000	1.0000	1.0000
2	2.0400	2.0450	2.0500	2.0550	2.0600	2.0650	2.0700
3	3.1216	3.1370	3.1525	3.1680	3.1836	3.1992	3.2149
4	4.2465	4.2782	4.3101	4.3423	4.3746	4.4072	4.4399
5	5.4163	5.4707	5.5256	5.5811	5.6371	5.6936	5.7507
6	6.6330	6.7169	6.8019	6.8881	6.9753	7.0637	7.1533
7	7.8983	8.0192	8.1420	8.2669	8.3938	8.5229	8.6540
8	9.2142	9.3800	9.5491	9.7216	9.8975	10.0769	10.2598
9	10.5828	10.8021	11.0266	11.2563	11.4913	11.7319	11.9780
10	12.0061	12.2882	12.5779	12.8754	13.1808	13.4944	13.8164
11	13.4864	13.8412	14.2068	14.5835	14.9716	15.3716	15.7836
12	15.0258	15.4640	15.9171	16.3856	16.8699	17.3707	17.8885
13	16.6268	17.1599	17.7130	18.2868	18.8821	19.4998	20.1406
14	18.2919	18.9321	19.5986	20.2926	21.0151	21.7673	22.5505
15	20.0236	20.7841	21.5786	22.4087	23.2760	24.1822	25.1290
16	21.8245	22.7193	23.6575	24.6411	25.6725	26.7540	27.8881
17	23.6975	24.7417	25.8404	26.9964	28.2129	29.4930	30.8402
18	25.6454	26.8551	28.1324	29.4812	30.9057	32.4101	33.9990
19	27.6712	29.0636	30.5390	32.1027	33.7600	35.5167	37.3790
20	29.7781	31.3714	33.0660	34.8683	36.7856	38.8253	40.9955
21	31.9692	33.7831	35.7193	37.7861	39.9927	42.3490	44.8652
22	34.2480	36.3034	38.5052	40.8643	43.3923	46.1016	49.0057
23	36.6179	38.9370	41.4305	44.1118	46.9958	50.0982	53.4361
24	39.0826	41.6892	44.5020	47.5380	50.8156	54.3546	58.1767
25	41.6459	44.5652	47.7271	51.1526	54.8645	58.8877	63.2490
26	44.3117	47.5706	51.1135	54.9660	59.1564	63.7154	68.6765
27	47.0842	50.7113	54.6691	58.9891	63.7058	68.8569	74.4838
28	49.9676	53.9933	58.4026	63.2335	68.5281	74.3326	80.6977
29	52.9663	57.4230	62.3227	67.7113	73.6398	80.1642	87.3465
30	56.0849	61.0071	66.4388	72.4355	79.0582	86.3749	94.4608
31	59.3283	64.7524	70.7608	77.4194	84.8017	92.9892	102.0730
32	62.7015	68.6662	75.2988	82.6775	90.8898	100.0335	110.2182
33	66.2095	72.7562	80.0638	88.2248	97.3432	107.5357	118.9334
34	69.8579	77.0303	85.0670	94.0771	104.1837	115.5255	128.2588
35	73.6522	81.4966	90.3203	100.2514	111.4348	124.0347	138.2369
36	77.5983	86.1640	95.8363	106.7652	119.1209	133.0969	148.9135
37	81.7022	91.0413	101.6281	113.6373	127.2681	142.7482	160.3374
38	85.9703	96.1382	107.7095	120.8873	135.9042	153.0269	172.5610
39	90.4091	101.4644	114.0950	128.5361	145.0584	163.9736	185.6403
40	95.0255	107.0303	120.7998	136.6056	154.7619	175.6319	199.6351
41	99.8265	112.8467	127.8398	145.1189	165.0477	188.0480	214.6096
42	104.8196	118.9248	135.2317	154.1004	175.9505	201.2711	230.6322
43	110.0124	125.2764	142.9933	163.5760	187.5076	215.3537	247.7765
44	115.4129	131.9138	151.1430	173.5726	199.7580	230.3517	266.1209
45	121.0294	138.8500	159.7001	184.1191	212.7435	246.3246	285.7493
46	126.8706	146.0982	168.6851	195.2457	226.5081	263.3357	306.7518
47	132.9454	153.6726	178.1194	206.9842	241.0986	281.4525	329.2244
48	139.2632	161.5879	188.0254	219.3683	256.5645	300.7469	353.2701
49	145.8337	169.8593	198.4266	232.4336	272.9584	321.2954	378.9990
50	152.6671	178.5030	209.3480	246.2174	290.3359	343.1796	406.5289

Future Value Annuity Factors

YEAR	7.5%	8.0%	8.5%	INTEREST RATE 9.0%	9.5%	10.0%	10.5%
1	1.0000	1.0000	1.0000	1.0000	1.0000	1.0000	1.0000
2	2.0750	2.0800	2.0850	2.0900	2.0950	2.1000	2.1050
3	3.2306	3.2464	3.2622	3.2781	3.2940	3.3100	3.3260
4	4.4729	4.5061	4.5395	4.5731	4.6070	4.6410	4.6753
5	5.8084	5.8666	5.9254	5.9847	6.0446	6.1051	6.1662
6	7.2440	7.3359	7.4290	7.5233	7.6189	7.7156	7.8136
7	8.7873	8.9228	9.0605	9.2004	9.3426	9.4872	9.6340
8	10.4464	10.6366	10.8306	11.0285	11.2302	11.4359	11.6456
9	12.2298	12.4876	12.7512	13.0210	13.2971	13.5795	13.8684
10	14.1471	14.4866	14.8351	15.1929	15.5603	15.9374	16.3246
11	16.2081	16.6455	17.0961	17.5603	18.0385	18.5312	19.0387
12	18.4237	18.9771	19.5493	20.1407	20.7522	21.3843	22.0377
13	20.8055	21.4953	22.2109	22.9534	23.7236	24.5227	25.3517
14	23.3659	24.2149	25.0989	26.0192	26.9774	27.9750	29.0136
15	26.1184	27.1521	28.2323	29.3609	30.5402	31.7725	33.0600
16	29.0772	30.3243	31.6320	33.0034	34.4416	35.9497	37.5313
17	32.2580	33.7502	35.3207	36.9737	38.7135	40.5447	42.4721
18	35.6774	37.4502	39.3230	41.3013	43.3913	45.5992	47.9317
19	39.3532	41.4463	43.6655	46.0185	48.5135	51.1591	53.9645
20	43.3047	45.7620	48.3770	51.1601	54.1222	57.2750	60.6308
21	47.5525	50.4229	53.4891	56.7645	60.2639	64.0025	67.9971
22	52.1190	55.4568	59.0356	62.8733	66.9889	71.4028	76.1368
23	57.0279	60.8933	65.0537	69.5319	74.3529	79.5430	85.1311
24	62.3050	66.7648	71.5832	76.7898	82.4164	88.4973	95.0699
25	67.9779	73.1059	78.6678	84.7009	91.2460	98.3471	106.0522
26	74.0762	79.9544	86.3546	93.3240	100.9143	109.1818	118.1877
27	80.6319	87.3508	94.6947	102.7232	111.5012	121.1000	131.5974
28	87.6793	95.3388	103.7438	112.9682	123.0938	134.2100	146.4151
29	95.2553	103.9659	113.5620	124.1354	135.7877	148.6310	162.7887
30	103.3994	113.2832	124.2147	136.3076	149.6875	164.4941	180.8816
31	112.1544	123.3459	135.7730	149.5752	164.9079	181.9435	200.8741
32	121.5659	134.2136	148.3137	164.0370	181.5741	201.1378	222.9659
33	131.6834	145.9506	161.9204	179.8004	199.8237	222.2516	247.3773
34	142.5596	158.6267	176.6836	196.9824	219.8069	245.4768	274.3520
35	154.2516	172.3168	192.7017	215.7108	241.6886	271.0245	304.1589
36	166.8205	187.1022	210.0814	236.1248	265.6490	299.1269	337.0956
37	180.3320	203.0703	228.9383	258.3760	291.8856	330.0396	373.4907
38	194.8569	220.3160	249.3980	282.6299	320.6148	364.0436	413.7072
39	210.4712	238.9413	271.5969	309.0666	352.0732	401.4480	458.1465
40	227.2565	259.0566	295.6826	337.8825	386.5201	442.5928	507.2518
41	245.3008	280.7811	321.8156	369.2920	424.2396	487.8520	561.5133
42	264.6983	304.2436	350.1700	403.5283	465.5423	537.6372	621.4722
43	285.5507	329.5831	380.9344	440.8458	510.7688	592.4010	687.7268
44	307.9670	356.9497	414.3138	481.5219	560.2919	652.6411	760.9381
45	332.0645	386.5057	450.5305	525.8589	614.5196	718.9052	841.8366
46	357.9694	418.4261	489.8256	574.1862	673.8990	791.7957	931.2295
47	385.8171	452.9002	532.4608	626.8630	738.9194	871.9753	1030.0086
48	415.7534	490.1323	578.7200	684.2807	810.1168	960.1729	1139.1595
49	447.9349	530.3428	628.9112	746.8659	888.0779	1057.1902	1259.7713
50	482.5300	573.7703	683.3686	815.0839	973.4453	1163.9092	1393.0473

Future Value Annuity Factors

				INTEREST RATE			
YEAR	11.0%	11.5%	12.0%	12.5%	13.0%	13.5%	14.0%
1	1.0000	1.0000	1.0000	1.0000	1.0000	1.0000	1.0000
2	2.1100	2.1150	2.1200	2.1250	2.1300	2.1350	2.1400
3	3.3421	3.3582	3.3744	3.3906	3.4069	3.4232	3.4396
4	4.7097	4.7444	4.7793	4.8145	4.8498	4.8854	4.9211
5	6.2278	6.2900	6.3528	6.4163	6.4803	6.5449	6.6101
6	7.9129	8.0134	8.1152	8.2183	8.3227	8.4284	8.5355
7	9.7833	9.9349	10.0890	10.2456	10.4047	10.5663	10.7305
8	11.8594	12.0774	12.2997	12.5263	12.7573	12.9927	13.2328
9	14.1640	14.4663	14.7757	15.0921	15.4157	15.7467	16.0853
10	16.7220	17.1300	17.5487	17.9786	18.4197	18.8726	19.3373
11	19.5614	20.0999	20.6546	21.2259	21.8143	22.4204	23.0445
12	22.7132	23.4114	24.1331	24.8791	25.6502	26.4471	27.2707
13	26.2116	27.1037	28.0291	28.9890	29.9847	31.0175	32.0887
14	30.0949	31.2207	32.3926	33.6126	34.8827	36.2048	37.5811
15	34.4054	35.8110	37.2797	38.8142	40.4175	42.0925	43.8424
16	39.1899	40.9293	42.7533	44.6660	46.6717	48.7750	50.9803
17	44.5008	46.6362	48.8837	51.2493	53.7391	56.3596	59.1176
18	50.3959	52.9993	55.7497	58.6554	61.7251	64.9681	68.3941
19	56.9395	60.0942	63.4397	66.9873	70.7494	74.7388	78.9692
20	64.2028	68.0051	72.0524	76.3608	80.9468	85.8285	91.0249
21	72.2651	76.8257	81.6987	86.9058	92.4699	98.4154	104.7684
22	81.2143	86.6606	92.5026	98.7691	105.4910	112.7015	120.4360
23	91.1479	97.6266	104.6029	112.1152	120.2048	128.9162	138.2970
24	102.1741	109.8536	118.1552	127.1296	136.8315	147.3199	158.6586
25	114.4133	123.4868	133.3339	144.0208	155.6195	168.2080	181.8708
26	127.9988	138.6878	150.3339	163.0234	176.8501	191.9161	208.3327
27	143.0786	155.6369	169.3740	184.4013	200.8406	218.8248	238.4993
28	159.8173	174.5351	190.6989	208.4515	227.9499	249.3661	272.8892
29	178.3972	195.6067	214.5828	235.5079	258.5834	284.0306	312.0936
30	199.0209	219.1015	241.3327	265.9464	293.1992	323.3747	356.7867
31	221.9132	245.2981	271.2926	300.1897	332.3151	368.0303	407.7369
32	247.3236	274.5074	304.8477	338.7135	376.5160	418.7144	465.8200
33	275.5292	307.0758	342.4295	382.0526	426.4631	476.2408	532.0348
34	306.8374	343.3895	384.5210	430.8092	482.9033	541.5333	607.5197
35	341.5896	383.8793	431.6635	485.6604	546.6808	615.6403	693.5725
36	380.1644	429.0254	484.4632	547.3679	618.7493	699.7517	791.6726
37	422.9825	479.3633	543.5988	616.7889	700.1867	795.2182	903.5068
38	470.5106	535.4901	609.8306	694.8875	792.2109	903.5726	1030.9977
39	523.2667	598.0714	684.0103	782.7485	896.1983	1026.5549	1176.3373
40	581.8261	667.8496	767.0915	881.5920	1013.7041	1166.1398	1342.0246
41	646.8269	745.6524	860.1425	992.7910	1146.4856	1324.5687	1530.9080
42	718.9779	832.4024	964.3596	1117.8899	1296.5288	1504.3855	1746.2351
43	799.0655	929.1287	1081.0828	1258.6262	1466.0775	1708.4775	1991.7080
44	887.9626	1036.9785	1211.8127	1416.9544	1657.6676	1940.1219	2271.5470
45	986.6385	1157.2310	1358.2302	1595.0737	1874.1643	2203.0384	2590.5636
46	1096.1688	1291.3125	1522.2179	1795.4579	2118.8057	2501.4485	2954.2425
47	1217.7473	1440.8135	1705.8840	2020.8902	2395.2504	2840.1441	3368.8364
48	1352.6996	1607.5070	1911.5901	2274.5015	2707.6330	3224.5635	3841.4734
49	1502.4965	1793.3704	2141.9809	2559.8141	3060.6252	3660.8795	4380.2796
50	1668.7711	2000.6079	2400.0187	2880.7909	3459.5065	4156.0982	4994.5187

Index

S

4 WAYS TO ORDER

CALL 800-543-0874

CLICK www.NationalUnderwriterStore.com

MAIL TO: The National Underwriter Co.
Orders Department
P.O. Box 14448
Cincinnati, OH 45250-9786

FAX your order form to 800-874-1916
(Please include your return fax number)

SHIPPING & HANDELING			
Order		**Total**	**S&H**
$0	to	$39.99	$6.50
$40.00	to	$64.99	$8.50
$65.00	to	$109.99	$11.50
$110.00	to	$154.99	$13.50
$155.00	to	$199.99	$15.50
$200.00	to	$249.99	$17.50

For expedited shipping
information, call
1-800-543-0874

SALES TAX

Sales tax is required
for residents of the
following states:
CA, CT, DC, FL,
GA, IL, KS, KY, NJ,
NY, OH, PA, TX, WA

*MAKE CHECKS PAYABLE TO

The National Underwriter Company

**CVV INFORMATION

For Visa/MC, the three-digit CVV#
is usually printed on the back of
the card.

For AmEx, the four-digit CVV# is
usually on the front of the card.

PAYMENT INFORMATION & GUARANTEE

Shipping and handling rates for
the continental U.S. only. If your
order exceeds total amount listed
in chart or for overseas rates, call
800-543-0874. Any discounts do
not apply to shipping and handling. Unconditional 30 day guar-
antee. Product(s) damaged in
shipping will be replaced at no
cost to you. Claims must be made
within 30 days from the invoice
date. Prices, information and availability subject to change.

Your Job Function
(please check one)
☐ Owner/Principal/GA
☐ Agent/Broker
☐ Financial Advisor
☐ Adjuster/Claims
☐ Other

Your Business Type
(please check one)
☐ Agency/Brokerage
☐ Financial Planner/
Advisor/Registered Rep
☐ Home Office
☐ Risk Management
☐ Other

Your Business Line
(please check one)
☐ Life & Health
☐ Property & Casualty
☐ Multi-Lines
☐ Other

_____ Copies of Ultimate IRA Resource #210003K $74.95
(includes Including the Ultimate IRA Calculator)

Method of Payment: ☐ Check enclosed* ☐ Bill Me ☐ Call Me

Name _____ Title _____

Company _____

Street Address _____

City _____ State _____ Zip _____

Business Phone (___) _____ Fax (___) _____

E-mail _____ ☐ May we contact you via e-mail?

BUSINESS REPLY MAIL

FIRST-CLASS MAIL   PERMIT NO 68   CINCINNATI OH

POSTAGE WILL BE PAID BY ADDRESSEE

CUSTOMER SERVICE
THE NATIONAL UNDERWRITER COMPANY
PO BOX 14448
CINCINNATI OH 45250-9786